A Different Way of Being

Towards a Reformed Theology of Ethnopolitical Cohesion for the Kenyan Context

I0127966

David Kirwa Tarus

Langham

MONOGRAPHS

Published 2019 by Langham Monographs
An imprint of Langham Publishing
www.langhampublishing.org

Langham Publishing and its imprints are a ministry of Langham Partnership

Langham Partnership
PO Box 296, Carlisle, Cumbria, CA3 9WZ, UK
www.langham.org

ISBNs:
978-1-78368-580-6 Print
978-1-78368-581-3 ePub
978-1-78368-582-0 Mobi
978-1-78368-583-7 PDF

British Library Cataloguing-in-Publication Data
A catalogue record for this book is available from the British Library

ISBN: 978-1-78368-580-6

Cover & Book Design: projectluz.com

Dr Tarus's work is an exemplary piece of historical, systematic, and contextual theology. He shows that a Christian theology of the divine image (drawing especially on Calvin's theology) provides a foundation for overcoming ethno-political conflict in Kenya. Where class and ethnic differences too often fuel conflict, corruption, intolerance, and violence, Tarus argues that the Christian theology that all people bear the divine image anchors a vision for social and political unity that also recognizes, respects, and integrates diversity within that community. Tarus sets his constructive contribution in conversation with key voices in the history of African political theology. He also identifies and analyzes the challenges facing Christian political engagement in Kenya. Tarus writes, moreover, with an irenic, thoughtful, and compelling style.

Steven M. Studebaker, PhD
Howard and Shirley Bentall Chair in Evangelical Thought
Associate Professor of Systematic and Historical Theology,
McMaster Divinity College, Hamilton, Canada

Would you like to understand the genesis of ethno-political violence in Kenya and how you can address the vice by renewing God's image in you? In this well-researched, interesting, objective and revolutionary book, Dr David Tarus invites theologians, religious leaders and scholars of religion, historians, and all Kenyans of goodwill to exercise heroic faith to remove any public leader who does the honor God. He challenges all Christians at the individual level to demonstrate Christian love which is extended beyond close kin and kith. This is a must-read for every Kenyan interested in "Unity, Peace and Liberty, Justice to be found within our borders."

Eunice Kamaara, PhD
Professor of Religion, Ethics, and Gender Development,
Moi University, Kesses, Kenya

To my mom who is now with Jesus.

Contents

Abstract xi

Acknowledgments xiii

Chapter 1 1

Introduction

    The Need for the Book 1

    Definition of Key Terms 3

        Ethnopolitical Conflict and Ethnopolitical Cohesion 3

        Ethnicity/Ethnic Group 4

        Tribalism/Negative Ethnicity/Ethnocentrism/Ethnicism 7

    Literature Review 8

        On Ethnopolitical Conflict in Kenya 8

        On Church and Ethnopolitical Conflict in Kenya 14

        On Liberation Theology in Kenya: The Role of Women

            Theologians 15

        On Reformed Theological Anthropology and Politics 19

    Research Methodology/Model/Framework 23

    Structure of the Book 28

Chapter 2 31

History of Ethnopolitical Conflict in Kenya: 1895–2013

    The Roots of Ethnopolitical Conflict in Kenya: The "Colonial

      Situation" 31

    The Mau Mau Uprising and the Freedom of Kenya 44

    The Roots of Ethnic-Based Coalitions and Political Parties

      in Kenya 46

    Ethnopolitical Conflict during President Jomo Kenyatta's Era

      (1963–1978) 47

    Ethnopolitical Conflict during President Daniel Arap Moi's Era

      (1978–2002) 53

    Ethnopolitical Conflict during President Mwai Kibaki's Era

      (2002–2013) 59

    Conclusion 62

Chapter 3 65

The Church and Ethnopolitical Conflict in Kenya: 1982–2013

Ethnopolitical Conflict and the Church in Kenya: A Unified
  Voice (1982–2002)...66

Ethnopolitical Conflict and the Church in Kenya: A Divided
  Voice (2001–2008)...79

Ethnopolitical Conflict and the Church in Kenya: On the Road
  to Recovery (2008–2013)...84

Conclusion 87

Chapter 4 89

*John Calvin's Doctrine of the Image of God as a Basis for a
Reformed Doctrine of Ethnopolitical Cohesion in Kenya*

Defining "Reformed Tradition" 90

Resourcing the Reformed Tradition 91

Reformed Churches in Kenya 93

A Brief Biographical Sketch of John Calvin............................95

  Calvin's Ministry..97

  A Reconstruction Theologian or a Dictator? 99

  Calvin's Publications 100

  The Biblical Material and the Diversity of Opinions on the
    Image of God..102

  Theories of the *Imago Dei* 104

Calvin's Doctrine of the Image of God..................................108

  Previous Scholarship 108

  Calvin's Engagement with Other Views 112

  The Soul, the Body, and the Image of God 114

  The Image of God after the Fall 122

  Implications of Calvin's Doctrine of the Image of God 124

Conclusion 130

Chapter 5 131

*John Calvin's Doctrine of the Christian Life in Relation to His
Anthropology and Its Relevance for Ethnopolitical Cohesion in Kenya*

The Role of an Individual Believer 132

Necessary Resources in the Renewal of God's Image 137

  The Role of Christ 138

  The Role of the Holy Spirit...141

  The Role of the Word of God 144

  The Role of the Church 146

The Implications of Calvin's Doctrine of the Christian Life............152

Conclusion 158

Chapter 6 159

John Calvin's Political Theology in Relation to His Anthropology
and its Relevance for Ethnopolitical Cohesion in Kenya

    The Overall Shape of Calvin's Political Thoughts..........................159

    Calvin on Christianity and Culture..162

        Two Major Approaches..162

        Calvin and the Two Kingdoms..168

    The Source and Justification for Civil Government 172

        The Purpose and Role of Government 177

        Duties of Citizens towards Civil Authority 179

    Insights and Limitations of Calvin's Political Theology for the

        Kenyan Context 183

        Inspiration for Sociopolitical Engagement 183

        Basis for a Prophetic Critique of Ethnic-Based Politics............186

        Basis for a Prophetic Critique of Politics as Eating 187

        Inspires Charity and Compassion and an Ethic of Work..........196

    Conclusion 200

Chapter 7 201

"A Hungry Stomach Has No Ears": The Political Theology of
David Gitari and Henry Okullu as Theological Responses to
Ethnopolitical Conflict in Kenya

    Bishop John Henry Okullu...202

        Okullu's Political Theology 203

    Archbishop David Mukuba Gitari..210

        The Mode of Gitari's Public Engagement.................................213

        Gitari's Model of Public Engagement.......................................216

        The Theological Basis for Gitari's Political Engagement...........218

    Okullu, Gitari, and Calvin...227

    Conclusion 230

Chapter 8 231

Jesse Mugambi's Theology of Reconstruction as a Theological
Response to Ethnopolitical Conflict in Kenya

    A Brief Biography of Jesse Mugambi 232

    The Roots of African Theology of Reconstruction 233

    From Liberation to Reconstruction: The Thesis and

        Methods of ATOR 236

        Personal Reconstruction...242

        Cultural Reconstruction 243

        Ecclesial Reconstruction 244

        Socio-economic Reconstruction...246

Support and Critique of Mugambi's Reconstruction Theology 247
Contribution of Mugambi's Reconstruction Theology to the
    Quest for Ethnic Cohesion 255
        Mugambi and Calvin 258
    Conclusion 259

Chapter 9 261
John Mbiti's Theologies of Identity, Culture, and Community as
Theological Responses to Ethnopolitical Conflict in Kenya
    A Brief Biography of John Samuel Mbiti 262
    The Identity Question of Africa 265
        Mbiti's Concept of the Indigenous African Identity 274
    Mbiti's Theology of Culture 280
    Mbiti's Theology of Community 283
    Mbiti and Calvin 287
    Conclusion 288

Chapter 10 289
Conclusion, Limitations, and Further Research
    Limitations of the Book 291
    Further Research and Engaging Non-Christian Audiences 292

Appendix 295
Response to Reinhold Niebhur's Moral Man and Immoral Society

Bibliography 299

Index of Subjects 341

Index of Names 345

Abstract

This book provides a theological basis for social-political cohesion of Kenyan communities based on a study of the Reformed (John Calvin's) theological anthropology, Christian life, and politics. The book also examines the works of four Kenyan theologians from a Reformed perspective. Its thesis is that the search for ethnic cohesion in Kenya is a theological task that calls for a new theological anthropology and politics. A new future in Kenya calls for a new way of being human, which can only be availed of when the Kenyan people respond to the divine call and grace and by learning to challenge the inherited visions of the world. The response to God's call and grace means that the Kenyan people can look at their lives, their identities, in a new way. They can question and interrogate their allegiance to their ethnic communities and political parties and live differently. Only by looking deep into these realities can the Kenyan people find the lasting solution to the challenge of ethnopolitical conflict and, indeed, other social evils such as corruption, intolerance, and violence.

Acknowledgments

I owe a debt of gratitude to the faculty of McMaster Divinity College for the support and help accorded to me throughout my PhD studies. In particular, I want to thank my supervisor, Dr Steven M. Studebaker, and second reader, Dr Gordon L. Heath, for their immense support, guidance, and patience during the research and writing of my dissertation from which this book is developed. I would also like to thank my church families at Africa Inland Church, Chebaywo, Uasin Gishu, Kenya, and Mission Baptist Church, Hamilton, Canada, for their support and prayers. In particular, I thank my home church in Kenya for supporting me in prayer and financially at Scott Christian University where I undertook my undergraduate studies and from where my theological journey started. I thank my parents so much for their hard work, prayers, support, and above all, for nurturing my siblings and me in the ways of the Lord. I thank Langham Partnership International, ScholarLeaders International, and the family of Luke Baer, for providing the financial support that I needed for my studies. Without their help, I could not afford to study at McMaster even if I sold everything I own back in Kenya. Berur and Tala, my sons, I thank you so much. I lack words to express how much I love you. You always put a smile on my face even when I am tired and frustrated with research. Jeane, my dear wife, you have been my cheerleader and a close companion. *Achamok mising*.

CHAPTER 1

Introduction

The introductory section of the book has five parts. First, it highlights the need for the study. Second, it defines key terms such as ethnopolitical conflict/cohesion, ethnicity/ethnic group, and tribalism/negative ethnicity/ethnocentrism/ethnicism. Third, it offers literature review in three major areas: ethnopolitical conflict in Kenya in general; the role of Kenyan churches in responding to ethnopolitical conflict; and Reformed theological anthropology and politics. Fourth it presents the research methodology and framework. Fifth, it presents the structure of the book.

The Need for the Book

A few years ago, a Kenyan Christian posted on Facebook a post that encapsulates the struggle of the church in Kenya in regard to ethnicity and politics. He wrote, "For many Kenyan Christians, our commitment and allegiance follows the order below: (1) Tribe, (2) political party, (3) Christ."[1] Unfortunately, the Kenyan people's allegiance to their ethnic groups and political parties has resulted in animosity, bigotry, and often violence. Consequently, theological conversations on building a cohesive Kenyan society must, of necessity, address ethnic identity and political mobilization.

Building a cohesive Kenyan society is a key agenda of the National Commission on Integration and Cohesion (NCIC), established through an act of parliament (the National Cohesion and Integration Act, 2008), as part of the Kenya National Dialogue and Reconciliation Agreement signed in Nairobi on 1 February 2008, which sought to end the post-election ethnic

---

1. Kevin Okwara, Facebook post, retrieved 27 March 2016.

conflict that had engulfed the country from December 2007.[2] Although this book does not examine the work of NCIC, it provides the theological justifications for the overall agenda of NCIC, having a cohesive Kenyan society.

Though ethnopolitical conflict has been a part of Kenya's political history since 1963, and especially after the promulgation of multiparty democracy in 1991, there is a lacuna of Kenyan theologies of ethnicity and politics.[3] However, the dearth of theological responses to ethnopolitical conflict is not a Kenyan problem. John de Gruchy recognizes the absence of theological responses to ethnopolitical conflict all over Africa when he writes, "Although there has been courageous Christian opposition to unjust regimes, African theologians outside southern Africa have not generally developed a critical political theology able to help the churches resist tyranny, overcome ethnic tension, and establish a just democratic order."[4] As de Gruchy observes in his book, published in 1995, it is true that whenever the church in Kenya succeeded in engaging politically in the 1980s and 1990s, it was mainly in regard to activism against unjust political systems; little was written on the theological bases and justifications for the church's sociopolitical engagement.

Consequently, this study provides a theological basis for social-political cohesion of Kenyan communities. The thesis is that the search for ethnic cohesion in Kenya is a theological task that calls for a new theological anthropology and politics. Thus, a new future in Kenya calls for a new way of being human, which can only be availed of when the people respond to the divine call and grace. The response to God's call and grace means that the Kenyan Christians can look at their lives, their identities, in a new way. They can question and interrogate their allegiance to their ethnic communities and political parties and live differently. Only by looking deep into these realities can the Kenyan people find a lasting solution to the challenge of ethnopolitical conflict and, indeed, other social evils such as corruption, intolerance, and violence.

---

2. National Cohesion and Integration Commission, *Building a Cohesive Kenyan Society*, 1.

3. Lumumba, ("Electoral Justice," 147–167) argues that out of the ten elections held in Kenya since 1963, only the 1963 and the 2002 elections were credited fair and democratic. The rest were marred by irregularities.

4. de Gruchy, *Christianity and Democracy*, 191–192.

Definition of Key Terms

The following section defines several terms that are critical to this book. The terms include ethnopolitical conflict, ethnopolitical cohesion, ethnicity, ethnic group, and tribalism. This section also explains the positive dimension of ethnicity as construed from a Christian theological perspective. The section begins by defining "ethnopolitical conflict" and "ethnopolitical cohesion."

Ethnopolitical Conflict and Ethnopolitical Cohesion

Ethnopolitical conflict is the violence and or tension caused by allegiance to ethnicity and politics. As Kimani Njogu explains, ethnopolitical conflict takes different forms, which include "disruption of campaign rallies, eviction of citizens from their homes or constituencies, verbal threats, and intimidation, looting, abductions, arson and destruction of property, torture, physical assault, obstruction of voting or nomination processes and death."[5] Njogu adds that ethnopolitical conflict "is preceded by ethnic hate speech, distribution of leaflets warning of dire consequences if targeted individuals and communities do not vacate their homes and extensive political mobilization based on ethnic identity."[6] Ethnopolitical conflict is not a Kenyan problem. Different parts of the world struggle with it. Daniel P. Moynihan identifies ethnic-based conflict as a "world-wide pandemonium."[7] However, even though ethnopolitical conflict is a global problem, its destructive nature is most felt in Africa, a continent with multiple ethnic communities.

The term "ethnopolitical cohesion" as used in this book means social co-existence that transcends the divisions of ethnicity and politics. Another way to understand the term is to see it in terms of "community cohesion" or "social cohesion" but with a clear emphasis on ethnic and political issues (thus "ethnopolitical"). The term "community cohesion" became popular after being used in the United Kingdom following riots in northern cities of England (Oldham, Burnley, and Bradford) in the summer of 2001.[8] Ted

---

5. Njogu, "Prologue to Ethnic Diversity," vii.

6. Njogu, vii.

7. Moynihan, *Pandemonium*, xiii.

8. The riots were between police, white groups, and South Asian men. Following the riots, Ted Cantle was chosen to head a team to investigate the causes of the riots and to make recommendations to the UK government. Four reports were produced in 2001. As David Herbert (*Creating Community Cohesion*, 54) notes, following Ted Cantle's report (and

Cantle observes that prior to 2001, the term "community cohesion" had not been used to shape government policy on race relations in the UK.[9] Cantle distinguishes between the terms "community cohesion" and "social cohesion." He writes,

> *Social cohesion reflects divisions based on social class and economic factors and is complemented by social capital theories relating to the "bonding" between people and the presence of mutual trust. It is seen to be undermined by the social exclusion experienced by individuals or groups, generally defined by their social class and economic position.*
>
> *Community cohesion reflects divisions based upon identifiable communities, generally on the basis of faith or ethnic distinctions. It is also complemented by the social capital theory of "bridging" between communities. It is undermined by the disadvantage, discrimination, and disaffection experienced by the identifiable community as a whole.*[10]

The two terms above reflect the need to help communities to live in peace and harmony with one another. Since the original use of the term "community cohesion" as Cantle explains, was in regard to faith and ethnic issues, and not ethnic and political issues, the book forgoes its use and sticks to "ethnopolitical cohesion" because the term is precise in delineating the type of cohesion needed in Kenya. Certainly, ethnicity and politics are not the only factors contributing to conflict in Kenya, but they are the major factors.

Ethnicity/Ethnic Group

Scholars recognize that the term "ethnicity" is difficult to define precisely.[11] For this study, the term "ethnicity" means the subjective perception or the phenomenon of belonging to a particular ethnic group.[12] Elaine Burgess

---

other subsequent reports), the concept of "community cohesion" became key to subsequent government policies on community relations until 2010.

  9. Cantle, *Community Cohesion*, 48.

  10. Cantle, 52, emphasis original.

  11. Sparks, *Ethnicity and Identity*, 1; Eller, *From Culture to Ethnicity to Conflict*, 7.

  12. Several scholars point to the subjective nature of ethnic identification. See, Eller, *From Culture to Ethnicity to Conflict*, 11; Horowitz, *Ethnic Groups in Conflict*, 7. These scholars

defines "ethnicity" as "the character, quality, or condition of ethnic group membership, based on an identity with and/or a consciousness of group belonging that is differentiated from others by symbolic 'markers' (including cultural, biological, or territorial), and is rooted in bonds to a shared past and perceived ethnic interests."[13] The term "ethnic group" refers to "a group of people who have a shared history (through a common myth of origin), cultural heritage, economic circumstances, language, territory, and political organizing."[14] Ethnicity is not a negative reality.

Ethnicity is a key component of someone's identity. As Jolle Demmers asserts, "ethnic attachments answer to people's need to belong, to have a place in the world, a sense of destiny, immortality and continuity."[15] Furthermore, ethnicity is a positive force that can unite people for a common cause. In democracies such as Kenya, the most powerful unifying factor is not the nation but the kin group and the tribe. This union is often the only way a community survives the injustice of those in power. Ogot notes, "Kenya's rulers have chosen to distribute Kenya's limited resources on the basis not of equity and fairness but by favouring selected groups based on a recognition of their ethnic identity."[16] In such cases, ethnic communities form efficient social networks for humanitarian purposes because they cannot rely on the government. Thus, as a cultural phenomenon, ethnicity brings people together for the preservation of communal values, artifacts, histories, and for humanitarian purposes. However, as a political factor, ethnicity is malleable and often damaging. This is particularly true in democracies where people compete for scarce resources and politics operate within a framework in which the winner takes it all.

From a Christian theological perspective, ethnic diversity is part of the beautiful creation of God. Scripture establishes a trajectory, which moves from a mono-ethnic garden of Eden to a multi-ethnic city of God, a place where a great multitude of people from all tribes and nations are brought

---

argue that ethnic identity is something that is fluid and malleable. It is acquired through a process of socialization.

13. Burgess, "Resurgence of Ethnicity," 270.

14. Munene-Karega, "Production of Ethnic Identity," 43.

15. Demmers, *Theories of Violent Conflict*, 34.

16. Ogot, *Kenyans Who Are We?*, 14.

together to worship the Lamb (Rev 7:9–12).[17] Ethnic diversity is not a postlapsarian reality. Before the fall, God's creation is depicted as an intricate world of vibrant diversity in which humans existed in an interdependent relationship with one another and with God's other creation. The fall greatly distorted this unique diversity but did not eradicate it. God told Abraham that he would be the father of many nations (Gen 15:5; 22:17–18) and reminded the Jews to treat the foreigners as citizens (Lev 19:34), to love the stranger (Deut 10:18–19), and to be hospitable to the needy stranger (Lev 19:9–10; 23:22). Furthermore, the Jews were explicitly prohibited from oppressing the foreigner (Exod 23:9; Deut 24:14) or denying them justice (Deut 24:17–18). The prophets too emphasized justice, mercy, and compassion to the foreigner (e.g. Jer 7:6).[18]

Genesis 10 affirms that all human beings are all related. However, this story is immediately followed by the Tower of Babel (Gen 11), which shows how fallen humanity seeks an identity that is apart from God's intended purpose. But the New Testament story of Pentecost reverses the curse of Babel. The Pentecost narrative affirms ethnic and linguistic diversity as part of the renewed people of God. The reversal of Babel was not about obliteration of ethnic identities but in fact was an affirmation and a renewal of them. In Acts 2, "God does not reverse Babel by removing ethnic or linguistic diversity. Rather Spirit-filling enables people to hear and declare God's greatness in every language (a foretaste of heaven – Rev 5:9, 10)."[19] At Babel, people sought homogeneity outside God's intended purpose; Pentecost restored unity-in-diversity as God intended. This restoration begins with the church and culminates in the eschatological city of God, the new Jerusalem, where

---

17. Manickam, "Race, Racism, and Ethnicity," 723.

18. Van Es, "Hosting a Stranger," 36–46.

19. Rasmussen, "What Are We Going to Do," 214. Similarly, Walls (*Missionary Movement*, 51) adds, "Conversion to Christ does not isolate the convert from his or her community; it begins the conversion of that community. Conversion to Christ does not produce a bland universal citizenship: it produces distinctive discipleships, as diverse and variegated as human life itself." For the Kenyan context, the challenge is how to assist these "distinctive discipleships," Christians from various ethnic communities to love one another and to not let their ethnicities and political identifications define how they relate with each other.

God's creation is restored once again to the beauty of diversity.[20] The new Jerusalem bears close resemblance to the garden of Eden. The only difference is that it is a sanctified city.[21]

Thus in God's eschatological kingdom, all nations (ethnic communities) are reconciled in Christ. Thus ethnicity, which is part of God's original creation, is not a negative reality but becomes negative when used as a marker of exclusion of people or to inspire physical or non-physical conflict between ethnic groups. Unfortunately, in Kenya ethnicity has often been used as a marker of exclusion and not as a positive force.

Nelson Kasfir pays attention to the polarizing nature of ethnicity when he argues that the "markers" of ethnicities such as common ancestry, language, territory, cultural practices and the like, "are perceived by both insiders and outsiders as important indicators of identity, so that they can become the bases for mobilizing social solidarity and which in certain situations result in political activity."[22] The resultant political activity in many cases intensifies to political conflict, especially if political actors manipulate ethnicity to attain, retain, or monopolize power. John Lonsdale refers to this form of manipulation of ethnicity for political gain as "political tribalism" or "political ethnicity," which "determines how 'we' behave in relation to 'other' in the arena of a multi-ethnic state."[23] Chapter 2 of this book delves into the history and manifestation of political tribalism in Kenya.

Tribalism/Negative Ethnicity/Ethnocentrism/Ethnicism

The above terms connote the negative aspects of ethnicity. They represent the viewpoint that an ethnic group is superior to other ethnic groups. Dawn Nothwehr defines "tribalism" as "the attitude and practice of harboring such a strong feeling of loyalty or bonds to one's tribe that one excludes or even demonizes those 'others' who do not belong to that group."[24] Similarly, D. W. Waruta asserts, "Tribalism is a pernicious moral problem because it means not only a very strong feeling of loyalty or a very strong bond to one's tribe

---

20. Manickam, "Race, Racism, and Ethnicity," 723; Wolters, *Creation Regained*, 91; Yong, *Missiological Spirit*, 42–47.

21. Studebaker, "Servants of Christ," 61.

22. Kasfir, *Shrinking Political Arena*, 77.

23. Lonsdale, "Moral and Political Argument," 73.

24. Nothwehr, *That They May Be One*, 5.

but also harbouring a favourable attitude and partial treatment towards members of one's tribe at the expense of those who do not belong to one's tribe."[25] Some scholars prefer the terms "negative ethnicity," "ethnocentrism," and "ethnicism" instead of "tribalism" because of the negative connotation that the term "tribe" carries. For many scholars, the word "tribe" is pejorative and connotes primitive, savage, barbaric, or regressive communities.[26]

Literature Review

This section reviews the literature relevant to the book. The review focuses on four major areas: ethnopolitical conflict in Kenya in general, the various responses of the Kenyan church to ethnopolitical conflict, liberation theology particularly the work of the Circle of the Concerned African Women Theologians, and Reformed theology (theological anthropology, Christian life, and political theology). The book's chapters also provide review of other relevant literature that is not outlined here, and there is no need to repeat the materials below. The review begins with scholarship on ethnopolitical conflict in Kenya.

On Ethnopolitical Conflict in Kenya

Scholarly works on ethnopolitical conflict in Kenya are numerous. Thus, the review cannot possibly cover all the materials but focuses on major sources. Bruce Berman and John Lonsdale's *Unhappy Valley: Conflict in Kenya and Africa* is a standard reference.[27] The book contains several articles written separately or jointly by the two western scholars since the 1970s on various issues such as the nature and development of the colonial State, the creation of Kenya's political elites, the Mau Mau emergency, and political violence. Lonsdale challenges Kenyans to reject what he calls "political tribalism" and to embrace "moral ethnicity," the moral compass or set of standards through which to judge the actions of political elites.[28] Lonsdale admits that moral

---

25. Waruta, "Tribalism as a Moral Problem," 120.

26. On the negative connotation of the terms "tribe," see Wamwere, *Towards Genocide*, 95–97; Waruta, "Tribalism as a Moral Problem," 120–121; Chege, "Ethnic Pluralism," 3–17; Munene-Karega, "Production of Ethnic Identity," 43; Berman and Lonsdale, "Nationalism," 313.

27. Berman and Lonsdale, *Unhappy Valley*.

28. Berman and Lonsdale, 466; Lonsdale, "Moral and Political Argument," 77.

ethnicity may not be a powerful institutional force against political abuse of power, "but it is the nearest Kenya has to a national memory and a watchful political culture."[29] Lonsdale's recommendation is indeed what Kenya needs, especially his call for a watchful political culture. Indeed, as Lonsdale asserts, Kenyans, especially Christians, must become tough critics of culture and must embody a different way of practicing relationships and politics.

Ethnicity and Democracy in Africa edited by Bruce Berman, Dickson Eyoh, and Will Kymlicka, has three essays on ethnicity and democracy in Kenya: John Lonsdale's "Moral and Political Argument in Kenya," E. S. Atieno Odhiambo's "Hegemonic Enterprises and Instrumentalities of Survival: Ethnicity and Democracy in Kenya," and Githu Muigai's "Jomo Kenyatta and the Ethno-Nationalist State in Kenya." The essays cover how Kenyan politicians capitalize on ethnicity for State and regime building. Odhiambo's essay covers the growth of resistance movements to ethnic-based politics in Kenya while Muigai, who was the Attorney General of Kenya until February 2018, examines the role played by Kenya's first president, in establishing the place of ethnicity and ethnic sub-nationalism in the politics of contemporary Kenya.[30] Odhiambo highlights the role of the clergy, reformist-constitutionalist lawyers, reformist politicians, and university lecturers and students in critiquing ethnic-based politics.[31] He also highlights the growth of negative ethnic sentiments in regard to Gikuyu-Luo relationships.

Myles Osborne's *Ethnicity and Empire in Kenya*, which is a revision of his thesis, traces the development of Kamba (Akamba) ethnic identity as "martial" and "loyal" over the past two hundred years.[32] Osborne examines how the Kamba people came to embrace martial and loyalty as definitive of "Kambaness." Additionally, the book shows how the Akamba capitalized on loyalty and military prowess to gain favors from the colonial regime, which employed Kamba men to fill the ranks of police and colonial soldiers. Furthermore, the book investigates the politicization of Kamba ethnicity in post-colonial Kenya. Osborne shows that in the mid-nineteenth century, ethnicity rarely organized the Kamba people. For example during the

---

29. Berman and Lonsdale, *Unhappy Valley*, 467.

30. Muigai, "Jomo Kenyatta," 200.

31. Odhiambo, "Hegemonic Enterprises," 168–172.

32. Osborne, *Ethnicity and Empire in Kenya*.

famine of the 1920s the Kamba fled west and "became" Kikuyu.[33] Kamba ethnic identity solidified through the various programs of the colonial government such as the *kipande* (identity cards) and forceful removal of the Kikuyu people from Ukamba Province, which became a province inhabited by Kamba alone.[34] The creation of an ethnic-based political organization, Ukamba Members Association (UMA) in 1938, bolstered ethnic consciousness among the Kamba.[35] Finally, Osborne shows that the Kamba have been less involved in post-election violence, attributed to various factors including the loyalty of the Kamba to the government.[36]

Chapter 7 of Edmond J. Keller's *Identity, Citizenship, and Political Conflict in Africa* is titled, "Kenya: Citizenship, Land, and Ethnic Cleansing."[37] In the chapter, Keller traces the roots of ethnic grievances to the colonial period, particularly the displacement of indigenous people from their ancestral lands in the Rift Valley and central provinces, the "White Highlands." Keller correctly argues that land, ancestral land in particular, carries more significance to the Kenyan people more than legal definitions of citizenship. Thus most of the ethnic tensions and conflict are associated with land problems.[38] Keller also examines the ethnic factor in the founding of Kenya's first political parties and Kenya's post-independence governments.

Jacqueline M. Klopp's "Kenya's Internally Displaced: Managing Civil Conflict in Democratic Transitions" is an important essay on the internal displacement of people following ethnic-based violence. The essay is found in

---

33. Osborne, *Ethnicity and Empire in Kenya*, 14. Bethwell Ogot, (*Kenyans, Who Are We?*, 20–30) also offers a similar argument about the malleability of Kenya's pre-colonial communities. Ogot writes, "By the end of the Nineteenth Century, the African communities in the future Kenya were already all contaminated by each other in a complex interdependent word. There were no watertight ethnicities. Clans and lineages expanded and contracted, gaining and losing members across porous and cultural frontiers" (20). Ogot gives the examples of the different ethnic communities that peacefully intermingled, intermarried, and "became" new ethnic communities, even producing new languages.

34. Osborne, *Ethnicity and Empire in Kenya*, 96–97.

35. Osborne, 109.

36. Osborne, 245.

37. Keller, *Identity, Citizenship, and Political Conflict*, 104–124.

38. Other essays that deal with land and conflict in Kenya include, Klopp, "Pilfering the Public"; Ndung'u, "Land and Violence in Kenya," 57–69; Sesi, "Ethnic Conflicts in Africa," 131–151.

East Africa and the Horn: Confronting Challenges to Good Governance.[39] Klopp has written other important articles on ethnic violence in Kenya.[40] Klopp defines "Internally Displaced Persons" (IDPs) as "people forced to leave their homes by coercion but who remain within their national borders."[41] Klopp's essay is important given that Kenya has experienced violence every five years following a national election and thousands of Kenyans have been displaced from their homes. Klopp examines the IDP crisis from 1991 to 2004. She writes, "By 2004 roughly 350,000 to 600,000 people, approximately one in every sixty Kenyans, continued to suffer from lack of redress for the violent displacement, loss of property and livelihood, but also murder or mutilation of loved ones they experienced during the clashes."[42] It is unfortunate that just two years after Klopp wrote the essay, Kenya experienced the worst IDP crisis in which more than 650,000 people were internally displaced.[43] Klopp's essay shows the important work the church plays in the aftermath of such a crisis. For Klopp, without the role of the church in Kenya in helping provide humanitarian relief, more IDPs, especially women and children, would die.[44]

The 2007–2008 post-election violence was a watershed moment in Kenya's history. Before the violence, Kenya was a safe haven for many refugees from the neighboring nations of Sudan, Ethiopia, and Somalia. Several works focus on the 2007–2008 violence. They include, *Healing the Wound: Personal Narratives about the 2007 Post-Election Violence in Kenya, Defining Moments: Reflections on Citizenship, Violence, and the 2007 General Elections in Kenya,* both edited by Kimani Njogu, and *(Re)membering Kenya: Identity, Culture, and Freedom* edited by Mbugua wa-Mungai and George

---

39. Klopp, "Kenya's Internally Displaced," 59–80. Other scholarly works on the refugee and IDP crisis in Kenya include, Abdullahi, "Ethnic Clashes, Displaced Persons"; United Nations Office for the Coordination of Humanitarian Affairs, *Affected Populations*; Intermediate Technology Development Group (ITDG), *Conflict in Northern Kenya*; Norwegian Refugee Council, "Kenya: Speedy Reform Needed"; Norwegian Refugee Council, *Internally Displaced People*; Obeng, "Religious Dimensions of Refugee Suffering," 121–133; Houle, "Empowering the Victims," 164–185.

40. Klopp, "Can Moral Ethnicity Trump Political Tribalism?"; Klopp, "NCCK and the Struggle"; Klopp, "Pilfering the Public."

41. Klopp, "Kenya's Internally Displaced," 60.

42. Klopp, 64.

43. Norwegian Refugee Council, "Kenya: Speedy Reform Needed," 7.

44. Klopp, "Kenya's Internally Displaced," 66.

Gona.[45] These books are part of a series of materials produced by Twaweza Communications, a Nairobi-based strategic communications company. *Healing the Wound* contains personal narratives of Kenyans who were victims of the 2007–2008 post-election violence, those who showed mercy and gave hope, and those who perpetrated the violence. The narratives show that the violence was not just about the presidential results, but was also about historical injustices in Kenya. *Defining Moments* has eight essays about the 2007–2008 ethnic violence. The essays revisit the factors that contributed to the violence and what Kenya should do to avoid recurrence of conflict in the future. *(Re)membering Kenya* critically examines the history of ethnicity and violence in Kenya, what it means to be a Kenyan, generational competition, the contribution of diasporic Kenyans to ethnic violence in Kenya, the role of Kenya's media in conflict resolution, and the success and failures of the Truth, Justice, and Reconciliation Commission (TJRC).

In addition to scholarly works, other materials detail ethnopolitical conflict in Kenya. These resources include the Truth, Justice, and Reconciliation Commission (TJRC) Report (3 volumes),[46] the Akiwumi Commission of Inquiry into Tribal Clashes,[47] the Waki Commission of Inquiry into Post-Election Violence,[48] the *Report of the Parliamentary Select Committee on Ethnic Violence*,[49] the Report of the Ndungu Commission on Illegal and Irregular Allocation of Public Land,[50] and the National Cohesion and Integration Commission (NCIC).[51] Human Rights Watch has also produced important

45. Njogu, ed., *Healing the Wound*; Njogu, *Defining Moments*; Gona and wa-Mungai, eds., *(Re)membering Kenya*. Other works on the 2007–2008 violence include, Nyaundi, "Walking the Slippery Road," 115–129; Nason, "Ethnic Violence in Kenya," 99–113; Ngaruiya, "Multifaceted Genesis," 82–89; Nasimiyu-Wasike, "Moral and Religious Implications," 120–128; Gathogo, "Meddling on to 2008," 143–154.

46. Truth, Justice, and Reconciliation Commission, *Summary: Truth Justice Reconcilaition Commission*, available online, http://www.acordinternational.org/silo/files/kenya-tjrc-summary-report-aug-2013.pdf.

47. Government of Kenya, *Akiwumi Report*.

48. Government of Kenya, *Waki Report*.

49. Government of Kenya, *Report of the Parliamentary Select Committee*.

50. Government of Kenya, *Ndung'u Report*.

51. National Cohesion and Integration Commission, *Building a Cohesive Kenyan Society*; National Cohesion and Integration Commission, *Status of Social Cohesion*.

documents on ethnic-based and post-election violence in Kenya.[52] Another important resource is the United States' House of Representatives records of the hearing of Subcommittee on Africa and Global Health, titled, "The Political Crisis in Kenya: A Call for Justice and Peaceful Resolution" written in February 2008.[53] The resource presents witness reports of a few Kenyans, the diplomatic community, and international humanitarian agencies on the post-election violence of 2007–2008. The National Council of Churches of Kenya (NCCK) has also produced several reports, letters, and press statements on ethnic violence.[54] In addition, Kenyan periodicals cover ethnopolitical conflict on a regular basis.

Although the Kenyan government purports to address the problem of ethnocentrism in all sectors of the Kenyan public, ethnocentrism continues to be a major problem, so much in fact that two Kenyan scholars believe Kenya is dangerously courting genocide. Koigi Wamwere, a former Member of Parliament and a political exile, encapsulates this dangerous path in his *Towards Genocide in Kenya: The Curse of Negative Ethnicity*.[55] Likewise, Peter Kagwanja, a notable Kenyan intellectual, also sums up Kenya's path to genocide in his "Courting Genocide: Populism, Ethno-Nationalism and the Informalisation of Violence in Kenya's 2008 Post-Election Crisis."[56] Wamwere's and Kagwanja's claim that Kenya is courting genocide is not farfetched. In *Kenya: A History since Independence*, Charles Hornsby observes, "The problem of ethnically focused political violence in Kenya has come to world attention in 1969, 1991–1993 and 2007–2008; each time worse than the last."[57] If indeed the severity of ethnopolitical violence has been intensifying since 1969, then Kenya must address the crisis or else the coming years will be dark.

---

52. Human Rights Watch, *"All the Men have Gone"*; Human Rights Watch, *Turning Pebbles*; Human Rights Watch, *Divide and Rule*; Human Rights Watch, *Playing with Fire*; Human Rights Watch, "High Stakes"; Human Rights Watch, *Playing the "Communal Card,"* 97–112; Kenya Human Rights Commission, *Killing the Vote*; Tostensen, Andreassen, and Tronvoll, *Kenya's Hobbled Democracy*.

53. US Government Printing Office, *Political Crisis in Kenya*.

54. NCCK, *Kairos for Kenya*; NCCK Executive Committee, "Hope for Kenya."

55. Wamwere, *Towards Genocide*.

56. Kagwanja, "Courting Genocide."

57. Hornsby, *Kenya*, 2.

On Church and Ethnopolitical Conflict in Kenya

Scholarly works on the church and ethnopolitical conflict in Kenya are numerous. Chapters 7 to 9 of this book examine and critique various theological responses of the church in Kenya to ethnopolitical conflict. The chapters examine and critique the contributions of David Gitari and Henry Okullu, Jesse Mugambi, and John Mbiti respectively, to ethnopolitical cohesion in Kenya. The said chapters, therefore, provide a review of publications by and on the above Kenyan scholars. Also, chapter 3 engages responses of the NCCK, the EFK (EAK), and various individuals to the problem of ethnopolitical conflict.

The following review provides other key publications on the responses of the church in Kenya to ethnocentrism and politics. *Contested Space: Ethnicity and Religion in Kenya* has thirteen essays on the responses of the church in Kenya to ethnic conflict.[58] Another relevant book is *Peacebuilding in East Africa: Exploring the Role of the Churches*, which has ten essays on the cultivation of peace and justice in East Africa.[59] Anne Nasimiyu-Wasike's essay, "Moral and Religious Implications for the Kenyan 2007 Post-Election Violence: The Role of the Church in National Healing" focuses specifically on Kenya.[60] Nasimiyu-Wasike argues that the church in Kenya must be at the forefront of the healing process following the 2007–2008 post-election violence.

Two essays in *Moral and Ethical Issues in African Christianity* are pertinent to the book.[61] The essays are D. W. Waruta's, "Tribalism as a Moral Problem in Contemporary Africa," and Peter Kanyandogo's, "Who Is My Neighbour? A Christian Response to Refugees and the Displaced in Africa."[62] Waruta begins by defining the terms "tribe" and "tribalism." He identifies colonialism as the origin of tribalism in Africa.[63] He also highlights the ethnic factor in Africa's politics, religions, institutions, and other sectors of the public life. Concerning religion, he asserts, "Most religious groups and denominations,

---

58. Chemorion, Mombo, and Peter, eds., *Contested Space*.
59. Musana, *Peacebuilding in Africa*.
60. Nasimiyu-Wasike, "Moral and Religious Implications," 120–128.
61. Mugambi and Nasimiyu-Wasike, *Moral and Ethical Issues*.
62. Waruta, "Tribalism as a Moral Problem"; Kanyandogo, "Who Is My Neighbour?"
63. Waruta, "Tribalism as a Moral Problem," 121–126.

closely scrutinized, are very tribal in their composition and leadership. Those that happen to be multi-ethnic with a national outlook are plagued with internal inter-tribal conflicts and strife which often attract the media as they take each other to the law courts for redress."[64] Waruta is right as chapter 3 of this book shows (see for example the case of the Anglican Church). Waruta proposes eight solutions to tribalism.[65] The proposals focus on the role of citizens, academic institutions, and the government in exposing tribalism as a moral problem.

The second essay is by Peter Kanyandogo. The essay claims that refugees must be treated not as numbers for statistical purposes but as brothers and sisters created in the image of God, and who share the same identity, dignity, and destiny as other fellow human beings.[66] Thus the refugee problem poses serious moral and anthropological questions. Kanyandogo challenges the church in Africa to embrace a theology of hospitality and compassion that recognizes the humanity of the refugees and the internally displaced. Certainly, this book follows Kanyandogo's proposal in affirming the image of God as the basis for affirming the humanity of all the people of Kenya, thus transcending ethnic divisions. By studying Calvin's political theology, this book affirms such important virtues as compassion and justice especially for the poor and the dispossessed such as the IDPs.

On Liberation Theology in Kenya: The Role of Women Theologians

African women's theology is an important strand of Christian engagement with culture in Kenya. African women's theology gained prominence through the work of Mercy Amba Oduyoye, a Ghanaian theologian who founded an organization called the Circle of the Concerned African Women Theologians (hereafter the Circle) in 1989. Other key women who have been in the helm of leadership of the Circle include Musimbi Kanyoro, from Kenya, and Isabel Phiri, from Malawi. Several women theologians from Kenya are members of the Circle. Among them are Esther Mombo, Eunice Kamaara,

---

64. Waruta, 127.
65. Waruta, 131–133.
66. Kanyandogo, "Who Is My Neighbour?," 173.

Philomena Njeri Mwaura, Teresia Hinga, Mary Getui, and others.[67] These women have published widely on Christianity and culture, especially on gender issues in the African context. The absence of women's theology in African Christian theology motivated the beginning of the Circle. Circle theologians compared African theology at that time to a bird with only one wing, noting that African theology was missing the perspective of African women. The Circle therefore sought to supply African theology with the missing dimension, the voices of African women thus creating "a two-winged theology."[68]

Circle theologians employ various methodologies when they theologize, and they approach scripture and theology from different perspectives.[69] Consequently, a great diversity exists in their works but they share the following theological conventions. Foremost, they resource African indigenous culture (proverbs, folktales, and stories) in their theologizing in order to contest gender discrimination. They also treat the Bible as God's story that has potential for transforming individuals as well as communities but can also be used to further oppression.[70] Their main goal is to redefine the meaning of being human in the world. Oduyoye argues that the responsibility to redefine humanity falls on men and women who must, together, reject anthropologies that affirm dichotomies and hierarchies as intrinsically necessary.[71] Thus they counter anthropologies that put prominence on ethnicity, race, and gender. Therefore even though Oduyoye asserts that Circle theology "adopts a perspectival approach rather than analysis and critique of existing

---

67. Their publications include, Kanyoro, *Introducing Feminist Cultural Hermeneutics*; Kanyoro, "Engendered Communal Theology"; Kanyoro, "African Women's Quest"; Chemorion, Mombo, and Peter, *Contested Space*; Kamaara, "Towards Christian National Identity"; Mwase and Kamaara, *Theologies*; Mwaura, "Human Identity"; Hinga, "African Feminist Theologies"; Getui and Kanyandogo, *From Violence to Peace*.

68. Njoroge, "New Way," 29.

69. Ogbu ("Daughters of Ethiopia," 265–266) expresses this diversity when he writes, "some women choose to be *rejectionist* by rejecting the Bible as canon; others are *radical reformers* who mine the radical elements within the gospel for empowerment; and still others have deployed Biblicism as the mooring for *loyalist* postures" (emphasis original).

70. For re-reading the Bible from an African women's perspective see Masenya, "Reading the Bible"; Dube, *Postcolonial Feminist Interpretation*; Dube, "Rereading the Bible"; Dube, *Other ways of Reading*.

71. Oduyoye, *Hearing and Knowing*, 132–135.

works,"[72] for its aim is to share the perspective of women on issues that affect women in Africa and around the world, Circle theologians have also intentionally criticized the works of male theologians whenever it falls short.[73] Thus as Maluleke observes, Circle theologians "are mounting a critique of both African culture and African Christianity in ways that previous African theologies have not been able to do."[74]

Circle theology is multicultural, multi-religious, multi-ethnic, and multi-racial; it is intentionally dialogue-oriented and pluralistic in approach. Members of the Circle include women from around the world who share the same goal of countering patriarchy in the world through research and publishing. Members come from different religions. The main dialogue partners for Christian Circle theologians are their counterparts in African Traditional Religion and African Indigenous Churches (AICs). The multi-faceted nature of Circle theology reflects in its commitment to the idea of community, hospitality, and equality. In fact, the name "Circle" itself echoes the equality between members and the primacy of dialogic communication.[75]

Circle theology is communal theology. Oduyoye asserts that African women's theology is "a theology of relations" because "African culture is very community-oriented."[76] Their theologies are also praxis-oriented. They have organized academic and non-academic conferences on Christianity and culture in Africa. They have also organized meetings geared towards addressing violence against women. Most of those meetings have been held at the *Talitha Qumi* Center for Women in Religion and Culture at Trinity College in Accra. Furthermore, they encourage reading the Bible with people in rural villages and emphasize that popular reading and academic reading should be encouraged.

Circle theology is greatly shaped by feminist perspectives and can be termed as feminist theology from an African context. However, Circle theologians prefer other titles such as "Circle theology," "communal theology,"

---

72. Oduyoye, Introducing *African Women's Theology*, 11.

73. An example is Oduyoye's critique of Mbiti's view of marriage in Oduyoye, "Critique of John Mbiti's View," 341–365 and Musa Dube's critique of J. N. K. Mugambi's theology of reconstruction in Dube, "Jesse Mugambi."

74. Maluleke, "Half a Century," journal article, 22.

75. Vähäkangas, "African Feminist Contributions," 171.

76. Oduyoye, *Introducing African Women's Theology*, 17.

"Bosati theology," "engendered communal theology," "sister theology," or "African women theology" as alternatives to "feminist theology" because of the negative connotations associated with the term "feminism" especially in Africa.[77] But what exactly is feminist theology from an African perspective?

For Oduyoye, African feminist theology is simply letting African women solve issues African women encounter in their day-to-day lives. African women must not wait for African men to solve women's problems because as she writes, "African men carry none of the life-giving burdens that African women carry. Women with babies on their backs and yams, firewood, and water on their heads [are] the common image of African women in real life as in art."[78] The main goal of Circle theology, therefore, is to address practical issues that Africans, especially women and children, face. Oduyoye asserts, "African women's theological reflections intertwine theology, ethics, and spirituality."[79] Kanyoro adds, "for us in Africa, it does not matter how much we write our theology in books, the big test before us is whether we can bring change to our societies. This is the tall order and we agonise about it."[80] The above efforts by Circle theologians show that their interest in the entire theological enterprise goes beyond academic theology, that is, reading, reflecting, and writing, to a practical theology that addresses real life issues of women and others who are oppressed in Africa.

This book aligns with the overall agenda of the Circle that seeks to redefine the meaning of being human in the world especially in the context of violence. For Christian Circle theologians, this redefinition of humanity is an ecclesio-theological task. Its center is the doctrine of the image of God for in it is the affirmation of the sacredness of human life. Circle theologians call for an anthropology that views all people as created in God's image. This book is, like the work of the Circle, a project in contextual theology for it responds to a specific need within a certain context, in this case, Kenya. Furthermore, the book aligns with the agenda of the Circle of working for

---

77. Oduyoye, *Hearing and Knowing*, 121; Kanyoro, "Engendered Communal Theology"; Gibelini, *Paths of African Theology*, 167. For the negative perception of feminism in Africa, see Oduyoye, "Feminist Theology," 166–167.

78. Oduyoye, "Feminist Theology," 174.

79. Oduyoye, *Introducing African Women's Theology*, 16.

80. Kanyoro, "African Women's Quest," 82.

the sociopolitical transformation of the African continent. Even though Circle theologians are particularly interested in elevating the place of women in society, they are also interested in overcoming all other dehumanizing structures in societies. Circle theologians advocate for justice, reconciliation, and transformation of the world by way of doing theology. They particularly speak to evangelical churches in Kenya to consider social engagement part of their mission agenda. Thus, although this project does not particularly resource the work of Circle theologians, it continues its goals of furthering the dignity of all people through calling for an end to discrimination based on gender, race, ethnicity, or political affiliations.

On Reformed Theological Anthropology and Politics

Theological works on theological anthropology and political theology are extensive, and thus, it is not possible to review all of them. The review focuses only on materials that center on the image of God and the Reformed doctrines of the Christian life and political theology. Chapters 4, 5, and 6 engage with various publications on Calvin's theological anthropology, the Christian life, and political theology respectively, and therefore, shall not repeat the review here. The review that follows is limited to a few materials on theological anthropology in general and specifically on the *imago Dei*.

Douglas John Hall's *Imaging God: Dominion as Stewardship* examines the biblical, historical, and theological meaning of *imago Dei* in view of addressing the challenge of environmental degradation. Hall begins by asserting that the Western interpretation of the *imago Dei* as dominion has resulted in abuse of the environment.[81] Hall emphasizes *imago Dei* as relational, not as something to be possessed. He treats "endowments" or "substance" of the image as secondary. The book is useful in its deep historical development of the doctrine of the *imago Dei* and shows that theological musings on the relevance of the image of God to contemporary human problems are not far-fetched.

Stanley J. Grenz's *The Social God and the Relational Self: A Trinitarian Theology of the Imago Dei* is an important resource on relational theological anthropology. Grenz notes that his work "seeks to extend the insights of contemporary Trinitarian thought to theological anthropology, with the goal of

---

81. Hall, *Imaging God*, vii.

developing a social or communal understanding of the concept of the *imago Dei* as a response to the dissipation of the self of modernity."[82] In regard to *imago Dei*, Grenz asserts that the three understandings of the image of God, that is, substantialist, relational, and eschatological models are insufficient. He proposes an alternative option, which is relating image of God to *imago Christi*.[83] He argues that the Old Testament looks forward to Christ, the perfect image of God who establishes an eschatological community, the new humanity with God. "Consequently, the humankind created in the divine image is none other than the new humanity conformed to the *imago Christi*, and the *telos* toward which the Old Testament creation narrative points is the eschatological community of glorified saints who have joined their head in resurrection life by the power of the Spirit."[84] Grenz also provides various practical significance of the image of God that is rooted in Christ. The book is significant in developing further the thought on the practicability of the image of God for today, which is the overall goal of this book.

Howard I. Marshall's "Being Human: Made in the Image of God" explores "the concept of the image of God in human beings in the light of the evidence in the OT and also in the NT where believers are conformed to the image of Christ and draws out the implications for what it means to be truly human."[85] In regard to what it means to say that Christ is the image of God and Christians are being re-created in Christ's image, Marshall asserts: "This new image is related to character and glory. It begins with inward transformation, which must surely have outward expression, and it leads to transformation of the body into a glorious body."[86] Marshall also discusses five implications of the doctrine of the image of God: (1) the creatureliness of humanity; (2) dominion as responsible stewardship; (3) human dignity rooted in the image of God and redemption in Christ; (4) body as dignified; (5) rejection of social boundaries. In conclusion, Marshall attempts to develop the practical consequences of the concept of the image

---

82. Grenz, *Social God*, 3.
83. Grenz, 142.
84. Grenz, 231.
85. Marshall, "Being Human," 47.
86. Marshall, 60.

as the capacity for personal relationships and concludes that being human is being like Jesus.[87]

In *Reforming Theological Anthropology: After the Philosophical Turn to Relationality*, F. LeRon Shults, a Reformed systematic theologian, argues that theological anthropology needs to be reformed in the wake of the "philosophical turn to relationality" in philosophy, psychology, and science. To achieve this task, Shults engages in interdisciplinary studies of philosophy, educational psychology, cultural anthropology, and theology. Of special interest to the book is chapter 10, "Relationality and the Doctrine of the *Imago Dei*." In this last chapter, he argues that *imago Dei* understood relationally and eschatologically, provides the church with a hope-filled way of life. A hope-filled life is "a proleptic participation (*koinonia*) in divine glory," rather than a life preoccupied with self-glory and self-aggrandizement.[88] Shults examines and critiques how the image of God has been interpreted in Christian history, from church fathers to medieval theologians to modern thinkers.

J. Richard Middleton's, *The Liberating Image: Imago Dei in Genesis 1* (2005) is a reference material on scholarship in the image of God. Middleton examines the doctrine of the image of God from an interdisciplinary approach. In addition to biblical exegesis, Middleton resources the ancient Near East culture that formed the context of Genesis. Middleton converses with theologians and ethicists on ways the image of God is relevant for the world. Indeed, his intention is stated as interdisciplinary "an attempt to bridge the disciplinary gap between systematic theology and Old Testament studies, as it applies specifically to the *imago Dei*."[89] Middleton also examines the various views on the image of God. His study is significant for understanding the image of God, the social context of Genesis 1, and the relevance of the doctrine of the image of God for ethics, power, and violence.

David P. Gushee's *The Sacredness of Human Life: Why an Ancient Biblical Vision is Key to the World's Future* provides the practicability of the doctrine of the image of God, showing that the doctrine is still relevant today.[90] In this book, David Gushee defines and defends the concept of the sacredness

---

87. Marshall, 63–67.

88. Shults, *Reforming Theological Anthropology*, 241.

89. Middleton, *Liberating Image*, 32.

90. Gushee, *Sacredness of Human Life*.

of human life. He digs into scripture, historical theology, Christian history, and present-day ethical issues to establish that sacredness of human life has always been part of Western history. Gushee examines theological themes of creation, *imago Dei*, liberation, justice, incarnation, and *imago Christi* in attempt to prove the sacredness of human life.

Philip Tachin's article, "Humanity in the Image of God: Towards Ethnic Unity in Africa" is an important essay for two reasons.[91] First, it discusses the problem of ethnic conflict in Africa. Second, it presents the doctrine of the image of God as a theological basis for ethnic integration in Africa. His overarching thesis is that when Africans see each other as made in God's image, they will see those of other ethnicities as extensions of themselves and so work together with one another for peace and reconciliation. Tachin focuses on the Nigerian context. He concludes with the following piercing but generalizing statement: "There is no continent on earth in the twenty-first century where people of similar cultures would hunt down and kill fellow humans as they do animals, except Africa. Africans apply the same hunting mood for animals to their fellow Africans in all kinds of violent conflicts."[92] Tachin's assertion ignores the reality of conflict in other parts of the world such as the Middle East. Tachin asserts that secular anthropology has not helped resolve Africa's ethnic problems; "Christian anthropology offers a better perspective that should be accepted and inculcated into younger generations to prepare them for a better future for African nations."[93] He considers the image of God to encompass both the ontological and functional aspects of a human being. For Tachin, affirming the image of God in humanity guarantees the dignity of all human beings. Tachin also emphasizes the role of redemption in Christ in helping humanity transcend ethnic divisions. The book develops Tachin's thesis further by including political dimensions of ethnicity and emphasizing the renewal of humanity in Christ.

Marc Cortez's two books on theological anthropology are good reference materials for the book. The first book is *Theological Anthropology: A Guide for the Perplexed* and *Christological Anthropology in Historical Perspective*.[94]

---

91. Tachin, "Humanity in the Image of God."

92. Tachin, 72.

93. Tachin, 73.

94. Cortez, *Theological Anthropology*; Cortez, *Christological Anthropology*.

In the first book, Cortez covers various aspects of theological anthropology such as the *imago Dei*, sexuality, mind and body, and free will. He notes that theological anthropology begins with the divine-human relationship and more specifically, with Jesus Christ, "the one who is both fully human and fully divine, the true image of God, the redeemer of humanity, and the teleological focus of all creation."[95] Precisely, theological anthropology "is the area of Christian reflection that seeks to understand the mystery of humanity by reflecting theologically – and thus, christologically – on the human person in constant and critical dialogue with the other anthropological disciplines."[96]

Cortez's second book delves deeper into what exactly entails a christologically focused anthropology. He examines the Christologies of Gregory of Nyssa (the incarnation), Julian of Norwich (God's love displayed on the cross), Martin Luther (the righteousness of Christ that becomes ours), Friedrich Schleiermacher (Jesus's unique God-consciousness), Karl Barth (the doctrine of election), John Zizioulas (true personhood), and James Cone (Jesus's liberating activity on behalf of the oppressed).[97] In studying each historical figure, Cortez provides various ways Christology informs theological anthropology. Furthermore, each figure examined address the *imago Dei* in light of ethics and Christology. The starting points of each figure also lead to various anthropological conclusions.

Research Methodology/Model/Framework

The book is a project in interdisciplinary and contextual theology. It is interdisciplinary because it draws from the fields of sociology (ethnic violence) and theological anthropology as well as contemporary (e.g. Mugambi) and historical theology (i.e. Calvin). It is contextual because it starts with and endeavors to address a specific issue within Kenyan society and Christianity. Since the book is contextual theology, starting with the context is important.[98] Contextual theology intentionally works out of a particular cultural place.

---

95. Cortez, *Theological Anthropology*, 5.

96. Cortez, 7.

97. Cortez, *Christological Anthropology*, 219.

98. Contextual theology focuses on the context first before explicating how theology speaks to the context. See, Schreiter, *Constructing Local Theologies*, 4; Pears, *Doing Contextual Theology*, 13; Bevans, *Models of Contextual Theology*, 1–2.

For this book, the starting point is the history and contemporary reality of ethnopolitical violence in Kenya. This focus on history of ethnopolitical conflict in Kenya and the subsequent solution through a study of a historical figure (Calvin), coheres with the African traditional milieu that respects the past. African people believe that the past (*zamani*) and the present (*sasa*) are mutually connected.[99] A history of a particular community, for example, defines how a community lives in the present time. Thus, to neglect the past is to neglect the present. The past, a people's history, is "a constant source of new beginnings, of ontological renewal" and there is no such a thing as factual history for history's own sake.[100] In traditional Africa, history was viewed as "a normative and living record" that had a rich, practical significance to contemporary life.[101] Thus for many traditional African communities, history is not about a dead past. History is alive. This book works from this view of history. Chapters 2 and 3 tell the story of ethnopolitical conflict in Kenya so that contemporary Kenyan Christians can learn from the past and so re-define their lives in the present. Chapters 4 to 6 resource John Calvin, a man who belongs to a different generation and culture, but his theology is part and parcel of the story of the Reformed movement in Kenya and thus must be told. Chapters 7 to 9 resource four major theologians from Kenya as part of the contemporary story of Christian political engagement in Kenya and in view of addressing the problem of ethnopolitical conflict. The intersection of Calvin and the Kenyan theologians is on the main issues that the Kenyan theologians tackle (practical sociopolitical engagement – Okullu and Gitari; sociopolitical reconstruction – Mugambi; and identity, culture, and community – Mbiti). The focus on these four theologians shows that a Reformed theology for the Kenyan context is not one-directional (Calvin to Kenya) but two-way. The Kenyan context has something to say about theological and sociopolitical issues in Kenya.

Whereas the book resources Calvin's theology for the Kenyan context, it recognizes that the African worldview has important resources that can

---

99. John Mbiti was the first person to popularize the twin ideas of *zamani* and *sasa* in his *African Religions and Philosophy* (1969). (The first edition is used in this study unless otherwise stated).

100. Ray, *African Religions*, 41.

101. Ray, 42.

nourish and enrich theology especially in its quest to address sociopolitical issues. The book works from the framework that understands the whole of life as interconnected. The African traditional life embraces this holistic nature of life. For the African, the sacred and the secular, the supernatural and the natural, are inextricably linked and cannot be separated. J. N. K. Mugambi and John Mbiti emphasize this holistic nature of African worldview (chapters 8 and 9 respectively). Because the African traditional cosmology values interconnectedness of life, it opposes dichotomization of life into sacred and secular. For the African culture, space was sacred, holy, and symbolic (contrary to Calvin).[102] For Africans, objects and nature, events and actions were viewed from a religious perspective and carried a symbolic message. African philosophy (ethnophilosophy), aesthetics, art, music, and politics and so forth, are intimately linked to religion because African people are by nature "notoriously religious."[103] Consequently, the idea that the sacred and the secular or church and State, do not meet, is antithetical to the African worldview.[104] The analogy of currents that flow into each other, nourishing, invigorating, and even disturbing each other in the process, and yet distinct from each other has been used to explicate this interconnectedness typical of the African traditional worldview.[105]

Another important contextual resource is the concept of *ubuntu*. The term "*ubuntu*" is a Bantu ontological noun describing the essence of being

---

102. Dyrness ("Spaces for an Evangelical Ecclesiology," 268) argues that Protestant Reformers "explicitly denied that any particular 'spaces' had symbolic significance. Calvin's locked church became a metaphor for a space that was symbolically vacant." Reformers emphasized the preaching of the Word and the administration of sacraments. What the church did was considered very important. Consequently, "objects and actions filled Protestant spaces but they did not have intrinsic religious significance" (268). Dyrness believes that this outlook shaped Evangelical consciousness and resulted in a disembodied spirituality. Dyrness adds, "For the church is not simply gathering of believers into the body of Christ by the power of the Spirit to the glory of God, not even those theologically important activities which constitute worship; it is also an historically and culturally situated institution that presents some shape to the world" (255).

103. Mbiti, *African Religions and Philosophy*, 1.

104. Chapter 3 shows that whereas Kenyan politicians are fond of telling the church to stay away from politics, what they mean by "stay away from politics" is mainly that the clergy must not preach against social injustice and must not challenge their congregations to hold politicians and the government accountable. Politicians would still find a way to co-opt the church in order to win votes.

105. For more on this idea of "currents" see Okesson, "Sacred and Secular Currents."

human.[106] A person with *ubuntu*, Desmond Tutu explains, is generous, hospitable, friendly, caring, and compassionate.[107] *Ubuntu* is about human life as a dynamic movement towards becoming more human; a person with *ubuntu* works towards becoming a better person.[108] As a person treats others with respect, they become a better human being. However, not all people act human, others, especially those who harm people, are considered inhuman (cruel/barbaric) or unhuman (bearing animal-like characteristics). The Kalenjins categorize such inhuman/unhuman persons as *sorin* (*sorik*), "evil" people, or *bik che matinye koroti* ("people with no human blood"). A Kalenjin proverb puts it this way: *Ma chi chi nengero ko chi ama chi* (a person is not a person who does not act like a person). Thus, a person has to act humanely to be considered human. However, though inhuman people are perceived as unhuman, and they may indeed be unhuman because of their actions, their actions, nevertheless, do not obliterate *ubuntu*. *Ubuntu*, like *imago Dei*, is a permanent irreversible essence of human life (chapter 4). Human actions have the potential of darkening *ubuntu* but cannot completely alienate it.[109] For African people, a person regains his or her noble status as a bearer of *ubuntu* only through actualizing *ubuntu*. In summary, a person is fully *umuntu* (human) when they treat other human beings as *abantu* (humans) and not as *infintu* (things).[110] This sacred character of human life coheres with the Christian affirmation that all human beings are created in God's image and so deserve honor (chapters 4 to 6). Humans are persons, not things, to be used or to be abused.

The book draws from library and archival research for chapter 2 and 3. It draws on the following primary sources: colonial reports, Kenyan periodicals, the reports of the Truth, Justice, and Reconciliation Commission (three volumes), the report of the Akiwumi Commission of Inquiry into Tribal Clashes, the report of the Waki Commission of Inquiry into Post-Election Violence, the report of the *Parliamentary Select Committee on Ethnic*

---

106. Hankela, *Ubuntu, Migration, and Ministry*, 50. Other synonyms of *ubuntu* include *botho* in Setswana and Sesotho, *utu* in Swahili, and *unhu* in Shona.

107. Tutu, *No Future*, 31.

108. On this aspect of becoming more human, Ezigbo, *Re-imagining*, 268–269; Hankela, *Ubuntu, Migration, and Ministry*, 52; Ng'weshemi, *Rediscovering the Human*, 15.

109. Hankela, *Ubuntu, Migration, and Ministry*, 53.

110. Kapolyo, *Human Condition*, 19–27.

Violence, and the report of the Ndung'u Commission on Illegal and Irregular Allocation of Public Land, and various documents of the Human Rights and Kenya Human Rights Commission. The book also draws from various documents produced by the National Council of Churches of Kenya (NCCK) and the Evangelical Alliance of Kenya (EAK).[111]

The second step is constructive (chapters 4 to 6). It draws on Calvin's theological anthropology, Christian life, and political theology to propose a solution to ethnopolitical violence for the Kenyan Reformed churches. Specifically, this section applies Calvin's theology of the divine image, the Christian life, and political life to the problem of ethnopolitical conflict in Kenya. The book shows that affirming the doctrine of the image of God sustains a view of the Christian life and political theology that helps people live peacefully with one another. Douglas John Hall, in *Imaging God*, demonstrates a present-day scholarly legitimacy of using the *imago Dei* as an interpretive lens to address modern concerns such as the ecological crisis, ethics, and human conflict.[112] The book, therefore, follows Douglas Hall's methodology. Furthermore, the book follows in the footsteps of Reformed theologians who affirm the destructive power of sin, the redemption, not only of individual believers, but of culture as well, and bearing witness to a different way of life. Thus the book follows the strand of Reformed scholarship, which recognizes salvation as holistic and stresses that Christians are not spectators but active agents in the transformation of their communities, including the political life.[113]

The third step is to set forth previous proposals for dealing with the problem of ethnopolitical violence (chapters 7 to 9) from Kenya and responding to them from a Reformed perspective. This step is essential in order to examine the contributions from Kenyan theologians. It is also essential because it locates the book within the current field of scholarship in Kenya. Thus, more than being descriptive, the chapters analyze, critique,

---

111. I am thankful to ScholarLeaders International for awarding me a research grant, which covered most of the expenses of my research work in Nairobi.

112. Hall, *Imaging God*, 66.

113. Not all Reformed theologians affirm cultural transformation. VanDrunen, (*Natural Law and the Two Kingdoms*), for example, opposes Christian culture making emphasizing instead, the redemption of people not culture.

and synthesize the major theologies of ethnopolitical cohesion from Kenya, from a Reformed perspective.

The research uses historical theology to study Calvin's doctrine of the divine image, the Christian life, and political theology. Calvin's *Institutes of the Christian Religion* (1559 edition) is the main primary source of this study. This book relies on Calvin scholars in order to identify the major parts of Calvin's works that are relevant. Thus, this research is informed by a host of secondary literature related to the topics of study.

Structure of the Book

The book has ten chapters. Chapter 1 is the introduction. Chapter 2 provides a broad descriptive analysis of ethnopolitical conflict in Kenya. It examines the contributions of the British colonial government and Kenya's post-colonial governments, i.e. Kenyatta regime (1963–1978), Moi regime (1978–2002), and Kibaki regime (2002–2013), to the current problem of ethnopolitical conflict. The chapter shows that even though ethnopolitical conflict is rooted in the colonial past, pre-colonial governments have also helped entrench it in Kenya's culture.

Chapter 3 examines the roles the mainstream Protestant, Evangelical, and Roman Catholic churches and their umbrella organizations, the National Council of Churches of Kenya (NCCK), the Evangelical Fellowship of Kenya (EFK, now called Evangelical Alliance of Kenya), and the Kenya Catholic Episcopal Conference (KCEC) – now known as the Kenya Conference of Catholic Bishops (KCCB) – played in their quest for ethnopolitical cohesion. The chapter shows that the church in Kenya was *generally* united in its prophetic engagement between 1990 and 2002, but lost its prophetic voice from 2002 to 2008. Following Kenya's tumultuous conflict in 2007–2008 and the subsequent apology of the KCCB to the Kenyan people, the church is on the way to recovery (2008–2013).

Chapters 4 to 6 propose a theology of ethnopolitical cohesion based on a constructive appropriation of John Calvin's theology of the divine image, the Christian life, and political theology. Based on Calvin's anthropology, chapter 4 shows that affirming humanity's creation in the image of God not only challenges the Kenyan people to value each other, it also inspires them to work towards peace and dignity. Calvin's theology of the image of God also shows the importance of humanity's reconciliation with God. Chapter 5 deals with Calvin's view of the Christian life as a renewal of God's image in believers. The chapter shows that for Calvin, the Christian life is holistic. The chapter argues that ethnic reconciliation is ultimately about the transformation of the human person. Chapter 6 examines the relevance of Calvin's political theology for ethnopolitical cohesion in Kenya. It argues that contrary to the politics of self-aggrandizement and corruption that prevail in Kenya, which results in manipulation of ethnicity for political gain thus causing ethnic conflict, politics is about the public good, not self-enrichment.

Chapters 7 to 9 examine three theological responses to ethnopolitical conflict from Kenya. Chapter 7 examines the work of Archbishop David Mukuba Gitari and Bishop John Henry Okullu to the Kenyan church's quest for ethnopolitical cohesion. The two clerics were among the most active in Kenya in the 1980s and 1990s. The chapter shows the theological underpinnings of the two bishop's social engagement. Chapter 8 focuses on the work of Jesse Mugambi who advanced a theology called African Theology of Reconstruction (ATOR) in the 1990s and after in response to poverty in Africa. Although ATOR focuses on socio-economic challenges that the African people in general, and the Kenyan people in particular, face, it is relevant for addressing ethnopolitical conflict. Poverty, conflict, and underdevelopment lead to ethnopolitical conflict. Chapter 9 examines John Mbiti's views of identity, culture, and community and their relevance for a theology of ethnopolitical cohesion in Kenya. Ethnopolitical conflict in Kenya is strongly tied, not only to politics, but also to identity, culture, and community. Chapter 10 is the concluding chapter.

CHAPTER 2

History of Ethnopolitical Conflict in Kenya: 1895–2013

This chapter provides a broad descriptive analysis of ethnopolitical conflict in Kenya from 1895 to 2013. It examines the contributions of the British colonial government and Kenya's post-colonial governments to the current problem of ethnopolitical conflict. The chapter shows that colonialism is the root cause of Kenya's ethnic problems. When the colonialists left in the early 1960s, post-independence governments capitalized on ethnicity to acquire and/or keep power. The chapter follows the following order: colonialism as the root cause of tribalism in Kenya, the Mau Mau uprising and the freedom of Kenya, the roots of ethnic-based political parties in Kenya, and the various faults of three post-independence Kenyan governments in regard to ethnocentrism: the Kenyatta regime (1963–1978), the Moi regime (1978–2002), and the Kibaki regime (2002–2013).

The Roots of Ethnopolitical Conflict in Kenya: The "Colonial Situation"

Ethnic conflict in Kenya has its roots in the "colonial situation."[1] Prior to the establishment of the British East Africa Protectorate on 1 July 1895, a territory that, after 1920, became known as Kenya Colony, the so-called Kenyan tribes, the forty-two or so sociocultural communities, were not

---

1. Leys, *Underdevelopment*, 108–206; Nnoli, *Ethnic Conflicts*, 290; Muigai, "Jomo Kenyatta," 200; Wrong, *Our Turn to Eat*, 47–49.

identified as "tribes" living within an exclusive boundary unit.[2] The colonialists assumed that the different ethnic communities had to be categorized
according to the languages they spoke, places they lived, their occupations
(i.e. pastoralists, hunters, farmers and so on), physical characteristics, and
put into neatly drawn boundary units.[3] They ensured that the categorized
groups stayed within their political units. Thus the tribes rarely interacted
with one another as they did before. Ultimately, ethnic consciousness and
rivalry between the various communities increased.

Professor Bethwell Ogot notes that by categorizing communities, the
colonialists "often confused language, ethnicity, and culture by attempting
to combine linguistic, cultural, ethnic and geographic elements to create
homogenous administrative and local government units."[4] Indeed, for the
colonialists, this process of categorization and combining of different ethnicities was an "experiment" in itself, a process of trial and error.[5] As the case of
the Kalenjin and Luhya communities explained below shows, these ethnic
communities neither had a unifying language nor a centralized form of

---

2. For example, Huntingford, (*Nandi*, 4) wrote in 1950 about the idea of "tribe"
among the Nandi:

The Nandi have no word for "tribe." The word emet . . . does not mean "tribe,"
and it is impossible to translate word for word into Nandi the Swahili phrase kabila
gani? "What is your tribe?" If a Nandi wanted to ask this question, he would say, I
chii ne inye? "What sort of man are you?" or ipo ono inye? "Where are you from?"
There is, in fact, no need for the Nandi to have a word for "tribe."

3. Thus Huntingford (*Nandi*, 4) explains what he thinks the Nandi people envisioned
in terms of their own identity as a tribe: "The definition of a tribe in the Nandi group is based
on this attitude: It is a community bearing a name common to all its members in which they
can take pride, speaking its own language, and occupying its own territory." See also the
"Geographical and Tribal Studies, Kenya Colony and Protectorate" which gives a detailed
picture of the distribution of the population of Kenya by location and tribe; summarized in
Her Majesty's Stationery Office, *Colonial Report, 1954*, 11–12.

4. Ogot, *Kenyans, Who Are We?*, 43.

5. Consider for example the report of the District Commissioner of Mumias, dated
16 September 1909 (*Handing Over Reports: North Kavirondo District*) Where he wrote the
following about the Bantu and the Nilote (Luo/Jaluo):

A great deal of "fetina" exists unfortunately between Ngonga & Wanyandi [two
chiefs]. Wanyandi's people are Bantu, whilst the people of Alego are Jaluo, and
this fact in itself appears to me sufficient to cause trouble between Ngonga &
Wanyandi, who was placed under the former only quite recently. It is my firm
conviction, that though we may eventually succeed in administering Wanyandi's
country through Ngonga, *the experiment* is not worth attempting, and I would
most earnestly recommend that in this case we return to the "status quo ante" and
endeavour to rule Usonga by itself. (emphasis added)

political governance. Thus the colonial classifications of them were arbitrary and misguided. The colonialists turned simple communities into political units as the colonial report of 1949 admits,

> The people whom the explorers found in the interior were of many different races, but in no case except in Uganda had their society advanced beyond the simple tribal state. The population was small for the area, both on account of the inhospitable environment and also on account of the slave trade. Tribe fought tribe sometimes for cattle but often also to obtain captives which the chiefs sold to Arab slave traders in return for arms and spirits.[6]

Except for the above-mentioned form of tensions, the communities lived in peace with one another. The tensions over boundaries or cattle rustling never became protracted hostilities. Thus as Michela Wrong observes, "While the Kikuyu, Maasai, and Kamba frequently fought each other over women and cattle, they also traded with one another, intermarried and exploited the same lands, with the pastoralist Maasai, for example, often relying on the agriculturalist Kikuyu to feed their families when drought killed their herds."[7] Thus inter-ethnic relations in Kenya were a common phenomenon among the different ethnic communities. Among the Highland Bantu, particularly the Kikuyu, Kamba, Meru, and Embu, trade, intermarriage, and patronage, "knew no confines."[8] Among the Nandi-speaking tribes, later renamed the Kalenjin, tensions with their neighbors focussed on farmlands and pasture because they were pastoralists, while among the inhabitants of the Lake Victoria basin and the Western Highlands, trade was a daily occurrence. The Bantu-speaking Luhya and Kisii and the Nilotic Luo communities traded with the southern inhabitants, particularly the Maasai of Kenya and the neighboring Tanzania (then the German East Africa).

The British colonialists created tribal boundaries drawn on a map, and implemented on the ground, without paying due attention to pre-existing forms of tribal governance, inter-ethnic relations, shared history and origin,

---

6. Great Britain Colonial Office, *Colonial Report, 1949*, 97.

7. Wrong, *Our Turn to Eat*, 48.

8. Lonsdale, "Conquest State," 19.

and sacred community spaces.[9] The colonialists ignored a very important traditional belief about land, that is, the ancestral land is the place where the spirits of the ancestors reside, and allowing other communities to occupy it, especially by force, is a gross violation of the sacredness of their land and may lead to serious problems for the community.[10] Even worse, the colonialists ensured that the communities stayed within their territories.[11] Ogot notes that prior to the boundary mapping, a buffer zone separated the various ethnic communities. The groups respected these buffer zones, and since they were not based on ethnic or linguistic demarcations, Africans could cross the "borders" without any fear or restrictions.[12] The colonialists

---

9. Sir Arthur Hardinge was the man responsible for the creation of provinces and districts in Kenya.

10. The TJRC (*Report of TJRC, Vol. III*, 13) mentions that during their witness hearing in Eldoret, a witness to the Commission expressed the traditional spiritual belief about land among the Kalenjin Community and why it is important to preserve the traditional order for peace to prevail between the Kalenjin and the Kikuyu. The witness said,

From the Kalenjin perspective, the soil is alive. The soil has its spirit. That is where languages clash. The soil is alive and it knows its owners and its name. However, when somebody else brings a name, there is a clash. The soil says, "What is this name? What is your totem? What is your clan?" I do not blame the Kikuyu Community. However, we would like to tell them that the names they have given the lands they have occupied continue to create conflict in the spiritual realm. For that reason, conflict demonstrates itself practically.

11. See for example the following excerpt from a letter dated 21 October 1909 written by the District Commissioner, Kisumu, (*Handing Over Report: North Kavirondo District*) quoted as follows:

With reference to your letter No. 3065/1, I find that Mr. Evans visited Kakumega some months ago. He found that 107 of Chief Schvatsi's people were living in the Kakumega district which has been placed under Mumias. He ordered Schivatsi to get his people back into his own territory. I expect what has happened is much the same as has occurred between Owurr of Kajulu and Ogola of Kano, that is, that the latter has been told on two occasions by Officers to remove his people from Kajulu.

The Commissioner was basically saying that the two communities, Luhya in Kakumega, and the Luo in Kajulu and Kano, cannot coexist together. Each much stay within their own territories. Osborne, (*Ethnicity and Empire in Kenya*, 96–97) explains that the colonial regime employed the same policy among the Kamba. He writes,

European-authored texts published at the time give the impression that missionaries, anthropologists, and administrators oversaw a system of neatly organized tribes. Administrative decrees built and bolstered such order: Male migrant laborers were issued with identity cards (*kipande*) after the war that identified them as "Kamba." And the provincial system was altered in December 1919 to produce neater ethnic lines: Kikuyu living in Kiambu were removed from Ukamba Province, which became a province inhabited by "Kamba" alone.

12. Ogot, *Kenyans, Who Are We?*, 30.

disturbed this peaceful order by crafting administrative boundaries based on language and ethnicity. This caused massive displacement of communities and created animosity. Also, the various tribes started to fight to protect their boundaries from outsiders. The fights intensified with the advent of competitive multiparty politics.

Several reports from District and Provincial Commissioners demonstrates post-colonial boundary disputes. For example, the Provincial Commissioner of Nyanza province reported in 1966 of tribal disputes in the re-organization of administrative boundaries noting, "boundary disputes remained on and off in certain areas."[13] To date, Kenyan tribes view other tribes with suspicion. This negative perception of other communities yields dangerous stereotypes and sentiments, which fuel ethnic hatred or even ethnic cleansing.[14]

The colonial government also displaced the native people in their quest for fertile lands. They particularly targeted the rich fertile plateau of the Rift Valley, the Nyanza province, the Western province, the Central province, some parts of the Eastern province, and Taitaland. According to the British colonial government, all land belonged to Her Majesty having been allegedly surrendered to the Crown by the Imperial British East Africa Company, which had entered into a number of treaties with chiefs of various tribes and who supposedly surrendered themselves and all their territories to the Company.[15] At this point, the land reverted from the original inhabitants to the colonial government as "Crown lands."

The term "Crown lands" was first used in 1901 where it is defined as "all public lands within the East Africa Protectorate, which for the time being are subject to the control of His Majesty by virtue of any treaty, convention, or agreement, or of His Majesty's Protectorate, and all lands which have been or may hereafter be acquired by His Majesty under the lands Acquisition Act, 1894, or otherwise howsoever."[16] Thus the colonial government had

---

13. Murgor, *Nyanza Province Annual Report 1966*, 5. This problem of tribal boundaries persisted as attested in the annual report of 1972. See Cheluget, *Nyanza Province Annual Report, 1972*, 7.

14. See Tarus and Gathogo, "Conquering Africa's Second Devil," 8–9.

15. Government of Kenya, *Kenya Land Commission Evidence*, vol. 1, 45–46.

16. Government of Kenya, 47.

the sole jurisdiction to allocate land as it wished.[17] Consequently, it allocated lands to European farmers as ninety-nine year leaseholds. The 1915 Land Ordinance increased the lease years from ninety-nine to 999 years.[18] The Commission of Inquiry into the Illegal/Irregular Allocation of Public Land established in 2003 to inquire into land allocations in Kenya, asserts that it is the history of colonial direct allocation of public land that "later facilitated the massive illegal and irregular allocation of public land by the Government after independence."[19]

Furthermore, the 1915 Ordinance also established the Reserves or Native Land Units or Closed Districts (land reserved for Africans only).[20] This means that the native Africans were rendered landless thus losing their sole economic base, their farms. Poverty deepened, ultimately leading to tensions and conflict as the communities fought to protect the small farms remaining. Other communities became squatters while others, notably the Kikuyu, became traders spreading themselves all over the country. Consequently, the settlement of the Kikuyu in areas outside their homelands generated and continue to generate resentment of the local communities.[21]

---

17. Government of Kenya, 47 says, "This order [Lands Acquisition Act, 1894] vested the control of all Crown lands in the Protectorate in the Commissioner, and authorised him to make grants or leases of any Crown lands on such terms and conditions as he thought fit, subject to any directions of the Secretary of State."

18. On this issue, Ogot, (*Kenyans, Who Are We?*, 40) observes, "By the beginning of the First World War, the total European population of the Protectorate was about 5,438, while the number of farmers and planters did not exceed 1,000. To this small population, about 5,000,000 acres of land had been alienated by the end of 1914, and the 1915 Crown Land Ordinance increased agricultural leases to 999 years."

19. Government of Kenya, *Commission of Inquiry into the Illegal*, 7.

20. These native reserves were declared unsuitable for the European settlers mainly because of tsetse flies. Therefore it was dehumanizing and unjust for the settlers to force Africans to live in these places. See Truth, Justice, and Reconciliation Commission, *Report of TJRC, Vol. II A*, 12.

21. A letter dated 18 December 1962 written by the Branch Secretary of the Kenya African Democratic Union, Uasin Gishu District Branch, a Mr Richard A. Tarus, clearly warns against the reception of Kikuyu people into the Rift Valley. The letter is hereby quoted in full:

On behalf of the Kalenjin Political Alliance Executive Committee Members Uasin Gishu District, I as the Hon. Secretary of the abovementioned Union and as well as an Organiser of Kenya African Democratic Union Uasin Gishu Branch have been instructed to write as follows:

"That we Kalenjin-Masai have declared to the last Boundary Commission Kenya, that Kalenjin-Masai will have the right of possessing all lands within the proposed

When the natives refused to move from the fertile lands where they had settled from time immemorial, the colonialists used brutal force to repatriate them to native reserves. Indeed, for Sir Arthur Hardinge, the first Protectorate Commissioner, Africans could only understand "submission by bullets."[22] His successor, Sir Charles Eliot, continued the trend of forceful evictions of Africans from their farms.[23] Using force was a total disregard of the Crown Lands Ordinance enacted in 1902, which made provisions for the safeguarding of the rights of the natives: "In all dealings with Crown land regard shall be had to the rights and requirements of the natives, and in particular the Commissioner shall not sell or lease any land in the actual occupation of the natives."[24] Also the Crown Lands Ordinance, 1902, section 16 (*b*) clearly stipulated the rights of the natives: "That the lessee, his servants and agents will not interfere with the settlement or villages of natives or with the land allotted for native settlement or villages, and so far as possible will avoid all quarrels with natives in or near the land leased."[25]

In a letter dated 23 October 1903 to Sir Charles Elliot, Mr John Ainsworth, the sub-Commissioner, Ukamba Province, legitimized the expatriation of Africans from their farms. According to him, the natives had no rights to own such fertile lands unless they were willing to cultivate in the manner the Europeans had taught them. He wrote,

---

Region (Rift Valley) and as such the Kalenjin-Masai are opposed to the action taken by present Coalition Government by allowing the Kikuyus to buy land within Uasin Gishu District which is completely annoying the tribes concerned, therefore we strongly warn the Minister concerned to remove un required buyers from the District within a period of fifteen days as from today 18th day of December, 1962, otherwise we Kalenjin-Masai will as a group remove unrequired land buyers and will be unresponsible for the result. We also warn the management of land Bank from giving unnecessary loans to these un required tribes." See, Tarus, "Sales of Lands in Rift Valley."

This problem was not unique to Uasin Gishu District. Mr T. L. Edgar, the District Commissioner, Kajiado, wrote to the officer of Mtego wa Simba Prison saying, "I regret that I am instructed by my Provincial Commissioner not to accept any Kikuyu into this District. It is a Masai District and the African District Council would also refuse consent." See, Edgar, "KPF Convict."

22. Truth, Justice, and Reconciliation Commission, *Report of TJRC, Vol. II A*, 5.

23. Truth, Justice, and Reconciliation Commission, 6.

24. The Crown Lands Ordinance, 1902, cited in the Government of Kenya, *Kenya Land Commission Evidence*, vol. 1, 47.

25. Cited in the Government of Kenya, *Kenya Land Commission Evidence*, vol. 3, 2151.

> Tribes like the Kikuyu, who are blessed with a very fertile land, and who in their own state, cultivate in the most reckless manner, scattering their shambas [farms] about all over the country and allowing land which from the time of its reclamation has perhaps only borne two or three crops to run fallow for one or two years, require showing that their just and ample requirements can be met by their being restricted to much more limited areas.[26]

Consequently, Africans were restricted to limited areas called native reserves. Examples of such reserves include the Kikuyu Native Reserve allotted in 1903, the Mua (Wakamba) Native Reserve allotted in 1911, the Elgeyo Native Reserve allotted in 1911, the Londiani Native Reserve allotted in 1911, the Kaimosi Native Reserve allotted in 1912, the Sotik Native Reserve allotted in 1911, and the Nandi Native Reserve first allotted in 1907 but settled in 1926 because of disputes.

Maloba asserts that whereas the colonial government was quick to draw boundaries for the native reserves, they delayed drawing boundaries for their own "White Highlands" (the fertile lands they had acquired from the Africans) until 1939, "because the colonial government accepted the settler argument that land found suitable for permanent European settlement should be added to the highlands, whenever it became available."[27] Thus the Europeans kept looking for more arable lands. They committed great injustice in the process. The implication of this colonial capitalism to modern day Kenya is obvious. The research highlights examples of the Maasai, Sabaot, and Nandi ethnic communities and consequences the alienation from their lands has had on them.

From 1904 to 1913, through a series of several expatriations, the Maasai were forcefully moved from the Central Rift Valley (Eldama Ravine, Nakuru, and Naivasha) and the Northern Rift Valley (Laikipia) to the South Rift (Mau Narok and Trans Mara). A District Commissioner's letter dated 25 September 1911 details the removal of the Maasai from their original

---

26. Government of Kenya, *Kenya Land Commission Evidence*, vol. 1, 55.
27. Maloba, *Mau Mau and Kenya*, 26.

grazing lands of Laikipia, Nakuru, Naivasha, Elementaita, and Njoro.[28] Consequently, they were sent to the Mau Narok (Inesoit) area, a place the District Commissioner repeatedly refers to as the "Promised Land" notwithstanding that the Southern Maasai, who had moved from the Uasin Gishu region, were already the occupants of this "Promised Land."[29] Also, the Maasai living among the Kamba people were forcefully moved south of the Kenya-Uganda Railway.[30] The colonial government was basically forcing the Maasai communities to coexist in total disregard of their differences in terms of the clan, dialect, and their way of life.

An Assistant District Commissioner by the name of E. C. Crewe-Read noted in his diary dated 19 September 1911 that he followed up to ensure that the Maasai arrived at the Southern destinations and never went back to their ancestral lands.[31] To date, the Maasai are still aggrieved. They have gone to court several times seeking justice. Even more significant is the ethnic tensions and conflicts between the Maasai, the Kipsigis, and the Dorobo (their neighbors in the South Rift).[32] To date, tensions exist between these communities. For example, on 24 December 2015 violence broke out at Olposimoru in Narok County between Maasai and Kipsigis communities and by the end of the three-day conflict, two people had been killed, 2000 displaced, and twelve injured.[33]

It was not only the Maasai who suffered colonial injustice, the same was the case with the Sabaot people. The Sabaot people were forcefully removed from the arable areas of Trans-Nzoia district of the Rift Valley in the 1920s and the 1930s. This case is particularly important because of the recent conflicts in the Mount Elgon area.

The Sabaot community was moved to Chepkitale and Chepyuk. Despite their grievances to the Kenya Land Commission in 1932, this community

---

28. Colonial Report, *Masai Move*.

29. Colonial Report.

30. Government of Kenya, *Kenya Land Commission Evidence*, vol. 2, 1175–1266.

31. Colonial Report, *Masai Move*, Section 35–46. For more on this injustice committed against the Maasai, see, Hughes, *Moving the Maasai*.

32. See Ochieng, *Modern History of Kenya*, 90; Truth, Justice, and Reconciliation Commission, *Report of TJRC, Vol. II A*, 9.

33. Sayagie, "Narok Violence"; Saysagie, "Fear Grips Village"; Kerich, "Livestock, Land Feuds."

never received any compensation.[34] In 1968 the Kenyatta government annexed a greater portion of the Chepyuk land as a game reserve, forcing the inhabitants to leave. When the inhabitants complained, the government initiated a resettlement program in 1971 which forced the Chepkitale Sabaot to live among the Chepyuk Sabaot. However, this resettlement program was unsuccessful. The government tried several times to implement new ways of settling the communities, such as phase 2 and 3 of the Chepyuk Settlement scheme in 1989, but because of corruption and politicians wanting to gain from the conflict, the land problem escalated into a tribal conflict.[35]

Ethnic tensions amplified following the introduction of political pluralism in 1991 when a group of Sabaot men armed with poisoned bows and arrows attacked the Luhya and Bukusu ethnic groups.[36] Tensions also escalated in the December 2002 general election leading to the formation of the Sabaot Land Defense Force (SLDF), a militant group. The SLDF committed great atrocities between 2006 and 2008. They displaced more than 200,000 people, recruited more than 650 children as child soldiers, and killed more than 615 people.[37] The government of Kenya deployed the Kenyan army to regain control of Mt. Elgon in a joint operation with the Kenya police called Operation Okoa Maisha (Operation Save Lives). The operation was brutal and unjust. Several people were killed.

Another example is the repatriation of the Nandi to the Nandi Native Reserve. A document from 1910 shows several correspondences between the District Commissioner and Provincial Commissioner of Nandi and Nyanza in regard to the removal of the Nandi into a Reserve and the creation of clear-cut boundaries.[38] Prior to this, the Nandi had waged war against the British starting in 1895 to 1905 being led by Koitalel Arap Samoei. Ogot notes that the British mastered the strongest army to fight the Nandi warriors,

---

34. Human Rights Watch, *"All the Men have Gone"*, 12.

35. Human Rights Watch, 12–13.

36. The Weekly Review, "Troubled Areas Relatively Calm," 9–10; Weekly Review, "A New Angle to the Strife," 13–14; Weekly Review, "Fresh Outbreak of Violence," 15–16; Weekly Review, "Turmoil in Bungoma District," 19–20; Weekly Review, "Mt. Elgon," 23.

37. Human Rights Watch, *"All the Men have Gone"*, 20. The report also shows that the SLDF was responsible for intimidations, rape, torture, mutilation, illegal taxation, sabotage of water pipes, theft of land and cattle, and burning of houses (19–25).

38. Provincial Commissioner's Report, *Boundaries General*.

"compromising 60 European army officers, 1500 troops from 1st and 3rd Kings African Rifles, 200 Indian soldiers, 1000 Maasai levies, 500 armed porters, 300 Sudanese volunteers, 10 machine gun sections, and two armored trains."[39] More than 100,000 Nandis were killed, including their spiritual leader, Koitalel Samoei.[40] The tensions between the Nandi and their Luo and Luhya neighbors can be attributed to this colonial injustice against them.[41]

Another way the colonialists contributed to Kenya's ethnic problems is through the creation of powerful politico-administrative authorities. The colonialists created these centers of power in order to coalesce power and to subjugate the indigenous communities.[42] These powerful authorities included administrative chiefs, sub-chiefs, and community elders (headsmen), all answerable to the District Commissioners. It also included 141 African courts appointed by and answerable to the Provincial Commissioners.[43] The African courts exercised jurisdiction over Africans only. Before this form of leadership, spiritual leaders such as Koitalel Arap Samoei, led their own people, including resolving judicial cases. The institution of chiefdom was foreign to most African communities.[44] But even more significant to modern-day Kenyan politics is the association of leadership to money, land, and power. The native chiefs and sub-chiefs were empowered to collect hut and poll taxes. They would go around counting the huts and administering taxation thus paving way for corruption and abuse of office. They acquired huge parcels of land for themselves. Being a native chief became a very lucrative

---

39. Ogot, *Kenyans, Who Are We?*, 39.

40. Ogot, 39. Huntingford (*Nandi*, 108) writes of this Nandi defeat,

After their defeat in the war of 1905–1906 the Nandi began to settle down in the diminished territory which was confirmed to them as a permanent Reserve, and they accepted British rule simply because they had the sense to realize that continued resistance would do them nothing but harm. For the next fourteen years there was peace in Nandi.

41. See Government of Kenya, *Report of the Parliamentary Select Committee*.

42. Oyugi, "Ethnic Politics in Kenya," 290.

43. See, Her Majesty's Stationery Office, *Colonial Report, 1954*, 107.

44. Maloba, *Mau Mau and Kenya*, 27.

business.[45] This form of leadership intensified competition for power and favors among the leaders and their constituents.

When the struggles for supremacy intensified among the tribes, the colonialists created Tribal Police Units, Tribal Police Reserves, and Tribal Guards, armed with rifles and other forms of weaponry and tasked with ensuring law and order within particular tribal territories.[46] Oyugi notes that the recruitment of the police units and the armed forces favored two particular communities, the Kamba and the Kalenjin because, for the British, these two communities were the "martial tribes."[47] But even more significant is that this form of political arrangement ensured the people were governed in their own tribal-linguistic units further promoting ethnic consciousness among the tribes. Thus African leaders became tribal kingpins and the local governments became tribal enclaves.

Transcending this ethnocentric form of local government became a major challenge for the post-independence Kenya.[48] The consequence of this historical reality has been extensive. Kenyan tribes have since then unified themselves for the sake of political interests. These forms of competitions are further intensified by the form of political structure in play in Kenya: the winner-takes-all political system. Tribal groups, whose elites are in power,

---

45. Thus Maloba, (*Mau Mau and Kenya*, 23, 27) asserts about the colonial chiefs:

> These men owed their offices to British colonial administration and not to the traditional institutions. They were government appointees and served without being unduly worried about their popularity with their subjects. The most significant acquisition of these chiefs was land. They acquired this land as individuals, and it became their personal property and not that of their *mbari* ["a lineage group of all Kikuyu who traced their descent through the male line from a known ancestor"] or any traditional association.

46. Great Britain Colonial Office, *Colonial Report, 1949*, 84; Her Majesty's Stationery Office, *Colonial Report, 1954*, 1. According to the *Colonial Report*, of 1954, by 1954, there were 3,877 Tribal Police, 118 Kikuyu Guards, and 22,000 joint Kikuyu, Embu, and Meru Guards. Preparations were in place to recruit 6,400 Tribal Police Reserves by 1955. See, Her Majesty's Stationery Office, *Colonial Report, 1954*, 115.

47. Oyugi, "Ethnic Politics in Kenya," 291. An annual provincial report of 1957 seems to support the British assertion that the Kalenjin have an affinity to join the military as compared to the other tribes. The District Commissioner of Kericho reports: "The general standard of smartness and alertness is high and there is a very real spirit of the esprit de corps. A few new recruits were taken on during the year and as usual vast numbers of Kipsigis turned up to apply for the very few vacancies available." Loyd, *Nyanza Province Annual Report 1957*, 7.

48. For more on this, see, Ogot, *Kenyans, Who Are We?*, 44–45.

dominate all major public sectors and have a major say in what kind of policies are implemented. Those who lose elections are marginalized and are soon forgotten until the next national election. Thus, of paramount importance to Kenya's ethnic communities is how to enable many of their own to be in government. This requires a lot of ethnic calculation. An example of the Luhya and the Kalenjin ethnic groups illustrates this point.

The Luhya tribes consist of sixteen groups speaking the same language though in different dialects.[49] Before colonialism, these ethnic communities existed as separate ethnic entities. The Luhya became a unified ethnic entity in 1940 when these sixteen communities decided to come together as one community in order to have political say.[50] Even to date, Luhya politicians still call for Luhya unity so as to win national elections. Recently, former presidential hopeful, Mr Musalia Mudavadi, called for the Luhya people to unite ahead of the 2017 general election.[51] Ababu Namwamba, the former member of parliament for Budalangi Constituency, also issued a similar call terming the Luhya unity the "Mulembe consciousness."[52]

Similarly, the Kalenjin consist of eight tribal groups also speaking the same language though in different dialects.[53] Like the Luhya, in pre-colonial period, the Kalenjin were not a unified ethnic community. The label "Kalenjin," which literally means, "I tell you," is a recent invention first used in the late 1950s by a group of young Kalenjin elites who were trying to find a common term to unify the eight tribes for political interests.[54] Prior

---

49. These communities include Bukusu, Samia, Tachoni, Dakho, Kabras, Khayo, Nyole, Kisa, Marachi, Maragoli, Marama, Nyala, Tiriki, Tsotso, and Wanga.

50. Oyugi, "Ethnic Politics in Kenya," 288. The Luhya unity has been a major rallying cry for Luhya politicians. For the 1992 general election and the Luhya unity, see, The Weekly Review, "Luhya Factor"; Weekly Review, "Luhya Dilemma"; Weekly Review, "Strike!"

51. Wafula and Kagonya, "Mudavadi Tours Counties," 32.

52. Citizen TV, *Western Kenya Intrigues*.

53. These communities include Nandi, Kipsigis, Keiyo (or Keyo), Marakwet (or Markweta), Pokot (or Suk), Tugen, Sabaot (or Sabiny), Dorobo (or Ogiek), and Terik. The writer of this book is from the Nandi ethnic community; thus, a Nandi speaking person (a *Mnandi*).

54. Kipkorir, *People of the Rift Valley*; Kipkorir and Welbourn, *Marakwet of Kenya*, 1; Lynch, *I Say to You*.

to the amalgamation of the nine Kalenjin dialects, the Kalenjins were still referred to as the "Nandi-speaking people."[55]

As the Kalenjin and Luhya tribal alignment for political reasons illustrates, the 1950s was a time of preparation to take over power from the colonial government. Powerful Kenyan politicians were positioning themselves to lead the country while the British colonial administrators, especially those who intended to remain behind, were, in turn, recruiting individuals who would protect them and their wealth upon their ascent to power.[56] Indeed the colonialists needed protection especially from radical movements such as the Kenya Land and Freedom Army (KLFA) also known as Mau Mau. The Mau Mau was a radical group that sought to free Kenya from the colonial masters but also committed great atrocities in the process. A quick note about the movement follows below.

The Mau Mau Uprising and the Freedom of Kenya

The Mau Mau armed struggle started in 1948 but did not gain momentum until 1952. It maintained over 35,000 guerilla fighters in the forests and many thousands more in the urban areas.[57] The Mau Mau fighters had one agenda in mind: *ithaka na wiyathi* (land and freedom), and nothing could stop them from achieving this goal. Initially, the movement began as a homegrown response to the imperialist's quashing of nation-wide political associations, racial injustice, land grabbing, and economic degradation; though more than five million Africans lived in the colony, only 29,000 European settlers controlled the economy and political space in Kenya.[58] Thus the first task of the KLFA was to secretly develop new communication links with all people of Kenya and assist in the liberation of Kenya.[59]

---

55. According to Huntingford, (*Nandi*, 19–20) the "Nandi-speaking peoples" included the Suk sub-group of Uasin Gishu area (the Kadam or Entepes, the Pokwut or Suk, the Endo, the Marakwet), the Elgon sub-group (il-kony of Elgon, the Pok or Lago, the Kamechak, the Mbai, the Sabaut, the Kipsorai or Sore), the Rift Valley sub-groups (the Tuken or Kamasya, the Kabarnet, the Keyo or Elgeyo), the Kipsikis-Nandi sub-groups (the kipsikis or Lumbwa, the Terik or Nyang'ori, the Nandi), and finally, the Dorobo.

56. Oyugi, "Ethnic Politics in Kenya," 293.

57. Durrani, *Kimathi*, 9.

58. Anderson, *Histories of the Hanged*, 9.

59. Durrani, *Kimathi*, 12.

However, the colonial government responded to this quest with brutal force. Thus the struggle turned exceedingly violent and bloody, a form of terrorism, according to Falola and Harr.[60] Indeed the Secretary of State for the Colonies, Oliver Lyttleton, in his address to the House of Commons, in London in 1952, labeled the Mau Mau fighters terrorists.[61] According to the British settlers, the Mau Mau followers were scarcely human, and in the words of Frank Loyd, who served the British Empire in the heartlands of the Kikuyu territory where the Mau Mau war was fought, the Mau Mau was "bestial" and "filthy," "an evil movement" that had to be "eliminated at all costs."[62]

As indicated, the Mau Mau wanted to destroy the colonial regime and establish an African (mainly Kikuyu) government. However, with time, they expanded their fight beyond the colonial regime. In addition to fighting the European settlers, the Mau Mau committed massive atrocities against Africans loyal to the British colonial government, Christians, and others deemed to be in opposition to their agenda. According to the Truth, Justice, and Reconciliation Commission (TJRC) set up in 2008 to investigate historical injustices in Kenya since independence, the Mau Mau carried out "decapitation and general mutilation of civilians, torture before murder, bodies bound up in sacks and dropped in wells, burning victims alive, gouging out of eyes and splitting open the stomachs of pregnant women"[63] By the end of their fight, the Mau Mau had caused the death of at least 14,000 Africans, twenty-nine Asians, and ninety-five Europeans.[64]

The colonial government responded with brutality. Sir Everlyn Baring declared a state of emergency on 20 October 1952, paving way for a counterinsurgency measures against the movement.[65] Elkins observes, "From the moment Baring declared the state of Emergency, the treatment of Mau Mau suspects, with rare exception, was devoid of any humanity."[66] Indeed,

---

60. Falola and Haar, *Narrating War and Peace*, 65–67.

61. BBC, "Kenyatta Arrested in Security Raid."

62. Elkins, *Imperial Reckoning*, 48.

63. Truth, Justice, and Reconciliation Commission, *Report of TJRC, Vol. II A*, 14.

64. Truth, Justice, and Reconciliation Commission, 14.

65. Maloba, *Mau Mau and Kenya*, 2, 7; Truth, Justice, and Reconciliation Commission, *Report of TJRC, Vol. II A*, 13–16.

66. Elkins, *Imperial Reckoning*, 55.

the colonial government, and afterward President Jomo Kenyatta's government, resorted to horrendous brutality to suppress the Mau Mau. By 1956, "A total of 430 [Mau Mau] detainees were shot 'trying to escape,' and more than 1,000 executions had been carried out."[67] David Anderson gives the precise number of executions as 1,574.[68] In total, more than 50,000 people died in the Mau Mau conflict.[69]

Yet it was not only the loss of lives that occurred during this time. Ethnicity became deeply ingrained in political associations. Here is the reason why. Still recovering from the Mau Mau war, the colonial government thought all political associations would disseminate the Mau Mau agenda. Thus they banned all colony-wide associations paving way for regional associations. The regional associations became ethnic-based political parties.

The Roots of Ethnic-Based Coalitions and Political Parties in Kenya

In 1953 the colonial government banned the only truly nationalist political party, the Kenya African Union (KAU), paving way for the formation of ethnic-based district political organizations, all strictly under the management of the British colonial government.[70] Consequently, the political parties formed thereafter, such as the Nairobi District African Congress later to become Nairobi People's Convention Party, the Mombasa African Democratic Union, the Nakuru African Progressive Party, the Abaluhya Political Union, the Abagusii Association of South Nyanza, the Taita African Democratic Union, the Kilifi African People's Union, the North Nyanza District Congress, the Somali National Association, the Kalenjin Political Alliance Party, the Baringo District Independence Party, European New Kenya Group (NKG), Kenya Asian Party, and the Maasai United Front were regionally based ethnic associations.[71] The loss of nationalism is the major legacy of these regional associations; people favored ethnic loyalties to

---

67. Finlayson, "Kenya: Mau Mau," 323.

68. Anderson, *Histories of the Hanged*, 6.

69. Oyeniyi, "'Glocalization' of Terrorism," 231.

70. Oyugi, "Ethnic Politics in Kenya," 293; Anderson, "Struggle for Majimbo," 551; Ogot, *Kenyans, Who Are We?*, 55–58.

71. Oyugi, "Ethnic Politics in Kenya," 293; Muigai, "Jomo Kenyatta," 209–211.

national interests. Thus from 1963 to date, ethnicity has remained a salient element in the formation and the execution of political parties in Kenya.[72]

The Kenya African National Union (KANU) and the Kenya African Democratic Union (KADU) emerged from such a background. Those among the Kikuyu and the Luo who had opposed the Mau Mau struggle started KANU, while those among other tribes who feared the Kikuyu-Luo dominance united to form KADU. *Majimbo* (regionalism/federalism) became the major agenda of KADU.[73] Under the *majimbo* system, prominence is given to ethnicity and ethnic boundaries as the solid base for socio-economic progress and political mobilization.[74] The logical outcome of *majimboism,* as is popularly known in Kenya, is ethnic cleansing because at its core, it insists on ethnic purity and exclusivity and generates a culture of "us" versus "them" or "our zones" versus "their zones" and ultimately the expulsion of those who do not belong. The next section explains the role the Kenyatta's presidency had on the ethnopolitical conflict in Kenya.

Ethnopolitical Conflict during President Jomo Kenyatta's Era (1963–1978)

Johnstone Kamau Ngengi also known as Jomo Kenyatta (1891–1978), began his political career in a regional political association called the Kikuyu Central Association (KCA) in 1924.[75] The Kikuyu people had started KCA in 1922 to represent their interests. Kenyatta rose through the ranks of KCA to become the association's Secretary General in 1927. In 1929 he went to present the Association's grievances to the colonial department in London. He ended up enrolling at the London School of Economics where he studied social anthropology under Bronisław Malinowski from 1929 to 1946. He returned to Kenya in 1947 but by that time the colonial government had already banned KCA. He joined the Kenya African Union (KAU), but then, again, the colonial government banned KAU in 1953. However, KAU later

---

72. Oloo, "Party Mobilization," 32; Hornsby, *Kenya,* 9.

73. Ogot, *Kenyans, Who Are We?,* 58.

74. Klopp, "Can Moral Ethnicity Trump Political Tribalism?," 272; Weekly Review, "Ethnic Strife," 11; Weekly Review, "Onslaught on Kalenjin Leaders," 19.

75. Muigai, "Jomo Kenyatta," 201.

re-emerged as the Kenya African National Union (KANU) in May 1960 under the leadership of James Gichuru, Tom Mboya, and Oginga Odinga.[76]

Kenyatta became the President of KANU on 28 October 1961; he had just been released from prison where he had served a seven-year sentence for his alleged involvement in the Mau Mau freedom struggle. He completed his sentence on 14 April 1959 but he was still under restrictions until August 1961. KANU formed the first indigenous Kenyan government after winning the country's first general elections in May 1963 with Kenyatta as the Prime Minister. On 1 June 1964, Kenya became a Republic within the Commonwealth with Kenyatta as the president.[77]

As already stated, at the time, the colonial government did not allow Africans to form colony-wide political associations. Thus Kenyatta came to power through a regional political association. Furthermore, as Githu Muigai observes, Kenyatta "inherited from the colonial government a political culture and a political class that placed ethnicity at the heart of politics and conspired to derail the nationalist agenda at every turn."[78] Kenyatta's major challenge was to ensure that he was indeed the "father of the nation" as he was so famously called. Indeed in his speech addressed to parliament on 14 August 1964, he promised to help draft a functional constitution that would ensure the protection of all the people of Kenya.[79] However, Kenyatta did not serve the interests of all the Kenyan people as promised.

Kenyatta's active role in Kenya's ethnic politics started as an ideological warfare between him and his deputy, Jaramogi Oginga Odinga.[80] Odinga was then the vice president of Kenya and the vice president of KANU. Odinga and his ally Bildad Kaggia advocated for the nationalization of foreign companies and for the redistribution of Kenya's wealth upon independence among the less privileged, while Kenyatta and his ally Tom Mboya, on the other hand, believed that only hard work and one's work ethic should buy

---

76. Muigai, 209.

77. The drafting of the Republican Constitution caused the one year delay in shifting from Prime Minister to President. See Kenya News Agency, "Prime Minister's Statement."

78. Muigai, "Jomo Kenyatta and the Ethno-Nationalist State in Kenya," 200.

79. See Kenya News Agency, "Prime Minister's Statement."

80. Branch, *Kenya*, 10.

one's freedom from poverty.[81] Odinga intensified the ideology when he appealed to pro-Communist states such as China and Russia for support.[82] The communists helped Odinga organize a student airlift to Russia and China and assisted him to build the Lumumba Institute, a school established to train KANU party officials in the hope that they would one day get into power and help him champion his redistribution of wealth cause.[83]

In time, Odinga's efforts came to the attention of senior KANU officials who suspected him of planning a coup.[84] The KANU politicians pressured the president to suppress him. This marked the beginning of Kenyatta's intolerance towards non-conformists such as Odinga. Odinga's allies lost their jobs in the civil service. Several politicians were assassinated: Pio Gama Pinto (1965), Tom Mboya (1969), and Josiah Mwangi (J. M.) Kariuki (1975).[85] Several politicians were detained without trial. Such include Odinga himself, Martin Shikuku, Peter Kibisu, Chelagat Mutai, George Anyona, and Jean Marie Seroney.[86] Several intellectuals such as Ngugi wa Thiong'o and Koigi Wamwere went into exile abroad. Eventually, Odinga was hounded out of KANU in a heavily rigged party election at Limuru in 1967.[87] Odinga formed a new party, Kenya People's Union (KPU) as the next phase of championing his call for redistribution of wealth. The formation of KPU intensified ethnic politics in Kenya.

KPU was popular among people from Nyanza province, the tribe of Odinga. The Luo people felt that they had a legitimate grievance against the government because from independence, the Central and Eastern provinces received favors from the government since the majority of KANU officials, including the President, hailed from the region. Compared to the Nyanza province, members of the former regions enjoyed good road infrastructure,

---

81. Branch, 10, 63; Truth, Justice, and Reconciliation Commission, *Report of TJRC, Vol. II A*, 18.

82. Branch, *Kenya*, 41; Truth, Justice, and Reconciliation Commission, *Report of TJRC, Vol. II A*, 18.

83. Branch, 41, 50.

84. Branch, 48.

85. Branch, *Kenya*, 45, 79, 113; Gitari, *Troubled but Not Destroyed*, 33–34; Muigai, "Jomo Kenyatta," 213.

86. Truth, Justice, and Reconciliation Commission, *Report of TJRC, Vol. II A*, 23.

87. Branch, *Kenya*, 58.

access to Nairobi city markets, and competitive prices for their agricultural produce.[88] There was a sense in the country that KANU favored the Kikuyu and its analogous Bantu-speaking communities such as the Embu, while the Luo from Nyanza were disfavoured. Under Kenyatta, major sectors of the Kenyan economy became "Kikuyuised," meaning being taken over by the Kikuyu tribe.[89] By default, then, KPU became the party of choice among people from Nyanza and other Western Kenya regions.[90] Thus by marginalising Western and Nyanza provinces and by his intolerance to differing ideologies Kenyatta fractured the already fragile social cohesion of the country.

The simmering discontent with Kenyatta's government among the Luo turned hostile upon the assassination of Tom Mboya in 1969. From 1968, Kenyatta had started ailing and it was clear that his succession was the most important matter for discussion. Two candidates stood out, Daniel Toroitich Arap Moi from Rift Valley (a Kalenjin) and Tom Mboya from Nyanza (a Luo). Tom Mboya was at that time the KANU secretary general. Tom Mboya had lived in Nairobi for most of his life but identified with his original homeland, Nyanza province. Thus based on his ethnic roots, he being a Luo and considering the tension that the formation of KPU had caused, Kenyatta favoured Moi as his successor because Moi was not a threat to the Kikuyu insiders since he came from a very tiny Kalenjin tribe and Moi was considered a possible loyalist to Kenyatta's policies, including land settlement plans.[91]

Kenyatta's allies started organizing constitutional amendments to deny Mboya the chance to be president. They raised the minimum age requirement from thirty-five to forty (Mboya was thirty-eight years old). However, Mboya proved to be a very strong rival to Moi still. In Nairobi, he had been a champion for trade union rights against the colonialists. He had been forced to sever and destroy the ties upon joining the government. However, he could capitalize on the growing discontent against Kenyatta's government

---

88. Branch, 61–62.

89. On the "Kikuyuisation" of Kenya, see Branch, *Kenya*, 63; Hornsby, *Kenya*, 254–258.

90. Branch, *Kenya*, 63–64.

91. Hornsby, *Kenya*, 165.

among minor ethnic communities in Nairobi. In addition, Mboya had a cosmopolitan appeal as he had lived in Nairobi and worked in Nairobi with other communities for most of his life. Thus his assassination on 5 July 1969 could only be interpreted as curtailing the Luo people from the presidency.

Several protestors from the Luo community encircled the hospital for hours "shouting anti-government and anti-Kikuyu slogans."[92] The crowd chased out a Kikuyu priest who had been called to administer the last rites. The crowd also denied Moi the permission to view the body. When president Kenyatta arrived to pay his respects to Mboya at a requiem mass held three days later, an angry section of the crowd pelted his motorcade with stones.[93] The next day, at Dagoretti, the Kikuyu harassed Luo mourners as the cortege passed through the town. They were not happy with how the Luo had treated President Kenyatta. Tensions between Kikuyu and Luo communities did not dwindle after Tom Mboya's funeral on 11 July 1969. Mboya's death unified the Luo but widened the gap between the Luo and the Kikuyu.

Tom Mboya's assassination sparked a wave of ethnic violence in the Rift Valley, especially in Turbo and other settlement schemes where the Kikuyu people lived. Kalenjin youths attacked Kikuyu settlers at Kaptebei, Lumbwa, and Londiani.[94] Fearing that he would lose the support of his community because of the violence, President Kenyatta resorted to oathing rituals.[95] The rituals were meant to signify the Kikuyus' willingness to fight to the death for their hold on power. the Kikuyu vowed not to marry from another tribe, especially from the Luo community.[96] In addition to oathing, Kenyatta wooed the Central and Eastern Bantu communities for his support. From 1969 to 1970, Kenyatta transported representatives from the Kikuyu, Meru, Embu, and Kamba to his home in order to convince them to support his presidency.[97] Branch puts the total number of those transported to Kenyatta's Githunguri home at 300,000.[98] They were made to swear never to vote for a

---

92. Branch, *Kenya*, 80.

93. Branch, 80.

94. Branch, 84–85.

95. Truth, Justice, and Reconcilitaion Commission, *Report of TJRC, Vol. III*, 21; Branch, *Kenya*, 85; Muigai, "Jomo Kenyatta," 206.

96. Truth, Justice, and Reconciliation Commission, *Report of TJRC, Vol. III*, 21.

97. Muigai, "Jomo Kenyatta," 210.

98. Branch, *Kenya*, 85.

non-Kikuyu nor to pledge allegiance to a party that was not led by a Kikuyu and in return the president would reward them with government positions and their communities would enjoy several development projects.[99]

Kenyatta clashed with the Luo again in October 1969 in his visit to Kisumu to open a hospital.[100] Violence erupted during his speech as a result of his public rebuke of Odinga and his "stupid supporters."[101] The comment angered the audience who started pelting stones at the president. Kenyatta's bodyguards killed several angry protesters who were trying to block the president's motorcade. After the incident, Kenyatta ordered the detention of KPU leaders and banned KPU. The Kisumu massacre, as is widely referred to, amplified the tension between the Kikuyu and Luo and their other ethnic supporters. For example, the Nandi declared the Nandi District a Nandi-only zone. In July 1969, a Kalenjin Member of Parliament, Jean Marie Seroney, led the Nandi Hills Declaration which vowed to cleanse all Nandi District of all non-Nandi, individuals, corporates, or otherwise, unless they proved their loyalty to the Nandi.[102]

The problem of land distribution intensified ethnic tensions during Kenyatta's presidency. As European settlers gave up their lands, new settlement schemes were created. Kenyans and diplomats argued that a large portion of the settlement schemes were allotted to the Kikuyu only.[103] Indeed, Kenyatta had used land allocation to gain support among his Kikuyu strongholds. Besides land, Kenyatta awarded government positions to his Kikuyu supporters and friends. He argued that the Kikuyu deserved a bigger share of land because of their fight for freedom during the Mau Mau insurgency.[104] Kenyatta solidified his grip on the Kikuyu people through the formation of the Gikuyu, Embu, and Meru Association (GEMA), with a two-fold mission, "to strengthen the immediate ethnic base of the Kenyatta State by incorporating the Embu and Meru into a union with the Kikuyu, and to circumvent KANU's party apparatus in the mobilization of political support

---

99. Branch, 85.
100. Branch, 88.
101. Branch, 88.
102. Branch, 87.
103. Branch, 96.
104. Branch, 102.

among these groups."[105] Branch concludes that Kenyatta had "abandoned all but the most perfunctory pretense that his was a government for all Kenyans."[106]

Kenyatta's rule continued on until 22 August 1978 when he collapsed and died in his beach home in Mombasa. His reputation as the "father of the nation" had diminished because of his intolerance to dissents and opposition members and also because of his favoritism of his ethnic community.

Ethnopolitical Conflict during President Daniel Arap Moi's Era (1978–2002)

Kenyatta's vice president, Daniel Toroitich Arap Moi, took over as the president of Kenya. President Moi was born on 2 September 1924. He studied at Kapsabet High School and later attended Tambach Teachers Training College where he received a Diploma in Education. After a brief career in teaching, Moi started politics as an elected member of the legislative council for the Rift Valley Province. He formed the Kenya African Democratic Union (KADU) party alongside members of smaller ethnic groups to counter the Kenya African National Union (KANU) party, a party of the larger and more economically powerful and educated Kikuyu and Luo communities.

Kenyans saw President Moi as the answer to Kenya's quest for ethnic cohesion because of several factors. First, Moi came into power as an ardent churchman. He went to church every Sunday and he donated funds towards building churches, Christian hospitals, and schools.[107] Second, Moi came from a minority group, the Kalenjin community, and specifically a marginal and poor Kalenjin sub-tribe, the Tugen. Third, Moi was outside of Kenyatta's

---

105. Muigai, "Jomo Kenyatta," 214.

106. Branch, *Kenya*, 102. Muigai, ("Jomo Kenyatta," 215) observes that Kenyatta "totally failed to address adequately the problem of ethnic coalition. In fact, he served to entrench ethnicity as the dominant basis of political mobilization. By his complex web of ethnic coalitions he created a false sense of both nationhood and political stability, which he carefully grafted onto simmering ethnic tensions based on unfulfilled ethnic claims to power and resources." Muigai continues to assert that the ethnic discontent Kenyatta bequeathed Kenyans "remains unresolved" (215).

107. Okullu, "Render unto Caesar," 149.

inner circle of elites commonly known as the "Kiambu Mafia."[108] In fact, Moi's popularity and ultimate ascension to power disconcerted many of Kenyatta's allies who called him a "passing cloud."[109] But Moi was not a passing cloud. As already shown, Moi had carefully positioned himself to capture the presidency. Indeed he stayed in power for twenty-four years, retiring in 2002.

Moi's reign began with a call for nationalism and social cohesion. On 12 December 1978, he endorsed this call when he released all political detainees imprisoned during Kenyatta's presidency. To please the Kikuyu elites who still commanded a lot of influence in government, President Moi retained many of them in power but he ensured that his first cabinet was as multi-ethnic as possible. Thus his first cabinet consisted of Kenyans from eleven ethnic communities: "eight Kikuyu, three Kalenjin, three Luhya, three Luo, two Kisii, and one Maasai, Taita, Kamba, Embu, Digo, and Meru."[110] Furthermore, Moi promised to advance President Kenyatta's economic agenda popularly known in Swahili as *nyayo* ("follow in the footsteps").[111] The Nyayo philosophy, as it was referred, stood for peace, love, and unity and the needed war against poverty, ignorance, and disease.

Moi's regime started off peacefully, until 1 August 1982 when a section of the Kenya Air Force led by Hezekiah Ochuka, attempted a coup. The plot failed. Following the failed coup, Moi became utterly paranoid, taking several steps to curtail dissent and to consolidate power. First, he presided over a constitutional amendment which made Kenya a *de jure* ("by law") one-party State. Second, he surrounded himself with members of his Kalenjin community whom he rewarded with powerful government leadership positions.[112] Third, like his predecessor, President Moi became very intolerant to critics of his rule. Vocal critics were either detained, tortured, assassinated or

---

108. Truth, Justice, and Reconciliation Commission, *Report of TJRC, Vol. III*, 21; Muigai, "Jomo Kenyatta," 211.

109. Oluoch, *Christian Political Theology*, 8.

110. Truth, Justice, and Reconciliation Commission, *Report of TJRC, Vol. III*, 23.

111. Branch, *Kenya*, 136.

112. Oluoch, *Christian Political Theology*, 14; Truth, Justice, and Reconciliation Commission, *Report of TJRC, Vol. III*, 23.

mysteriously disappeared. Others went into self-exile abroad.[113] The assassination of foreign affairs minister Robert Ouko on the night of 12 February 1990 is one case that attracted national and international attention. The mysterious death of Bishop Alexander Muge, a firm critic of Moi, through a road accident, is another example of mysterious deaths of prominent personalities during Moi's presidency. Fourth, President Moi also solidified his presidential base by unifying the main ethnic communities from his home province of Rift Valley, that is, the Kalenjin, the Maasai, the Turkana, and the Samburu, forming what was popularly known as KAMATUSA, an acronym for the four ethnic communities.

Moi faced external and internal pressure from political activists, clergy, and politicians to repeal the law and allow multiparty democracy. In November 1991, donor agencies such as the World Bank and the International Monetary Fund (IMF) cut off their aid to Kenya to pressurize KANU to allow for multiparty democracy. Finally, in December 1991 Moi yielded to this pressure by repealing Section 2 (A) of the constitution which had hitherto prohibited political pluralism. This paved way for the registration of other political parties and the first multiparty national election since 1964.[114] However, Moi warned that multiparty democracy would entrench ethnic animosity and lead to violence. During a meeting with the president of the International Red Cross, Dr Cornelio Summaruga, President Moi argued that multiparty democracy "will definitely trigger chaotic situations which would be difficult to reverse."[115] He repeated the same message again later that week, saying that multiparty politics would "cause tribal friction."[116] Similarly, his most staunch supporter, the Mombasa KANU chairman, Sharif Nassir, told the United States ambassador to Kenya, Mr Smith Hempstone, when he went to visit the KANU office in Mombasa that Kenya was not ready for multiparty democracy; "We are too young a nation with different

---

113. See Oluoch, *Christian Political Theology*, 18; Institute for Education and Democracy, *1997 General Election*, 28–29.

114. Institute for Education in Democracy, *1997 General Election*, 29. Prior to the 1992 election, Kenya had held six elections (1963, 1969, 1974, 1979, 1983, and 1988)

115. Weekly Review, "A Heated Debate," 23.

116. Weekly Review, 23.

tribes. To introduce a multi-party system at this stage will mean inviting bloodshed."[117]

With the intensity and the competition characteristic of multiparty politics, Moi and Sheriff's prediction became true as multiparty politics overlapped the eruption of ethnic violence in Rift Valley, Nyanza, Coast, and Western provinces.[118] Politicians fuelled the violence as they exploited ethnic identity to win votes in the 1992 election and the subsequent elections.[119] The first recorded clash was at Meteitei farm in Nandi District on 29 October 1991.[120] The clashes were between the Kalenjin and the Luo communities though it escalated to other regions and by the end of it, more than 300,000 people had been displaced.[121] Victims of the ethnic clashes claimed that the violence was directed at non-Kalenjins who were accused of failing to vote for Moi's KANU party in the 1992 election.[122]

After the clashes, the Government and the Opposition blamed each other. On one hand, the government accused the opposition, especially FORD, the main opposition party, for plotting to "unleash a wave of terror with the aid of a section of Kenya's military members."[123] FORD, on the other hand, claimed that the government fanned the violence in order to "find a pretext to declare a state of emergency and ban all opposition political parties."[124] Following the violence and a public outcry, the government set up a parliamentary select committee (PSC) chaired by Mr Kennedy Kiliiku to

---

117. Weekly Review, "A New American Assertiveness," 14.

118. A newspaper report from that time asserts:

From early November last year a wave of ethnic clashes has led to the massive displacement of people from different communities living around the border areas of the Rift Valley, Nyanza, and Western provinces. The affected areas include the Kericho-Kisii, Kericho-Kisumu, Nandi-Kakamega, and Kakamega-Uasin Gishu border areas, as well as parts of Trans Nzoia and Mt. Elgon areas bordering Bungoma District. (Weekly Review, "Ethnic Strife," 10).

119. As to the political connection to ethnic violence, see, for example, Weekly Review, "Government Statement on Ethnic Clashes," 16–21; Weekly Review, "Ford's Response to the Government Statement," 23–24; Weekly Review, "Ethnic Violence," 14.

120. Human Rights Watch, *Divide and Rule*, 25.

121. Human Rights Watch.

122. Weekly Review, "Ethnic Violence," 14; Weekly Review, "Ethnic Strife," 6.

123. Weekly Review, "Ethnic Strife," 6.

124. Weekly Review, 6.

probe the clashes.[125] After a fact-finding tour of the clash-hit areas the PSC presented its report, popularly known as the Kiliku Report, to parliament. Among those implicated in the report were some high-ranking ministers and powerful figures in the KANU regime. The KANU majority parliament voted out the report.

Indeed, the results of the 1992 election attest the reality of ethnic-based politics in Kenya. The results show that the small ethnic communities made alliances, under KANU, against the two dominant ethnic communities, the Kikuyu and the Luo represented in the presidential race by Kenneth Matiba (a Kikuyu), Mwai Kibaki (a Kikuyu), and Oginga Odinga (a Luo). The Members of Parliament from the opposition parties namely the Forum for the Restoration of Democracy, Kenya (FORD Kenya), the Forum for the Restoration of Democracy-Asili (FORD Asili), and the Democratic Party (DP), were predominantly from the tribes of the party leaders.[126] A political commentator gave an accurate analysis of the major political parties in the 1992 general election as follows,

> To say that most of the political parties in Kenya are based on tribal sentiments is a tenable argument. Let us take the "big four" – Kanu, Ford Kenya, the DP and Ford Asili – for examples. Each of them has tacitly allotted itself some geographical regions that its members often refer to as "our zones." It is not by coincidence that the predominant ethnic group in those "zones have their tribesmen at their higher echelons of the respective parties. It is often said that, where the Kikuyu are predominant, the DP and Ford Asili have strong backing there for the simple reason that the two parties are led by Kikuyus – Mr. Mwai Kibaki and Mr. Kenneth Matiba respectively; where Luos are predominant Ford Kenya has the strongest support since its chairman, Mr. Oginga Odinga, is a Luo. Tribes that have no leaders in any of the opposition parties have chosen to stick with Kanu and form alliances with the Kalenjin; Note

---

125. Government of Kenya, *Report of the Parliamentary Select Committee.*
126. Oloo, "Party Mobilization," 37.

that the Kalenjin stayed in Kanu to "protect" President Daniel arap Moi.[127]

Another commentator expressed the same sentiments when he wrote, "Assessing the voting pattern of 1992, one gets the impression that 'tribal sycophancy or sycophantic ethnic bloc voting smacks of majimbo voting that produces a pattern of consolidated votes within any one community. The analysis of the 1992 election, therefore, depicts multiparty politics in Kenya as a glorification and strengthening of ethnic alliances."[128] As the two commentators asserts, multiparty democracy deepened the ethnicization of politics in Kenya. Violence intensified as politicians delineated certain areas as belonging to a specific political party. For example, some Rift Valley MPs declared the Rift valley as a KANU zone.[129] The implication of such a declaration is extensive. With such categorization came ethnic cleansing as communities demanded of others to vote for their own person and their party or move out of the region. In the Rift Valley, non-Kalenjins with the exception of the KAMATUSA communities were expelled after the 1992 elections.[130] Several Kalenjin MPs urged Kalenjin youths to protect KANU's hold over the region.[131] Such "protection" implied the removal of Luo, Kikuyu, Kisii, and Luhya communities because they were in the wrong parties, the opposition, FORD Kenya, FORD Asili, and DP.[132]

Similar trends were observed in the 1997 general election. President Moi of KANU competed against Mwai Kibaki of DP and Raila Odinga of the National Development Party of Kenya (NDPK) and twelve other candidates. Ethnicity became a major issue at play during their campaigns.[133] In the months leading to the December election, several leaders instigated violence through hate speech. For example, Francis Lotodo, the then Minister for Home Affairs and National Heritage, and William Ole Ntimama, the then

127. Mutai, "A House Divided," 32.

128. Mugivane, "Not Ready for Democracy," 16.

129. Weekly Review, "Spectre of Majimboism," 6–8.

130. Weekly Review, "Reality of Ethnic Politics," 6.

131. Weekly Review, "Volatile Politics," 15.

132. See for example what happened in Laikipia District, Rift Valley Province in The Weekly Review, "Tribal Trouble in Laikipia," 15.

133. Weekly Review, "Tribal Factor in Elections," 3; Weekly Review, "Playing the Tribal Card," 11–12.

Minister for Environment, both declared in 1997, that all non-indigenous communities living in the Rift Valley will have to leave upon the implementation of *majimbo*.[134] Similarly, the call for the expulsion of non-indigenous communities also prevailed in Mombasa with KANU party taking the blame for condoning hate speech.[135] Such utterances had serious consequences for soon after the elections, ethnic violence started in the Rift Valley and by the end of the clashes 1,500 had been killed and 300,000 displaced.[136]

As President Moi neared retirement in 2002, a KANU delegates' conference was convened at Kasarani stadium on 14 October 2002. During the conference, President Moi endorsed Uhuru Kenyatta, the son of Jomo Kenyatta as KANU's presidential candidate. This move greatly angered the other potential candidates; Raila Odinga, Kalonzo Musyoka, William Ole Ntimama, and Moody Awori walked out of the conference. Shortly, they joined the Rainbow Coalition movement. Mwai Kibaki became the flag-bearer of the Rainbow Coalition. Under his leadership, Rainbow won the December 2002 national elections and Mwai Kibaki was sworn in as the next president of Kenya.

Ethnopolitical Conflict during President Mwai Kibaki's Era (2002–2013)

Thousands of people attended President Kibaki's swearing-in ceremony optimistic that the country was finally triumphing over ethnocentrism. This optimism was based on several positive issues. First, the incoming president had won the national election (2002) under a coalition party, the National Rainbow Coalition (NARC), a multi-ethnic coalition. All ethnic groups voted for either Mwai Kibaki of NARC or Uhuru Kenyatta of KANU despite both of them coming from the Kikuyu community. In fact, Kenyans voted for Kibaki despite his fragile state due to a motor accident a few months to the election. Second, for the first time in history, a ruling party had been defeated and conceded defeat. President Moi and his KANU party

---

134. Weekly Review, "Spectre of Majimboism," 6.

135. Weekly Review, "Likoni Mystery," 4–6; "Dangerous Development," 3.

136. Weekly Review, "Oh, Not Again!," 4–6; Weekly Review, "Call to End the Violence," 7; Patel, "Multiparty Politics in Kenya," 159.

were finally out of power after leading for twenty-four years (KANU was in power for more than three decades). Third, the 2002 election was also historic because, for the first time since independence, Kenya experienced peace after a national election. Peace prevailed throughout the campaigns, election day, tallying, and the announcement of the results.

However, the national enthusiasm and confidence waned as the president gave in to ethnocentric forms of governance. The GEMA communities benefited from State appointments.[137] Furthermore, the president functioned in total disregard of the coalition partners. This impunity fractured the coalition and caused tensions throughout the country. Tensions escalated as the country prepared for the 2005 referendum on the Draft Constitution. Politicians resorted to ethnic sentiments during the campaigns for or against the Draft Constitution.[138] The country became highly polarized along ethnic lines. All the provinces except President Kibaki's Central Province overwhelmingly opposed the Draft Constitution.[139]

Ethnic tensions continued throughout the 2007 campaign periods culminating in the worst ethnic violence ever experienced in Kenya. The incumbent president, President Mwai Kibaki, ran for office under the Party of National Unity (PNU) against Raila Odinga of Orange Democratic Movement (ODM) and Kalonzo Musyoka of Orange Democratic Movement-Kenya (ODM, Kenya). Raila Odinga led in vote counting by midnight of 27 December 2007. But trouble started when on 29 December 2007 the margin narrowed down to only 38,000 votes with over 90 percent votes counted.[140]

---

137. Kanyinga and Okello, ("Contradictions of Transition," 10) asserts that during Kibaki's presidency, the GEMA community benefited from top government positions,

> members of the Gikuyu/GEMA community dominated the security, finance, and justice and law institutions—ministries where real state power is domiciled. In the ministries of finance, and security, both the Minister and the Permanent secretary were from one community, as was most of the heads of departments and directorates. In the justice sector, the Minister and the Chief Justice were also from the same community, and a purge of the judiciary that saw many judges removed from office was seen as an "ethnic cleansing" move in the judiciary, even though there were legitimate concerns about the integrity of that institution.

138. The Truth, Justice, and Reconciliation Commission (TJRC) formed after the post-election violence of 2007/2008, blamed "corruption, hate speech, and negative ethnicity" for the mayhem. See, Truth, Justice, and Reconciliation Commission, *Report of TJRC, Vol. 1*, 13.

139. Oloo, "Party Mobilization," 38–39.

140. Kagwanja and Southall, "Introduction," 5.

Coupled with delays of results from some regions where the president was considered to be most favored, and with the Electoral Commission of Kenya (ECK) chairman, Mr Samuel Kivuitu, saying the votes were "cooked," tensions in the country simmered and by the evening of 29 December 2007, nationwide protests and violence had erupted. The violence continued as Kenyans were deprived of news as media stations were locked out of the tallying center. The State Corporation, the Kenya Broadcasting Corporation (KBC), was the only station allowed into the center. The ECK chairman finally announced that President Kibaki had won the elections and within minutes of the announcement, he was hurriedly sworn in to serve his second term as the president of Kenya.[141] Countrywide violence escalated into an ethnic conflict. The hardest hit regions were Eldoret, Mombasa, Naivasha, Nakuru, and some parts of the Coastal region. By the end of the ethnic chaos, at least 1,133 people had been killed, 650,000 internally displaced, and 78,000 houses burnt down.[142] The violence also resulted in the destruction of properties worth billions of shillings. The following table shows the number of deaths per province.[143]

Rift Valley	744
Nyanza	134
Central	5
Western	98
Coast	27
Nairobi	125
TOTAL	1,133

Fearing that Kenya was on the precipice of a genocide, the African Union (AU) authorized a panel of Eminent African Personalities under the leadership of former UN Secretary-General Kofi Annan, to mediate a truce between the contending teams, the Government (PNU) and the opposition

---

141. Kagwanja and Southall, 4–5.
142. Norwegian Refugee Council, "Kenya: Speedy Reform Needed," 7.
143. Government of Kenya, *Waki Report*, 310.

(ODM).[144] On 28 February 2008, PNU and ODM reached a power-sharing agreement.[145] They agreed to end the violence and to share power equally between Mwai Kibaki who retained the presidency, and Raila Odinga who became the prime minister. The coalition agreed on the following four agendas to be implemented: (1) to cease violence against and between communities; (2) to resolve the post-election humanitarian crisis and to foster national healing, calm, and reconciliation; (3) to overcome the political crisis; and (4) to address long-term historical issues and to find durable solutions by means of constitutional, institutional, and legal reforms.[146] The PNU-ODM survived for five years, albeit with serious disagreements, till Kenya went into polls to choose the next leader. Uhuru Kenyatta, the son of Kenya's first president, won the election against Raila Odinga, the immediate prime minister and the son of Oginga Odinga, Kenya's first vice president.

Uhuru Kenyatta won the election held on 4 March 2013 under the Jubilee Coalition which is primarily a coalition of the Kikuyu and the Kalenjin communities. Kenyatta brought in the GEMA communities while his running mate, William Samoei Ruto, brought in the KAMATUSA communities. They also mobilized communities from the Coast and the North-Eastern region to join the coalition. Together they won the election against Raila Odinga of Orange Democratic Movement (ODM), a coalition primarily of Luo and Luhya communities. Uhuru Kenyatta and William Ruto, popularly known as UhuRuto, won the elections despite both of them, then, facing charges at the International Criminal Court (ICC) at The Hague for their alleged roles in crimes against humanity allegedly committed during the post-election violence of 2007–2008. The ICC withdrew the cases due to lack of evidence.

Conclusion

The chapter examined the contributions of the British colonial government and Kenya's post-colonial governments to the current problem of

---

144. The other team members included Benjamin Mkapa (former President of Tanzania) and Madam Graça Machel (formerly married to Samora Machel, President of Mozambique, then to President Nelson Mandela of South Africa)

145. For more on the mediation process, see, Khadiagala, "Forty Days and Nights."

146. Norwegian Refugee Council, "Kenya: Speedy Reform Needed," 8.

ethnopolitical conflict. The chapter shows that colonialism is the root cause of Kenya's ethnic problems, and the various historical factors that have contributed to ethnopolitical conflict in Kenya. The chapter also shows that by dispossessing the various ethnic communities of their ancestral lands and forcing them to move to different locations, the colonialists enhanced ethnic consciousness and contributed to the culture of negative ethnicity, which have always degenerated into conflict. Also, by demarcating ethnic-based boundaries, the colonialists killed the spirit of inter-ethnic relations that existed between the communities. The chapter also contends that tribalism is a salient problem in Kenya and it is particularly linked to politics: campaigns, mobilization, and voting. Thus, ethnic identity is entrenched in Kenya's politics and no politician wins elections without appeal to ethnic loyalties. In fact, nobody wins elections in Kenya without first gaining the support of his or her ethnic community. Even political parties subscribe to ethnicity rather than ideology albeit the well-written manifestos, party constitutions, and policy documents they launch every election year. Newspaper articles confirmed the reality of ethnopolitical tensions as Kenya headed toward the 2017 general election.[147] Therefore it is important that the Kenyan people seek a solution to this volatile problem. The next chapter shows the role the Kenyan church played in either stopping or promoting ethnopolitical violence in Kenya from 1982 to 2013.

---

147. Examples include, Gaitho, "We Do Ourselves a Disservice," 12; Ochieng, "Will Kenyans Ever Manage," 13; Murunga, "We Must Let Peace Prevail," 14; Daily Nation, "These Leaders Must Not," 14; Atieno, "Counties Turn Down Medics," 4; Ngwiri, "Where Are We Headed?," 12; Coredo, "Kenyans Can Replace," 16; Nyarora and Ageta, "Ruto Preaches Unity," 2; Murunga, "We Must Rise Above," 14; Ngwiri, "Why Kenyan's Have Little Faith," 12.

CHAPTER 3

The Church and Ethnopolitical Conflict in Kenya: 1982–2013

This chapter examines the role of the church in addressing the problem of ethnopolitical conflict in Kenya from 1982 to 2013. Though ethnocentrism within the Kenyan Christian community goes beyond the years cited to the colonial period and the immediate years following independence, the intensity of the problem after 1982 calls for special attention.[1] As argued in the previous chapter, President Kenyatta and his successor President Moi deepened the problem of negative ethnicity in Kenya. The single event that marks political change in Kenya is the 1982 attempted coup. Although this was not successful, the coup heightened opposition against Moi's rule. Thus, 1982 marks the beginning of the recent history of Kenya, a history in which three phases may be identified in the relationship between church and State:

---

1. For instance, the "missionary factor" is an important historical root of ethnocentrism within the Kenyan church that cannot be ignored. By the "missionary factor" the writer means the inheritance of ethnically divided churches from missionaries. In other words, the missionaries planted seeds of ethnocentrism by concentrating their efforts on certain communities while neglecting other communities. For instance, the Africa Inland Mission concentrated mission work among the Kamba and the Kalenjin; the Friends Mission among the Luhya; Methodist Mission among the Ameru people; Church Missionary Society among the Luo, Kikuyu, and Coastal areas; Seventh Day Adventist among the Gusii people; the Church of Scotland missionaries among the Kikuyu, Embu, and the Ameru. When missionaries left, Kenyan Christians had to find ways of making their churches multiethnic. This is still an ongoing challenge. For more on this "missionary factor" see Sesi, "Ethnic Realities," 25–39. Tostensen, Andreassen, and Tronvoll, (*Kenya's Hobbled Democracy*, 31), also highlight the ethnic factor in the founding of the various Christian denominations. Another historical issue that needs to be examined is the relationship between church leadership, ethnicity, and political governance. Oluoch (*Christian Political Theology*, 32) observes that whenever church lay leaders of the president's ethnic community held influential positions in government, the church rarely engaged the State. This scenario was particularly true during Kenyatta and Moi eras.

a generally united church (1982–2002); a divided church (2002–2007); and a recovering church (2008 onwards). The thesis of the chapter is that the church in Kenya generally exhibited a robust sociopolitical engagement in the 1980s and 1990s but lost its prophetic voice from 2002 to 2008 mainly because of ethnocentrism and the co-option and compromise of the clergy by the government and the opposition. The chapter, which is based on archival and library materials, broadly examines the roles the mainstream Protestant, Evangelical, and Roman Catholic churches and their umbrella organizations, the National Council of Churches of Kenya (NCCK), the Evangelical Fellowship of Kenya (EFK) – now called the Evangelical Alliance of Kenya, (EAK), and the Kenya Catholic Episcopal Conference (KCEC) – now called Kenya Conference of Catholic Bishops (KCCB), played in their quest for social cohesion. In doing so, the chapter highlights the failures of Kenyan churches in addressing the problem of ethnopolitical conflict.

Ethnopolitical Conflict and the Church in Kenya: A Unified Voice (1982–2002)

The period 1982–2002 saw a generally unified church against social injustice including tribalism. The church spoke in one voice in most cases. Protestant bishops teamed up to push for justice, democracy and ethnic cohesion especially during the years preceding the introduction of a multi-party political system in Kenya. Bishop Timothy Njoka of the Presbyterian Church of East Africa (PCEA), Bishop Zablon Nthamburi of the Methodist Church in Kenya (MCK), and Bishops John Henry Okullu, Alexander Kipsang Muge, and Archbishops Manasses Kuria, and David Gitari of the Church Province of Kenya (CPK) were instrumental in pushing for social justice, cohesion, and democracy in Kenya.[2] The bishops used the media (television and radio), publications, and their pulpits to achieve this purpose.[3] Bishop

---

2. Weekly Review, "Outspoken Clergyman," 5–6; Weekly Review, "Okullu Ready for 1994," 3–5; Weekly Review, "Njoya at it Again," 3–6; Weekly Review, "Okullu's Volley," 6–9.

3. Such include, among others, the NCCK newspaper *Target/Lengo*, and the various talk shows delivered at the state-owned Voice of Kenya (VOK) (later renamed Kenya Broadcasting Corporation). Gitari (*Troubled but Not Destroyed*, 33–34) observes that he delivered six live talks at VOK after the assassination of J. M. Kariuki in 1975.

Gitari summarized this sociopolitical engagement and the risks it caused with the following words:

> Bishop Okullu was very vocal. Bishop Muge was very vocal. Timothy Njoya was very vocal. I spoke out at every occasion. There was great reluctance by the government to enter into dialogue with church leaders. Live broadcasts of church services were stopped. Only churches who praised the government were allowed on the air. There was a lot of stiffening of the part of the government.[4]

Bishop Njoya led in preaching fiery sermons against Moi's one-party regime. In a new year's (1 January 1990) sermon preached at St Andrews PCEA in Nairobi, Njoya audaciously compared Kenya's one-party rule to the monolithic communist regimes in Eastern Europe, which, for him, would one day collapse as Nicolae Ceausescu's regime had collapsed in Romania.[5] Thus Njoya avowed that Kenya had no option but to embrace multiparty-ism. In addition, he condemned patronage and tribalism, which had derailed Kenya's progress.[6] Similarly, Bishop Okullu preached a comparable sermon at St Stephen's Cathedral in Kisumu.[7] Their courageous sermons had two major effects.

First the sermons rallied the KANU government against Njoya, Gitari, Kuria, Okullu, and Muge, the five most vocal clergymen.[8] These five clerics had been outspoken since the 1980s resisting the *mlolongo* (queue-voting) system of the KANU regime and urging Christians to set a good example of neighborliness. In the *mlolongo* system, voters would line up behind their preferred candidate and then the election presiding officer would do a head

---

4. Crouch, *Vision of Christian Mission*, 95–96.

5. Weekly Review, "Njoya at it Again," 3.

6. Weekly Review, 6.

7. Ngotho, "Day Democracy Visited," online edition; Weekly Review, "Clerics kick up storm," 5–6; Oluoch, *Christian Political Theology*, 20. Bishop Okullu, ("Theological and Ethical Considerations," 103), offers why he opposed single-party system of government: "I am infinitely suspicious of one-party system of government being capable of safeguarding and promoting human rights, because it is there to promote a colonization of the mind and to assist its leaders in staying in power for life. One party government only encourages idolization of leaders and the party and non-accountability to the people."

8. Weekly Review, "Question of Opposition," 8.

count before declaring the winner. In most cases, the candidate with the shortest line got declared the winner. Bishop Manasses Kuria termed the voting system "unchristian, undemocratic and embarrassing" while Bishop Muge referred to it as totalitarian.[9] Bishop Okullu said the queue system "produced some of the most blatant and cruel vote rigging and cheating that has been practiced in Kenya."[10] NCCK leaders urged KANU "to find an alternative method" of voting or otherwise they will ask Kenyan Christians to refrain from taking part in elections.[11]

Because of their resistance, the bishops were condemned. Bishop Okullu was branded a "prophet of doom who should be shunned by every peace-loving Kenyan"[12] while Timothy Njoya was referred to as a "tribalist bent on causing chaos in Kenya."[13] Gitari said that he "was in several instances referred to as a tribalist, a political activist, a champion of political groupings, a member of *Mwakenya* (the underground political movement) and a messenger of foreign masters."[14] These criticisms did not deter the clerics from critiquing the KANU regime.

Second, the sermons rallied the opposition against the KANU government and bolstered the push for multiparty democracy. The opposition team, the civil society, and the church united to oppose the dictatorial trends of the KANU regime and to push for multiparty politics. Even the then US Ambassador, Smith Hempstone, agreed with the clerics that Kenya must accede to multiparty democracy.[15] Several politicians including Kenneth Matiba, Paul Muite, Philip Gachoka, Charles Rubia, and Bishops Henry Okullu and David Gitari held night meetings to strategize how to plan campaigns for multiparty democracy.[16] These meetings resulted in several rallies and street protests.

In response, the KANU regime marshaled its forces to stop the protests. For instance, on 7 July 1997 hundreds of demonstrators who had met at

---

9. Weekly Review, "Queue-Voting Furore," 19.

10. Oluoch, *Christian Political Theology*, 17.

11. Oluoch, 85–86.

12. Weekly Review, "Dissenting Patriot," 15.

13. Weekly Review, "Heated Debate," 23; Weekly Review, "Njoya at it Again," 6.

14. Gitari, *Troubled but Not Destroyed*, 240.

15. Hempstone, *Rogue Ambassador*; Ngotho, "Day Democracy Visited," 5.

16. Gitari, *Troubled but Not Destroyed*, 256.

Uhuru Park grounds in Nairobi were brutally assaulted including those who sought refuge at the All Saints Cathedral, a church adjacent to the park.[17] Several clergies including Timothy Njoya and the provost of the cathedral, Rev Peter Njoka, were beaten up. The clergy and the opposition condemned the brutality as a sign of the government's infringing on religious freedom, suppression of its citizens, and disregard for the sanctity of human life.[18] Following the incident, Archbishop Gitari called for a "cleansing" service of the cathedral. Thousands of people attended the televised meeting. Gitari preached from the book of Daniel 5, warning President Moi that God's hand would soon write "Mene, Mene, Tekel, Parsin" on the wall of State House if he continues to hinder reforms.[19]

However, not all Protestant bishops accepted multi-party democracy. Bishop Lawi Imathiu of MCK and Bishop Muge of CPK issued a joint press statement supporting one-party rule.[20] They contended that multiparty system would precipitate ethnic conflicts in Kenya. Interestingly, Bishop Imathiu had served as a nominated Member of Parliament during Kenyatta's presidency (1974–1979) and the MCK had benefited a lot from both Kenyatta and Moi's governments. This historical reality might have informed Imathiu's non-confrontational stance against the Moi regime.[21]

However, even though Imathiu and Muge did not support multipartyism, they, especially Muge, condemned ethnocentrism in Kenya. Bishop Muge, who at the time was the chairman of NCCK's Justice, Peace, and Reconciliation, paid a heavy price for his opposition to KANU.[22] On 12 August 1990, Peter Habenga Okondo, the Labor Minister, issued a warning to both Bishop Okullu and Bishop Muge that they "would see fire and

---

17. The Uhuru Park grounds has been a venue for so many other political rallies. The 7 July 1990 meeting, and other subsequent meetings every 7 of July, referred to as Saba Saba (Seven Seven), borrowing from Tanzania's revolution day, which falls on the same day, inspired great struggles for justice in Kenya. For more on the Saba Saba struggles, see, The Weekly Review, "Strike for Freedom," 3–6; Weekly Review, "Show of Force," 4–6.

18. Weekly Review, "Strike for Freedom," 6; Weekly Review, "Blessing for the Mothers," 17.

19. Gitari, *Troubled but Not Destroyed*, 260.

20. Weekly Review, "Heated Debate," 23.

21. Okullu, *Quest for Justice*, 128.

22. His courageous actions are recorded in Otieno, *Beyond the Silence of Death*.

may not come out alive" if they went to Busia district for a church service.[23] Bishop Muge defied him and attended the service at St Stephen's Church in Busia on Sunday 14 August 1990. On his way to Eldoret, Muge was killed through a road accident. Muge joined the list of other prominent personalities assassinated in Kenya.

According to Crouch, Muge died "a champion of justice, peace, and human rights," and "a true nationalist, a martyr to the truth."[24] He was not afraid to speak his mind against tribalism in all areas, including the church and NCCK. At one time he wrote, "The NCCK in Kenya is like a rotten apple. To the best of my knowledge, the NCCK has nothing to lecture our nation because all the evils, which eat our nation such as tribalism, favoritism, nepotism, and other-isms, have found shape in NCCK."[25] He was truly a Christian martyr according to many ACK Christians in Eldoret, where Muge is buried.

Comparable to the activist-oriented Protestant churches, the Roman Catholic Church also united in pushing for socio-economic justice, democracy, and social cohesion in Kenya. Under the leadership of Cardinal Mourice Michael Otunga, Archbishop Rafael S. Ndingi Mwana a'Nzeki, Archbishop Zacchaeus Okoth, and Archbishop John Njue, the Roman Catholic Church produced several pastoral letters highly critical of the government and KANU.[26] For example, in February 1992, the Roman Catholic bishops issued a joint statement saying, in part, "The continuation of Kanu rule is a hazard to the genuine evolution of democracy in Kenya as evidenced by the brutal tribal clashes West of Nakuru."[27] On 22 March 1992, eighteen Roman Catholic bishops issued another pastoral letter accusing the government of complicity in the violent ethnic clashes prevalent in parts of western Kenya since October 1991 where more than sixty-five people had died and thousands rendered homeless.[28]

---

23. Okullu, *Quest for Justice*, 120.
24. Crouch, *Vision of Christian Mission*, 158.
25. Weekly Review, "Controversial Churchman," 5–7.
26. See Gifford, *Christianity, Politics*, 36–39; Weekly Review, "Church Factor," 5.
27. Weekly Review, "New Radicalism," 11.
28. Weekly Review, "Moving Into the Political Arena," 20.

Individual bishops issued similar calls. Bishop Mwana a'Nzeki condemned the Meteitei ethnic strife of 1992 saying, "These tragic happenings are orchestrated by irresponsible statements made in Kapsabet, Kapkatet, Kericho, and Narok."[29] Bishop Manasses Kuria declared that all peace loving Kenyans should resist politicians who capitalize on ethnicity for personal gains; "anything that is likely to cause disharmony, strife and chaos is evil; it is even satanic" and must be stopped.[30] Likewise, Bishop Cornelius Korir of the Roman Catholic Diocese of Eldoret and Bishop Longinus Atundo of the Bungoma Diocese condemned ethnic-based violence in the Rift Valley and Western provinces.[31]

During this pro-liberation struggle, the Kenyan church worked together across their denominational divides. The NCCK and the Catholic Church formed the National Ecumenical Civic Education Programme (NECEP) to provide civic education to Kenyan voters and politicians. Bishop Henry Okullu was elected chairman of NECEP.[32] In addition to civic education, NECEP coordinated two inter-parties symposiums in May and June of 1992 "to discuss national issues, particularly the spate of ethnic clashes" prevailing throughout the country.[33] NECEP joined hands with other concerned citizens to form the National Election Monitoring Unit (NEMU), with the idea of monitoring the General Election scheduled for 29 December 1992. Peace, order, and democracy during the election were NEMU's primary concern.[34]

The Catholic Church and the NCCK, under the leadership of the chairman of the Kenya Episcopal Conference, Archbishop Zacchaeus Okoth, and the Very Rev George Wanjau, respectively, took a strongly worded joint statement to State House titled, "People Have Lost Confidence in You" addressed to President Moi condemning the violence of 1992.[35] The statement is hereby quoted in part:

---

29. The Nairobi Law Monthly, "Nandi Clashes," 19.

30. Gatabaki, "Peace," 37.

31. Weekly Review, "Fresh Outbreak of Violence," 16; Weekly Review, "Lawlessness," 19.

32. Okullu, "Render unto Caesar," 151.

33. Weekly Review, "Church Factor," 3; Weekly Review, "United by a Common Cause," 16.

34. Okullu, "Render unto Caesar," 152.

35. Weekly Review, "People Have Lost Confidence," 21; Weekly Review, "Dressing Down," 20.

What [brings] us here is nothing less than the life or death of Kenya, the question of the lives and future of hundreds of families who have been treated inhumanly, butchered, slaughtered. The scenes are truly heartbreaking. No human being can be left unmoved. Anyone who carries responsibility before the nation, even more before our God and Father, must be forced to stop the bloodshed and human misery at once . . . Unless you change your present policies, Kenya will not be Kanu but a cemetery for thousands of its sons and daughters . . . Why do you not commit your administration officers, your police, and army to capturing these men? . . . Why have leading government ministers who made provocative statements and ordered non-Kalenjins out of Rift Valley province at public meetings in Kapsabet, Kaptagat, and Narok in September 1991, not been prosecuted or censured in any way? Your Excellency, you cannot deny what we have seen . . . whether you like it or not the truth is that the people have lost confidence in you and those close to you.[36]

The bishops went ahead to make public the details of the joint statement, and this greatly angered President Moi terming it a "violation of secrecy and trust."[37] But for Archbishop Manasses Kuria, "the statement concerned a grave matter of public national interest" and thus the bishops' actions was "a divine right and most patriotic."[38] For Linus Mwangi of the PCEA, "anything whispered in secret would be shouted on the rooftops."[39] However, not all bishops supported the publicity of the statement. Others, like Bishop John Njue of the Embu Catholic Diocese, Bishop Longinus Atundo of the Bungoma Diocese, and Rev Stephen Njenga of the CPK Kasarani, Nairobi, condemned the leak as unethical and a breach of trust.[40]

Only a few churches mainly evangelical churches such as the Africa Inland Church (AIC), the Deliverance Church (DC), and the Redeemed Gospel

---

36. Weekly Review, "People Have Lost Confidence," 21.
37. Weekly Review, "Violation of Secrecy," 21.
38. Weekly Review, 21.
39. Weekly Review, 21.
40. Weekly Review, 21–22.

Church (RGC), did not want to be part of the pro-liberation movements. They protested the so called social-oriented NCCK, especially its engagement in politics, while preferring the gospel-oriented Evangelical Fellowship of Kenya (EFK).[41] However, several authors contend that NCCK's sociopolitical engagement did not drive evangelical churches out of the NCCK; other reasons were predominant.

First, evangelical churches were pro-establishment while NCCK was pro-opposition.[42] Bishop Arthur Kitonga of the RGC urged Kenyan Christians "to preach obedience to the government and the established political order" while Bishop Japhet Omucheyi of the Overcoming Faith Church of Kenya and Fr. Juma Pesa of the Holy Ghost Coptic Church urged Christians "to desist from involving themselves in politics."[43] Bishop Ezekiel Birech of AIC told Margaret Crouch that the AIC prefered to critique the government "in love" as opposed to "shouting it from the rooftops" as the NCCK does.[44] Thus these churches did not take an active approach to critique the State as the NCCK did.

Second, ethnicity shaped the political leanings of evangelical churches. For instance, the AIC, which has a significant Kalenjin and Kamba presence, supported President Moi, a Kalenjin. A columnist noted, "The complete antithesis of the likes of Kuria, Okullu, and Nzeki are the AIC's Bishop Ezekiel Birech [a Kalenjin] and the Rev. Jones Kaleli [a Kamba], as is evident from the sermons they deliver at the televised religious services attended by President Moi every Sunday."[45] This ethnic factor was not unique to evangelical churches. As the next section shows, ethnicity shaped political choices of Anglican and Catholic Christians, greatly intensifying during President Kibaki's presidency, especially from 2002 to 2008.

Third, biblical and missional reasons shaped the evangelical position on social engagement. Evangelicals argued that the church, as Paul teaches in Romans 13, is called to pray and to support the government and not to

---

41. Weekly Review, "Honest Broker," 6. See also Okullu, *Quest for Justice*, 120.

42. See Oluoch, *Christian Political Theology*, 33; Weekly Review, "Church Factor," 3–5; Weekly Review, "Partisan Role in Politics," 12.

43. Weekly Review, "Honest Broker," 6.

44. Crouch, *Vision of Christian Mission*, 139.

45. Weekly Review, "Honest Broker," 7.

oppose it.[46] Also, since power comes from God, no one should resist those in leadership. Thus opposing the ruling government is equal to opposing God. Therefore, they argued that civil disobedience, protests, and other forms of agitation are uncharacteristic of biblically-centered Christians. On the missional front, evangelical churches perceived their call to be that of saving souls, which for them, must be clearly distinguished from sociopolitical engagement.[47] The primary task of the church is to win souls not to engage in politics.

Fourth, self-interest and the desire for state patronage shaped evangelicals' political leanings. Many church leaders argued that the growth of the church and its programs depended on the support of the government. Thus resistance and agitation against the government hinders outreach and mission work. A happy and peaceful government equals a happy and a peaceful church. Thus the government must be supported. Therefore evangelicals supported the government and in return the government supported evangelical churches and their programs. For example, President Moi allocated several tracts of land to the AIC church and the Africa Brotherhood Church (ABC) to build churches, schools, and hospitals.[48] Several Pentecostal churches too received huge sums of money from the president.[49]

The breakaway evangelical churches joined the Evangelical Fellowship of Kenya (EFK). EFK and NCCK differ in their social engagement. The prevailing notion at that time was that EFK was gospel-oriented while NCCK was social-oriented. This is not to say that NCCK did not have gospel at heart. On the contrary, they affirmed that social engagement, evangelism,

---

46. Gifford, *Christianity, Politics*, 217.

47. Parsitau, "From Prophetic Voices," 251. See also, Oluoch, *Christian Political Theology*, 32. On this point, Okullu ("Render unto Caesar," 148) observes,

Some churches have left the Council [WCC] over these issues [political engagement] . . . These church leaders tend to be more conservative evangelicals who see the Gospel message as for only saving souls. In some of these churches it is largely a question of the leadership. The AIC, for example, is one of the largest Protestant churches in Kenya. Many ordinary folk in that church expressed sorrow that the church pulled out of the Council. They are convicted that NCCK is doing the right thing, and that conviction extends to the political arena as well as ecumenical. It is the church leadership that is not enlightened enough to interpret these issues.

48. See Gifford, *Christianity, Politics*, 220–221.

49. Gifford, 215–220.

and missions are intertwined. Thus it is this kind of sociopolitical theology, which drove NCCK's public engagement. While the NCCK participated in pro-reforms movements, the EFK stayed away from them. In fact the EFK under the leadership of Rev Jonah Chesengeny and Rev Isaac Simbiri condemned the NCCK as "arrogant and anti-government."[50] According to Rev Arthur Kitonga, the NCCK's public engagement is an example serious loss of spiritual vision.[51]

The NCCK condemned hate speech utterances prevalent during the pre-election campaigns of 1992. Under the leadership of Rev George Wanjau of PCEA, the NCCK's task force named and condemned several politicians known for instigating ethnic violence.[52] Also during the meeting, the chairman of the NCCK's Justice, Peace and Reconciliation Commission, Bishop Henry Okullu, harshly criticized the opposition parties for their failure to unite together for the sake of the Kenyan people; "Our people are asking," he said, "What has gone wrong?" "Where shall our true liberators come from?" "Must we be condemned to walk in the darkness of oppression for yet another decade?" "Must we move from dictatorship to anarchy?"[53]

Since it was clear NCCK was more in tune with the opposition than the KANU government, the NCCK bore the brunt of Moi's presidency to the extent that it was almost deregistered.[54] Soon after the inter-parties symposium the NCCK published a document, *A Kairos for Kenya*, similar to what their counterparts in South Africa had published calling for the end

---

50. Weekly Review, "Partisan Role in Politics," 12. See another critique of the NCCK and the Roman Catholic church because of their pro-opposition stance in Weekly Review, "Poor Pastoral Strategy," 3.

51. Weekly Review, "Partisan Role in Politics," 12. See also Weekly Review, "Honest Broker," 6.

52. Weekly Review, "Report on Ethnic Violence," 14. See also Weekly Review, "Stop This Heinous Atrocity," 10–11.

53. Weekly Review, "United by a Common Cause," 16.

54. Weekly Review, "Partisan Role in Politics," 12.

of apartheid.[55] The *A Kairos for Kenya* called for political reforms and the necessity of a "Kenya We Want" national convention.[56]

During the 1997 national election, the NCCK, the Roman Catholic Church, and the Institute for Education of Democracy formed an election monitoring group to monitor the elections. The Joint Election Monitoring group, as it was named, published a report on the elections titled, "Report in the 1997 General Elections in Kenya."[57] Jacqueline Klopp asserts that the NCCK was the first ever church-based organization to "document the nature, dynamics, and human consequences of the [ethnic] violence [in Kenya]."[58] However, the report downplayed ethnic-based violence. It only reported such issues as intimidation and corruption, gender-based violence, and youth violence.[59] Factually, as the next paragraph attests, there were ethnic-related violence in the Coastal and the Rift Valley provinces during pre-election period. It is incomprehensible how these church organizations could overlook this ethnic-related violence in its reporting. In Part Four of the Report, "Conclusions and Recommendations," subheading, "Evaluating the Integrity of the Electoral Process," ethnic violence and any matters "tribal" are conspicuously missing except it's mention of political hotspot such as Laikipia, Njoro, and Baringo, the only places where post-election violence occurred.[60] The omission makes the campaign period seem tranquil when in reality there were cases of violence reported in several parts of the country. For example, The Human Rights Watch reported that in mid-1997, in the run-up to the General Election, armed raiders with backing from KANU party activists and some officials targeted potential opposition voters in weeks leading up to election in the Coast Province.[61]

---

55. With a foreword by John W. de Gruchy, the South African document (*The Kairos Document*), was signed by 156 individuals representing twenty denominations and focused on calling the church and State to engage in social-political reforms in South Africa. The Kenyan document was focused on conquering one-party dictatorship. Drawing from the South African experience, the NCCK contended that the Government of Kenya oppressed the people just like apartheid oppressed the people of South Africa.

56. NCCK, *A Kairos for Kenya*.

57. Institute for Education in Democracy, *1997 General Election*.

58. Klopp, "NCCK and the Struggle," 193.

59. Institute for Education in Democracy, *1997 General Election*, 64.

60. Institute for Education in Democracy, 64.

61. Human Rights Watch, *Playing with Fire*, 21.

Though the church organizations downplayed ethnic-based violence in the run-up to the 1997 General Election, they spoke with one voice during the post-election ethnic violence, which followed. On Tuesday 27 January 1998, two hundred Catholic priests, nuns, and brothers from the Nakuru Diocese, under the leadership of Bishop Peter Kairu, presented a protest letter to the Rift Valley provincial commissioner, Mr Nicholas Mberia, in which they condemned the Government of Kenya for its complicity in the ethnic strife.[62] Other Catholic Bishops issued a joint statement condemning the violence as did the NCCK.[63]

More than condemning the violence, the church did something to help the victims of the ethnic strife who numbered about 200,000 people.[64] The Roman Catholic Church put up several camps for the internally displaced in several parts of the country, including Thessalia in Kericho, Kamwaura and Elburgon in Nakuru, and Burnt Forest in Eldoret.[65] Similarly, NCCK sponsored camps in Eldoret town, Soi, and Turbo, while the Quakers had camps in Chwele and Bungoma.[66]

Though the church united in its condemnation of ethnopolitical conflict in the 90s, it oftentimes failed to exemplify ethnic cohesion. A few examples illustrate this failure. First, there were reports of impartiality during the relief

---

62. See Weekly Review, "Oh, Not Again!," 6.

63. The statement from the Catholic Bishops is hereby quoted in part as follows:

It is against this background, and out of our steadfast love and genuine concern for this nation that we are compelled to make the following appeals to the president: 1) To fulfil the pledges that he made to Kenyans as he sought their votes, to unite the country and to bring lasting peace in his last tenure of office, as his legacy; 2) To put an end to the violence immediately, because we know that he is able if he so wishes; 3) To dismiss from his cabinet those well-known ministers who have hitherto uttered inflammatory statements that have always led to ethnic violence. There must be firm action if he wants to put an end to impunity and enhance respect for the law; 4) To respect and accept defeat from certain areas and from certain communities, which did not vote for him in the recently concluded general election, in the same way that they have accepted the presidential results; 5) To concretely assure Kenyans that ethnic violence will not spread to other areas as is now feared; 6) To respect the oath of office that he took barely three weeks ago even if he is not eligible for re-election in the next general elections.

The Weekly Review, "A Call to End the Violence," 7. For the NCCK statement, see, Weekly Review, "Oh, Not Again!," 5.

64. See, Weekly Review, "Oh, Not Again!," 4.

65. Weekly Review, 5.

66. Weekly Review, 5.

efforts offered to victims of ethnic violence. Bishop Ndingi Mwana a'Nzeki of the Catholic Diocese of Nakuru allegedly concentrated relief work on the mostly Kikuyu Nakuru District, while neglecting the predominantly Kalenjin, Kericho District.[67]

The second example is the election of bishops. The election of Bishop Stephen Kewasis, a Pokot, to replace Bishop Alexander Muge, a Nandi, of the CPK Eldoret Diocese, is a good example of a church election decided on the basis of ethnicity. The Nandi Christians of the Anglican Diocese of Eldoret rejected the election of Kewasis just because he was not a Nandi, though Kewasis finally became the bishop through a court verdict.[68] In Kajiado, the Maasai rejected the election of Rev Bernard Njoroge, a Kikuyu, from being the first bishop of the newly created Kajiado Diocese, threatening "that fresh tribal clashes would erupt in Kajiado if Njoroge attempted to discharge his duties as bishop in the new diocese."[69] The Maasai Anglican Christians rejected Bishop Njoroge because "he is a stranger in the diocese."[70] After two years of resistance, the Maasai Christians finally got one of their own, Rev Jeremiah Taama, as the Bishop.[71]

Another example is the creation of several dioceses in the CPK Church. Ethnicity dominated the creation of Katakwa Diocese in Busia District. For more than five years, the Teso-dominated Katakwa region fought a dramatic and protracted battle to break away from the Luhya-dominated Nambale Diocese of Bishop Isaak Namango. Finally, the CPK leadership under Archbishop Manasses Kuria granted the Teso Christians their own diocese of Katakwa on 1 January 1991 under the leadership of Bishop Eliud Okiring.[72] This ethnicization of ecclesiastical leadership in the Anglican Church affected its credibility. It also provided precedence for the church

---

67. Weekly Review, "Honest Broker," 6.

68. Weekly Review, "Stormy Enthronement," 18.

69. Weekly Review, "Controversy Deepens," 14. See also, Weekly Review, "Ethnicity in the CPK," 12–14.

70. Weekly Review, "Controversy Deepens," 14.

71. Although Rev Jeremiah Taama is not a Maasai but a Kamba, he was nevertheless considered a Maasai because he had lived among the Maasai for many years and spoke the language very well.

72. Weekly Review, "Stormy Enthronement," 18; Weekly Review, "Katakwans To Do It," 13–15.

for aggrieved Christians from a particular community to use ethnicity to create a new diocese for themselves from any of the existing dioceses that currently encompass disparate ethnic communities within their jurisdiction.

The Anglican bishops also divided along ethnic lines in their support of political leaders.[73] Archbishop Manasses Kuria preferred to support Ford Asili chairman, Kenneth Matiba a fellow Kikuyu, for the presidency, while Henry Okullu, the bishop of Maseno South openly supported Ford Kenya's Oginga Odinga, a fellow Luo.[74] The Rev Elijah Yego of the Eldoret Diocese, a man who had earlier opposed the election of Bishop Stephen Kewasis because he was not a Nandi, supported President Daniel Arap Moi, a fellow Kalenjin. Reverend Yego called all non-Kalenjins to vote for Moi "or be prepared for eviction from the district if he loses."[75] Ironically, Rev Yego had earlier on, in March 1992, condemned the government for "not doing enough to quell the fighting in which the Luo have been the main victims."[76]

The foregone account shows that the Kenyan church actively engaged in political and social reforms in the 1990s. However, the church was not completely free of ethnic-based conflict. The next time period (2001–2008) marked the demise of the prophetic voice of the church in Kenya mainly because of negative ethnicity. The next section examines ethnopolitical conflict and the church in Kenya from 2001–2008.

Ethnopolitical Conflict and the Church in Kenya: A Divided Voice (2001–2008)

Ethnic divisions and conflict tore the church apart from 2002 to 2008. The period began with great hope for the country as it marked the end of President Moi's twenty-four-year rule. However, his successor, President Mwai Kibaki, though he campaigned on the platform of ethnic unity, failed to unify the country. Kibaki's government continued to polarize the country along ethnic lines. In the same manner, churches, both mainline, Evangelical, and Pentecostals, during this time, were greatly divided.

---

73. Weekly Review, "Of Clergymen and Tribalism," 12–13.

74. Weekly Review, 12.

75. Weekly Review, 12.

76. Weekly Review, "Ethnic Strife," 5.

The first division occurred during the struggle for constitutional review. For many years the opposition, civil societies, and the church had been pushing for a constitutional review. In 2001, President Moi allowed them some latitude to constitute a forum for constitutional changes. This caused a massive rift between the major church organizations. On one hand, the Forum for Restoration of Democracy (FORD) and NCCK wanted a review process that consulted Kenyans from all sectors, from the civil society to professional bodies to the clergy. On the other hand, evangelicals and a few opposition members such as Raila Odinga wanted a parliamentary-led review process. The NCCK under the leadership of the General Secretary, Rev Mutava Musyimi, proposed a merger between NCCK and the Parliamentary review team. The group referred to as "Ufungamano Initiative" (after the Ufungamano House, a church-owned premise that was a venue for most of the meetings), would lead the constitutional review process. The evangelicals, under the leadership of Archbishop Samson Gaitho, the Bishop of the African Independent Pentecostal Church, went to court because they wanted to be included in the team.[77] Archbishop Gaitho bolstered his point by noting that the NCCK represented "few than 40 bodies" while the evangelicals comprised of "more than 800 registered denominations."[78]

Reverend Musyimi defended the Ufungamano Initiative arguing that they were not being partisan.[79] Similarly, Archbishop Gitari responded to the Evangelicals describing them as "probably confused because their theology is faulty."[80] Gitari argued that evangelicals were aloof during the campaign for multiparty democracy in the early 90's, and when Kenyans were struggling for constitutional review, "they only wanted to support the government, whether it was right or wrong."[81] He also added, "They kept away from us and even held rallies against Ufungamano, now that the war is almost won, it's not sincere of them to appear at the eleventh hour with all manner of conditions."[82]

77. Thuku, "Churches in Threat of Merger," 5.

78. Thuku, 5.

79. Daily Nation, "Musyimi Clears Air," 4.

80. Gachamba, "Gitari Tells Off Churches Group," 1.

81. Gachamba, 3–4.

82. Gachamba, 5.

This rift between churches did not go unnoticed. In an editorial cartoon in the *Daily Nation* on 7 May 2001, the cartoonist drew two goats dressed in the manner likely to suggest that they were prelates, complete with a miter. Chained to each other but pulling in different directions, each endeavoring to reach a pot of water labeled constitutional reforms, albeit the pot being out of reach. This derision of the church highlighted the zero sum game of each camp's attempts to block each other from working towards constitutional reform. The constitutional reforms did not continue until after the election of December 2002.

After the election, the Kibaki Presidency constituted the Kenya Review Act, Chapter 3A, which established the Kenya Review Commission under the chairmanship of Professor Yash Pal Ghai, and mandated it to carry on the constitutional review process. The Commission held their meetings at the Bomas of Kenya in Nairobi from 2002 to 2005 producing the Draft Constitution (Bomas Draft), which was debated at the Kenya Constitutional Conference at Bomas and later organized as the Proposed New Constitution to be voted "yes" or "no" at a national referendum in 2005.

During the campaigns for the referendum, the church divided along ethnic, denominational, and party lines. For instance, a group of Catholic bishops from the Central Province under the leadership of Cardinal John Njue, also from the Central province (Embu), defended President Kibaki's presidency arguably because he was Catholic and from the Central province.[83] Their support came at a time when Kibaki was facing resistance from the Opposition because of his rejection of *majimbo* (regionalism). Thus Cardinal Njue's rejection of *majimbo*, though he claimed to be informed by national cohesion, was interpreted as support for Kibaki.[84] Accordingly, Njue was accused of being a "central Kenya mouthpiece" and a "Kibaki sympathizer."[85] Another Catholic Bishop, Archbishop Zacchaeus Okoth of Kisumu, distanced himself from Cardinal Njue's position by openly supporting the opposition. Here too, Kenyans saw ethnicity as informing Okoth's view

---

83. Gifford, *Christianity, Politics*, 40; Gekara, "Religious Leaders," 19; Gekara, "Cardinal Njue's Leadership," 15.

84. Njue is reported to have said: "I have no apologies to make on the *majimbo* stand. I stood for what I thought was right at the time and what was important for national unity." See, Gekara, "Cardinal Njue's Leadership," 15.

85. Gekara, "Cardinal Njue's Leadership," 15.

because he was from Nyanza, and him being a Luo, the community of the opposition leader, Raila Odinga.

As to the matter of the Bomas Draft constitution, Cardinal Njue encouraged Kenyan Catholics to vote "with their conscience."[86] The other denominations, except ACK who also encouraged their members to "vote with their conscience," were openly campaigning against it because it permitted abortion under certain circumstances and it favored Islam by recognizing the formation of Kadhi courts operated through tax payer's money. Njue's word had great authority not only because he was the one in charge of the Catholic Church at the time but also because he was a Constitution of Kenya Review Commission national delegate at the Bomas of Kenya representing the Catholic Church. Kenyans voted to reject the Bomas Draft constitution on 21 November 2005.[87] It can be argued that Njue's recommendations to the Catholics played a part in this defeat. On this note, Chacha avows, "the defeat of the new constitution was overwhelmingly not only along ethnic lines but religious too, undoubtedly on the side of Kibaki, who was continually viewed by the Catholics as a prominent member."[88]

Similarly, the Government and the Opposition co-opted some clergy to their sides. President Kibaki appointed Rev Mutava Musyimi, the NCCK undersecretary and hitherto a tough critic of the Moi regime, as the head of the Steering Committee on Anticorruption (he went on to contest a parliamentary seat on the president's party soon after resigning from NCCK and becoming a Member of Parliament). Gifford observes that "the NCCK under Musyimi changed its stance from 'principled opposition' during the Moi administration to 'principled cooperation' towards Kibaki's."[89] Raila Odinga of the newly formed Orange Democratic Movement (ODM), brought in Bishop Margaret Wanjiru, a prominent televangelist with a congregation of at least 20,000 people, to most of his political rallies. Wanjiru later vied

---

86. Parsitau, "From Prophetic Voices," 256; Gifford, *Christianity, Politics*, 59.

87. A banana was the symbol for "yes" and an orange, a symbol for "no." When Kenyans voted NO against the Draft Constitution, their decision inspired the formation of the Orange Democratic Movement (ODM) under the leadership of Raila Odinga. Later on, the ODM campaigned vigorously against the Party of National Unity (PNU), leading to a much-contested election in 2007 and the subsequent violence.

88. Chacha, "Pastors or Bastards?," 114.

89. Gifford, *Christianity, Politics*, 43.

for a parliamentary seat on the ODM party and won. Several clergies also sought elective positions in government but the majority of them lost. Thus the church failed because of co-option and compromise of the clergy by the government and the opposition.[90]

The years 2006 and 2007 also intensified partisanship in the church to a point where "Caesar and God spoon-fed each other" as Chacha observes.[91] The church was divided along tribal and party lines. The church's lack of voice and clear ethnic division disappointed the Kenyan people. Frequent newspaper columns and letters to the editor written during this time clearly show the disappointment. Editorials appeared with titles such as, "The church is not our voice anymore;"[92] "No longer the beacon of morality;"[93] "Heal yourself first, dear clerics;"[94] "Kenya badly in need of new leaders;"[95] "House of God divided;"[96] "When the shepherds led their flock astray;"[97] "How clergy took battle to Grim Reaper;"[98] "Church embedded long before elections;"[99] "Ethnicity in the church comes of age;"[100] "Church's worrying slide to silence;"[101] "political bishops betraying the people;"[102] "Kenyan 'prophets' who won no respect;"[103] "Did church leaders fail Kenyans?"[104] One author commented that church leaders used their pulpits "to beat drums of ethnic hatred, which fueled the post-election chaos."[105] And another writer said, "They preached poison from the pulpits, these men and women of God! They asked their communities to arm themselves and attack their fellow

---

90. Parsitau, "From Prophetic Voices," 251–252.

91. Chacha, "Pastors or Bastards?," 114.

92. Oloo, "Church is Not Our Voice."

93. Ogola, "No Longer the Beacon."

94. Oriang, "Heal Yourself First."

95. Opanga, "Kenya Badly in Need," 14.

96. Ngesa, "House of God Divided," 13.

97. Daily Nation, "When the Shepherds Led," 10.

98. Osanjo, "How Clergy Took Battle," 22.

99. East African Standard, "Church Embedded."

100. Wamanji, "Ethnicity and the Church."

101. Onyango, "Church's Worrying."

102. Nyatete, "Political Bishops Betraying."

103. Ogutu, "Kenyan 'Prophets.'"

104. Daily Nation, "Did Church Leaders Fail."

105. Gekara, "Cardinal Njue's Leadership," 15.

Kenyans. Yes, the clergy set community against community and brother against brother."[106]

In the wake of 2007/2008 post-election chaos, the clergy tried to urge people to embrace peace, but they were ignored. In fact, more than ten churches nationwide were burnt down.[107] The burning of thirty-five women and children who had sought shelter in an Assemblies of God church in Eldoret embodied the force of this national acrimony against the Church. By being partisan, the Church had lost its prophetic voice and could not be trusted to provide moral and spiritual direction.

Ethnopolitical Conflict and the Church in Kenya: On the Road to Recovery (2008–2013)

Soon after the 2007 General Election, the church discovered that it had lost its prophetic stand and had no authority to offer moral and spiritual guidance to the people of Kenya. The recovery of their prophetic place began with a formal apology from the NCCK entitled, "Hope for Kenya" on 15 February 2008. The NCCK apology is hereby quoted in part:

> We regret that we as church leaders were unable to effectively confront these issues because we were partisan. Our efforts to forestall the current crisis were not effective because we as the membership of NCCK did not speak with one voice. We were divided in the way we saw the management of the elections; we identified with our people based on ethnicity; and after the elections, we are divided on how to deal with the crisis. As a result, we together with other church leaders have displayed partisan values in situations that called for national interests. The church has remained disunited and its voice swallowed in the cacophony of those of other vested interests. We call on church leaders to recapture their strategic position as the moral authority of the nation. We have put in place measures to enable us overcome the divisive forces, and set off on a new

---

106. Opanga, "Kenya Badly in Need," 14.
107. Chacha, "Pastors or Bastards?," 126.

beginning. As the church, we will do our best in helping achieve the rebirth of a new Kenya.[108]

Another apology from the NCCK came in August 2008 at the NCCK General Assembly at Kabarak University, a meeting where more than 1,300 clergies attended. Reverend Canon Peter Karanja convened the meeting to give the clerics "a chance to reflect, repent, pray together and be transformed in the power of the Holy Spirit to become agents of healing and reconciliation to the nation."[109] During the meeting, the "Clergymen admitted to blessing warriors to engage in violence and inviting politicians to disseminate hate messages that incited people against members of various communities."[110] The confession was in line with the theme of the meeting, which was "the truth shall set you free."

The Catholic bishops became the second religious group to confess. Their public confession came in March 2008. Cardinal Njue offered a formal apology at the Holy Family Basilica in Nairobi at a thanksgiving service offered for the establishment of a grand coalition government. Cardinal Njue said, "We (the Catholic Church) did not listen to the voice of the shepherd, who is Jesus Christ. We failed to love one another. We sinned by failing to love one another."[111] Similarly, at a meeting to welcome the Pope's representative in Kenya, Archbishop Alain Paul Lebeaupin, Cardinal Njue confessed, "We may have taken sides, we may have gone wrong, but we have to turn around now. Let us embrace the idea of a coalition government because it is through it that we can ensure the government does not serve the interests of a single individual or community."[112]

Several other churches and organizations joined the NCCK and the Catholic bishops in apologizing to the country and calling for national healing. For instance, during a prayer meeting for the Sachang'wan fire tragedy victims in which more than 111 people lost their lives, religious leaders sought forgiveness for "leaving the people of Kenya dispersed like lost sheep

---

108. NCCK Executive Commitee, "Hope for Kenya."
109. Daily Nation, "Clergymen Own Up."
110. Daily Nation.
111. As quoted in Chacha, "Pastors or Bastards?," 129.
112. Mathenge, "Clerics Push for 'Faster Healing,'" 6.

without a shepherd" during the 2007 General Election.[113] Similarly, the Evangelical Alliance of Kenya was instrumental in the formation of a lobby group to mediate national cohesion and healing following the post-election chaos. The group met three times with the former UN Secretary General Kofi Anan in their attempt to broker a national accord.[114]

After the post-election chaos, the new Grand Coalition government appointed a commission of experts to draft a new constitution. When the Members of Parliament could not get the required signatures to amend the 150 contentious clauses, the proposed constitution was passed as it was. The Attorney General presented it to be voted either "yes" or "no" at a referendum on 4 August 2010. The church at this time united with ODM party to campaign against it. The issue of Kadhi courts and abortion triggered the church's rejection of the proposed constitution. All the church bodies (NCCK, EAK, and KCEC) urged their member churches to reject it. On 30 July 2010 the Christian leaders issued a joint statement urging their members "to exercise their democratic right to vote, and to display their patriotism for our country and convincingly vote NO to this flawed proposed constitution."[115] Again, on 31 July 2010, the Kenya Episcopal conference issued a statement signed by all the twenty-five Roman Catholic bishops to reject the proposed constitution because it permitted abortion.[116]

However, not all leaders supported the "no" campaign. Retired Archbishop Gitari urged the Anglican Christians to vote "yes" because the proposed constitution was by far better than the Lancaster House constitution that Kenya had used since independence.[117] Gitari gained the support of Bishop Peter Njoka, the Anglican Bishop of Nairobi and Bishop Lawi Imathiu of the Methodist church. At the end of the campaign, the "yes" camp won. Kenya promulgated a new constitution on 27 August 2010. Even though the "no" team was defeated, the unity of the church was clearly manifest during this time. For the first time in several years, the church rose above ethnic divides. Indeed, the church could be said to be "on the road to recovery." Even the

---

113. Gekara, "Religious Leaders," 19.
114. Chacha, "Pastors or Bastards?," 129.
115. Gitari, *Troubled but Not Destroyed*, 284–285.
116. Gitari, 285.
117. Gitari, 287–289.

Kenyan bishops who had no moral ground to talk to Kenyans regained respect in national issues. For instance, the Kenya Conference of Catholic Bishops issued a pastoral letter urging Kenyans to "to embrace peace and co-existence."[118] Maseno West Anglican bishop urged Kenyans to "stand up and say no to the culture of negative ethnicity, land grabbing, hate speech, and impunity because the country cannot continue to live in the past."[119]

Conclusion

This chapter argued that the church in Kenya commanded a great influence in the 90s but lost its prophetic voice in the years 2002 to 2008 mainly because of ethnocentrism and the co-option and compromise of the clergy by the Government and the Opposition. Mainline Protestant churches, especially the CPK and PCEA, under the auspices of the NCCK, called for justice, democracy, and ethnopolitical cohesion. Similarly, the Roman Catholic Church actively engaged in the sociopolitical transformation of Kenya. However, evangelical churches, especially the AIC, RGC, and DC, under the umbrella organization, the EFK (now EAK), steered away from social-political engagement. After the post-election skirmishes, which followed this period and the church's subsequent apologies to the Kenyan people, the church is now on the road to recovery. The next three chapters provide a Reformed theological response to the problem of ethnopolitical conflict in Kenya.

---

118. Vatican Radio, "Kenya Bishops Call for Unity."
119. Juma, "Crack Whip on Hate Mongers," 9.

John Calvin's Doctrine of the Image of God as a Basis for a Reformed Doctrine of Ethnopolitical Cohesion in Kenya

This chapter examines Calvin's doctrine of the image of God as a theological basis for ethnopolitical cohesion in Kenya. The study is based on the 1559 edition of the *Institutes of the Christian Religion* (hereinafter, *Institutes*).[1] Alister E. McGrath contends that Calvin stressed that his readers should treat the *Institutes* as "the primary resource for his religious thought" and "as the primary source of his theology."[2] The book also consults Calvin's biblical commentaries.[3] The thesis is that Calvin advanced a relational view of the image of God rooted in the restoration of humanity's relationship with God. This chapter shows that the heart of Calvin's theological anthropology is soteriology, precisely, restoration of the image of God in believers. In Christ, Christians are remade in God's image and then sent as God's image bearers to the world. The contemporary practical implication of this restoration of the image of God in Christ, for the Kenyan context, is to enable Christians to transcend hate and violence through respect and honor of those from other ethnic communities and divergent political views. The chapter has four sections. First, it presents the Reformed tradition and Reformed churches

---

1. Five editions of Calvin's *Institutes of the Christian Religion* exist. The editions are 1536, 1539, 1543, 1550, and 1559. Unless otherwise indicated, quotations are from Ford Lewis Battles's translation (Library of Christian Classics series), the 1559 edition. The acknowledgments are in the following format: Book, Chapter, Section; for example I.1.15.

2. McGrath, *Life of John Calvin*, 138, 146.

3. Quotations of Calvin's commentaries are from the *500 Years Anniversary Edition* (23 volume set) of various translators acknowledged in the following order: Volume, page number.

in Kenya. Second, it introduces Calvin, his ministry, and his publications. Third, it examines Calvin's doctrine of the image of God within the context of the historical interpretation of the doctrine. Fourth, it offers three implications of affirming the image of God in Kenya.

Defining "Reformed Tradition"

The Reformed tradition, also known as "Calvinism" or "Reformed Protestantism," refers to the ecclesial-theological tradition, which has its roots in the work and teachings of the Swiss Reformers (mainly Huldrich Zwingli, John Calvin, and Heinrich Bullinger) and Scottish Reformers (particularly John Knox).[4] Thus the Reformed tradition has two streams, Scottish and Dutch. Both differ in theological emphasis. The Scottish Tradition, through the teachings of John Knox and the Scotts Confession of Faith (1560), emphasized the doctrines of predestination, salvation, and order of salvation, while the Dutch Tradition, through the teachings of Zwingli, Calvin, and Bullinger, and the Belgic Confession, Heidelberg Catechism, and the Westminster Confession of Faith, emphasized cultural engagement and the lordship of Jesus over all of life.[5] Historically, the Reformed tradition owes its origins to the Protestant Reformation that Martin Luther started in Germany in 1517.[6]

No single theological affirmation encapsulates the Reformed Tradition. In addition to affirming the Reformation's *sola scriptura* (by scripture alone), *solus Christus* (through Christ alone), *sola fide* (by faith alone), *sola gratia* (by grace alone), *soli Deo Gloria* (for the glory of God alone), the Reformed tradition also emphasizes that Christians play a significant role in the cultural

---

4. Paul Helm, (*Calvin*, 9) presents other notable Reformed thinkers most of whom Calvin corresponded with to include: Jerome Zanchius (1516–1590), Peter Martyr Vermigli (1500–1562), Guillaume Farel (1489–1565), Pierre Viret (1511–1571), Theodore Beza (1519–1605), John Knox (1514–1572), and Zachary Ursinus (1534–1583).

5. Holcomb, "Two Major Streams"; Leith, *Introduction to the Reformed*, 31–40.

6. Though the Protestant Reformation gained traction through Luther's initiative, the reformation of the Roman Catholic Church predates Luther. Key figures of the Roman Catholic Church were already involved in reforming their church. In addition to Lutheran and Reformed traditions, the Protestant Reformation also produced other traditions such as the Anabaptist/Radical Reformation and the British/English Reformation. The Catholic (Counter) Reformation, specifically, the Council of Trent, is an important stream of the Reformation.

transformation of their communities. This particular belief is rooted in the Reformed tradition's emphasis on God as creator and redeemer of culture.[7] The Reformed tradition believes that "the full spectrum of human life is called towards the realization of the demand for obedience to the command-ments of God and his Word."[8] They reject dichotomizing of life into secular and sacred and emphasize that God permeates all spheres of human life.

The version of the Reformed tradition embraced in Kenya blends both the Scottish emphasis on salvation (with less emphasis on election/predestina-tion), including the Puritan focus on spiritual and moral renewal, and the Dutch, especially Kuyperian emphasis on Christ's influence in the different spheres of human life. As shown below, the Reformed movement in Kenya arrived via the work of missionaries from United States of America, Scotland, and South Africa. However, little has been published on the influences of their theological inclinations on the shape of Reformed theology in Kenya. Much of what Reformed Christians in Kenya know about Reformed theol-ogy is gained through preaching and the internet. Hence there is a need to resource the Reformed tradition for the Kenyan audience.

Resourcing the Reformed Tradition

The Reformed tradition, like any other tradition, has its achievements and flaws. For good, the Reformed tradition was responsible for various eco-nomic, social, and intellectual reforms in various countries. Calvin himself pioneered the Academy of Geneva, and wherever the Reformed communi-ties came into existence, they started schools, hospitals, and other projects. For bad, the Reformed tradition was responsible for legitimating apartheid in South Africa.[9] Calvinist Boers in South Africa legitimated their segrega-tion of blacks using the Bible (for example arguing that Africans were a "cursed race") and an interpretation of John Calvin's doctrines of election and

---

7. Leith, *Introduction to the Reformed*, 188.

8. Botha, "Christian-National," 472.

9. Several publications provide a theological critique of the Calvinist theology that shaped apartheid in South Africa. Notable ones include Bax, *Different Gospel*; Boesak, *Black and Reformed*; de Gruchy, *Liberating Reformed Theology*.

predestination, which excluded the black people.[10] Similarly, Presbyterians in the Southern states of USA ignored the segregation of black people because of an erroneous ecclesiology (the doctrine of "spirituality of the church"), political theology, and a theological anthropology that supported segregation of races.[11] However, despite this negative legacy, the Reformed tradition has positive implications today.

John de Gruchy argues that tradition shapes identity, beliefs, and actions; "even when we are critical of parts or reject it as a whole; it is our story and inheritance."[12] According to him, traditions are alive because adherents read and re-examine them in light of contemporary situations.[13] Similarly, John Leith observes that gratitude for tradition should be balanced by critical judgment of it because "every tradition has its share of false starts, mistaken judgments, and betrayals of its own best convictions."[14] André Biéler has a similar perspective when he proposes "creative imagination" in the study of Calvin because not everything in Calvin's theology is beneficial for a contemporary audience.[15] According to David Hester, the assumption that critical engagement of tradition should balance an appreciation of it is a key ethos of the Reformed tradition.[16] Hence it is important to balance appreciation of tradition with critical engagement.

An example of a critical engagement of theological tradition is found in South Africa. In the midst of misinterpretation of Calvin, which legitimated oppression of black people through apartheid, other scholars offered an alternative interpretation of Calvin, which fostered the dignity of black people and ultimately their liberation.[17] De Gruchy observes that other contextual

---

10. John Baur, (*2000 Years of Christianity*, 191–192) asserts that the Calvinist Boer's own superiority "was for them a clear confirmation of the 'indubitable certainty of grace' in which all heirs of Calvin believed more than he himself did. For Calvin the community of the elect formed the invisible church, but they identified it with their racial community sojourning in a heathen land."

11. On this issue, see, Borneman, "All Things Turned"; Borneman, "Presbyterians, Civil Rights."

12. de Gruchy, *John Calvin*, 24.

13. de Gruchy, 24.

14. Leith, *Introduction to the Reformed*, 7.

15. Biéler, *Social Humanism of Calvin*, 65.

16. Hester, "Sanctified Life," 196.

17. de Gruchy, *John Calvin*, 12.

questions are currently shaping Reformed theology in South Africa, for example, questions regarding the role of the ancestors or the "living dead."[18] Similarly, Dieumeme Noelliste believes that some elements of Calvin's theology "can be salvaged for our time" especially in the Majority World "where issues of political liberty, economic justice, and overall social well-being have taken on greater urgency than in the Western world."[19] In this regard, this book draws from this process of resourcing tradition although it recognizes as Noelliste suggests, that not everything in Calvin's thought is appropriate for today.[20] However, before resourcing Calvin's heritage, a brief introduction of Reformed churches in Kenya is necessary.

Reformed Churches in Kenya

Several churches in Kenya trace their denominational legacy to the Reformed wing of the Protestant Reformation. The first is the Presbyterian Church of East Africa (PCEA), which was started in 1891 through the work of various missionaries from Scotland, Britain, and South Africa.[21] It has a membership of over 4.3 million and an annual growth rate of 5 percent.[22] The Reformed Church of East Africa (RCEA), started in Eldoret in 1944 by the Dutch Reformed Church of South Africa, is another Reformed denomination. It has a membership of around 400,000. The Dutch Reformed Church handed over the mantle of leadership of RCEA to the Reformed Mission League of the Netherlands. The RCEA became independent in 1963. However RCEA split due to differences in its missionary focus, to form the Christian Reformed Church in Eastern Africa (CRCEA) in 1992, another Reformed denomination with a membership of 100,000.[23]

---

18. de Gruchy, 23.

19. Noelliste, "Exploring the Usefulness," 221.

20. Noelliste, 240.

21. Parsitau, "Pentecostalising the Church of Scotland?," 229; Hart, *Calvinism*, 202.

22. Parsitau, 229; Mohr, *Enchanted Calvinism*, 5.

23. Benedetto and McKim, *Historical Dictionary*, 153. Followers of the CRCEA wanted to extend missionary outreach beyond Kenya to Uganda, Tanzania, and Congo.

Africa Inland Church (AIC) is another Reformed denomination.[24] It started in 1895 through the work of Peter Cameron Scott, the founding director of the Africa Inland Mission (AIM). Scott was a member of the Presbyterian Church in America. AIM wanted to focus their missionary efforts in the interior of Africa. Prior to them, several mission agencies, like the Church Missionary Society (CMS), had concentrated their efforts along the coastline of Mombasa, but none had ventured to the hinterlands of Kenya. Though Scott died of Blackwater fever only a year after his arrival in Kenya having managed to convert a handful of Africans, the AIC denomination has grown to more than five-million members and has spread to Tanzania, Uganda, South Sudan, and Congo.[25]

Reformed churches in Kenya struggle to overcome ethnocentrism. As argued earlier, missionaries to Kenya precipitated the volatile problem of tribalism in Kenya by concentrating their outreach among specific ethnic communities while neglecting others. The Church of Scotland missionaries concentrated their work among the Kikuyu, and thus PCEA has remained predominantly a Kikuyu church. When Kikuyu people spread to other parts of the country, they pioneered PCEA churches. However, these congregations remained exclusively for members of the Kikuyu community to the extent that the service is often held in the Kikuyu language even in urban churches such as St Andrews in Nairobi.[26] Similarly, AIM missionaries worked among the Kamba and Kalenjin communities. Consequently, the AIC denomination, the daughter church of the AIM, is mainly found within

---

24. It is important to say that the AIC is Reformed in the sense that it was founded under Calvin's legacy. It has, however, diverted from the Reformed tradition in liturgical, organizational structure, and in embracing adult baptism.

25. Omulokoli, "Foundational History," 45–50; Gehman, "Spreading Vineyard."

26. Parsitau, "Pentecostalising the Church," 231; Khasandi-Telewa, "'She Worships,'" 295. Whereas Parsitau, in this cited essay, concludes that the PCEA "is either unable or unwilling to shed off its ethnic label" (232), Khasandi-Telewa concludes from her study of the use of the Kikuyu language among believers of the PCEA that Kikuyu Christians, even those who live in the diaspora, prefer to worship in churches that use the vernacular (294–300). Thus the use of vernacular is not the major problem, but the problem is the exclusion of those who do not speak the language. Some churches overcome this problem by having a blended service (vernacular and Swahili/English) where they use a translator or by having two services.

these two communities.[27] The Dutch Reformed Church of South Africa and the Dutch Reformed Church of the Netherlands focused their attention among Kalenjin and Luhya communities. Consequently, the Reformed Church of East Africa is mainly found among these two communities.[28]

Considering that ethnocentrism is a real challenge to Kenyan churches how would churches overcome it? What kind of theological perception should Kenyan Christians embrace that would compel them to view each other with utmost respect and to live in peace with one another? How would Reformed Christians in Kenya exemplify the meaning of love to the neighbor of a different ethnic background and political affiliation? The way forward is to draw from Calvin's theological anthropology, which has implications for personal and communal relationships, leadership (whether civil or ecclesial), and the quest for justice and peace among all God's people. Doing this enables an emphasis on the recreation of a new view of humanity capable of transcending ethnic divisions. The following section introduces John Calvin and his publications.

A Brief Biographical Sketch of John Calvin

John Calvin (as his name is known in English; Jean [Jehan] Cauvin in French; Ionnis Calvinus in Latin) was born on 10 July 1509 in Noyon, France, to a devout aristocratic Catholic family. Calvin's father, Gérard Cauvin, served as a canon lawyer and estate administrator of the bishop of Noyon. Gérard shaped his son's future career as a theologian. First, he sent him to College de Montaigu to acquire pre-university education in logic and literary studies under the tutelage of Mathurim Cordier.[29] Afterward, in 1524, Calvin joined College de la Marche of the University of Paris to study Greek, Hebrew, and Classical Philosophy in preparation for a clerical vocation, graduating in 1528 with a Master of Arts degree.[30] In the same

---

27. A few AIC churches are found in the Coast, Nyanza, and North-Eastern counties of Kenya. The AIC, through one of its departments, the Africa Inland Church Mission Department (AICMD), has send missionaries throughout the country and beyond. However, the AIC is still perceived as a Kalenjin and a Kamba denomination.

28. Sesi, "Ethnic Realities," 29.

29. Torrance, *Hermeneutics of John Calvin*, 96.

30. Hiagbe, *Reconciled to Reconcile*, 49.

year, Gérard encouraged his son to join the University of *Orléans* to study law under Pierre de l'Estoile. However, a year later, Calvin moved to the University of Bourges to study under Andrea Alciati, an outstanding jurist and humanist scholar.[31] Calvin graduated with an equivalent of a Master of Law degree in 1532 and began to teach at the University of *Orléans*.

In the same year (1532), Calvin published his first book, a commentary on Seneca's *De Clementia* ("On Clemency"), which was a diplomatic protest against religious intolerance. However, the book, which embraced Stoic philosophy, did not receive the popularity Calvin expected. Scholars observe that it is this failure that might have prompted Calvin to consider Protestantism thus shifting his interest from Stoic philosophy to biblical authority and theology.[32]

Calvin converted to Protestantism in 1532. Philip Schaff asserted that "Calvin's conversion was a mere change from Catholicism to Protestantism, from papal superstition to evangelical faith, from scholastic traditionalism to biblical simplicity."[33] Schaff's assertion that the conversion was "a mere change from Catholicism to Protestantism" underplays the significant experience of Calvin's conversion. Calvin's own life, his emphasis on piety and total surrender to God, and his own ministry as a pastor attests to a different form of conversion. It was not a mere conversion from Catholicity to Protestantism. In the preface to his commentary on Psalms, Calvin mentioned his conversion as conversion to "a teachable frame" the outcome of which was an "inflamed" and "intense" desire to pursue godliness. Thus Calvin's conversion was not a mere change of denominational allegiance.[34]

Calvin's conversion almost cost him his life. The Catholic Church persecuted him for his faith ultimately leading to his escape from France. The persecution intensified when the French authorities, suspicious of the rising aggressiveness of the reforming movement in France, thought Calvin wrote the inaugural address that his friend Nicolas Cop, the Rector of Royal

---

31. Witte, *Reformation of Rights*, 42; Steinmetz, *Calvin in Context*, 7; Bouwsma, *John Calvin*, 114.

32. Hiagbe, *Reconciled to Reconcile*, 49; Torrance, *Hermeneutics of John Calvin*, 96; Hughes, "Pen of the Prophet," 74–75.

33. Schaff, *History of the Christian Church*, vol. 8, 310.

34. Calvin, *Commentary on Psalms*, 1:25.

College, delivered on All Saints Day, 1533, at the college.[35] The Parliament of Paris issued an arrest warrant for Cop. Fearing for his life, Cop fled to the Protestant city of Basel. Calvin later joined him in Basel, severing his ties with the Roman church for life.

In 1536, Calvin decided to move to Strasbourg. However, the direct route from Noyon to Strasbourg was impassable due to an outbreak of war between Francis I of France and Emperor Charles V of Germany. Calvin was forced to make a detour, which brought him to Geneva. Upon hearing of Calvin's arrival, Guillaume (William) Farel, the father of the Reformation in Geneva, compelled him to remain, threatening him with God's punishment should he refuse to stay.[36] Geneva became Calvin's home for the rest of his life except for a period of three-year exile in Strasbourg (1538–1541).

Like Geneva, Strasbourg was home to international refugees. Calvin ministered to them for three years. During the course of his ministry in Strasbourg, Calvin married Idelette de Bure Stordeur, a widow with two children from her first marriage to Jean Stordeur, an Anabaptist refugee who had converted to Reformed Christianity under Calvin's witnessing, and who was a member of Calvin's church. She bore Calvin a son who died shortly after a premature birth. Idelette died in 1549.[37] Calvin died on 27 May 1564 and was buried in an unmarked grave in Geneva. Theodore Beza (1519–1605) took over as the leader of the Genevan church.

Calvin's Ministry

Calvin's initial intention was to be a quiet scholar in Strasbourg.[38] However, the plans changed when Farel urged him to remain in Geneva. Between writing academic and lay materials, Calvin preached at least eight times a week; twice on Sunday and each weekday morning every other week, to local citizens, international refugees, pastors in training, and intellectuals

---

35. Hiagbe, *Reconciled to Reconcile*, 52.

36. Selderhuis, *Calvin Handbook*, 30–37; Hiagbe, *Reconciled to Reconcile*, 52; van der Walt, "School That Calvin Established," 306.

37. In his letter to Viret, dated 7 April 1549, written from Geneva (Calvin, *Reflection Book*, 91–92), Calvin describes his grief upon the loss of his wife: "And truly mine is no common source of grief. I have been bereaved of the best companion of my life . . . During her life she was the faithful helper of my ministry."

38. Calvin, *Reflection Book*, 11; Benoit, "Pastoral Care," 52; Hughes, "Pen of the Prophet," 71–72.

who attended Saint Pierre church where he served.[39] He also supervised the catechetical instruction of young children every Sunday afternoon, having published the catechism used for this purpose. He also offered pastoral care to parishioners, the sick, prisoners, and refugees. Pastoral care provided Calvin an opportunity to affirm abundant life in the midst of the poverty of Geneva. It was also an occasion to showcase the sovereignty of God and the reign of Jesus Christ in the midst of life-threatening challenges in Geneva. Calvin also corresponded with several friends on a wide array of issues.[40]

In Geneva, Calvin saw his ministry as extending beyond spiritual matters. He believed that salvation had sociopolitical implications. As such, Calvin enforced socio-religious and economic reforms in Geneva. He desired to govern Geneva through the Word of God and obedience to Christ. Thus in addition to the Lutheran two marks of the church (preaching of the Word and administration of sacraments), Calvin added discipline as the third mark.[41] In order to establish this discipline, Calvin created the Consistory of Geneva to adjudicate various cases and to excommunicate unrepentant sinners.[42] It was because of these reforms that Calvin was called "the dictator of Geneva."[43]

---

39. Godfrey, *John Calvin*, 61–62.

40. On pastoral care, see Benoit, "Pastoral Care" and on Calvin's correspondence with others, see, Swanepoel, "Calvin as a Letter-Writer."

41. Lambert and Watt, *Registers of the Consistory*, x–xi. Of discipline, Calvin, (*On the Christian Life*, 110) says, "As the saving doctrine of Christ is the soul of the Church, so discipline forms the ligaments, which connect the members together and keep each in its proper place."

42. The blurb of Lambert and Watt, (*Registers of the Consistory*) succinctly captures the first two years of the Consistory with the following description:

Within the first twenty-four months of the Consistory's existence, almost 850 people were called to appear from a total population of less than 13,000. Besides the expected pursuit of *paillards*, the Consistory heard the cases of drunkards, blasphemers, usurers, wastrels, beggars, dancers, singers of "improper songs," healers, magicians, gamblers, and other "evil livers." The Consistory, charged with repressing the beliefs and practices of the old faith, also investigated numerous cases of recidivist Catholics, from those who continued praying to Mary and the saints to those who refused Reformed communion.

43. Kingdon, *Transition and Revolution*, 97–103; Naphy, *Calvin and the Consolidation*; McGrath, *Life of John Calvin*, 2.

A Reconstruction Theologian or a Dictator?

In an article titled, "Reading John Calvin in the African Context: Any Relevance for the Social Reconstruction of Africa?" a Kenyan theologian suggests that John Calvin fits the status of a reconstruction theologian.[44] Reconstruction theology focuses on the spiritual, economic, ecclesial, and sociopolitical renewal and reforms of communities emerging out of devastation. Susan Schreiner observes that "Calvin sensed that the foundations of the late 'medieval' world had crumbled. The portals of change had been opened and threatened to sweep everything away. In the face of such chaos, Calvin encouraged his audience to hold to the Word of God."[45] Thus the Word of God was the pillar of reconstruction in Calvin's program of renewal and transformation of Geneva.

Despite this commendable effort of reforming Geneva through God's Word, some scholars depict Calvin negatively. Carter Lindberg observes that Calvin is portrayed as "a narrow dogmatist," "a ruthless inquisitor," "an ascetic, cold authoritarian," and "a rigorous individualist."[46] To Roland Bainton, Calvin symbolized "the peak of Protestant intolerance."[47] Will Durant concludes his history of John Calvin with the following words: "we shall always find it hard to love the man who darkened the human soul with the most absurd and blasphemous conception of God in all the long and honored history of nonsense."[48] Calvin's intolerance to Hieronymus Bolsec and Philibert Berthelier both banished from Geneva, and Michael Servetus whose execution Calvin allowed albeit reluctantly, are the main points of reference on Calvin's tyrannical leadership.

Some of the criticisms are a misinterpretation of Calvin's character and personality as well as his theology and the events of history. Allister McGrath argues that the image of Calvin as the "dictator of Geneva" bears no relation to the known facts of the sixteenth-century Geneva, especially how the city was governed.[49] He argues that Calvin's authority in civic matters

---

44. Gathogo, "Reading John Calvin," 220.
45. Schreiner, *Theater of His Glory*, 3.
46. Lindberg, *European Reformations*, 250.
47. Bainton, *Travail of Religious Liberty*, 52.
48. Durant, *Reformation*, 490.
49. McGrath, *Life of John Calvin*, 109.

was limited to personal and moral issues, and thus despite Calvin's power of influence through his moral authority, "he had no civic jurisdiction, no *right*, to coerce others to act as he wished."[50] It was the Genevan city council, Messieurs de Genève, which had civic jurisdiction.[51] This "council had no intention of surrendering its hard-won rights and privileges to anyone, let alone one of its employees – a foreigner devoid of voting rights, whom they could dismiss and expel from the city as they pleased."[52] McGrath contends that except for the Consistory and the Venerable Company of Pastors, no part of the Genevan laws owed their origin to Calvin.[53] Thus the laws Calvin implemented were not his laws, but the city's laws.

Calvin's Publications

The commentary on Seneca's *De Clementia* published in April 1532, was Calvin's first published work.[54] Calvin wrote the commentary on the Roman philosopher, for the benefit of scholars of classics, but the book gained no popularity and cost him his life savings.[55] Though he gained minimal financial profit from this work, Calvin sharpened the skill of persuasion through words. He deployed this skill in later publications such as the *Institutes of the Christian Religion* first published in Latin in 1535.[56] Calvin published the second edition of the *Institutes*, also in Latin, in 1539; it contained seventeen chapters. In 1541, he produced the French edition, followed by another Latin edition in 1543, and the final Latin edition in 1559.[57] The *Institutes* has been expanded, reprinted, and translated into French (1560), Spanish (1540), Italian (1557), Dutch (1560), and English (1561).[58] Calvin declared that he wrote the *Institutes* to prepare and instruct future pastors

---

50. McGrath, 109.

51. McGrath, 108.

52. McGrath, 109.

53. McGrath, 109.

54. Torrance, *Hermeneutics of John Calvin*, 96. See, Calvin, *Commentary on Seneca*.

55. McGrath, *Life of John Calvin*, 60–61.

56. Lindberg, (*European Reformations*, 254) observes that the first edition of the *Institutes* consisted of "six chapters on the Law, the creed, the Lord's prayer, the sacraments of baptism and the Lord's Supper, arguments against the remaining sacraments, and a discussion of Christian Liberty."

57. Greef, "Calvin's Writings," 42–43.

58. Steinmetz, *Calvin in Context*, 18.

in sacred theology.[59] In addition to intellectual rigor, Calvin expected the pastoral candidates to exhibit pious attitude, humble disposition, and obedience towards instruction.[60]

Calvin also wrote other publications such as commentaries on all but two books of the Bible, catechetical materials, sermons, tracts and letters, and books on various topics such as prayer, faith, and the Christian life. Scholars differ on whether Calvin had a single unifying theology in his writings. The first school of thought points to a single principle. Loraine Boettner identifies predestination while Benjamin Milner identifies the correlation between the Spirit and the Word.[61] Edward Dowey and T. H. L. Parker identify the doctrine of the knowledge of God.[62] Thomas Torrance identifies anthropology, David Willis and Wilhelm Niesel identify Christology, while Susan Schreiner focuses on the doctrine of creation as the theater of God's glory.[63] Benjamin Warfield and Gwyn Walters identify the doctrine of the Holy Spirit as the center of Calvin's theology.[64]

Other scholars disagree that there is a unifying theology in Calvin. François Wendel asserts, "If we want to speak of a 'system' of Calvin, we must do so with certain reservation, owing to the plurality of themes that imposed themselves simultaneously upon its author's thinking."[65] McGrath also avows, "There is no 'hard core,' no 'basic principle' or 'central premise,'

---

59. In the Preface to the 1559 edition titled, "John Calvin to the Reader" Calvin (*Institutes of the Christian Religion*, 4) clearly presents his intention of writing the *Institutes*:

> Moreover, it has been my purpose in this labor to prepare and instruct candidates in sacred theology for the reading of the divine Word, in order that they may be able both to have easy access to it and to advance in it without stumbling. For I believe I have so embraced the sum of religion in all its parts, and have arranged it in such an order, that if anyone rightly grasps it, it will not be difficult for him to determine what he ought especially to seek in Scripture, and to what end he ought to relate its contents.

60. As for the spiritual dispositions see for instance, Calvin, *Institutes*, I.13.24 and I.15.2. As to the intellectual capacities, Calvin observes that he wrote for the "moderately discerning reader" (Calvin, *Institutes*, II.10.20).

61. Boettner, *Reformed Doctrine of Predestination*; Milner, *Calvin's Doctrine*, 190.

62. Dowey, "Knowledge of God," 41–49; Parker, *Calvin's Doctrine*.

63. Torrance, *Calvin's Doctrine of Man*; Willis, *Calvin's Catholic Christology*; Schreiner, *Theater of His Glory*; Niesel, *Theology of Calvin*, 247.

64. Warfield, *Calvin as a Theologian*, 5; Walters, "Doctrine of the Holy Spirit," 332.

65. Wendel, *Calvin*, 357.

no 'essence' of Calvin's religious thought."[66] Thus this school of thought does not see any theological principle unifying Calvin's arguments.

The third group of scholars argue that it is possible to identify a single principle or dogma in Calvin's thought without necessarily asserting that Calvin's entire argument rests on the said dogma. These scholars pick one doctrine, for example, union with Christ, as the basis for examining the *Institutes*.[67] This book follows these later scholars in asserting the centrality of the doctrine of the image of God in Calvin's theological anthropology without arguing that the doctrine influenced the shape of Calvin's other doctrines. The main purpose of such a framework is to show the centrality of a certain doctrine without excluding other doctrines. The next section examines the nature of Calvin's theological anthropology particularly the doctrine of the image of God and its relevance for the Kenyan context. However, before examining Calvin's doctrine of the image of God, a brief introduction to the biblical material and the various theories of the image of God is necessary.

The Biblical Material and the Diversity of Opinions on the Image of God

Genesis 1:26–27 affirms that humanity is created in the image and likeness of God. Other direct references to image of God in the Old Testament are found in Genesis 5:1 and Genesis 9:6. Psalms 8:4–6 alludes to the image of God. The New Testament mentions the image of God in connection with human beings as God's image (1 Cor 11:7; Jas 3:9), Jesus Christ as the image of God (2 Cor 4:4; Col 1:15; Heb 1:3), and restoration of the image of God in believers (Rom 8:29; 1 Cor 15:49; 2 Cor 3:10; Eph 4:22–24; Phil 3:21; Col 3:10). The Apocryphal writings also allude to the *imago Dei* in Wisdom 2:23–24 and Ecclesiasticus 17:1–12.[68]

---

66. McGrath, *Life of John Calvin*, 149.

67. See Partee, "Calvin's Central Dogma Again," 193 for example. In this article, Partee identifies union with Christ as the basis for surveying Calvin's *Institutes* (194, 196).

68. In keeping with the Protestant tradition, the writer does not affirm the canonicity of apocryphal writings. However, apocryphal writings are important documents in presenting important elements of the Jewish history and tradition especially during the intertestamental period.

According to J. Richard Middleton, the word "image" occurs seventeen times in the Hebrew Bible and has three primary meanings of which the first meaning refers to the physical cult statues of various false gods, condemned in the Old Testament (Num 33:52; 2 Kgs 11:18; 2 Chr 23:17; Ezek 7:20; 16:17; Amos 5:26).[69] The second meaning refers to physical representations that are not cult statues of deities, "(raised-relief) wall carvings of Babylonian soldiers (Ezekiel 23:14) and golden copies of the mice and tumors that afflicted the Philistines and that were offered as a guilt offering to YHWH to avoid judgment (1 Samuel 6:5, 11)."[70] The third use designates "the fleeting nature of human existence, likening it to a shadow (Ps. 39:6) or to the residue of a dream that remains after one awakes (Ps. 73:20)"[71] In contrast, the word "likeness" occurs twenty-five times, mostly in the book of Ezekiel, and is used in an abstract sense to describe a thing being similar to or having an "appearance" or "form" of another.[72] Scholars observe the ambiguity of both these phrases but note the significant contribution of the doctrine of the image of God.

Scholars convey their ideas on the *imago Dei* by responding to such questions as what does it mean to be created in the image of God? Is the phrase "image and likeness of God" an anthropological or a theological statement? (i.e. is it a statement about humans or about God? Is there a distinction between "image" and "likeness" of God?). Are both male and female created in the image of God? Where in humanity is the image of God located? What did sin do to the image of God? (i.e. did sin efface or deface the image?) What is the relationship between the image of God and image of Christ? How can the image of God in humanity be restored? Answers to these questions are diverse, and as Karl Barth and David Clines argues they mirror the dominant anthropology and intellectual biases of the scholars.[73] The next section briefly presents three interpretations of the *imago Dei*

---

69. Middleton, *Liberating Image*, 45.

70. Middleton, 45–46.

71. Grenz, *Social God*, 186.

72. Middleton, *Liberating Image*, 46; Grenz, *Social God*, 187.

73. Barth, *Church Dogmatics*, vol. 3, part 1:192–94; Clines, "Image of God," 68.

proposed in the various time periods of Christianity, in view of situating Calvin's doctrine of the image of God within the history of the discussion.[74]

Theories of the *Imago Dei*

The Substantial View

Paul Ramsey defined the substantial (or substantialist[75] or structuralist[76]) view of the image as the view that "singles out something *within* the *substantial form* of human nature, some faculty or capacity man [sic] possesses, and identifies this as the thing, which distinguishes man from physical nature and from other animals."[77] Throughout the history of Christianity, theologians have singled out intellect as the main "substance" of the image of God, resulting in varied forms of anthropological affirmations. In addition to reason, theologians single out conscience, aesthetic sense, dominion, spiritual awareness, immortality, freedom, personhood, and moral capacity as other substantial characteristics of human nature that were the "stamp" of the *imago Dei*. According to the substantial view, to image God is to possess one or all of these qualities. The substantial view of the *imago Dei* dominated Western Christianity for more than 1500 years and is particularly evident in the works of Saint Augustine and Thomas Aquinas.[78] The substantial view emphasizes the uniqueness of human beings as compared to other creatures who do not seem to possess the capacity for self-consciousness as do human beings.

However, the substantial approach is problematic for several reasons. First, it fosters individualism because of the emphasis on what an individual person is endowed with. Second, it supports a dualism of the mind and the body in its emphasis on inner capacities of human nature (i.e. personhood,

---

74. These views on the image of God are not the only ones that have been advanced. However, they are the major views.

75. Hall, *Imaging God*, 89.

76. Brunner, *Christian Doctrine*, 59.

77. Ramsey, *Basic Christian Ethics*, 250.

78. Hall, *Imaging God*, 92; Kilner, *Dignity and Destiny*, 178; Grenz, *Social God*, 143; Vliet, *Children of God*, 60; Blomberg, "True Righteousness and Holiness," 68. However, Matthew Drever, ("Redeeming Creation," 135–153) argues for a relational view in Augustine's doctrine of the image of God. He argues that although Augustine emphasized intellectualism in his anthropology, he did not ignore moral and soteriological aspects.

soul, mind, spirit), resulting in the denigration of the body, and a spiritualist focus of human life.[79] Third, in its emphasis on reason as the distinguishing mark between humans and animals, the substantial view creates a dichotomy between humans and non-human creation, which may ultimately lead to the abuse of creation and which is inconsistent with Genesis that links human life and other forms of life. Fourth, substantial view isolates human beings who cannot live up to perfection, for example, the mentally handicapped, resulting in their denigration and their abuse as it happened in Germany during Hitler's time or in Uganda during Idi Amin's.[80] Fifth, this view falls apart in explaining what sin did to the mind (if reason is the main substance of the image of God, then, did the fall render reason obsolete?). The answer to this question is either a denial of the fall or offering a distinction between the words "image" and "likeness."[81] John Kilner argues that this distinction between "image" and "likeness" ultimately leads to the classification of human beings into those who have the image and likeness of God more and those who have it in a lesser degree, consequently legitimating their exploitation or even death.[82]

The Royal Functional View

The royal functional approach is rooted in the dominion perspective, which dates back to Chrysostom.[83] Middleton notes that the royal functional approach "designates the royal office of calling of human beings as God's

---

79. See Kilner, *Dignity and Destiny*, 180.

80. Reynolds, (*Vulnerable Communion*, 177–187) argues convincingly that the doctrine of the image of God, if not interpreted correctly, leads to dehumanization of the disabled. For the case of dehumanization in Germany, see Kilner, *Dignity and Destiny*, 21. Idi Amin Dada loaded the disabled into trucks and dumped them into the River Nile. His action was informed by his belief that the disabled were subhuman.

81. Fairbairn, *Life in the Trinity*, 60.

82. Kilner, (*Dignity and Destiny*, 19) argues that Aquinas believed that the mentally handicapped did not have the image of God at all. He cites *Summa Theologica*, I.93.8. Aquinas might have reached this conclusion because of his belief in the gradations of the image of God. Thomas explained this gradations of the image in terms of three levels: natural humanity have the image in a lesser degree; redeemed (but imperfect) humans have a higher image compared to natural humans; redeemed humans i.e. the "just" or those who are "knowing and loving God perfectly" have the "image by likeness of glory." (See Thomas, *Summa Theologica*, 1.93.4).

83. Frederick McLeod, (*Image of God*, 236) argues that the Antiochene Fathers (Diodore of Tarsus, John Chrysostom, Theodore of Mopsuestia, Nestorius, and Theodoret) established a form of the functional/dominion theory of the image. To image God, therefore, for the

representatives and agents in the world, granted authorized power to share in God's rule or administration of the earth's resources and creatures."[84] In other words, human beings are God's royal representatives. To arrive at this conclusion, biblical scholars link "in our image" and "let them rule" in Genesis 1:26, arguing that the later defines the former.

However, because the text does not say exactly what imaging God means, Old Testament scholars look to the ancient Near East (ANE) societies for some clues on the meaning of this symbol.[85] Thus Claus Westermann notes, "the background of Gen. 1:26f is what Egypt and Mesopotamia say about the king as the image of God. A person as the image of God corresponds to the king as the image of God; both are God's viceroy or representative."[86] Christoph Barth notes, "Ancient Sumerian, Babylonian, and Egyptian texts speak of kings being shaped in the image of their gods. Mesopotamian kings are hailed as the image of Bel or Shamash, Egyptian kings may boast of being the holy image of Re."[87] Conversely, even though biblical scholars resource the ANE background to understand Genesis, they also explicate the radical difference between the Genesis account and the ANE creation accounts. For example, while the ANE limits image bearing to kings and priests, Genesis opens up the notion of imaging God to include all humanity. Men and women, kings and ordinary people, are image bearers of God. In addition, as Middleton shows, the Genesis account of creation also depicts creation as harmonious and very good in contrast to the violent and tragic ANE creation accounts.[88]

In addition to the above conclusions from biblical scholars, it is clear that the evidence from ANE also supports communion with God as important in imaging God. Ancient accounts show that kings were embodied

---

Antiochenes is to "serve in creation as a concrete, living, and visible symbol that points to the existence of God and moreover that he shares in His power."

84. Middleton, *Liberating Image*, 27.

85. Middleton, ("Liberating Image?," 18) explains that the ancient Near Eastern societies are "Mesopotamian (that is, Sumerian, Babylonian or Assyrian), West Semitic (that is, Canaanite), or Egyptian."

86. Westermann, *Genesis 1-11*, 152.

87. Barth, *God with Us*, 27. For more on the ancient Near East context as a proof for royal functional view of the image, see Clines, *On the Way*, vol. 2, 475–480.

88. Middleton, "Liberating Image?," 17.

manifestations of the divine. The king represented and mediated the deity's presence on a given territory because the deity empowered the king to do so. From this, it can be concluded that to image God rests on communion with God. Communion with God enables image bearing. Without communion with God humans cannot fulfil the divine mandate of being representatives and agents of God on earth. It is in this communion with God that humans are shaped into beings that faithfully exercise their God-given mandate of being God's representatives on earth through ruling (stewardship) of the earth and of their own lives. The relational view emphasizes this communion aspect of God's image.

The Relational View

The relational view stresses the fundamental relationship between the human creature and the Creator, which shapes other forms of relationships.[89] This emphasis on the relationship with God was the main focus of the Protestant Reformers, particularly Luther and Calvin.[90] Mainly, the Reformers emphasized the moral aspects of the image of God. The Reformers also maintained the substantial view of the image. Luther maintained that reason was the chief part of a human being because reason elevates human beings above non-human creation.[91] Although Luther affirmed reason as an important element of God's image, relationship with God was more important.[92] John Calvin believed that the image of God is the original righteousness human beings lost because of their fall into sin. For Calvin, humans regain their original godly status through regeneration and sanctification, which is equivalent to the renewal of God's image.

The relational view also emphasizes the active nature of imaging God. According to Douglas Hall, to be created in the image of God "does not

---

89. Ramsey, *Basic Christian Ethics*, 254; Grenz, *Social God*, 142; Schwöbel, "Human Being As Relational," 142; Hall, *Imaging God*, 98; Gunton, *Christ and Creation*, 99–127; Cortez, *Theological Anthropology*, 24.

90. Grenz, (*Social God*, 162) argues that Calvin in particular represents "the birth of the relational *imago*." Similarly, Hall, (*Imaging God*, 101) observes, "While Luther implies the relational concept of the imago Dei throughout his scriptural commentaries and elsewhere, John Calvin expresses it directly." Also, Cairns, (*Image of God*, 144) notes that Calvin emphasized the relational aspects of the image more than any other theologian in Christian history.

91. Luther, *Luther's Works*, vol. 1, 137.

92. Bell, "Man is a Microcosmos," 162.

mean to have something but to do something: to image God."[93] For Ramsey, to image God is to reflect God's glory in life and actions.[94] Thus the relational view also emphasizes the ethical implications of bearing God's image. One of the key emphasis, especially for Calvinists, is cultural engagement and transformation. To bear God's image is to participate in the God-given vocation of being God's faithful representatives on earth. The chapter now examines Calvin's doctrine of the image of God.

Calvin's Doctrine of the Image of God

Previous Scholarship

There are three major clusters of scholarship on Calvin's doctrine of the image of God. The first school of thought emphasizes the relational aspects of the image of God in Calvin. Gerrit Berkouwer, Thomas Torrance, Wilhelm Niesel, Brian Gerrish, Richard Prins, and Randall Zachman argue that Calvin discussed the image of God in order to explain the redemption of humanity from sin through Christ.[95] Thus according to them, Calvin's theological anthropology should not be underscored apart from his Christology and soteriology. Following Calvin, Berkouwer asserts that the image of God can only be clearly defined in connection to conformity to God (*conformitas cum Deo*), which occurs through Christ, the image of God.[96] Torrance also argues that Christian anthropology, for Calvin, played two significant roles: "by pointing believers to their original creation in the image of God to produce gratitude, and by pointing [them] to [their] present miserable condition to produce humility."[97] Richard Prins argues that Calvin's view of the image of God should be understood within the larger framework of his view of restoration in Christ.[98] Prins explains binary aspects of restoration

---

93. Hall, *Imaging God*, 98.

94. Ramsey, *Basic Christian Ethics*, 254.

95. Torrance, *Calvin's Doctrine of Man*; Niesel, *Theology of Calvin*; Gerrish, "Mirror of God's Goodness"; Prins, "Image of God"; Zachman, "Jesus Christ"; Zachman, *Image and Word*.

96. Berkouwer, *Man*, 107.

97. Torrance, *Calvin's Doctrine of Man*, 13. See also Gerrish, "Mirror of God's Goodness," 212 for an emphasis on this dual nature of human self-knowledge.

98. Prins, "Image of God in Adam," 39.

that occurs through Christ as restoration to the full Adamic integrity (pre-fall conditions) and restoration unto Christ. He asserts that although Calvin emphasized this dual nature of redemption, he was focused on restoration unto Christ, not a restoration back to the Adamic nature.[99] Thus this group of scholars emphasize redemption in Calvin's theological anthropology, including his view of the image of God.

The second school of thought focuses on the two aspects of the image of God (substantial and relational) in Calvin's thought. They argue that scholars who limit Calvin's anthropology to Christology ignore the other dimensions of Calvin's anthropology, precisely, the substantial aspects of the image of God and Calvin's emphasis on the ethical implications of the doctrine. David Cairns, Jelle Faber, Jakobus Vorster, Ronald Wallace, and Yosep Kim argue that Calvin presents his theological anthropology in other contexts than Christology.[100] These contexts include human dignity, morality, and practical living, for example, service and charity to the neighbor. Vorster argues that Calvin laid the foundation for a Reformed ethic of human dignity and social concern based on his doctrine of the image of God.[101] In his explication of Calvin's doctrine of the Christian life, Wallace argues that Calvin saw the obligation of service and charity to neighbor as an outcome of a renewed life.[102] Thus Calvin did not examine the doctrine of the image of God based on Christology alone.

The third school of thought points to the lack of clarity in Calvin's thought concerning the image of God and seeks to understand why.[103] Mary Potter Engel, Jason Van Vliet, David Cairns, and William Bouwsma seek to establish the context and objective of Calvin's ideas of the image of God.[104] As to Calvin's inconsistency, Engel asserts, "Calvin's anthropology contains

---

99. Prins, 32–44.

100. Cairns, *Image of God*; Faber, *Essays in Reformed Doctrine*; Vorster, "Calvin and Human Dignity"; Wallace, *Calvin's Doctrine*; Kim, *Identity and Life*.

101. Vorster, "Calvin and Human Dignity," 197–213.

102. Wallace, *Calvin's Doctrine*, 299–312.

103. Kim, (*Identity and Life*, 22) argues that these scholars "moves the centre of attention from Calvin's definition of the *imago Dei* to the context in which he employs this concept."

104. Engel, *Calvin's Perspectival Anthropology*; Vliet, *Children of God*; Cairns, *Image of God*; Bouwsma, *John Calvin*.

such a definite and constant set of shifting perspectives that are contradictory yet complementary."[105] Similarly, Susan Schreiner observes that it is not clear whether Calvin focuses on "the right spiritual attitude," or "gratitude," or "reflecting God's glory," or "mirroring God's image," or whether the image of God is "immortality of the soul" or includes the body.[106] Likewise, Cairns argues that Calvin's view of the image of God "is not exhaustive" for at certain instances Calvin talked about the obliteration of God's image after the fall, while at certain points he assumed the image is still present after the fall.[107] These scholars assert that it is possible to explain the inconsistency in Calvin's view of the image of God through a study of the context of Calvin's work.

A good example of this contextual analysis is Jason Van Vliet's *Children of God: The Imago Dei in John Calvin and His Context*. In this book, Vliet studies the "historical, personal, cultural, collegial, and polemical" contexts that shaped Calvin's view of the image of God.[108] Similarly, Bouwsma proposes that pastoral concerns, especially his view of the fallen nature of people, shaped Calvin's view of the image of God.[109] Thus based on the study of the context, scholars arrive at various conclusions especially in respect to Calvin's apparent inconsistency on whether the image of God is still present in fallen humanity or it is totally obliterated. Foremost is Engel's "perspectival approach," in which according to Calvin, from God's perspective human beings lost the image, but from the relative perspective of humans, the image still remains.[110] Another approach is Yosep Kim's "teleological perspective," in which he argues that, according to Calvin, human beings lost their ability to glorify God as God intended when God created them.[111] David Cairns proposes soteriology in order to understand Calvin's view of the fall. He

---

105. Engel, *Calvin's Perspectival Anthropology*, xi. Engel also argues that at face value, it is not clear whether, according to Calvin, the image of God is found in all creation or only in human beings; whether the image of God is located in the soul or in the body; whether the image of God refers to natural or supernatural human endowments; whether the image of God is present in humans after the fall or totally destroyed; and whether the restored image in Jesus Christ takes precedence over the created image of God in Adam and Eve (38).

106. Schreiner, *Theater of His Glory*, 51.

107. Cairns, *Image of God*, 134; Hoekema, *Created in God's Image*, 43.

108. Vliet, *Children of God*, 252.

109. Bouwsma, *John Calvin*, 141–142.

110. Engel, *Calvin's Perspectival Anthropology*, 54–61.

111. Kim, *Identity and Life*, 34–35.

writes, "When Calvin talks of what God gives in the image, then he says it is not wholly lost, but when he speaks of what we contribute, then he must talk of it as obliterated in the natural man since the Fall."[112] Another approach is T. F. Torrance's psychological approach. He argues, "When Calvin uses quantitative terms such as portions or remnants it is clear that his mind is for the moment running on psychological rather than on theological lines, and he is thinking of our natural gifts, which, though they have been corrupted, still remain in man, for they are part of the groundwork of his creation."[113] In other words, in their fallen state, human beings continue to keep noetic aspects of the image, such as intellect and will, though even these are affected by sin, but they have lost the relational aspects (i.e. faith, love of God, and zeal for holiness and righteousness). Thus context of Calvin's works and his pastoral intentions reveals Calvin's view of what sin did to the image of God.

As the third group of studies shows, it is undesirable to derive a definite systematic definition of the "image of God" from Calvin's theological anthropology because Calvin himself did not offer such a definition.[114] Consequently, if Calvin did not offer a fixed definition of the doctrine of the image of God, it is also objectionable to cast aside the various ways of explaining Calvin's doctrine of the image of God. Thus the various schools of thought provide useful information to understand Calvin's anthropology. The first school of thought shows the importance of Christology and soteriology in Calvin's doctrine of the image of God. The second school of thought emphasizes other aspects of Calvin's anthropology such as ethics and social concern. The third school of thought emphasizes the context of his anthropology. Thus all the three schools of thought are beneficial for understanding Calvin's arguments. Therefore, this book draws from these three schools of thought. Yet it aligns more with the second school of thought in acknowledging that Calvin emphasized the "relational" and "structural" aspects of the image of God within the context of redemption.

Although Calvin retained the "structural" language in his theology of the image, his main focus was the relational, particularly, the relationship between believers and God, which manifests in a relationship with one another

112. Cairns, *Image of God*, 134–135.
113. Torrance, *Calvin's Doctrine of Man*, 95.
114. Kim, *Identity and Life*, 23.

in their particular sociopolitical environments. In regard to the methodology of studying the *Institutes*, the book assumes the division of the *Institutes* into four parts: creation of humankind (Book I), condition of humankind after the fall (Book II), redemption and regeneration of humankind (Book III), political implications of the Christian life (Book IV). The book now examines the various aspects of Calvin's doctrine of the image of God.

Calvin's Engagement with Other Views

Calvin began his discussion of the image of God by refuting erroneous views. Foremost, he rejected the Anthropomorphites' perspective, which located the *imago Dei* in the human body, and that argued that the *imago Dei* constituted a literal physical resemblance to God.[115] Calvin insisted that the soul is the location of the image of God.[116] Then Calvin rejected the views of Andreas Osiander (ca. 1498–1552) who claimed that human beings were created only in the image of the-yet-to-be-incarnated God.[117] Calvin differentiated between the image of God in creation and re-created image through Jesus Christ; humans can only be said to be created in the image of Christ in redemption not in creation.[118]

Additionally, Calvin opposed "the Manichean error" of Michael Servetus (ca. 1511–1553). Hall argues that Servetus hypothesized "an ontic connectedness (*analogia entis*) between God and the human creature at the point of the latter's psyche" thus fusing humanity together with God.[119] For Servetus, human beings were emanations of God. Calvin argued that human beings were creatures of God, not emanations of God; "We are God's offspring, but in quality, not in essence."[120] Calvin argued that Servetus misunderstood creation *ex nihilo* assuming that creation was an "inpouring" from God. In contrast, creation was "the beginning of essence out of nothing."[121]

---

115. Calvin, *Genesis*, 1:94. See also *Institutes*, I.13.1 and IV.17.23, 25. Battles (Calvin, *Institutes of the Christian Religion*, 121n4) notes that the sect was founded by Audius (d. 372) in Mesopotamia.

116. Calvin, *Institutes*, I.15.3.

117. See, Vliet, *Children of God*, 226. Calvin's refutation of Osiander's views are found in *Institutes*, I.15.3–5 and II.12.5–7.

118. Calvin, *Institutes*, II.12.7.

119. Hall, *Imaging God*, 102.

120. Calvin, *Institutes* I.15.5.

121. Calvin, I.15.5.

Next, Calvin rejected the distinction between the terms "image of God" and "likeness of God" that Irenaeus had proposed.[122] Irenaeus argued that God's image refers to something static and essential to human nature such as reason and free will, and remains after the fall, while God's likeness refers to something dynamic and accidental to human nature such as righteousness, lost after the fall.[123] On the contrary, Calvin argued that these terms are synonyms employed for emphasis. He wrote, "We also know that it was customary with the Hebrews to repeat the same thing in different words. Besides, the phrase itself shows that the second term was added for the sake of explanation."[124] Calvin noted that commentators who make a distinction between "image of God" and "likeness of God" engage in speculations.[125]

Calvin also rejected Augustine's speculation on an analogy of the Trinity in humanity's intellect, will, and memory.[126] Augustine believed that to be created in the image of God is to possess a rational (intellectual) soul, which enables humans to know and to love God.[127] He believed that the mind has three faculties: memory, intellect, and will, which correspond to the divine Trinity in that they are of one substance (essence), yet they are also distinct and mutually interrelated.[128] On the contrary, Calvin argued that Augustine was speculating. He cautioned against speculation insisting that whatever is claimed about the image of God must be in concert with the sound teachings of scripture.[129] According to Calvin, understanding and will are the only two faculties of the soul.[130]

Calvin rejected Chrysostom's view that dominion alone constitutes the image of God.[131] However, Calvin affirmed that dominion constitutes a

---

122. On Irenaeus's position see, Kilner, *Dignity and Destiny*, 197; Hoekema, *Created in God's Image*, 33–35; Shults, *Reforming Theological Anthropology*, 221. It is important to point out that other scholars such as Finch, ("Irenaeus on the Christological Basis," 87–90) argue convincingly for the synonymous interchangeability of the terms in Irenaeus's thought.

123. Shults, *Reforming Theological Anthropology*, 221; Kilner, *Dignity and Destiny*, 197.

124. Calvin, *Genesis*, 1:94; *Institutes*, I.15.3.

125. Calvin, *Genesis*, 1:93.

126. Calvin, *Institutes*, I.15.4.

127. Augustine, *Trinity*, 11–12.

128. Augustine.

129. Calvin, *Genesis*, 1:93.

130. Calvin, *Institutes*, I.15.7.

131. Calvin, I.15.4. See, McLeod, *Image of God*, 43–44.

small element of the image of God in humans.[132] It is important to mention what dominion is according to Calvin. Although Calvin asserted that the world was created to "tend to the happiness of man" and God appointed humans to be "lord of the world," he did not see dominion of creation as abuse of creation, but as stewardship, which is the expression of thankfulness for God's provision through his creation.[133] The exercise of stewardship distinguishes humans from other creatures, which cannot worship God.[134]

The Soul, the Body, and the Image of God

According to Calvin, a human being is composed of a soul and a body. Soul and body are two distinct "elements," "essences" or "substances" of a human being.[135] These distinct elements are not an outcome of the fall but belong to humanity by nature. Of these two natures, the soul is "the nobler part."[136] Consequently, the soul is the location, "the proper seat" of God's image.[137] For Calvin, the soul is an incorporeal substance containing two faculties, intellect (understanding) and will.[138] By "intellect" or "understanding" Calvin meant, all the functions, capacities, or acts, that contribute to knowledge, among which are reason and moral choices, and by "will" he meant freedom, decision making, and following the guidance of intellect.[139] Of these two faculties, intellect/understanding is "the governor of the soul."[140] However, because of the fall, intellect and will are corrupted and weakened, such that in regard to the "heavenly things," human beings are incapable as they were before the fall, to distinguish correctly and to choose rightly.[141] Consequently, even when humans know the truth they will suppress the moral implications of truth. Apart from God's gracious illumination of intellect and will,

---

132. Calvin, *Book of Joshua*, IV:308.

133. Calvin, *Institutes*, I.14.22; Calvin, *Commentary on Genesis*, 1:26.

134. Calvin, *Institutes*, I.15.3.

135. Calvin, II.15.1.

136. Calvin, I.15.2.

137. Calvin, I.15.3.

138. Calvin, I.15.7.

139. Stocker, "Calvin and Ethics," 136. See Calvin, *Institutes*, I.15.7.

140. Calvin, *Institutes*, I.15.7.

141. Calvin, II. 2.12, 13, 23. "Heavenly things" include "the pure knowledge of God, the nature of true righteousness, and the mysteries of the Kingdom of God." (II.2.13)

humans have no hope of rising above their fallen condition.¹⁴² It is only when faith "takes root in the depths of the heart" and reason is "subjected to the obedience of faith" that actual transformation occurs.¹⁴³

Although Calvin identified the soul as the location of the image, he talked about some sparks of God's image in the body. "And although the primary seat of the divine image was in the mind and heart, or in the soul and its powers, yet there was no part of man, not even the body itself, in which some sparks did not glow."¹⁴⁴ Yet these sparks of God's image cannot be regarded as God's image because the image of God is something internal and spiritual, not something physical.¹⁴⁵ The body, according to Calvin, acts as a temporary residence for the soul. The body fetters, imprisons, and weighs down the soul.¹⁴⁶ The body is earthly by nature while the soul is heavenly, and thus to "extend God's image both to the body and to the soul, mingles heaven and earth."¹⁴⁷ Human beings attain blessedness only by being transposed from their bodies into heaven, the true home of the soul.¹⁴⁸

There are two schools of thought concerning whether Calvin's anthropology presented above is purely platonic or has biblical support. Laetus Lategan, Stuart Fowler, and Roy Battenhouse insist that Calvin's view of the body is foreign to the Bible.¹⁴⁹ Charles Partee, Jason Vliet, Kyle J. Dieleman, and Adrian Hallet disagree arguing instead that Calvin borrowed Plato's language but contrasted with him considerably.¹⁵⁰ These later scholars cite three points in Calvin's teaching concerning the soul to buttress their point. Foremost, they cite Calvin's claim that the soul is not the whole human being, but a part of them.¹⁵¹ Furthermore, they point to Calvin's claim that the soul is not immortal in essence as Plato argued, but is created *ex nihilo* and

---

142. Calvin, *Institutes*, III.2.34.

143. Calvin, III.2.36; I.15.2.

144. Calvin, I.15.3.

145. Calvin, I.15.3. Fowler, "Persistent Dualism," 343.

146. Calvin, *Institutes*, I.15.2; I.15.4; II.13.4; III.2.19; III.9.4; III.6.5; III.25.1; V.15.11.

147. Calvin, I.15.3.

148. Calvin, II.2.12.

149. Lategan, "Significance of Calvin's Anthropology," 145; Battenhouse, "Doctrine of Man," 61; Fowler, "Persistent Dualism," 339–352.

150. Partee, *Calvin and Classical Philosophy*, 51; Vliet, *Children of God*, 258–260; Hallet, "Theology of John Calvin," 5–6; Dieleman, "Body and Resurrection," 157–164.

151. See Calvin, *Institutes*, I.15.3

has its existence in the absolute grace of God.[152] Finally, they cite Calvin's stress that the soul is estranged from God and must be redeemed from its fallen nature, as distinguishing Calvin's anthropology from Plato's.[153]

Notwithstanding the difference between Calvin's anthropology and Plato's, Calvin's dualism is problematic for several reasons. Foremost by its imagery of the body as a prison house of the soul denigrates the body and may lead to its abuse. Next, its emphasis on heavenly concerns leads to disengagement from earthly affairs and an escapist spirituality. As Howard Snyder and Joel Cross observes, "Faithful mission requires wholistic, earthed discipleship – a discipleship that rejects the divorce of heaven and earth and works for reconciliation."[154] Moreover, it may lead to violence against fellow humanity because it assumes the disposability of the body. If the body is not so noble, then whatever is committed against it is not so important.

The emphasis on the soul also has moral implications like committing sins of the flesh or physical abuse of the flesh such as flagellation. It also has sociopolitical implications. If Christians concern themselves with matters of the soul and neglect the bodily implications of their faith, they will basically be handing over the management of their bodies to another power. Dualism also does not have a strong biblical support and contradicts God's action in the incarnation. In Jesus Christ, God became human validating not only the beauty of the human body but also showing that redemption means the *redemption of the entire human person*, "the human person as a totality, a whole, a unitary being."[155] N. T. Wright argues that in the New Testament and the teachings of Jesus Christ, the word "soul," "though rare, reflects when it does occur, underlying Hebrew or Aramaic words referring not to a disembodied entity hidden within the outer shell of the disposable body but rather to what we would call the whole person or personality, seen as being confronted by God."[156] Historically, Christianity has embraced in varied forms this dualistic posture espoused by Calvin and other scholars. Several churches in Kenya embraced an escapist posture because of their

---

152. Partee, *Calvin and Classical Philosophy*, 63–64.

153. Calvin, *Institutes*, III.6.3

154. Snyder and Scandrett, *Salvation Means Creation Healed*, 132.

155. Hoekema, *Created in God's Image*, 210.

156. Wright, *Surprised by Hope*, 28.

theology, which assumed the main concern of the church was only to win souls and to prepare people to go to heaven. Such a posture neglected the body as well as the earth thus resulting in neglect of social responsibility. Thus a theological anthropology that provides a better way forward for the church in Kenya must neglect dualisms. It must value the body, the earth, as well as the spiritual life of people.

Calvin affirmed that the image of God is the original integrity of Adam's prelapsarian state, "the integrity with which Adam was endowed."[157] In this state, human beings possessed the "right understanding," their "affections kept within the bounds of reason," and had their "senses tempered in right order," and they "truly referred [their] excellence to exceptional gifts bestowed upon [them] by [their] Maker."[158] Calvin added, "Nevertheless, it seems that we do not have a full definition of 'image' if we do not see more plainly those faculties in which man excels, and in which he ought to be thought the reflection of God's glory."[159] These faculties included true knowledge, pure righteousness, and holiness.[160] Before the fall, the image of God was "visible in the light of the mind, in the uprightness of the heart, and in the soundness of all the parts."[161] In his commentary on Genesis 1:26, Calvin wrote, "in the mind perfect intelligence flourished and reigned, uprightness attended as its companion, and all the senses were prepared and moulded for due obedience to reason."[162] Thus according to Calvin the image of God is the original righteousness of human nature before the fall.

Calvin also affirmed the image of God as mirroring God. Torrance argues that "there is no doubt that Calvin always thinks of the *imago* in terms of a *mirror*."[163] Although the mirror metaphor is prominent in Calvin's thought, Calvin explicated the image of God in terms of other metaphors such as the

---

157. Calvin, *Institutes*, I.15.3.

158. Calvin, I.15.3. See also Calvin, *Genesis*, 1:94–95 for a similar assertion.

159. Calvin, *Institutes*, I.15.4.

160. Calvin, I.15.4

161. Calvin, I.15.4

162. Calvin, Commentary on Genesis, 1:26

163. Torrance, *Calvin's Doctrine of Man*, 36.

glory of God and inwards possessions of the soul as explained earlier.[164] The image of a mirror has two implications.

The first is the ability to mirror or to reflect God. Human beings are able to mirror God because God enables them to do so. By design, a mirror is able to reflect because it possesses certain inherent qualities that enable mirroring. Likewise, humans are able to mirror God because God created them with the ability to mirror God. In Calvin's view, this divine orientation is universal in scope. Calvin refers to this spiritual awareness as "some traces of God's glory,"[165] "an awareness of divinity,"[166] "seed of religion,"[167] "a sense of deity inscribed in the hearts of all,"[168] and "a certain understanding of his divine majesty."[169] Calvin noted that this sense of divinity is permanent.[170] However, sin destroyed this pre-fallen knowledge of God such that human beings cannot come to the true knowledge of God without God's active involvement through Christ.[171]

The second implication, which is the antithesis of the first one, is humanity's inability to mirror God because they are estranged from God. Though humans were created in the image of God to be a mirror that displays the glory of God, their sinful nature impairs them from actually fulfilling this role.[172] In their original perfection, humans could mirror God, but in their fallen state, they mirror whatever their hearts and minds are attuned to because it is only when a mirror is turned towards the object that it reflects the image of that object.[173] Because of sin, human beings are estranged from God and from one another. The more humans are alienated from God, the more they are alienated from other relationships. When the "mirror" turns

---

164. For the metaphor of a mirror, see for example, *Institutes*, I.5.1, 3, 11; I.14.1, 21; II.7.7; II.12.6; III.2.6; III.24.5; III.25.3. For more on this theme see, Gerrish, "Mirror of God's Goodness"; Keesecker, "John Calvin's Mirror."

165. Calvin, *Institutes*, I.15.3

166. Calvin, I.3.1.

167. Calvin, I.4.1.

168. Calvin, I.3.1.

169. Calvin, I.3.1

170. Calvin, I.3.3.

171. Calvin, I.1.2

172. Calvin, I.5.4; II.12.6.

173. Hall, *Imaging God*, 104; Torrance, *Calvin's Doctrine of Man*, 36.

away from God towards other priorities such as security, pleasure, and so on, it is disoriented from the source and ground of its existence.[174]

Calvin used the metaphor of a mirror in reference to other areas. The first is in regard to humanity's inability to fathom the infinite. Because humans are unable to understand God, God graciously accommodates himself to their frail understanding through his creation. Thus "this skillful ordering of the universe is for us a sort of mirror in which we can contemplate God, who is otherwise invisible."[175] Second, the law is a mirror of God's goodness.[176] To Calvin, the law accomplishes three functions: to reveal sin, to drive us to Christ, and to restrain sin in believers.[177] Since humans are born in a state of sin and are completely inclined to self-love, keeping the law enables love towards God and neighbor.[178] The "law of God contains the dynamic of the new life by which his image is fully restored in us."[179] So in other words, the law aids believers towards God. Third, the entire scriptures are "like a mirror in which faith may behold God."[180] Fourth, Jesus Christ, the Word incarnate, is another mirror of God's goodness to humanity through whom human beings draw closer to God.[181] Fifth, like creation, the sacraments of the church are "mirrors in which we may contemplate the riches of God's grace, which he lavishes upon us."[182] The sacraments are "a visible word" "for the reason that it represents God's promises as painted in a picture and sets them before our sight, portrayed graphically and in the manner of images."[183]

---

174. Hall, *Imaging God*, 106.

175. Calvin, *Institutes*, I.5.1.

176. Calvin, I.8.7. In the *Institutes*, I.14.1, Calvin observes, "In short, let us remember that the invisible God, whose wisdom, power, and righteousness are incomprehensive, sets before us Moses' history as a mirror in which his living likeness glow."

177. Calvin, II.7.5

178. Calvin, II.8.54

179. Calvin, *Golden Booklet*, 16.

180. Calvin, *Institutes*, III.2.6.

181. Calvin, III.24.5. Calvin (*Institutes*, III.25.3) believed that Jesus's resurrection was a mirror of the believer's own resurrection.

182. Calvin, *Institutes*, IV.14.6.

183. Calvin, IV.14.6.

Whereas, for Calvin, God's image is primarily in human beings, he also affirmed that non-human creation bear God's image in a secondary sense.[184] Calvin affirmed the image bearing character of non-human creation in his commentary in Psalms 19:1 whereby he observed that God's distinct image is engraved in creation.[185] In addition, Calvin asserted that God's creation reflects the glory of God: "it is certain that the lineaments of the Divine glory are conspicuous in every part of the world."[186] For him, all creation, including nature and animals, is a mirror of a "most glorious theater."[187] It is through creation that God's providence, wonder, and majesty are demonstrated.[188] Calvin also argued that creation does more than merely reveal God's majesty; creation awakens us to the worship of God.[189] However, sin greatly hinders human beings from beholding God through creation because instead of worshiping God the Creator, they worship or praise God's creation. Therefore, due to the damaging power of sin, human beings must go beyond beholding God through creation to beholding God through Christ.[190]

Randal Zachman presents three metaphors that Calvin employed to delineate the created order to include the theater of God's glory, the living image of God, and the beautiful garment of God.[191] Zachman concludes that these three metaphors emphasized that God seeks to draw humanity to himself. The universe as the theater of God's glory, the living image of God, and the beautiful garment of God, directs human beings to God, although it cannot lead them to eternal life because since the fall, the universe manifests

---

184. In *Institutes*, I.15.3 Calvin asserts without expounding what he means, that angels were created in God's likeness. This seems to contradict his view that it is only human beings who were created in God's image.

185. Calvin, *Book of Joshua*, IV:308.

186. As quoted in Hall, *Imaging God*, 103.

187. Calvin, *Institutes*, I.6.2.

188. Calvin, I.5.10. Susan Schreiner, (*Theater of His Glory*, 121) observes that Calvin thinks of nature in terms of "a mirror, a painting, and a theater of the divine glory." Similarly, Peter Huff, ("Calvin and the Beasts," 68) notes that Calvin extols the natural creation in his writings: "The power and variety of creation, including the beautiful, the violent, the charming, and the grotesque, are regularly set before the reader of his theology. In Calvin's mind, the world of nature is never separated from the realm of divine revelation."

189. Calvin, *Institutes*, I.5.10.

190. See, Calvin, *Institutes*, II.6.2; III.2.1; IV.8.5.

191. Zachman, *Calvin as Teacher*, 233–242.

the destructive power of the curse.[192] Zachman asserts that Jesus Christ as the living image of God is the only one to lead humans to eternal life.[193]

Calvin affirmed the image of God in both male and female. In his commentary on Genesis 2:18, Calvin wrote, "what was said in the creation of the man belongs to the female sex."[194] He also avowed that without the creation of a woman, man would be an incomplete being.[195] However, although Calvin affirmed God's image in women, he believed in the subjection of women especially in the realm of political order. Commenting on 1 Corinthians 11:7, which says, "A man ought not to cover his head, since he is the image and glory of God; but woman is the glory of man," Calvin wrote, "But the statement in which man alone is called by Paul 'the image and glory of God' and woman excluded from this place of honor is clearly to be restricted, as the context shows, to the political order."[196] Jane Dempsey Douglass explains that "political order" is "the whole realm of human governance where human beings are free to order their lives on the basis of divine guidance, the realm of human law rather than divine, eternal law."[197] Hence subjugation of women belongs to the realm of human governing and not the realm of eternal divine law. Douglas shows through a study of the various editions of Calvin's *Institutes* that according to Calvin, ecclesiastical polities should be respected for the sake of order and decorum in the church, but should be held with a free conscience, and should be amenable to change as circumstances require.[198]

---

192. Zachman, 243.

193. Zachman, 243–260.

194. Calvin, *Commentary on Genesis*, 1:129.

195. Blocher, "Calvin's Theological Anthropology," 80; Calvin, *Commentary on Genesis*, 1:97.

196. Calvin, *Institutes*, I.15.4.

197. Douglass, "Image of God," 193; see also Douglass, *Women, Freedom, and Calvin*, 47.

198. Douglass, *Women, Freedom, and Calvin*, 50. In Calvin, *Commentary to the Corinthians*, 10:472, (on 1 Cor 14:37), Calvin believes that Paul's recommendations to the church of Corinth was for the sake of order in the church. It was not meant to be an "inviolable law" applicable to all Christians everywhere.

The Image of God after the Fall

Calvin had a conflicted view of what sin did to the image of God. At one instance he spoke of the image as if it is totally obliterated and at certain points, he believed the image is still present. Using authoritative references from Calvin's commentaries and sermons, Hoekema asserts, "[Calvin] sometimes speaks of the image of God as having been *destroyed* by sin,[199] *obliterated* by the Fall,[200] *wiped out* or *lost* by sin,[201] *canceled* by sin,[202] 'as it were, *blotted out* . . . by Adam's sin,'[203] or *utterly defaced* by sin."[204] Indeed Calvin believed that "even though we grant that God's image was not totally annihilated and destroyed in him, yet it was so corrupted that whatever remains is a frightful deformity."[205] He added that the image of God, which "shone in Adam before his defection . . . was subsequently so vitiated and almost blotted out that nothing remains after the ruin except what is confused, mutilated, and disease-ridden."[206] However, Calvin also believed in "some remaining traces of the image of God."[207] In his commentary on Genesis 1:26 he calls these traces "lineaments,"[208] and "remnant" in his commentary on Genesis 9:6.[209] It is clear that Calvin maintained that the image is both defaced and effaced. Calvin's focus on these two dimensions of the damage caused to God's image highlights the destructive power of sin on God's image. The fall's corrupting effects on God's image is so real that Calvin can say that the image is defaced. If there are any traces of God's image in humanity after the fall, it is barely recognizable. It is only in Christ that human beings regain the lost image.

Calvin attributed the cause of sin to prideful rebellion or disobedience. He argued that the faith Eve had on the Word of God was the guardian

---

199. Calvin, Commentary on Genesis, 1:26.

200. Calvin, Commentary on Genesis, 3:1.

201. Calvin, Commentary on Ephesians, 4:24.

202. Calvin, Commentary on 2 Corinthians, 3:18.

203. Sermon on Job 14:16–17.

204. Sermon on Job 32:4–5; Hoekema, *Created in God's Image*, 43. Italics original. Footnotes 199–203 are part of the original quote.

205. Calvin, *Institutes*, I.15.4.

206. Calvin, I.15.4.

207. Calvin, II.2.17.

208. Calvin, *Genesis*, 1:153 (on Genesis 1:26).

209. Calvin, 1:153 (on Genesis 9:6).

of her heart but she gave up that protection when she disobeyed God. Consequently, "she corrupted both herself and all her senses, and depravity was diffused through all parts of her soul as well as her body."[210] Calvin asserted "Since the woman through unfaithfulness was led away from God's Word by the serpent's deceit, it is already clear that disobedience was the beginning of the Fall."[211] Elsewhere, he concluded, "Unfaithfulness, then, was the root of the Fall. But thereafter ambition and pride, together with ungratefulness, arose, because Adam by seeking more than was granted shamefully spurned God's great bounty, which had been lavished upon him."[212] Pride is now innate in all human beings such that human beings desire to be flattered.

Furthermore, the fall caused depravity, corruption, perversity, and wickedness of human nature.[213] Sin tainted the entire human being to the extent that the whole person "is of himself [or herself] nothing but concupiscence."[214] By asserting that the whole person "is of himself nothing but concupiscence" it means total depravity of a person's entire being. However, "total depravity" does not mean that everything a person does is evil, for Calvin affirmed that some people act in commendable virtue and character. "In every age there have been persons who, guided by nature, have striven toward virtue throughout life. I have nothing to say against them even if many lapses can be noted in their moral conduct."[215] Depravity is "total" in the sense that it encompasses a person's entire being. Every facet of human life is depraved and in need of salvation. Depravity is "total" also in the sense that it continually produces more sins, "acts of the flesh" or particular sins.[216]

For Calvin, sin did not end with Adam. Adam's posterity inherited a corrupted nature that continually breeds other sins.[217] Even infants "have

---

210. Calvin, 1:153 (on Genesis 3:6).

211. Calvin, *Institutes*, II.2.4.

212. Calvin, II.1.4.

213. Burns, "From Ordered Soul," 89.

214. Calvin, *Institutes*, II.1.8.

215. Calvin, II.3.3.

216. Calvin, *Institutes*, II.1.8. See also *Institutes*, II.2.4, II.1.5, II.1.7, II.1.8, II.1.9, and II.1.8.

217. Calvin, II.1.5.

the seed [of corruption] enclosed within them."[218] The seed of corruption continues to "burn" in humanity "just as a burning furnace gives forth flame and sparks, or water ceaselessly bubbles up from a spring."[219] Even the mind is now a "sink and lurking place for every sort of filth."[220] The mind is "weak and plunged into darkness"[221] and "it was partly weakened and partly corrupted so that its misshapen ruins appear."[222] The fallen mind and will lead people to idolatry and self-degradation.[223] Indeed, for Calvin, fallen human nature is a "perpetual factory of idols."[224] In other words a human being is a liturgical being as James K. A. Smith argues.[225]

Total depravity of human beings has implications for how humans come to know God in Christ. Since human free will "has been so enslaved," nobody can "turn to God for himself."[226] The will cannot turn to God without the grace of God.[227] Furthermore, since sin also affected feelings, for feelings do not always arise from a lawful cause and are not always directed to the lawful end, the Christian life, therefore, must be seen as exceeding intellectual knowledge.[228] The Christian life, as explained in the next chapter, is a reorientation of the entire life of a human being, not a mere depositing of correct beliefs on people. Affections must be subdued to Christ.[229]

Implications of Calvin's Doctrine of the Image of God

Being made in the image of God has important theological implications in Kenya, a country that has experienced the denigration of human life at various levels. The colonial experience, the wars of independence, the postcolonial governments that have fostered corruption and ethnic politics, and

---

218. Calvin, II.1.8.

219. Calvin, II.1.8.

220. Calvin, I.15.5.

221. Calvin, II.2.12.

222. Calvin, II.2.12.

223. Calvin, II.2.8.

224. Calvin, I.2.12.

225. See Smith, *You Are What You Love*, 23; Smith, *Imagining the Kingdom*, 3.

226. Calvin, *Institutes*, II.2.8.

227. Calvin, II.3.6. See also II.2.7, 8.

228. Calvin, *Commentary on John* 11:31. Calvin (*Institutes*, III.3.10) argues that feelings often result in desires that lure people to sin.

229. Calvin, *Institutes*, III.7.1.

the current waves of terror attacks, call for a re-evaluation of what it means to be human in Kenya. Particularly, Calvin's emphasis on the devastating effects of sin should be taken seriously. Human beings behave the way they do because of sinful nature. The inhumanity and atrocities committed against each other are the outcome of the fallen nature. Affirming the theological source of the problem bedeviling Kenya does not exclude other causes or factors that contribute or have contributed to inhumanity and atrocities against the Kenyan people. Such factors include social, economic, and political problems deriving from post-colonialism, and others. Theologically speaking, then, to mend broken relationships and to create long-lasting reconciliations requires the transformation of human beings, through the work of the Holy Spirit. Calvin's doctrine of the image of God has particular relevance to how Kenyans should treat one another. Kenyans should treat one another with respect, as people who bear God's image.

The Image of God as the Basis of Human Dignity, Fairness, and Love

Though the terms "human dignity" as understood today (its connection to constitutionalism), does not exist in Calvin's writings, the idea of the inherent sacredness or worth of human beings permeates his writings.[230] Jakobus Vorster argues that according to Calvin, human dignity is based on several reasons. The first is the image of God all human beings possess.[231] The second is the value God placed on human beings as the best of his creation. The third is the grace of God lavished on all people regardless of their station in life. The fourth is the common heritage and nature that all human beings share. The fifth is the equality of all human beings before God.[232]

Though Calvin was evidently pessimistic about human beings in their fallen state, he argued that all human beings, whether redeemed or fallen, bear the image of God. Therefore, to say that every person is created in the image of God is to affirm that all human beings, irrespective of race, gender, or ethnicity have an unconditional divine dignity, which no one can deny, and accordingly, all people merit honor and respect. Calvin asserted, "The

---

230. See Vorster, "Calvin and Human Dignity," 198.

231. Calvin, *Institutes*, III.9.40.

232. Vorster, "Calvin and Human Dignity," 201.

Lord has willed that we . . . reverence his image imprinted in man, and to embrace our own flesh in him."[233] Therefore, "if we do not wish to violate the image of God, we ought to hold our neighbor sacred."[234] Thus the commitment to prevent death, harm, and injury to our neighbors is rooted in the image of God in people. "To sum up, then, all violence, injury, and any harmful thing at all that may injure our neighbor's body are forbidden to us."[235] Instead of causing injury to others, people should foster one another's welfare: "We are accordingly commanded, if we find anything of use to us in saving our neighbor's lives, faithfully to employ it; if there is anything that makes for their peace, to see to it; if anything harmful, to ward it off; if they are in any danger, to lend a helping hand."[236] Thus the image of God makes humanity unique and gives humanity dignity and worth.

Calvin believed that how Christians treat one another validates their relationship with God. He argued that the lives of Christians "shall best conform to God's will and the prescription of the law when it is in every respect most fruitful for our brethren."[237] Therefore for Calvin, the best demonstration of the Christian life is to honor and respect fellow human beings. Honor and respect apply to every human being whether redeemed or unredeemed, a friend or an enemy.[238] For Calvin, Christians should lead the way in exemplifying what it means to be image bearers of God. In his commentary on John 13:34, "A new commandment I give unto you, that ye love one another," Calvin wrote, "Love is, indeed, extended to those outside, for we are all of the same flesh and are all created in the image of God. But because the image of God shines more brightly in the regenerate, it is proper that the bond of love should be much closer among the disciples of Christ."[239] Thus Christians should lead the way in showing what it is to be created in God's image.

---

233. Calvin, *Institutes*, III.9.40.
234. Calvin, III.9.40.
235. Calvin, II.8.39.
236. Calvin, II.8.39.
237. Calvin, I.8.50.
238. See Templin, "Individual and Society," 165.
239. As quoted by Hoekema, *Created in God's Image*, 101.

Calvin also affirmed that the image of God is the basis for treating our neighbors fairly. He contended that every human being "without exception" must be treated fairly.[240] One way of fulfilling this role is to adhere to the Golden Rule principle (Matt 7:12). It was in his exposition of the Golden Rule that Calvin condemned ethnic discrimination: "equity is to be cultivated constantly and toward all [human beings]."[241] He argued that the Israelites were "commanded to love strangers and foreigners as themselves."[242] Calvin added, "Hence it appears that the name of neighbor is not confined to our kindred, or such other persons with whom we are nearly connected, but extends to the whole human race."[243] Thus in Calvin's thought, there was no room for ethnic discrimination.

Calvin's theology of the image of God therefore addresses the wanton destruction of human lives through ethnopolitical conflict in Kenya. At the peak of the 2007–2008 post-election violence, about 1,200 Kenyans were killed, more than 400,000 were displaced, roads were blocked, railway lines uprooted, and hundreds of women and young girls were raped. Kenya has experienced violence every five years following a national election. Kimani Njogu observes, "In 1992, 1997, 2002, and 2007 elections in Kenya citizens have been internally displaced and many have been injured or killed because they have dared to show support, associate or vote differently in areas seen as not ancestrally theirs."[244] Termed as *madoadoa* (blemishes), "foreigners" are targeted for attack.

Recounting the massacre of thirty-five people at the Assemblies of God church in Kiambaa village near Eldoret, Pastor Stephen Mburu, the church's pastor, said that the attackers called the Kikuyu refugees "*ghasia, takataka, wezi, nyoka, madoadoa* (dirt, rubbish, thieves, snakes, and spotted hyenas)."[245] To the attackers, the Gikuyu refugees were subhuman because they belonged to a different ethnic community and political party and thus could be attacked and killed. Likewise, the Kikuyu retaliated by attacking non-kikuyu

240. Calvin, *Commentaries on the Four Last Books,* III:116, (on Lev 19:33–34).

241. Calvin, III:117, (on Lev 19:33–34).

242. Calvin, III:117, (on Lev 19:33–34).

243. Calvin, III:118, (on Lev 19:33–34).

244. Njogu, *Healing the Wound,* 3.

245. Wamwere, *Towards Genocide,* 3.

living among them. The case of Bernard Ndege Orinda, a Luo man who lost his entire family during the post-election violence, illustrates the severity of the Kikuyu retaliatory attacks. Before setting his home on fire, killing Orinda's two wives and eight children, the Kikuyu attackers were shouting *ihii, nyamu cia ruguru* ("uncircumcised boys," "animals from the west").[246] To them Orinda, just because he was a Luo, was nothing but an animals.

In *Exclusion and Embrace*, Miroslav Volf analyses the ideology behind ethnopolitical violence such as the ones explained above. Volf argues that ethnic cleansing feeds on the "logic of the 'politics of purity.'"[247] Through this logic, communities or individuals implement programs of territorial, tribal, and national purity. This logic insists on getting rid of heterogeneity and plurality in favor of homogeneity and unity.[248] Its vision is "one people, one culture, one language, one book, one goal" and whoever or whatever "does not fall under this all-encompassing 'one' is ambivalent, polluting, and dangerous" and must be reduced, rejected, segregated, dominated, or eliminated.[249] Volf also argues that this logic of "exclusionary practices" is successful because of "exclusionary language and cognition."[250] Before excluding others, people legitimate their actions through "dysphemisms" or derogatory names. Thus they brand the other as "outsiders," "dirty," "lazy," "parasites," and so on so that they can discriminate against, dominate, or drive them out.[251] More perniciously, getting rid of the other becomes a moral obligation to rid the community of "*agents corrupteurs*."[252] Volf also asserts that the "practice of exclusion" and the "language of exclusion" causes emotional reactions to the other ranging from hatred to indifference. Of the two, indifference is the most dangerous because it makes people view atrocities as something normal.[253] Thus people could be slaughtered in their hundreds and no one would care. Applying Volf's language to the Kenyan

---

246. Wamwere, 5.

247. Volf, *Exclusion and Embrace*, 74.

248. Volf, 74.

249. Volf, 74.

250. Volf, 75.

251. Volf, 76.

252. Volf, 76, emphasis original.

253. Volf, 77.

context illumines why the attackers behaved the way they did. When people are demonized or bestialized, killing them would not be a problem.

Volf's explanation on indifference also helps to shed light on why few Kenyans are aggrieved by the reality of lynching in Kenya. Lynching is a prominent form of "mob justice" in Kenya. It is carried out on witches, murderers, thugs, robbers; basically, anybody who is suspected of committing a crime and happens to fall in the hands of a mob would likely be lynched. This problem is so severe that after studying over 1,500 cases of lynchings in Kenya from August 1996 to August 2013, Robert McKee concludes that lynchings in Kenya have been accepted "for better or for worse, as part of [the] national culture."[254] Even the media treat this matter casually as McKee writes,

> Similarly, lynchings are seldom front-page news; they are likely, rather, to be reported as briefs, or as regional or local news, or as non-headline items in crime roundup articles. When reported as one of however many briefs – as, e.g., in a narrow vertical column of such – a lynching brief might appear anywhere from top to bottom in the column; when reported as a non-headline item in a crime roundup, the lynching item is often introduced—consistent with its relative lack of salience in the roundup – by a sentence beginning with "Meanwhile, . . ." or "Elsewhere, . . ." The text of some newspaper lynching reports is no longer than a single sentence.[255]

Why would the murder of another human being be taken so lightly? Why would Kenyans turn their eyes away from such atrocities? Volf suggests that viewing the other as more sinful than we are is also a powerful motivation for violence against them. This could be the reason why few Kenyans condemn lynching of those accused of a crime. Yet as Volf shows, and as Calvin did, all human beings are guilty of sin. The practice of pointing fingers at others justifies mistreatment or abuse of people. Volf argues that in any form of human violence there are three parties involved: the perpetrator, the victim,

---

254. Mckee, "Lynchings," 4.
255. Mckee, 6.

and the "third party" who is either a spectator watching from the sidelines or an activist trying to stop the violence.

Contrary to the wanton destruction of human life, Kenyans especially Christians should engender an alternative way of being human. Kenyans should offer an alternative narrative to the prevailing one of ethnic and political divisions. Kenyan Christians should embrace peace in place of violence, love in place of hatred, courage in place of fear, and humanity in place of inhumanness. It is possible to do so. In the wake of the 2007–2008 violence, several Kenyans exemplified *utu* (humanness), which is a chief characteristic of a person created in the image of God.[256] Several Kenyans risked their lives to hide their neighbors in their houses from those who were seeking to kill them. Several donated food, water, clothing and other items to the internally displaced persons in camps. The courageous actions show the importance of valuing one another especially in times of conflict.

Conclusion

This chapter has argued that Calvin advanced a relational view of the image of God rooted in the restoration of humanity's relationship with God. The chapter shows that Calvin's theological anthropology focuses on humanity's relationship with God, which occurs through salvation in Jesus Christ. Calvin did not expound his anthropology except in the context of saving humanity from sin. Thus anthropology is connected to other Christian doctrines such as hamartiology, soteriology, ecclesiology, and the Christian life. The chapter also showed Calvin's view of sin as the destruction of the image of God. Redemption, which occurs by the grace of God in Christ through the Holy Spirit, is the restoration of the image of God in believers. Finally, the chapter highlighted an implication of affirming God's image in humanity: the image of God as the basis for *utu* (human dignity) in Kenya. The following chapter provides more depth to the doctrine of renewal of God's image in believers according to Calvin. Particularly, the chapter emphasizes the role of the individual believer, the role of Christ, the role of the Holy Spirit, the role of scripture, and the role of the church.

---

256. See the various narratives of Kenyans who helped one another during the post-election violence in Njogu, *Healing the Wound*, 155–213.

CHAPTER 5

John Calvin's Doctrine of the Christian Life in Relation to His Anthropology and Its Relevance for Ethnopolitical Cohesion in Kenya

This chapter examines Calvin's doctrine of the Christian life in the context of his theological anthropology, precisely, humanity's relation with God and with one another, and its relevance for ethnopolitical cohesion in Kenya. Calvin believed that the Christian life is a renewal of God's image in believers, but the believer must actively participate in his or her spiritual renewal through the regenerative grace of God in Christ through the Holy Spirit in the context of the church. Since the Christian life is "a doctrine not of the tongue but of life," believers who are being transformed in God's image are to live out their faith in concrete ways.[1]

The chapter has three interconnected parts. Foremost it examines the role of an individual believer in the renewal of God's image. Additionally, the chapter studies the necessary resources in the renewal of God's image in believers. For Calvin, Christ and the Holy Spirit are the external means of the renewal of God's image in believers. The grace of God that is available to believers in Christ through the Holy Spirit is external to, or apart from, believers because human beings are sinners and cannot merit the benefits through their own effort. Therefore, although a believer must surrender to God, his or her renewal (sanctification) in God's image, is, according to

---

1. The phrase "a doctrine not of the tongue but of life," is from Calvin, *Institutes*, III.6.9.

Calvin, strictly and solely the work of God. In addition to Christ and the Holy Spirit, Calvin also emphasized the role of scripture and the church in the formation of believers in God's image. Thus the chapter also examines the role of scripture and the church in the renewal of God's image according to Calvin. The chapter shows that according to Calvin, the church plays the role of enabling believer's sanctification through the proclamation of God's Word, the administration of sacraments, and effecting discipline through the ordering of life in accord with the gospel. The chapter concludes with how Calvin's theology of the Christian life is relevant for Reformed churches in Kenya in their quest for ethnopolitical cohesion.

The Role of an Individual Believer

According to Calvin, a believer must deny oneself. Self-denial, which Calvin considered as "the sum of the Christian life," stems from an attitude of the heart, which recognizes that "we are not our own masters, but belong to God."[2] In his commentary on Matthew 16:24, Calvin described what it means to deny one's self: "This *self-denial* is very extensive, and implies that we ought to give up our natural inclinations, and part with all the affections of the flesh, and thus give our consent to be reduced to nothing, provided that God lives and reigns in us."[3] Writing to Farel in a letter dated August 1541 from Strasbourg, Calvin tells Farel, who had written to him urging him to return to Geneva following his dismissal from there, that if it was his choice he would not return to Geneva, "But when I remember that I am not my own, I offer up my heart, presented as a sacrifice to the Lord . . . I submit my will and affections, subdued and held fast, to the obedience of God."[4] Thus the recognition that we belong to God and not ourselves is a strong motivation for godly obedience.

A believer has to submit every facet of life to God. Believers undergo a transformation of their lives when they orient their lives such that they "think, speak, meditate, and do nothing except to [God's] glory."[5] Calvin

---

2. Calvin, *Institutes*, III.7.1.

3. As quoted in Pattison, *Poverty in the Theology*, 197, emphasis original.

4. Calvin, *Letters of John Calvin*, 256–257 as cited in Evans, "John Calvin," 89–90.

5. Calvin, *Institutes*, III.7.1.

noted, "We are God's: let all the parts of our life accordingly strive toward him as our only lawful goal."[6] Calvin also observed, "Therefore, he alone has duly denied himself who has so totally resigned himself to the Lord that he permits every part of his life to be governed by God's will."[7] As to the matter of the mind, Calvin condemned philosophers who elevate reason as the pinnacle of human success. For Calvin, Christians should surrender their minds to "the Holy Spirit so that the man himself may no longer live but hear Christ living and reigning within him [Gal 2:20]."[8] He reminded believers to surrender themselves "and all [their] possessions to the Lord's will, and to yield to him the desires of [their] hearts to be tamed and subjugated."[9] Calvin also argued that believers should surrender "contrary affections" to Christ.[10] Thus the mind, affections, and possessions must be surrendered to Christ

A believer must repent. Calvin viewed repentance broadly. For him, repentance encompasses conversion, salvation, and regeneration. Repentance results in regeneration also called new birth, sanctification, and imitation of Christ.[11] This broad understanding of "repentance" is clear in Calvin's definition of "repentance" as "the true turning of our life to God, a turning that arises from a pure and earnest fear of him; and it consists in the mortification of our flesh and of the old man, and in the vivification of the Spirit."[12] The Catechism of 1545, which Calvin wrote, defines repentance as "dissatisfaction with and a hatred of sin and a love of righteousness, proceeding from the fear of God, which things lead to self-denial and mortification of the flesh, so that we give ourselves up to the guidance of the Spirt of God and frame all the actions of our life to the obedience of the Divine will."[13] Thus repentance involves inward and outward transformation through Christ. The main purpose of it is restoring the image of God in believers that was damaged by sin.[14] As Leith explains, "repentance" according to Calvin is the

---

6. Calvin, III.7.1.
7. Calvin, III.7.10.
8. Calvin, III.7.1.
9. Calvin, III.7.8.
10. Calvin, III.8.10.
11. Calvin, III.4.1, 3. See Hoogerwerf, "Ecclesiology and Christian Nurture," 46.
12. Calvin, *Institutes*, III.3.5.
13. As quoted in Leith, *John Calvin's Doctrine*, 67.
14. Calvin, *Institutes*, III.3.9; III.6.1, 3.

whole process whereby a sinner turns to God and is renewed in God's image so that they may glorify God.[15] It is the recognition of sin and surrendering sin and sinful habits to God and consciously turning away from previous sinful habits and embracing a new way of life in Christ.

The process of turning away from previous sinful habits and embracing a new way of life does not mean obliteration of the old human self-identity. A Christian maintains his or her identity but forgoes old sinful habits while embracing new ones, which glorify God. The Christian life, therefore, is not the creation of a totally brand-new identity but the redemption of the old identity and forming it or re-forming it into the likeness of Christ. Thus, for example, by being a Christian, a Kalenjin person does not lose his or her identity as a Kalenjin but forgoes aspects of his or her "Kalenjiness" that are not aligned with God's will. A Kalenjin will reject all worldviews, systems, and values that are contrary to the new identity in Christ. As explained below, Calvin believed that the church with its spiritual practices such as scripture reading, preaching, sacraments, fellowship, worship, and others, is the place and means whereby believers are re-formed into new beings that glorify God. Thus, a believer must necessarily be a part of a church community.

According to Calvin, the renovation of God's image in believers is a progressive process.[16] Matthew Boulton asserts that Calvin understands the whole process of discipleship as *paideia,* "'formative education,' a sanctifying, disciplinary, recuperative path, and in that sense a humble and humbling return, little by little, to full humanity in Christ's image."[17] Thus sanctification, or Christian discipleship, is not instantaneous but is a day-by-day experience, which occurs as believers surrender their whole lives to God. The goal of discipleship should be to form believers in God's image so that they may go out into the world and be reflectors of God's being. Believers who are reformed in God's image inhabit a different way of being. They embody a different story and they live by a different set of standards. They

---

15. Leith, *John Calvin's Doctrine,* 66.

16. Hoogerwerf, ("Ecclesiology and Christian Nurture," 46) observes that according to Calvin sanctification is a dynamic response characterized by such words as "progress, advance, growth, journey, [and] formation."

17. Boulton, *Life in God,* 4.

do not allow the ungodly values of this world to form them, or in the words of Paul (Romans 12:2) to squeeze them into the world's mold, but rather they reform the world. They show the world a different kind of existence.

Sanctification involves mortification, which Calvin defined as "sorrow of soul and dread conceived from the recognition of sin and the awareness of divine judgment."[18] When someone is aware of the gravity of sin, the holiness of God, and the sheer despair of his or her inability to save himself or herself, then that person "begins truly to hate and abhor sin."[19] Hatred of sin is especially necessary because a believer is in constant battle with sin (i.e. the old nature) and the devil.[20] Thus the Christian life is a warfare against the forces of sin and the devil.[21] Self-denial results in victory over these powerful forces of darkness and their evil manifestation, for example, pride, self-love, and self-righteousness.[22]

A believer must bear the cross and follow Christ. For Calvin, the progressive sanctification of believers occurs as believers carry their own crosses and follow Jesus Christ.[23] The cross, which Calvin understood as suffering and affliction, is an important element of the Christian faith.[24] Without taking up the cross and following Jesus, a believer cannot be renewed in the image of God. In other words, taking up the cross is a means of believers to conform to the image of Christ.[25] Furthermore, it is through the cross of Jesus that humanity's incapacity and frailty before God is fully manifested so

---

18. Calvin, *Institutes*, III.3.3.

19. Calvin, *Institutes*, III.3.3.

20. Calvin, III.3.14. In the *Institutes* III.3.10, Calvin explains the fact that believers are always battling with sin: "We accordingly teach that in the saints, until they are divested of mortal bodies, there is always sin; for in their flesh there resides that depravity of inordinate desiring which contends against righteousness."

21. For more on Calvin's use of the military metaphors, see, Leith, *John Calvin's Doctrine*, 82–85; Kim, *Identity and Life*, 71–72. In addition to the military metaphor of "warfare" Calvin used other metaphors like "race" (*Institutes*, III.3.9), "journey/pilgrimage" (*Institutes*, III.6.5), and "hero" (*Institutes*, I.14.18).

22. Calvin, *Institutes*, II.1.1, 3; III.7.10 and III.7.2.

23. Calvin, III.8.1–2. For an exposition of Calvin's theology of the cross in the context of progressive sanctification, see Chung, "Taking up Our Cross," 164; Leith, *John Calvin's Doctrine*, 74–82.

24. For the idea of the cross as suffering, see Calvin, *Institutes*, III.8.1.

25. Calvin, *Institutes*, III.8.1, which states, "we share Christ's sufferings in order that as he has passed from a labyrinth of all evils into heavenly glory, we may in like manner be led through various tribulations to the same glory."

that believers may turn to God for help.[26] The cross, therefore, is the point of humanity's brokenness before God's majesty.

Self-denial has implications on social relationships. It is only those believers who have learned to subject their entire lives to God that are able to conquer the sin that vitiates human relationships. Through self-denial, believers surrender their selfish interests and foster the interests of others. "For, such is the blindness with which we all rush into self-love that each one of us seems to himself to have just cause to be proud of himself and to despise all others in comparison."[27] Because of self-love people "[wish] to tower above the rest, and loftily and savagely abuses every mortal man, or at least looks down upon him as an inferior."[28] Also, because of self-love and self-aggrandizement, people "covet wealth and honor, [and] strive for authority, [and] heap up riches" at the expense of relationships.[29] In other words, self-love damages relationships. The goal of self-denial is to conquer this selfish love and replace it with selfless love.

Self-denial produces respect, love, and humility and prompts a believer to think beyond their own interests to the interests of others. In addition, self-denial results in proper works of charity and compassion towards others.[30] Calvin asked, "For how can you perform those works which Paul teaches to be the works of love, unless you renounce yourself, and give yourself wholly to others?"[31] There is no other way for believers to fulfil Christian

---

26. Calvin, *Institutes*, III.8.3. Here, Calvin writes, "For, overturning that good opinion which we falsely entertain concerning our own strength, and unmasking our hypocrisy, which affords us delight, the cross strikes at our perilous confidence in the flesh. It teaches us, thus humbled, to rest upon God alone, with the result that we do not faint or yield." In the Preface to Psalms Calvin, (*Commentary on Psalms*, 1:23) Calvin writes,

> the bearing of the cross is a genuine proof of our obedience, since by doing this, we renounce the guidance of our own affections and submit ourselves entirely to God, leaving him to govern us, and to dispose of our life according to his will, so that the afflictions which are the bitterest and most severe to our nature, become sweet to us, because they proceed from him.

27. Calvin, *Institutes*, III.7.4.

28. Calvin, III.7.4.

29. Calvin, II.8.55.

30. According to Calvin, Christian charity is rooted in two theological foundations: God's generosity (providence) and God's image in all humanity. This point is discussed in the next chapter.

31. Calvin, *Institutes*, III.7.5.

charity other than for them to submit totally to the Lord so that they may be empowered to carry out this Christian responsibility.

It is through self-denial that believers serve God. "Let this, therefore, be the first step, that a man depart from himself in order that he may apply the whole force of his ability in the service of the Lord."[32] Calvin believed that God saves humans from the power of sin so that they may serve God in whatever work they do and wherever they live. Calvin defined "service" as absolute obedience to the Word of God and the Holy Spirit such that a believer "may no longer live but hear Christ living and reigning within him [or her]."[33] In other words serving God, for Calvin, has to do with surrendering everything for the Lord's use. It means devotion to God, which Calvin understood as dethroning the self and human ambition and elevating God's glory before any other thing.[34] Thus for Calvin, the Christian life is a life whereby God is the center of everything.[35] The next section examines the "external means" of renewal of God's image in believers.

Necessary Resources in the Renewal of God's Image

Although Calvin believed than an individual believer has a role to play in his or her own spiritual transformation, the Christian life is not possible without external aid. Thus Calvin avowed, "if we look to ourselves only, and ponder what condition we deserve, no trace of good hope will remain; but cast away by God, we shall lie under eternal death."[36] A believer is in need of assistance, which include Jesus Christ, the Holy Spirit, the Word, and the church.

---

32. Calvin, III.7.1.

33. Calvin, III.7.1.

34. Calvin, III.7.2.

For when Scripture bids us leave off self-concern, it not only erases from our minds the yearning to possess the desire for power, and the favor of men, but it also uproots ambition and all craving for human glory and other more secret plagues. Accordingly, the Christian must surely be so disposed and minded that he feels within himself it is with God he has to deal throughout his life.

35. Zachman, ("'Deny Yourself," 466–468) argues that Calvin's vision of the Christian life may be summarized as conquering the self-love, which greatly impairs believers from expressing the image and likeness of God.

36. Calvin, *Institutes*, III.2.1.

The Role of Christ

According to Calvin, Christ plays various roles in the renewal of God's image in the believer's life. Foremost, Christ enables true knowledge of God.[37] According to Calvin, the goal of human life is to know God. This idea is encapsulated in Calvin's opening statement of the *Institutes* that the sum of wisdom is knowledge of God and human self-knowledge. Human self-knowledge is twofold: knowing the worthy condition humans were before the fall and the despondent condition they are after the fall.[38] Humans can truly know themselves when they contrast their current state with the original state they were before sin. The more humans honestly examine themselves, the more they know they are in need of help. Calvin argued that "unless God confronts us in Christ, we cannot come to know that we are saved."[39] Knowing God is more than cognitive or factual knowledge. Knowing God is about having a deep spiritual relationship with God through Jesus Christ. For Calvin, faith is knowledge of God's will towards humanity perceived through God's Word and founded on God's truth.[40]

Christ also enables the renewal of God's image through offering salvation and victory from sin.[41] Calvin believed that human beings are in a state of perpetual enmity with God but Christ restores the damaged relationship with God and enables godly living.[42] Calvin termed the process in which Christ took on human nature in order to restore that which humanity had lost due to sin, as the wonderful exchange.[43] Through the wonderful exchange, what humanity was not able to achieve by their power, God achieved

---

37. Calvin, I.13.13; II.6.2. See also Faber, *Essays in Reformed Doctrine*, 233; Niesel, *Theology of Calvin*, 33; Dowey, *Knowledge of God*, 164; van Wyk, "Calvin on the Christian," 234–237; Zachman, "'Deny Yourself,'" 466.

38. Calvin, *Institutes*, II.1.3.

39. Calvin, II.6.4.

40. Calvin, III.2.6

41. Calvin, I.13.13

42. Calvin, I.15.4

43. Calvin, IV.17.2.

This is the wonderful exchange which, out of his measureless benevolence, he has made with us; that, becoming Son of man with us, he has made us sons of God with him; that, by his descent to earth, he has prepared an ascent to heaven for us; that, by taking on our mortality, he has conferred his immortality upon us; that, accepting our weakness, he has strengthened us by his power; that, receiving our poverty unto himself, he has transferred his wealth to us; that, taking the

for them through Christ. "Who could have done this had not the self-same Son of God become the Son of man, and had not taken what was ours so as to impart what was his to us, and to make what was his by nature ours by grace?"[44] The wonderful exchange therefore is the wonderful grace of God in action restoring humanity to a status they had lost.

Another way of understanding the wonderful exchange is Calvin's understanding of justification. Justification means, for Calvin, that God gathers the elect ones to himself out of compassion and grace and sees them as just, and for the sake of Christ, reconciles them to himself.[45] Justification, which is by faith alone and hinges on God's absolute sovereignty, is the judicial exchange of the human condition of sin with Christ's righteousness, which happens when believers unite with Christ.[46]

The wonderful exchange is possible because of the incarnation. In the event of the incarnation, Christ restored to humanity that which they had lost in Adam.[47] Christ removed the curse inflicted on humanity and the guilt and the condemnation that they carried within themselves. "This is our acquittal," Calvin wrote, that "the guilt that held us liable for punishment has been transferred to the head of the Son of God [Isa 53:12]."[48] Christ made children of Adam children of God. "His task was so to restore us to God's grace as to make of the children of men, children of God; the heirs of Gehenna, heirs of the Heavenly Kingdom."[49] Christ's death and resurrection manifested the grace of God to humanity. Through Christ's death "sin was wiped out and death extinguished;" through Christ's resurrection,

---

weight of our iniquity upon himself (which oppressed us), he has clothed us with his righteousness.

44. Calvin, *Institutes*, II.12.2. For more on the incarnation and the wonderful exchange, see, Zachman, "Jesus Christ," 50–51.

45. Wyk, "Calvin on the Christian," 235; Hunt, "Calvin's Theory," 60. On justification see, *Institutes*, III.11.2–4, 11, 16, 22; III.14.9; III.15.1.

46. In the *Institutes*, III.2.24, Calvin observes, "But since Christ has been so imparted to you with all this benefits that all his things are made yours, that you are made a member of him, indeed one with him, his righteousness overwhelms your sins; his salvation wipes out your condemnation; with his worthiness he intercedes that your unworthiness may not come before God's sight."

47. Zachman, "Jesus Christ," 53.

48. Calvin, *Institutes*, II.16.5.

49. Calvin, II.12.2.

"righteousness was restored and life raised up."[50] Christ's death and resurrection represent the passing on of the old life and the restoration of a new life.

Christ's death and resurrection also represent victory not only from sin and its power, but also from everything else that enslaves humanity. Jesus Christ confronted violence through compassion and love. On Calvary, Christ showed that evil does not have the last word. His resurrection is an indictment on the forces of evil. Christians can now work for justice in the world because the power of the resurrected Christ resides in them. Calvin avowed, "Christ enriches his people with all things necessary for the eternal salvation of souls and fortifies them with courage to stand unconquerable against the assaults of spiritual enemies."[51] For Calvin, greater victory is achieved in the ascension because it is a pledge that believers will inherit the kingdom of God.[52] The ascension is a mark of victory for the redeemed. It assures them that their salvation rests on a solid foundation of God's victory over sin, the world, and the devil.[53]

Christ plays the role of sanctifying or renewing believers in God's image by the power of the Holy Spirit.[54] For Calvin, the Christian life is renewal or restoration of God's image through Jesus Christ.[55] With Christ's intervention, human beings know God personally and are transformed in the image of God.[56] Thus transformation, which follows conversion, is the "restoration of the image of God in [believers]."[57] The sole end of regeneration is "to restore in us the image of God that had been disfigured and all but obliterated through Adam's transgression."[58] Christ is also the standard to which believers aspire to be like. "For we have been adopted as sons by the Lord with this one condition: that our life express Christ, the bond of our

---

50. Calvin, II.16.13.

51. Calvin, II.15.4.

52. Calvin, II.16.14. See, Zachman, "Jesus Christ," 59.

53. Calvin, *Institutes*, IV.1.3.

54. Calvin, I.15.4; III.1.1–4.

55. Wallace, (*Calvin's Doctrine*, 112) summarizes Calvin's view of the Christian life as, "to live a life ordered according to the image of God" and likewise, Leith, (*John Calvin's Doctrine*, 214) contends that the Christian life, according to Calvin, is "the reconstruction of the image of God which was defaced by the fall."

56. Calvin, *Institutes*, I.15.4.

57. Calvin, III.3.9.

58. Calvin, III.3.9.

adoption."[59] Calvin avowed that God renews believers in two inseparable ways; one is "by his Spirit," the other is "by his Word."[60] It is the role of the Holy Spirit in the renewal of the *imago Dei* in believers that we turn to next.

The Role of the Holy Spirit

Benjamin Warfield refers to John Calvin as "the theologian of the Holy Spirit" and Eifion Evans refers to Calvin as the "All-round theologian of the Holy Spirit."[61] Indeed in Book Three of the *Institutes*, Calvin focused on the Holy Spirit as the one to draw people to God. He believed that the Holy Spirit "is the bond by which Christ effectually unites us to himself."[62] The Holy Spirit "enflames our hearts with the love of God and with zealous devotion."[63] He also writes, the Holy Spirit "arouses hope of a full renewal."[64] The Holy Spirit "brings forth the buds of righteousness."[65] Christ "unites himself to us by the Spirit alone."[66] And "By the grace and power of the same Spirit we are made his members, to keep us under himself and in turn to possess him."[67] He also added, "faith is the principal work of the Holy Spirit" and the Spirit is the "inner teacher by whose effort the promise of salvation penetrates into our minds."[68] Nobody can understand the Word of God unless the Holy Spirit illumines him or her.[69] Therefore it is through the work of the Holy Spirit that believers are united to Christ who then unites them to God.

The Holy Spirit is active in awakening (vivifying) believers. Vivification is the process of "quickening" or "awakening" of humanity's spiritual

---

59. Calvin, III.4.3.

60. Calvin, II.5.5.

61. Warfield, *Calvin as a Theologian*, 5; Evans, "John Calvin," 93.

62. Calvin, *Institutes*, III.1.1.

63. Calvin, III.1.2

64. Calvin, III.1.2

65. Calvin, III.1.3.

66. Calvin, III.1.3.

67. Calvin, III.1.3.

68. Calvin, III.1.4. In his commentary on Ephesians 1:13, Calvin, (*Galatians and Ephesians*, 21:208) asserts, "The true conviction which believers have of the word of God, of their own salvation, and of religion in general, does not spring from the judgment of the flesh, or from human philosophical arguments, but from the sealing of the Spirit."

69. Calvin, *Institutes*, III.2.33. See also, *Institutes*, I.7.1, 4, 5.

consciousness to receive the gift of faith. Human beings need to be awak-
ened because they are in a state of spiritual slumber and in a state of spiritual intoxication.[70] It is the Holy Spirit who awakens human beings from
the slumber that sin causes in order that they may accept the grace of God
offered to them.[71] Spiritual quickening occurs when a person responds to
God with faith.[72] Then the Spirit produces an "inclination to righteousness, judgment, and mercy . . . that comes to pass when the Spirit of God
so imbues our souls, steeped in his holiness, with both new thoughts and
feelings, that they can be rightly considered new."[73] Thus salvation is only
possible through the work of the Spirit.

Furthermore, just as it is impossible to be redeemed without the Holy
Spirit, so it is impossible to be sanctified without the Holy Spirit.[74] For
Calvin, "the Spirit is not only the initiator of faith, but increases it by degrees, until by it he leads us to the Kingdom of Heaven."[75] Calvin defined
sanctification as a progressive or a day by day experience whereby believers
are renewed into the image of Christ.[76] Sanctification is also a pilgrimage
out of worldly desires that happens through mortification of the flesh.[77]
Sanctification is healing of the inherited corruption. Calvin asserted that
the goal of sanctification is "to restore in us the image of God that had been
disfigured and all but obliterated through Adam's transgression."[78] The out-

---

70. Calvin, *Institutes*, III.12.8.

71. Calvin, II.3.11. In *Institutes*, IV.1.21, Calvin asserts, "So, carrying, as we do, the
traces of sin around with us throughout life, unless we are sustained by the Lord's constant
grace in forgiving our sins, we shall scarcely abide one moment in the church."

72. Calvin, *Institutes*, III.3.3.

73. Calvin, III.3.8.

74. In the *Institutes*, IV.1.21, Calvin offers a trinitarian view of the Christian life:
"Consequently, we must firmly believe that by God's generosity, mediated by Christ's merit,
through the sanctification of the Spirit, sins have been and are daily pardoned to us who
have been received and engrafted into the body of the church."

75. Calvin, *Institutes*, III.2.33.

76. In his commentary on 2 Corinthians 3:18 Calvin wrote: "Observe, that the design
of the gospel is this, that the image of God, which had been effaced by sin, may be stamped
anew upon us, and that the advancement of this restoration may be continually going forward
in us during our whole life, because God makes his glory shine forth in us by little and little."
Calvin, *Commentary to the Corinthians*, 10:187.

77. Calvin, *Institutes*, III.7.3.

78. Calvin, III.3.9.

come of sanctification is "true piety, righteousness, purity, and intelligence."[79] Believers are able to manifest the fruit of the Spirit as the Holy Spirit enables them.[80] Renewal of the image of God is an ongoing lifetime process because believers are forever in conflict with the flesh, the world, and the devil. Once begun, it does not end, until the point of physical death.[81]

The Holy Spirit is the initiator and the sustainer of faith. Because of the Spirit, believers are sure of their salvation.[82] Calvin defined faith as "a firm and certain knowledge of God's benevolence toward us, founded upon the truth of the freely given promise in Christ, both revealed to our minds and sealed upon our hearts through the Holy Spirit."[83] From this definition, Calvin's view of faith is trinitarian. At the outset, God the Father is the source of faith, or in other words, faith is grounded in the Father's goodness. Second, faith comes to believers from the Father through Christ. In other words, Christ is the means of receiving faith from the Father.[84] Third, the Holy Spirit is the enabler of faith. Without the agency of the Spirit, believers cannot receive faith.

Receptivity to faith is only possible through the agency of the Spirit. Receptivity happens through the softening of the heart. Calvin reiterated that the knowledge of faith "is more of the heart than of the brain, and more of the disposition than of the understanding."[85] Hence, the benefits that come to believers from God, through Christ by the Holy Spirit, are external unless internalized.[86] The believer must have proper disposition or proper response to the Holy Spirit. They should actively participate in renewal by heeding to God, being obedient to the leadership of the Holy Spirit, and actively participating in the Christian community. Calvin did not separate

---

79. Calvin, I.15.4

80. See Calvin, *Institutes*, III.1.1.

81. Calvin, III.2.18, 21.

82. In his commentary on Ephesians 1:14, Calvin, (*Galatians and Ephesians*, 21:209) observes, "The Spirit, then, is the *earnest of our inheritance* of eternal life, *until the redemption*, that is, until the day of complete redemption is arrived." (Emphasis original).

83. Calvin, *Institutes*, III.2.7.

84. Calvin, III.2.8.

85. Calvin, *Institutes*, III.2.8. See also, I.5.9; III.2.33, 36.

86. McGrath, *Theology*, 9.

the role of the Spirit in sanctification from the role of the Scripture in the same. We turn now to the role of scripture in the renewal of God's image.

The Role of the Word of God

Calvin argued that the sum of wisdom consists in knowledge of God and humanity. Scriptures contain the knowledge of God and of humanity. Contrasted to what nature reveals about God, Calvin argued that nature reveals the transcendence and power of God while scripture reveal the loving, gracious, trinitarian God. Hence, for Calvin, scripture has greater authority than nature. It is only in the scripture, Calvin argued, that "God bestows the actual knowledge of himself upon us."[87] Calvin also argued that the Word of God is the solid foundation of doctrinal teachings.[88] Without God's Word, humanity is susceptible to error due to the sin that entangles them. It is the Word of God that will free humans from the power of sin.

> We must come, I say, to the Word, where God is truly and
> vividly described to us from his works, while these very works
> are appraised not by our depraved judgment but by the rule
> of eternal truth. If we turn aside from the Word, as I have just
> now said, though we may strive with strenuous haste, yet, since
> we have got off the track, we shall never reach the goal.[89]

Calvin emphasized that the image of God is renewed through the grace of God ministered through the Holy Spirit by way of Scripture. "God breathes faith into us only by the instrument of his gospel."[90] The Word of God is the foundation through which faith is built.[91] Faith is rooted in the Word of God (written and preached) established by the work of the Holy Spirit. Yet believers have a role to play; they must obey the Word of God.[92] Scripture

---

87. Calvin, *Institutes*, I.6.1.

88. Calvin, III.21.4 says, "I desire only to have them generally admit that we should not investigate what the Lord has left hidden in secret, that we should not neglect what he has brought into the open, so that we may not be convicted of excessive curiosity on the one hand, or of excessive ingratitude on the other."

89. Calvin, I.6.3.

90. Calvin, IV.1.5.

91. Calvin, III.2.6, 31.

92. Calvin, I.6.2. In his Calvin, *Commentary on Hebrews*, 4:12, Calvin says, "we shall never be renewed in the whole mind, which Paul requires, (Ephesians 4:23), until our old man be slain by the edge of the spiritual."

must be taken seriously, Calvin asserted, because "the Scriptures obtain full authority among believers only when men regard them as having sprung from heaven, as if there the living words of God were heard."[93] The study of the Word of God for Calvin, therefore was not something of mere speculation and intellectualism but of genuine encounter with God, which gives birth to piety and religion.[94] Calvin asserted, "For the Word of God is not received by faith if it flits about in the top of the brain, but when it takes root in the depth of the heart that it may be an invincible defense to withstand and drive off all the stratagems of temptation."[95]

However, the use of Scripture is not helpful to the Christian life without the efficacy of the Spirit.[96] Calvin believed Scripture was useful only in the Christian life as the Spirit works through it to guide and transform believers. Hence Calvin avowed that "no one can get even the slightest taste of right and sound doctrine unless he be a pupil of Scripture."[97] Elsewhere Calvin asserted, "The Word of God is like the sun, shining upon all those to whom it is proclaimed, but with no effect among the blind. Now, all of us are blind by nature in this respect. Accordingly, it cannot penetrate into our minds unless the Spirit, as the inner teacher, through his illumination makes entry for it."[98]

Because the task of interpretation of the Bible was significant, Calvin argued that believers should interpret the Bible with assistance of pastors and teachers.[99] Calvin strongly argued, and personally modeled, that preaching is significant whether people pay attention to the Word or decide to ignore it.[100] As already shown earlier, Calvin himself preached almost every day in

---

93. Calvin, *Institutes*, I.7.1.

94. Calvin, I.2.1.

95. Calvin, III.2.36.

96. Calvin, III. 2.33–37.

97. Calvin, I.6.2.

98. Calvin, III.2.34.

99. Calvin, IV.1.5.

100. Calvin, *Commentary on Isaiah*, 1:165, (on Isaiah 6:10).

But whatever may be the result, still God assures us that our ministrations are acceptable to him, because we obey his command; and although our labor appear to be fruitless, and men rush forward to their destruction, and become more rebellious, we must go forward; for we do nothing at our own suggestion, and ought to be satisfied with having the approbation of God.

Geneva. He believed that it is in the preaching of the Word of God that believers are transformed. Leith observes, "Calvin thought of preaching as the
primary means by which God's presence becomes actual to us and by which
God's work is accomplished in individual life and in the community."[101] Yet
for Calvin, preaching is meaningless unless the Spirit is active in the lives of
the hearers. "The foundation of faith would be frail and unsteady, if it rested
on human wisdom; and therefore, as preaching is the instrument of faith,
so the Holy Spirit makes preaching efficacious."[102] The efficaciousness of the
Word occurs because the Spirit imparts power to the Word of God so that
it may not be spoken in vain.[103] The Spirit also softens the heart so that it
may respond to the Word in obedience. Therefore actual transformation of
the church and society comes through the Word of God because the Word
transforms both the mind and the heart, the private as well as the public life.

The Role of the Church

Calvin's discussion on the subject of the church is found in Book Three and
Four of the *Institutes*. According to Calvin, the church, or the community of
the elect, is the earthly means by which God sanctifies and forms believers in
God's image and likeness.[104] The church carries out the process of enabling
believer's sanctification through the proclamation of God's Word, the administration of sacraments, and effecting discipline through the ordering
of life in accord with the gospel.[105]

Calvin understood the term "church" as the community of those whom
God has given the gift of faith, alive presently and those from the past,
residing in different parts of the world, and who are being sanctified by
Christ through the Holy Spirit.[106] In the *Institutes*, IV.1.7 Calvin asserted,

---

101. Leith, "Calvin's Doctrine of the Proclamation," 29.

102. Calvin, *Galatians and Ephesians*, 21:208; Calvin, *Commentary on Hebrews*, 4:12
asserted, "I indeed admit that the power does not proceed from the tongue of man, nor
exists in mere sound, but that the whole power is to be ascribed altogether to the Holy
Spirit; there is, however, nothing in this to hinder the Spirit from putting forth his power
in the word preached."

103. Calvin, *Institutes*, IV.1.6.

104. Calvin, IV.1.1, 2.

105. Hester, "Sanctified Life," 200.

106. Calvin, *Institutes*, IV.1.4, 7, 9.

> Sometimes by the term "church" it means that which is actu-
> ally in God's presence, into which no persons are received but
> those who are children of God by grace of adoption and true
> members of Christ by sanctification of the Holy Spirit. Then,
> indeed, the church includes not only the saints presently liv-
> ing on earth, but all the elect from the beginning of the world.
> Often, however, the name "church" designates the whole mul-
> titude of men spread over the earth who profess to worship
> one God and Christ.

Thus the church is both visible and invisible, local and universal, holy and unholy, and is solely a community of the elect.[107] Calvin employed various metaphors to explain the role of the church in nurturing faith within itself and in faithfully carrying out its tasks to the wider community.

The first metaphor is "the mother of all the godly." This metaphor is clear in the title "The true Church with which as mother of all the godly we must keep unity."[108] The church is the "mother of all the godly" in the sense that it is the fountain or the source through which God's grace operates in the world.[109] For Calvin, the free grace of God comes to humanity through the church. Calvin's emphasis on the "mothering" nature of the church is in line with the ancient dictum, *extra ecclesiam nulla salus* (there is no salvation outside the church).[110] "For there is no other way to enter into life unless this mother conceive us in her womb, give us birth, nourish us at her breast, and lastly, unless she keep us under her care and guidance."[111] Calvin added, "away from her [the Church's] bosom one cannot hope for any forgiveness of sins or any salvation [consequently,] it is always disastrous to leave the Church."[112] Calvin's "motherhood" metaphor also follow's Cyprian's dictum,

---

107. The doctrine of election is foundational to Calvin's ecclesiology in the *Institutes*. See *Institutes*, IV.1.2; III. 21.1; III. 24.6. For an explanation of the doctrine of election in Calvin's ecclesiology, see, Kroon, *Honour of God*, 147; Niesel, *Theology of Calvin*, 189; Leith, *John Calvin's Doctrine*, 168.

108. Calvin, *Institutes*, IV.1.1.

109. Kim, *Identity and Life*, 103.

110. Niesel, *Theology of Calvin*, 186; Wendel, *Calvin*, 294–295; Kim, *Identity and Life*, 101.

111. Calvin, *Institutes*, IV.1.4.

112. Calvin, IV.1.4.

"No longer can he have God for his father who has not the Church for his mother."[113] Thus, the church, for Calvin, is a "mother" because it is through the church that people come to faith, receive the forgiveness of sin, and are renewed in God's image and likeness.

The second metaphor is the church as a "school."[114] The metaphor of a "school" is closely connected to the metaphor of a "mother." As a mother, the church "gives birth" to believers, God's children. As school, the church is "the pillar and ground of the truth" where education, discipline, and nurture of believers happens.[115] Boulton argues that Calvin envisioned the church as a "gymnasium, a training ground, a school, a community of preparation and practice enrolled (we hope and pray) in God's sanctifying, transformative *paideia*."[116] The terms "gymnasium" and "school" presuppose rigorousness, discipline, habit formation, and spiritual workout. These images show that Calvin believed that believers must actively participate in their own spiritual workout.

Furthermore, since gymnasiums and schools are communal spaces, it means that spiritual formation occurs in community. Believers help one another to be who God created them to be by the power of the Holy Spirit. The church must not train the mind only, it must also help believers to re-form their old habits. Reforming themselves in God's image is necessary for Christians because of the deforming power of evil. James K. A. Smith argues that human beings are liturgical beings, "always worshipping, always pursuing something, a *telos*, or a certain 'kingdom.'"[117] Smith argued that the various cultural practices form or deform human beings. Therefore, the purpose of Christian discipleship, for Smith, is to re-orient (re-order, re-habituate, re-calibrate, re-form) human longings so that they align with

---

113. Cyprian, *De Unitate Ecclesiae*, VI.19. See Calvin, *Institutes*, IV.1.1, where Calvin says, "for those to whom [God] is Father the church may also be Mother." The main difference between Cyprian's and Calvin's ecclesiology is that whereas Cyprian was talking about the mystical or invisible church, Calvin's focus was the visible church. For Calvin, the visible church differs with the invisible church not only because of its concreteness but because the visible church is an imperfect church in need of God's sanctifying work through the Holy Spirit. The invisible church is the pure church.

114. Zachman, *Calvin as Teacher*, 7.

115. Calvin, *Institutes*, IV.1.10.

116. Boulton, *Life in God*, 230.

117. Smith, *You Are What You Love*.

God's intended plan for humanity.[118] Thus the church is the place of renewal, a place where Christians are formed into new beings.

The preaching of the word of God and the administration of sacraments, both communal practices, are the means through which believers are firmly grounded in their faith. "Wherever we find the word of God purely preached and heard, and the sacraments administered according to the institution of Christ, there, it is not to be doubted, is a church of God."[119] Preaching and sacraments effects the sanctification of believers because God connects the Spirit with the preaching and with the sacraments and causes change in the lives of the believers.[120] The Word of God and the sacraments must be received by faith. "The office of the sacraments is precisely the same as that of the word of God; which is to offer and to present Christ to us, and in him the treasures of his heavenly grace; but they confer no advantage or profit without being received by faith."[121] As Wilhelm Niesel puts it, according to Calvin, the Word of God can only have a meaningful impact in the lives of believers, when the believers are "mastered and claimed by the gospel."[122] Therefore, believers not only hear the preaching but must also respond to it in obedience.[123]

Calvin provided four ecclesiastical authorities for the purpose of church governance. These include pastors, doctors, elders, and deacons. The role of

---

118. Smith, 65.

119. Calvin, *Institutes*, IV.1.9. In his sermon on Galatians 4:26–31 (quoted in Kim, *Identity and Life*, 105), Calvin says,

> We need to be discerning, and not like animals who are led by the reins across the field. We need to be aware of what constitutes the true church . . . Wherever, his Word is preached faithfully without any human additions, his own people will be found. This will occur where the gospel is unadulterated, and where people are led directly to God seek in him all that they lack.

120. Leith, *John Calvin's Doctrine*, 170.

121. Calvin, *Institutes*, IV.14.17.

122. Niesel, *Theology of Calvin*, 183.

123. In the *Institutes*, IV.1.5 Calvin urges the congregation to obey God's Word:

> Among many excellent gifts with which God has adorned the human race, it is a singular privilege that he deigns to consecrate to himself the mouths and tongues of men in order that his voice may resound in them. Let us accordingly not in turn dislike to embrace obediently the doctrine of salvation put forth by his command and by his own mouth.

For more on the role of the congregation in responding to the preaching of God's Word, see, Parker, *Calvin's Preaching*, 57–64; Kim, *Identity and Life*, 110.

pastors is to preach the word and administer sacraments.[124] The "doctors" of the church are the specialists in studying scripture and exposing it. The role of elders is to implement discipline within the church, which includes, caution, rebuke, and in some cases, the excommunication of errant members.[125] The deacons are tasked with dispensing charity and compassionate ministries. However, the ecclesiastical officers do not operate in isolation from one another but with one another because the various ministries are communal ministries.

Indeed, Calvin abhorred isolationism. He believed that Christians must always work together for the glory of God. He rebuked those who are "led either by pride, dislike, or rivalry to the conviction that they can profit enough from private reading and meditation; hence they despise public assemblies and deem preaching superfluous."[126] Such kind of rebellion, Calvin noted, "is like blotting out the face of God which shines upon us in teaching."[127] In the same vein, Calvin rebuked anyone who abandons the faith. There is no life outside the church, "all that is out of Christ is hurtful and destructive."[128] In the church, one has spiritual food and everything necessary for salvation and growth.[129]

The third metaphor is "society of Christ" and "communion of saints."[130] These two metaphors denote the fellowship that believers have with God and with one another. Believers are the "communion of saints" in the sense that they are part of the invisible community of God.[131] Yet the church is also a "society of Christ." The use of the word "society" denotes that the church is called to faith from a wider community of humankind though not so that they can be isolated from that community, but so that they can

---

124. Calvin, *Institutes*, IV.1.1, 5.

125. Although Calvin believed that the church is composed of saints and sinners (IV.1.7), he also believed that "the openly wicked" should be removed from the church albeit very cautiously (IV.1.15). However, individual Christians have no right to decide who should be removed and who should not. The task "belongs to the church as a whole and cannot be exercised without lawful order.'" (IV.1.15).

126. Calvin, *Institutes*, IV.1.5.

127. Calvin, IV.1.5.

128. Calvin, Commentary on Ephesians, 4:13

129. See Calvin, *Institutes*, IV.1.10.

130. Calvin, IV.1.3.

131. Calvin, IV.1.7.

become the beacons of light and thereby draw humankind to God in Christ. Thus the "society of Christ" denotes the visible character of the church, the physical embodiment of the reality of salvation in Christ. Leith argues that Calvin did not distinguish between individual Christianity and communal Christianity. For Calvin, "The primary fact is the redemptive grace of God which calls the individual to a new life, which is always life in community."[132] Marijn de Kroon has a similar perspective when he observes that Calvin's ecclesiology has a strong focus on divine-human relationships that does not neglect the human-human relationships. "The bipolarity of the divine-human relation, however, does gain a new dimension: the connection with others, the communion of believers inasmuch as weak human beings cannot remain standing in the faith by themselves."[133] Therefore the faith Calvin envisioned is not one that isolates believers from one another but one that joins them together in fellowship. The Christian faith is also faith lived out in the wider community. The community of faith is part and parcel of the wider human society. Thus the church is a community within a community.[134]

The fourth metaphor is the imagery of a tree and its branches. This imagery denotes the communion between Christ and the church. In his commentary on Ephesians 4:16 Calvin avowed, "as the root conveys sap to the whole tree, so all the vigour which we possess must flow to us from Christ."[135] Two key points can be deduced from Calvin's statement above. To begin with, the spiritual life, which the church has is the life of Christ. In other words, Christ is the source and the origin of faith. Human initiative

---

132. Leith, *John Calvin's Doctrine*, 167.

133. Kroon, *Honour of God*, 148.

134. Several scholars emphasize the communal character of the church. The various proposals include the church as "covenant fellowship" (Webster, *Word and Church*); "a vehicle of true sociality," (Gunton and Hardy, *On Being the Church*, 5); "a Trinitarian community" (Harper and Metzger, *Exploring Ecclesiology*, 19; Volf, *After Our Likeness*); "a community for the kingdom of God" (Fuellenbach, *Church*); "a community of the Spirit," "A community of social relationships," "a community where Satan is disarmed," "a worshipping community" and "a sacramental community" (Harper and Metzger, *Exploring Ecclesiology*; Charry, "Sacramental Ecclesiology"); "the communion of equals" (Kärkkäinen, *Introduction to Ecclesiology*, 128.); "the coming together of 'relatives' of Christ" (Oduyoye, "African Family," 471); "a missional community" (Guder, "Church as Missional Community," 116; Wright, *Mission of God's People*; Bosch, *Transforming Mission*); "a cultural/counter-cultural and prophetic community" (Healy, *Church, World*; Harper and Metzger, *Exploring Ecclesiology*; Hauerwas, *Community of Character*).

135. Calvin, *Galatians and Ephesians*, 21:287, (on Eph 4:16).

does not give birth to faith; faith comes entirely from Christ through the Holy Spirit.[136] Faith is a gift of God. Thus the church does not possess an inherent spiritual life of its own. The life it possesses and displays before the world, is the life of Christ. In addition, since believers have a common source of spiritual life, communion between themselves is essential. Their life has one source, Jesus Christ. Thus Christians cannot purport to follow Christ and yet fight among themselves.

Calvin's emphasis on the common origin of the church adheres to his emphasis on the common origin of humanity. All human beings come from one source, God, and thus are all related.[137] Thus believers are to love each and every human being alike. However, they must love one another first.[138] Without mutual love, therefore, the health of the church, and other forms of human relationships, cannot be maintained.[139] Therefore believers must give support and care to one another because they are members of one family, God's family. Such support and care by itself is a means through which the grace of God comes to the church.[140]

The Implications of Calvin's Doctrine of the Christian Life

Calvin's strong focus on the need for redemption of humanity from sin and their sanctification (renewal in God's image) is relevant for Kenyan churches to embrace. Calvin deals with the problem of the human condition of sin in his emphasis on self-denial and wholehearted surrender to God. Sociopolitical theologies must not ignore the reality of human depravity. Ethnic cohesion can be enhanced by helping human beings deal with their own sinful condition. In addressing human sin, it is important to deal with individual as well as social (and systemic) sin. Ethnocentrism is both an individual and a social/corporate and systemic evil. A theological proposal

---

136. Calvin, *Institutes*, III.1.1.

137. Leith, *John Calvin's Doctrine*, 166; Wolterstorff, *Hearing the Call*, 126.

138. Calvin, *Institutes*, III.7.5.

139. Calvin, *Galatians and Ephesians*, 21:287 (on Eph 4:16). See also *Institutes*, III.7.7.

140. Calvin, *Institutes*, IV.1.5

of ethnopolitical cohesion, therefore, must emphasize the need for restoration of, not only the relationship with God but also between human beings.

The church must begin by acknowledging its own sinful character. As Nicholas Healy observes, the eschatological "not yet" character of the church "reminds us that until the end of the Church's time it remains imperfect and sinful, always *ecclesia semper reformanda* or *semper purificanda.*"[141] The church is always reforming itself through God's Word. For the church to lead others to repentance, it must itself be repenting and reforming. The African palaver is a useful resource for African churches in regard to repentance. African palaver is about brokenness, confession, and healing.[142] It is about confessing sin to one another and reintegration back to the community. Palaver is not about overlooking sin and crimes, but helping the victim and the perpetrator to find healing in the midst of evil. It was only when the church in Kenya confessed of its failings and sinfulness before the Kenyan people, that it regained its prophetic character. Thus ethnic reconciliation is ultimately about the transformation of the human person. As Calvin showed, the transformation begins with self-denial and wholehearted surrender of every facet of life to God's rule. This surrender inaugurates an ongoing process of being formed into a new humanity.

For Calvin, life is to be lived for the glory and honor of God alone. Calvin's emphasis on God as the center of human existence dethrones humanity from the center and places God at the center of all reality. African anthropology is anthropocentric; even God exists for the benefit of humankind. The God of African traditional religion is far removed from human experiences, but the God revealed in Jesus Christ is near and desires to fellowship with humanity. African anthropocentric anthropology is problematic not only because it yields pride and idolatry, but because anthropocentrism has profound ecological implications. If everything exists for the sake of human beings, then humans can use (and abuse) nature as they wish, thus contributing to an ecological crisis.[143] Indeed enthroning God as the center

---

141. Healy, *Church, World*, 10.

142. Bujo, *Foundations*, 45–48.

143. Hall, *Imaging God*, 24; LenkaBula, "Beyond Anthropocentricity," 375. Calvin's emphasis on the proper use of earthly resources addresses ecological degradation through showing that humans are part of the wider earth community (the church is a community within a community) and should therefore use the earthly resources in ways that glorify

of human existence is the proper way to live because it is, as Calvin emphasized, a mark of gratitude for God's sovereign presence in the world, and
it is the proper acknowledgment of humanity's sole dependence on God.

Calvin emphasized that every facet of human life is meant to glorify
God. There is no part of life that God does not speak to. Even the mind is
to be subjected to the lordship of Christ. Salvation, for Calvin, is holistic.
Believers must surrender everything including their wealth and work to
God.[144] Calvin's holistic spirituality impacts culture. Since every facet of life
is within the sphere of God's rule, culture, which is the product of human
action and decisions, is within God's rule as well. Thus the redeemed should
exercise their faith in tangible ways because the Christian faith has social
and political implications as the next chapter argues.

Though the church has an invisible character in the sense that God
knows those who are truly his, the church is nonetheless always a physical,
tangible, concrete community living within a particular cultural environment. Calvin's own practical initiatives, as well as his acts of compassion
to refugees in Geneva and Strasbourg, illustrates the importance of public
engagement. Redemption is not isolation. Thus the church in Kenya should
engage in the sociopolitical transformation of Kenya.

The christological emphasis in Calvin's doctrine of the Christian life
has important implications. First, Calvin stressed that Christ is the savior
of humanity. Calvin's doctrine of sin emphasized humanity's helplessness
before God. Without God's intervention in Christ, human beings are unable to free themselves from sin. Second, Calvin emphasized that believers
should pattern their lives after the life of Christ. For Calvin, Jesus Christ is
the true embodiment of what it means to be human.[145] There is one par-

---

God. Calvin stressed, against the Stoic and Augustinian philosophy, the proper enjoyment
of material goods not just merely for human sustenance, but because the goods themselves
have an inherent beauty (See, Calvin, *Institutes*, III.10.2). In *Institutes*, III.10.3, Calvin
noted, "Away, then, with that inhuman philosophy which, while conceding only a necessary
use of creatures, not only malignantly deprives us of the lawful fruit of God's beneficence
but cannot be practiced unless it robs a man of all his senses and degrades him to a block."

144. In the *Institutes*, III.10.6, Calvin emphasized that every work humans do is a
calling; "no task will be so sordid and base, provided you obey your calling in it, that it will
not shine and be reckoned very precious in God's sight."

145. Calvin, *Institutes*, I.13.13: "Moreover, if apart from God there is no salvation,
no righteousness, no life, yet Christ contains all these in himself, God is certainly revealed."

ticular implication from this christologically focused anthropology for the Kenyan context. For Kenyan Christians, Jesus embodied and enables what Kenyans are unable to, on their own, to achieve: peace, neighborliness, and love for one another. Kenyans, like all people of the world, long to live in peace with one another. However, as argued earlier, ethnic division is a grave reality in Kenya.

Kenyan communities have struggled to live in peace with one another. Even when peace seems to have been achieved, national elections reveal deep-seated ethnic sentiments, which often ignite violence. Thus, Kenyans have an eschatological vision, a longing for "the peaceful village," the place where people of all ethnicities and divergent political opinions live in peace with one another. The church is in some ways "the peaceful village" because Christ has already initiated his kingdom in the world manifested (in imperfect ways) through the church. However, churches in Kenya are marred by ethnic divisions and so have failed to model the ideal of a peaceful village. Ultimately the perfect "peaceful village" will be inaugurated in Christ's second coming. However, believers have the responsibility of participating in the already ongoing work of God in transforming the sinful world into a more "peaceful village." In other words, the church in Kenya must be a peaceful community so that it can help the wider society to become a peaceful village. In addition, the church must also work with other religious communities and non-religious communities to create in common such peaceful villages. This can be done through collaboration, dialogical communication, and support of grassroot peace initiatives.

Calvin emphasized the role of the Holy Spirit in the transformation of believers whether through the reading of God's Word, through preaching or through the work of Christ in believers. Human beings who have experienced the transforming power of Christ become sanctified daily to better reflect the image of God. The new humanity, the sanctified humanity, is enabled by the Holy Spirit to live out community beyond exclusive barriers. Thus, the church is the community of the Spirit. Without the Spirit of God, the church cannot be the church. The Holy Spirit invigorates spiritual disciplines so that it becomes disciplines that transform lives. In other words, "the spiritual disciplines are conduits of the Spirit's transformative grace."[146] In addition, the Holy Spirit works in the day-to-day lives of God's people. Spiritual transformation does not stop at the day of worship, but continues through ordinary mundane activities of life. God, through the Spirit, is always at work in the lives of God's people.

Calvin accentuated that the Spirit carries out the work of transforming believers through the church (preaching of God's Word and administration of sacraments). Thus Calvin's anthropology is also ecclesial (i.e. communal). Calvin's emphasis on the church as the place where God's people experience salvation is important. Through the church, people come to know Christ. The emphasis on the church as a redemptive community shows that the Christian life is to be pursued in the community not only for the benefit of those already in the church but also for those who are yet to come in. Eugene Peterson says it well, "there can be no maturity in the spiritual life, no obedience in following Jesus, no wholeness in the Christian life apart from an immersion and embrace of community. I am not myself by myself. Community, not the highly vaunted individualism of our culture, is the setting in which Christ is at play."[147] The church, or the elect community, though imperfect, is a visible manifestation of a new humanity being born. The church, therefore, should be a welcoming community.

In the church, redeemed persons are or ought to manifest qualities of redeemed humanity, such as truth, obedience, righteousness, and justice, or what Paul in Galatians 5:22–23 terms the fruit of the Spirit: love, joy, peace, forbearance, kindness, goodness, faithfulness, gentleness and self-control. As a community in God's image, the church ought to concretely embody God's presence in the world. Having experienced all the benefits of being in God's family, the church should live out those benefits so that those who are still outside God's family may be drawn to come in and experience *shalom*. The more the church faithfully lives out what it means to be humanity as the image of God, the more the circle of evil in the world is broken, and human flourishing is fostered.[148]

---

146. Smith, *You Are What You Love*, 68.

147. Peterson, *Christ Plays*, 226.

148. See appendix for a response to Reinhold Niebhur's *Immoral Man and Immoral Society* which espouses a divergent position.

Calvin accentuated that God is the originator and the sustainer of the christian community. The Christian community is not the outcome of humanity's own effort but a creation of God. Community is the outcome of humanity's response to God's grace and initiative. Many theologians have followed Calvin in asserting theocentric nature of the Christian community. These theologians include Stanley Grenz, Jean Vanier, Dietrich Bonhoeffer, Henri Nouwen, Thomas Reynold, Josiah Royce, John Ackerman, Eugene Peterson, and Emmanuel Katongole.[149] Henri Nouwen, for example, notes, "The basis of the Christian community is not the family tie, or social or economic equality, or shared oppression or complaint, or mutual attraction . . . but the divine call."[150] Similarly, Grenz observes, "We enter that community through our faith response to the proclamation of the salvific action of God in Christ, symbolized by baptism."[151] Josiah Royce explicates the Christian community as different from the "natural community" because the Christian community, "the Beloved Community," is characterized by love and bound by the Spirit of God, and was initiated and is being sustained by Christ.[152] Similarly, Eugene Peterson observes, "The resurrection of Jesus establishes the entire Christian life in the action of God by the Holy Spirit. The Christian life begins as a community that is gathered at the place of impossibility, the tomb."[153] However, although the church began "at the place of impossibility, the tomb" the church is the place of possibility, enabling the creation of a new humanity capable of embodying godly practices and leavening the world.

Thus, communion with God in Christ through the Holy Spirit, as Calvin explicated, is the only basis of authentic Christian community. When Christians respond to the divine call, they experience, not only the new birth, but also the Spirit's renewal that enables them to embrace new values which include esteeming God's people not because of their ethnic identities but because of who they are, God's people. This theocentric nature of

---

149. Grenz, *Theology for the Community*; Vanier, *Community and Growth*; Bonhoeffer, *Life Together*; Nouwen, *Reaching Out*; Reynolds, *Vulnerable Communion*; Royce, *Problem of Christianity*; Ackerman, *Listening to God*; Peterson, *Christ Plays*; Katongole, *Sacrifice of Africa*.

150. Nouwen, *Reaching Out*, 153.

151. Grenz, *Theology for the Community*, 7.

152. Royce, *Problem of Christianity*, 130.

153. Peterson, *Christ Plays*, 230.

community challenges the anthropocentric nature of African community that tends to yield ethnic allegiance, which then breeds tensions and all manner of problems.

Conclusion

This chapter examined Calvin's doctrine of the Christian life in the context of his theological anthropology. The chapter showed that Calvin talked about the Christian life as the renewal of God's image in believers, which is an ongoing process. The chapter also showed that an individual believer has a role to play in this renewal. The most important role is self-denial and wholehearted devotion to God. Even though a believer participates in their renewal, they are in need of external help. The help is from Christ, the Holy Spirit, the Word, and the church. The chapter also showed the practical implications of Calvin's doctrine of the Christian life. The next chapter examines about Calvin's political theology in the context of his anthropology.

CHAPTER 6

John Calvin's Political Theology in Relation to His Anthropology and its Relevance for Ethnopolitical Cohesion in Kenya

The chapter examines Calvin's political theology and its relevance for ethnopolitical cohesion in Kenya. After a brief introduction on the nature of Calvin's political theology and two views on Calvin's understanding of Christianity and culture, several issues are then examined, which include, Calvin's Two Kingdoms theology, the source and justification for civil government, the purpose and role of civil government, and the duties of citizens toward civil authority. Also, the chapter resources Calvin's political theology for ethnopolitical cohesion in Kenya arguing that contrary to the politics of self-aggrandizement and corruption that prevail in Kenya, which has resulted in manipulation of ethnicity for political gain thus causing ethnic conflict, politics is about the public good, not self-enrichment. Also, rather than leading to quietism and aloofness from social issues, Calvin's theology inspires sociopolitical engagement, curtails corruption, promotes an ethic of work, and supports acts of charity, justice, and compassion to the poor and the marginalized.

The Overall Shape of Calvin's Political Thoughts

Calvin did not offer an extensive treatise on political theology. His political thoughts are framed within other theological concerns such as the sovereignty of God, Christian freedom, care for the poor, and the diplomatic letters he wrote to princes and other civic leaders urging them to be tolerant to Protestant Christians.[1] The final edition of the *Institutes* (1559) contains a chapter "On Civil Government" in which Calvin presents his political thoughts within the two swords, two powers, two kingdoms, and two authorities tradition.[2] Calvin's political thoughts cohere with his overall theological vision, which centered on the glory and sovereignty of God.[3] This chapter studies Calvin's political views in the 1559 edition of the *Institutes* and relevant biblical commentaries.

Calvin, being a pastor, presented his theological thoughts within the context of the Christian life. Throughout, he maintained that human beings are created in God's image and so are honored above all creation. However, sin totally deformed God's image such that without God's intervention, human beings are estranged from God and from one another. Calvin called for a total surrender to Jesus Christ because it is only in surrendering to God that human beings are brought into a life of obedience so that they can participate, through God's help, in God's restorative and transformative work in the world. To be redeemed by Christ is to belong to the community of the church, the household of faith.[4] It is unto this community of faith that Calvin addressed in his writings.

Calvin's audience was primarily Christian laity and Christian rulers in Geneva and other surrounding Christian states.[5] Thus Calvin was concerned with politics in a Christian setting. Indeed Calvin worked with the assumption that religion takes precedence in a nation. "Since, therefore, among all philosophers, religion takes first place, and since this fact has always been observed by universal consent of all nations, let Christian princes and magistrates be ashamed of their negligence if they do not apply themselves to this concern."[6] However, Calvin also recognized that not all leaders give preference to religion. "If anyone could enter into the hearts of kings, he would

---

1. McNeil, "Introduction," viii–ix; Boulton, *Life in God*, 4.

2. Calvin, *Institutes*, IV.20.

3. Yong, *In the Days of Caesar*, 67; Hancock, *Calvin and the Foundations*, 164; Wolterstorff, *Until Justice*, 10; Spykman, "Sphere-Sovereignty in Calvin," 186–89.

4. Douglass, "Calvin's Relation," 128–129.

5. McNeil, "Introduction," xiii.

6. Calvin, *Institutes*, IV.20.9.

find scarcely one in a hundred who does not despise everything divine."[7] In his commentary on Micah 4 where Micah prophecies that nation will not take up sword against nation, nor will nations train for war anymore, Calvin avowed that the fulfillment of this prophecy occurs through the spiritual kingdom. He argued, "But this was not fulfilled, we are certain, at the coming of Christ, in a manner visible to men: we must, therefore, bear in mind what Micah has previously taught, – that this kingdom is spiritual; for he did not ascribe to Christ a golden sceptre, but a doctrine."[8] Calvin also contended that Christians remain a minority in the world and they undergo, in most cases, persecution and troubles. The kingdom of God, therefore, is not achieved through violence but through the word and Spirit through which God "bends the hearts of [people] to obedience."[9] Thus even though Christians may enjoy the freedom of worship, in some cases they will suffer under unjust governments, and may be forced to seek refuge elsewhere as Calvin did.

Several scholars argue that Calvin preferred and modeled, in Geneva, a theocratic form of governance.[10] The term "theocracy" can be understood narrowly or broadly. The first meaning, which is narrow, is a form of governance in which authority comes from God and is exercised through God's representatives such as the clergy.[11] Based on this narrow definition, Calvin did not prefer theocracy as a political form of governance because he clearly separated civil and ecclesial responsibilities. "Calvin's concern" John Bolt argues, "was rather clearly to distinguish the Church and the magistracy

---

7. Calvin, *On God and Political Duty*, 91.

8. Calvin, *Twelve Minor Prophets*, XIV:280, (On Micah 4:8).

9. Calvin, (*Twelve Minor Prophets*, XIV:260, [On Micah 4:3]) asserted,

the Church of God could not be otherwise formed than by the Word, and that the legitimate worship of God cannot be set up and continued, except where God is honoured with the obedience of faith; so now he shows that Divine truth produces this effect—that they, who before lived in enmity towards one another and burned with the lust of doing harm, being full of cruelty and avarice, will now, having their disposition changed, devote themselves wholly to acts of kindness.

10. Troeltsch, *Social Teaching*, 627; McGrath, *Reformation Thought*, 216; Collinson, *Reformation*, 81; Allen, *History of Political Thought*, 64; Jeong, "Calvin and the Two Kingdoms," 300. Yong, (*In the Days of Caesar*, 66), asserts that Calvin's Geneva was a "clerocracy," "a government deeply informed by ecclesial leadership."

11. Chenevière, "Did Calvin Advocate Theocracy?," 160; Larson, *Calvin's Doctrine*, 1.

in terms of their respective roles and tasks."[12] Indeed a pastor, for Calvin, should not at the same time be a civil magistrate because both offices "are so different that they cannot come together in one man."[13] Calvin also rejected Mosaic theocracy as normative everywhere. He argued that every nation is free to make their own laws as deemed fit for their context. However, the laws "must be in conformity to [the] perpetual rule of love."[14]

The second meaning of "theocracy" is broad. Broadly understood, theocracy is the assumption that everything is under the Word and authority of God.[15] Thus as Marc Chenevière argues, based on Calvin's belief that all authority, whether civil or ecclesiastical, operates within God's mandate and blessing, it follows that "human society, as conceived by Calvin, is a theocratic society in which all power proceeds from God and in which all power is exercised by His representatives."[16] Therefore based on this belief, Calvin embraced theocracy. Indeed Calvin rooted every single event on the glory and sovereignty of God. God is the pivot in which everything turns. Everyone and everything is under the rule of God. Even politicians are under God's rule. Politicians are God's servants answerable to God. The later parts of this chapter deals with Calvin's views on political accountability. Before examining Calvin's views on civil government, the ensuing section briefly presents two views on Calvin's doctrine of Christianity and culture.

Calvin on Christianity and Culture

Two Major Approaches

There are two major views on the interpretation of Calvin on Christianity and culture. The first stream is the traditional neo-Calvinism, represented by Abraham Kuyper and Herman Dooyeweerd and contemporary neo-Calvinism represented by Al Wolters, Cornelius Plantinga, Craig Bartholomew,

---

12. Bolt, "Background and Context," xx.

13. Calvin, *Institutes*, IV.11.8.

14. Calvin, IV.20.15.

15. Bolt, "Background and Context," xxi.

16. Chenevière, "Did Calvin Advocate Theocracy?," 160.

Michael Goheen, and others.[17] The second stream is the "Two Kingdoms" perspective within the discussion of the natural-law tradition represented by David VanDrunen.[18]

Neo-Calvinists hinge their interpretation of Calvin's views of culture on four theological foundations: the cultural mandate, sphere sovereignty, the antithesis, and common grace.[19] The cultural mandate is the affirmation that human beings as bearers of God's image are responsible stewards of God's creation (Gen 1:28). More than merely emphasizing filling, ruling, and subduing the earth, the Reformed tradition represented by Neo-Calvinists, emphasize the redemption of culture. They argue that God is redeeming not only human beings but the entire cosmos from the destructive power of sin.[20] They argue that since evil has affected every facet of human life, including culture and the natural world, redemption from evil must encompass redemption of every facet of human life, including culture and the natural world.[21] Having been redeemed, believers must participate with Christ, in the formation of a Christian culture. A Christian culture does not necessary

---

17. Kuyper, *Lectures on Calvinism*; Dooyeweerd, *Roots of Western Culture*; Wolters, *Creation Regained*; Plantinga, *Engaging God's World*; Goheen and Bartholomew, *Living at the Crossroads*.

18. Even though the natural-law tradition is often associated with Roman Catholicism, VanDrunen and other Reformed scholars have argued for it. VanDrunen's publications on natural law include, *Living in God's Two Kingdoms*; *Natural Law and the Two Kingdoms*; *Biblical Case*; "Two Kingdoms Doctrine." Other Reformed theologians who advance a theology of natural law from a Reformed perspective include, Schreiner, *Theater of His Glory*, 73–95; Schreiner, "Calvin's Use of Natural Law," 51–76; Holmes, "Human Variables," 63–79, and "Concept of Natural Law," 195–208. Stephen J. Grabill's *Rediscovering the Natural Law in Reformed Theological Ethics* provides a survey of the natural-law tradition in Reformed Protestant scholarship including the significance and influence of the Barth-Brunner debate of 1934. The debate centred on Brunner's support of the natural law based on a reading of John Calvin and Barth's wholesale rejection of it also based on a reading of John Calvin.

19. McIlhenny, "Introduction," xx. Goheen and Bartholomew, (*Living at the Crossroads*, 16) identify the themes of Neo-Calvinism as:

[1] In and through God's redemption in Christ, grace restores nature. Grace is like medicine that restores health to a sick body. Christ's work of salvation is aimed at the creation as a whole in order to renew it to the goal that God always had in mind for it. [2] God is sovereign and orders all of reality by his law and word. [3] The cultural mandate given in Genesis 1:26–28 (to exercise royal stewardship over the creation) has ongoing relevance: God calls humankind to develop his creation through history, to his glory.

20. This is also a key emphasis in the New Perspective on Paul as well as the emerging church movement.

21. Plantinga, *Engaging God's World*, xv; Wolters, *Creation Regained*, 73.

mean Christianization of culture, a vague ideology, which often mean the propagation of supposed "Christian" values.[22] For neo-Calvinists, culture making is part and parcel of being created in God's image. To create culture, is to reflect the creative character of God.[23]

However, VanDrunen rejects the redemption of culture. Even though the cultural mandate continued after the fall, cultural endeavors are plagued with sin. The end result of culture is destruction, not redemption. In terms of Christ's work, VanDrunen argues that Jesus Christ redeems people, not culture. Jesus completed the work of redemption nothing is left for human beings to do in terms of redeeming culture. Consequently, to affirm that "cultural obedience contributes to building the new creation is to compromise the all-sufficient work of Christ."[24] He also argues that though Christians should live out the implications of their faith at all times and in all places, a Christian, however, is under no obligation to redeem culture.[25] The main task of believers is to live out their faith within the church and society and not to expect that their creative activity in the world contributes in any way to the redemption of culture. Only God in Christ redeems culture.

VanDrunen's emphasis on the divine role in cultural redemption is important for it protects against the reduction of Christian responsibility to mere cultural engagement. As this book shows, Christians shape culture when they respond in obedience to God's saving and transforming grace and then participate through God's help in embodying the norms of the kingdom of God thus showing the fallen world a different way of existence and drawing many to God's kingdom. VanDrunen's argument also highlights the damaging effects of sin on culture and warns against usurping Christ's

---

22. Quoting James Bratt, (*Abraham Kuyper: A Centennial Reader*, 198–199) McIlhenny, ("Christian Witness," 264) says that according to Kuyper, "the designation 'Christian culture' does not mean that the society has already been transposed into the kingdom of heaven" but it does imply witnessing "to the fact that public opinion, the general mind-set, the ruling ideas, the moral norms, the laws and customs there clearly *betoken the influence of the Christian faith*." (Emphasis original). Thus according to Calvinists, the adjective "Christian" in "Christian culture" denotes Christianity's influence on the surrounding culture to the point that the culture reflects Christian values. However, the term "Christian values" is still vague. There is a need then, to critique the said values to make sure it is not values of a particular culture being baptized as Christian values.

23. Crouch, *Culture Making*, 104.

24. VanDrunen, *Living in God's Two Kingdoms*, 51.

25. VanDrunen, 15.

role in redemption. He shows that there is a limit to human achievements. Redemption is indeed God's doing. In addition, VanDrunen's argument cautions against the tendency within neo-Calvinism of speculating on the final destiny of specific cultural endeavors, particularly the products of human creativity; for example, what type of music, architecture, and art makes it into God's coming kingdom?

However, VanDrunen's sharp distinction between the "civil" or "natural" kingdoms and the "spiritual" or "ecclesiastical" kingdoms is problematic because it propagates a dualism of the kingdoms.[26] It renders the natural world unredeemable. Whereas neo-Calvinists see the redemption of Christ permeating both the civil and ecclesiastical kingdoms, VanDrunen insists that redemption only permeates the spiritual kingdom. For him, the attributes of the spiritual kingdom include "its redemptive character, its spiritual or heavenly identity, and its present institutional expression in the Church" while the attributes of the natural kingdom include "its non-redemptive character, its external or earthly identity, and its present (though not exclusive) expression in civil government."[27] For VanDrunen, the natural kingdom is headed for dissolution at Christ's second coming but the spiritual kingdom will endure forever.[28] However, as explained below, Calvin did not entirely hold to a clear dichotomy between the two kingdoms. Calvin believed that though the two kingdoms are separate, they are not antithetical and both are redeemable. God in Christ is redeeming creation.

Another point of concern is VanDrunen's argument that civil kingdom does not pertain to matters of "ultimate and spiritual importance."[29] For him, Christians should spend their time focusing "on things that are of ultimate and spiritual importance, the things of Christ's heavenly, eschatological kingdom."[30] However, earthly matters are matters of ultimate and spiritual importance as the life and teachings of Jesus shows. Furthermore, scripture shows the continued connection between creation and new creation and between salvation now and future salvation. God is not merely concerned

---

26. VanDrunen, *Natural Law and the Two Kingdoms*, 71–82.

27. VanDrunen, 6.

28. VanDrunen, *Living in God's Two Kingdoms*, 67.

29. VanDrunen, *Biblical Case*, 24.

30. VanDrunen, 24.

about redemption of human beings; He is also concerned about their existence on earth. Thus, a spirituality that ignores the spiritual significance of
earthly matters has serious theological implications such as constraining the
church's public ministry and fostering a neglect of ecological ethics. Calvin
affirmed that since every facet of human life was under the lordship of Christ,
every single thing, including political matters, is a matter of ultimate and
spiritual importance.[31]

Within the discussion on the connection between politics and theology,
VanDrunen's argument falls within the stream that maintains "a cordon
sanitaire" between politics and theology. In this framework, "the task of
political theology might be to relate religious belief to larger societal issues while not confusing the proper autonomy of each."[32] Though Calvin

---

31. Richard John Neuhaus, (*Naked Public Square*, 86) argues convincingly of the
dangers of excluding the State from the realm of spiritual concerns.

32. Scott and Cavanaugh, *Blackwell Companion*, 2. See also Kirwan, *Political Theology*, 9.
Though recent streams of political theology represented mainly by Stanley Hauerwas recognize
the distinction between the secular and the sacred, they also emphasize theology as critique of
the political. They assert that the church is a concrete political space. Thus theologians such
as Cavanaugh, *Migrations of the Holy*; *Theopolitical Imagination*; Katongole, *Sacrifice of Africa*;
Fitch, *End of Evangelicalism?*; Ward, *Politics of Discipleship*; O'Donovan, *Desire of the Nations*;
Bretherton, *Christianity and Contemporary Politics*; Hauerwas, *Community of Character* see
political theology as the theological analysis and critique of political arrangements in view of
providing an alternative theological, social-cultural, and political vision and practice. They are
wary of the traditional political theologies that acknowledged nation-states as necessary for
social order, particularly represented by the Reformation's two-kingdoms doctrine, Kuyper's
"sphere sovereignty," and by such scholars as Reinhold Niebuhr, (*Christianity and Power
Politics*; *Nature and Destiny of Man*). Contrary to politics as statecraft (Niebuhrian emphasis),
Hauerwasian scholars argue that the State is not the solution for the problems bedeviling
humanity, but the church is. The church, for them, is a counter-cultural, alternative, distinct,
countersign community. The church must be church so that the world may know itself
as the world. Granted, the church indeed must be a countersign for the world, but being
countercultural does not mean exclusion of the State from fostering human order and
flourishing. How would the church live out its message if the State does not foster peace and
order? The church exists within a broken world and without the State, as Calvin emphasized,
evil will hinder the church from carrying out its mission. Therefore though Hauerwasian
school of thought is appealing to this book mainly because of its call for the church to be the
church and to avoid being coopted by the state, its sectarian tendencies is problematic. Luke
Bretherton, (*Christianity and Contemporary Politics*) provides a way forward in his emphasis
on the necessity of the church to be part of the public and to avoid sectarianism. He shows
that it is possible for the church to maintain its witness as an alternative community, "and
yet at the same time cooperate with religious and non-religious others in pursuit of goods in
common" (18). Bretherton asserts, "The public work of the church is thus to be an agent of
healing and repair within the political, economic, and social order, contradicting the prideful,
violent, and exclusionary logics at work in the *saeculum* and opening it out to its fulfillment

distinguished between the two spheres, he also emphasized the lordship of Jesus Christ in every area of life, and urged believers to live out their faith in their various callings. This is what is beneficial for the Kenyan context, which maintains a close connection between the spiritual and the secular.

Neo-Calvinists affirm the sovereignty of God over every facet of life. This affirmation is also related to redemption of culture. The Christian faith, for Spykman, "impels Christians to reclaim every sphere of life for the King – home, school, Church, State, college, university, labor, commerce, science, art, journalism, and all the rest."[33] Each sphere possesses God-given authority, and "has its own identity, its own unique task, its own God-given prerogatives. On each God has conferred its own peculiar right of existence and reason for existence."[34] Thus each sphere is limited and subservient to the rule of God. Sphere sovereignty emphasizes that though the different spheres exercise authority independently of each other, they are nonetheless mutually interrelated.

The antithesis, according to the Reformed tradition, is the reality of opposing "world systems."[35] Christians live out their faith in the midst of opposing or competing world systems. The task of believers is to participate in the generation of a Christian worldview. This antithetical stance yields various responses. It may rally Christians to be active agents in the transformation of their cultures. However, this rallying posture may also become a crusading posture against the negative forces of culture. One manifestation of such crusading stance is unyielding conservatism, which tends to narrow the church's focus to a handful of issues prevalent in the day.[36]

In regard to common grace, neo-Calvinists insist that God restrains the destructive power of sin on creation as a whole and lavishes his grace

---

in Christ" (10). This book follows Bretherton's argument that the church should critique the State but should also work with the State when it fosters human flourishing.

33. Spykman, "Sphere-Sovereignty in Calvin," 166; Wallace, *Calvin, Geneva*, 27–28.

34. Spykman, "Sphere-Sovereignty in Calvin," 167.

35. Leading publications on Christian worldview include, Walsh and Middleton, *Transforming Vision*; Smith, "Reforming Public Theology"; Smith, *Desiring the Kingdom*; Smith, *Imagining the Kingdom*; Poythress, *Lordship of Christ*; Goheen and Bartholomew, *Living at the Crossroads*.

36. For a discussion of the varied responses of Western Christianity to culture, which includes the crusading stance, see Studebaker, "Servants of Christ," 53–56.

on everyone thus enabling the development of science, art, and culture.[37] Consequently all the activities of life such as farming, teaching, sports, and the arts fall under the realm of common grace. Related to common grace is the doctrine of special grace. Whereas common graces deals with the realm of everyday life and is available to all people, special grace deals with the realm of spiritual life and is offered by God only to the elect. Common grace is not salvific whereas special grace is salvific.

As this study argues below, contrary to this emphasis on the unsalvific nature of common grace, God's grace redeems the entirety of life. There is no sphere that is outside the realm of the salvific grace of God. The same Spirit that regenerates believers renews creation and will ultimately liberate it from the bondage of decay.[38] The grace of God liberates humans as well as the entire creation. The next section examines Calvin's doctrine of the two kingdoms.

Calvin and the Two Kingdoms

Several scholars agree that Calvin affirmed the two kingdoms doctrine.[39] However, in his classic classification of Christian cultural engagement, Richard Niebuhr placed Calvin in a different category from Luther's two-kingdom theology.[40] For Niebuhr, Calvin affirmed the transformation of culture. The doctrine of two kingdoms predates Calvin. Calvin's two kingdoms doctrine is an extension, although not necessarily identical, of Paul's concept of the two ages (this age and the age to come),[41] Augustine's two

---

37. McIlhenny ("Introduction," xxxii) defines the doctrine of common grace as:

(1) God's offering of his creation to all of humanity regardless of spiritual state; (2) God's restraining of the full devastating consequences of the fall (i.e., bridling the "perversity of nature, that it may not break forth into action," according to Calvin); and (3) the ability of the nonelect to have moments of clear insight regarding truth, justice, goodness, and beauty.

38. For more on the regenerative role of the Spirit in creation, see Studebaker, *From Pentecost*, 243–268; Studebaker, "Creation Care," 248–263.

39. Keddie, "Calvin on Civil Government," 44; Yong, *In the Days of Caesar*, 67; VanDrunen, *Living in God's Two Kingdoms*, 14; VanDrunen, *Natural Law and the Two Kingdoms*, 69; Tuininga, "Good News for the Poor," 221; Torrance, *Kingdom and Church*, 90–164; Tuininga, "Calvin as Two Kingdoms," 393–401; Spykman, "Sphere-Sovereignty in Calvin," 163–208.

40. Richard Niebuhr, *Christ and Culture*, 217.

41. VanDrunen, (*Living in God's Two Kingdoms*, 14n3), offers a helpful distinction between the "two kingdoms" and "two ages" ideas:

cities ("the city of God" and "the secular city")[42] and Martin Luther's two kingdoms doctrine.[43]

Calvin argued that human beings are under a twofold government, the "spiritual" and the "temporal" or the "heavenly" and the "earthly."[44] Earlier in the *Institutes*, II.2, when Calvin talked about total depravity and human inability to understand "heavenly things," he offered a clear distinction between the two realms: "I call 'earthly things' those which do not pertain to God or his Kingdom, to true justice, or to the blessedness of the future life; but which have their significance and relationship with regard to the present life and are, in a sense, confined within its bounds."[45] Calvin cited matters of policy and economy, household management, mechanical skills, and the liberal arts as examples of the earthly things.

For Calvin, the "heavenly things" include "the pure knowledge of God, the nature of true righteousness, and the mysteries of the Heavenly Kingdom" and "God's will, and the rule by which we conform our lives to it."[46] For

---

Whereas the two-kingdoms doctrine primarily explains the twofold way in which God governs this present world, the two-ages doctrine primarily concerns an eschatological distinction and tension between this world and the next. And whereas both of the two kingdoms are legitimate and divinely-ordained (though corrupted by sin in this world), Paul's presentation of "this age" focuses upon its evil and demonic character and its rebellion against God (e.g., see 2 Cor 4:4; Gal 1:4; Eph 2:2).

Thus Paul's "this age" idea focuses on the system of values contrary to God's values; in other words, it focuses on worldliness rather than that the world (John 18:36; Rom 12:2; Col 2:8; Jas 1:27, 4:4; 2 Pet 2:20).

42. Augustine, *City of God*, vol. 2, 1–511. William Cavanaugh, (*Migrations of the Holy*, 60) explains Augustine's "two cities" idea: "The two cities are not the sacred and the profane spheres of life. The two cities are the *already* and the *not yet* of the kingdom of God." Thus Augustine's "two cities" idea refers to the eschatological city of God, in which people are either members or are not. The city of God consists of believers destined for eternal blessing while the secular city consists of unbelievers and destined for eternal condemnation. A person is a member of one city, and one city only. See, VanDrunen, *Living in God's Two Kingdoms*, 14.

43. Luther's "two-kingdoms" doctrine is particularly developed in his 1523 treatise titled, *On Secular Authority* found in Luther, *Luther's Works*, 45:81–129. Publications on Luther's two kingdoms doctrine include, Frostin, *Luther's Two Kingdoms Doctrine*; Bornkamm, *Luther's Doctrine of the Two Kingdoms*; and Wright, *Martin Luther's Understanding of God's Two Kingdoms*.

44. Calvin, *Institutes*, III.19.15. Calvin's discussion of the spiritual kingdom appears within his discussion of the Christian life (Book III to IV.3–9) and his discussion of the "temporal" or civil government, appears in Book IV.20.

45. Calvin, *Institutes*, II.2.13.

46. Calvin, II.2.13.

Calvin, humans, in their fallen state, are unable to understand clearly the "heavenly things" because sin hinders them.[47] Therefore it is clear that Calvin associated the spiritual kingdom with what is heavenly and spiritual and the earthly kingdom with what is earthly and of the present life.

Calvin argued that the spiritual kingdom is concerned with the inner life of individuals while the political kingdom is concerned with the outward life.[48] Jesus Christ, through his death and resurrection, inaugurated the spiritual kingdom, which will be consummated in Christ's second coming. Though Christians are pilgrims heading to their true home in heaven, the present reality of the spiritual kingdom "is already initiating in us upon earth certain beginnings of the Heavenly Kingdom."[49] Thus being a citizen of heaven does not necessitate rejection of this world, but means living in light of the reality of the kingdom of God that is already effecting real changes on earth. Thus the spiritual kingdom impinges on the political kingdom.

Calvin claimed that the two kingdoms are separate but not antithetical.[50] Both kingdoms have their common origin in God and are united by a common interest, which is the glory of God. The church's mission is to witness to the world about Christ while the State's mission is "to cherish and protect the outward worship of God, to defend sound doctrine of piety and the position of the Church, to adjust our life to the society of men, to form our social behavior to civil righteousness, to reconcile us with one another, and to promote general peace and tranquility."[51] For Calvin, salvation only rests in the spiritual kingdom.[52] Salvation is found only in the altar of the church not from the king's throne. Similarly, the church advanced through

---

47. Calvin, II.2.13.

48. Calvin, III.19.15.

49. Calvin, IV.20.2. Calvin delineates the Christian life as a pilgrimage; see, *Institutes*, II.16.14; III.2.4; III.7.3; III.10.1; III.25.1-2; IV.20.2. See VanDrunen, *Natural Law and the Two Kingdoms*, 77n26.

50. Calvin, *Institutes*, IV.20.1, 2.

51. Calvin, *Institutes*, IV.20.2. As to the church's mission, Torrance, (*Kingdom and Church*, 148), observes, "In contrast to Luther, Calvin laid greater emphasis upon the *ecclesia externa sive visibilis*. The Kingdom of Christ consists not only in the Gospel, not only in a hidden community of believers, but in the historical communication of the Gospel, and the building up of the Church on earth by human agency *(humanitus)*."

52. "Through this distinction it comes about that we are not to misapply to the political order the gospel teaching on spiritual freedom . . ." (Calvin, *Institutes*, III.19.15).

the Word and the Spirit, not through the power of the sword. However, though the magistrates play no direct role in advancing the gospel, Calvin argued that the magistrates play a secondary role by virtue of their judicial and political offices, in protecting the church and its pastors from harm.[53]

Thus, the State, for Calvin, must not hinder the gospel; although it may be implored to stop erroneous doctrine from spreading.[54] Consequently, the modern doctrine of the radical separation of church and State, sacred and secular, was foreign in Calvin's thought.[55] William Mueller argues that according to Calvin and Luther, "The church and the State are both subject to the sovereign rule of God, the *regnum Dei et Christi*. The authority of both spheres inheres in the will and purpose of the living God."[56] Similarly Carew Hunt observes that according to Calvin, "Church and State are united and inseparable. To the State belongs all coercive authority. The sword of the Church is the word of God."[57] Thus though both kingdoms are separate, they are under God's rule. However, God governs the two kingdoms in two different ways. God governs the spiritual kingdom through ecclesiastical authorities such as pastors, elders, and deacons and governs the civil kingdom through the magistrates and human laws.

---

53. Tuininga, "Calvin as Two Kingdoms," 399.

54. Calvin, *Institutes*, IV.20.3. Tuininga, ("Calvin as Two Kingdoms," 395) argues that although Calvin, like his sixteenth-century contemporaries, supported to use of civil magistracy for curtailing the spread of heresy and blasphemy; he nonetheless, seems to hold reluctantly to the idea. For example, in the 1536 edition of the *Institutes*, when Calvin talks about the role of the civil government, "he says virtually nothing about religion, focusing instead on matters of justice and peace between human beings, a characteristic that, notably, carries into his commentary on Romans 13, published four years later in 1540." Furthermore, in Calvin's discussion of church discipline in the 1536 edition of the Institutes, Calvin does not approve the use of the sword.

55. Keddie, "Calvin on Civil Government," 23; Mueller, *Church and State*, 127; Boer, *Political Grace*, xviii; McNeil, "Introduction," viii; Bradstock, "Reformation," 71–72.

56. Mueller, *Church and State*, 127. Niesel, (*Theology of Calvin*, 230) makes a similar point when he writes, "There can be no decisive separation between State and church because the State has the same Lord as the church."

57. Hunt, "Calvin's Theory," 17. Yong, (*In the Days of Caesar*, 67) notes that "whereas Luther secularized the State, Calvin clericalized it." Boer, (*Political Grace*, xix) makes a similar observation: "Calvin did not make human life less religious; rather, the whole of human life became a monastery." He also adds that Calvin "sacralized" the whole life. Thus Calvin viewed the entire life as a sphere of God's influence. Like the African worldview that emphasizes religiosity of life, Calvin saw reality as religious. Kuyper, (*Lectures on Calvinism*, 34–35) affirmed that according to Calvin, human beings are inescapably religious. This assertion is similar to Mbiti's claim that African's are notoriously religious.

Contrary to Zwingli, Calvin rejected the idea that the New Testament offices of deacon and elder are now fulfilled by civil officers. For Calvin, there is a "great difference and unlikeness between ecclesiastical and civil power."[58] Similarly Calvin did not delineate specific ecclesial oversight over the State.[59] He expected the church primarily to bear testimony to Christ and not to engage in direct oversight of the State. The magistrate governs the State through the power of the sword.[60] Contrary to Rome, the church does not have the power to punish or restrain or coerce; this role only belongs to the magistrates.[61] Contrary to the Anabaptists, Christian freedom does not prevent magistrates from exercising their duty of punishment and coercion. The duties of magistrates and other public authorities are theologically justified as the next section shows.

The Source and Justification for Civil Government

Calvin's discussion of civil governments begun with a response to two extreme schools of thought. The first one rejected the necessity of civil government and the other praised the rulers without critiquing their excesses.[62] Calvin responded to these extremes. He argued that both extremes threatened the purity of faith.[63] On the first argument, Calvin contended that civil government is "divinely-established order" and thus to overturn it; even the mere thought "of doing away with it is outrageous barbarity."[64] Referencing Romans 13, Calvin asserted, "There are no powers except those ordained by God."[65] He also added, "Scripture expressly affirms that it is the providence

---

58. Calvin, *Institutes*, IV.11.3. For this idea, see, Tuininga, "Calvin as Two Kingdoms," 397.

59. Chenevière, ("Did Calvin Advocate Theocracy?," 111) asserts, "Calvin never claimed for the Church any power over the State, but placed it in the midst of the State as a spiritual guide commissioned to teach and preach the Word of God, and to enable the faithful to receive the grace transmitted in the sacraments."

60. Calvin, *Institutes*, IV.20.9–12.

61. Calvin, IV.11.3, 8, 9.

62. Calvin, IV.20.1. See also Calvin, *Commentary on Romans*, 19:477, (on Rom 13).

63. Calvin, *Institutes*, IV.20.1.

64. Calvin, IV.20.1, 3.

65. Calvin, IV.20.4; Calvin, *Commentary on Romans*, 19:478, (on Rom 13:2).

of God's wisdom that kings reign."[66] Civil government is therefore an outcome of God's providential care of the world.

Calvin believed that government is necessary because of the presence of evil in the world. Without civil government, evil remains unrestrained.[67] Thus Calvin located the political in postlapsarian order of creation.[68] Chenevière observes that according to Calvin, "the State is charged with the duty of restraining the anarchic and egotistical tendencies of human nature let loose by sin, and in the final resort of preventing the strong from taking advantage of the weak."[69] Civil government also plays a positive role, which is to ensure cohesion and peace required to sustain human order.[70]

Calvin affirmed the doctrine of "universal grace" (common grace), through which God continues to sustain the entire world. Because of God's sustaining grace, human beings, even though they are in a state of sin, are still able to perceive "certain civic fair dealings and order" and "various countries [are] ruled by various kinds of government."[71] Since all human beings are image-bearers of God, they have the capacity to grasp creational truths and to order their lives. God has planted in them "some seed of political order" and therefore "no man is to be found who does not understand that every sort of human organization must be regulated by laws."[72] Thus according to Calvin, God governs the world through the various civil leaders such as kings and magistrates who are primarily "ministers of God" entrusted with "the business of serving [God] in their office."[73] In his commentary on 1 Peter 2:13, Calvin observed, "God the maker of the world has not left the

---

66. Calvin, *Institutes*, IV.20.7.

67. In Calvin, *Commentary on Romans*, 19:480 (Rom 13:3). Here, Calvin wrote, "for except the fury of the wicked be resisted, and the innocent be protected from their violence, all things would come to an entire confusion." In his *Commentary on First Peter*, 22:82 (1 Pet 2:14) Calvin asserted, "it is a singular blessing of God, that the wicked are not allowed to do what they like."

68. This is in contrast with later theologians such as Abraham Kuyper who located the State in prelapsarian order of creation. For Kuyper, the political was inevitable and would have evolved from the family (Yong, *In the Days of Caesar*, 70).

69. Chenevière, "Did Calvin Advocate Theocracy?," 113. See also Biéler, *Social Humanism of Calvin*, 43.

70. Calvin, *Institutes*, IV.20.4, 5, 9.

71. Calvin, II.2.12; IV.20.8.

72. Calvin, II.2.13.

73. Calvin, IV.20.4.

human race in a state of confusion, that they might live after the manner of beasts."[74] Thus God orders the world through the government.

Civil governance is a calling. Calvin affirmed this vocational nature of civil government when he claimed: "Accordingly, no one ought to doubt that civil authority is a calling, not only holy and lawful before God, but also the most sacred and by far the most honorable of all callings in the whole life of mortal men."[75] Magistrates "have a mandate from God, have been invested with divine authority, and are wholly God's representatives."[76] Thus they are accountable to God alone. In the same manner, those under authority are also accountable to God alone.[77] Because "The Lord has declared his approval of their offices," civil authority and duties are not profane responsibilities; neither are they "alien to a servant of God."[78] Magistrates act "as [God's] vicegerents;" they are also "deputies," and "vicars of God," and "their judgment seat is the throne of the living God."[79] Thus when magistrates judge, they are rendering judgments on behalf of God.[80] They should, therefore, not take their duty lightly. Instead, they should fulfil their duties with "great zeal for uprightness, for prudence, gentleness, self-control and . . . justice."[81] The fact that magistrates are acting on behalf of God is not meant to make them superior to anyone or to trample on people in exercise of their power, but is meant to motivate them to fear God and to render just judgments.[82]

Instead of being corrupt, proud, or unjust, civic leaders should "represent in themselves to [humanity] some image of divine providence, protection,

---

74. Calvin, *Commentary on First Peter*, 22:81.

75. Calvin, *Institutes*, IV.20.4.

76. Calvin, *Institutes*, IV.20.4.

77. Calvin, IV.20.4, 6, 23, 32; Calvin, *Commentary on Romans*, 19:481.

78. Calvin, *Institutes*, IV.20.6.

79. Calvin, IV.20.4, 6.

80. Calvin, IV.20.10. "[A]ll things [done by magistrates] are done on the authority of God."

81. Calvin, IV.20.6.

82. Calvin, IV.20.6.

How will they have the brazenness to admit injustice to their judgment seat, which they are told is the throne of the living God? How will they have the boldness to pronounce an unjust sentence, by that mouth which they know has been appointed an instrument of divine truth? With what conscience will they sign wicked decrees by that hand which they know has been appointed to record the acts of God.

goodness, benevolence, and justice."[83] Stevenson argues that according to Calvin (*Institutes*, IV.20.6), a government mirrors and channels God's paternal care to all under its charge when it "take[s] especial pains to enfold and protect those most vulnerable to exploitation. Imaging God means imaging God's communal construction work in the world; it means joining in the work of 'edification.'"[84] Thus those in power should model how God expresses his power in the world through Christ. Indeed, for Calvin, Paul speaks of the "higher" not of the "highest" powers.[85] The supreme power in the world is God alone.[86] Every leader, therefore, must not abuse power, but must serve as serving God, the giver of power.

Calvin's justification of the power of the magistrates came about through his response to Anabaptist's rejection of the civil authority set out in The Seven Articles of the Anabaptist Schleitheim Confession (1527).[87] According to Calvin, the radical Anabaptist view was a threat to human order and must be avoided.[88] Indeed, when Calvin wrote, the memories of the Peasants' Revolt (1524–1525) led by Thomas Müntzer, which led to the great social disorder and the loss of lives, were still fresh.[89] Also, the Münster Revolution

---

83. Calvin, *Institutes*, IV.20.6.

84. Stevenson, "Calvin and Political Issues," 176.

85. Calvin, *Commentary on Romans*, 19:478, (on Rom 13:2).

86. On this point, André Biéler, (*Social Humanism of Calvin*, 24), asserts:

At all times and in all circumstances the Christian has only one Lord and Master, and he is Jesus Christ. The partial obedience which the Christian owes to his human masters, to his parents, to his teachers, to his wife or husband, to his employers, to his military superiors, and to state officials is only a derived and conditional obedience which is at all times subordinated to the only absolute authority, that of Jesus Christ.

87. For more on the Anabaptist views on the State, see, Calvin, *Treatises Against the Anabaptists*; Balke, *Calvin and the Anabaptist Radicals*, 193–195, 260–265; Friedman, "Doctrine of the Two Kingdoms," 105–118; Schreiner, *Theater of His Glory*, 83–86; Boulton, *Life in God*, 16.

88. Calvin, *Institutes*, I.9.1; II.10.1; III.3.14; IV.1.13; IV.12.12; IV.16.10–32. These citations are acknowledge in Boer, *Political Grace*, 13.

89. Thomas Müntzer was a controversial figure. Following the example of Luther, Müntzer posted the Prague Manifesto on the door of a centrally located church in Prague on All Saints Day, 1 November, 1521. The document presented a radical view of scripture, clergy, church, and eschatology. His theology demanded an unrealistic and an ungodly expectation from the masses. To him, the objective of the Reformation was to set up a vibrant and renewed church of the apostles. He felt that Luther had not gone far enough to achieve these objectives. John Hus, the Czech leader of the reformation in Bohemia, burned at stake by the Council of Constance in 1415, inspired Müntzer. Meic Pearse (*Great Restoration,*

(1534–1535) was ongoing at the time Calvin wrote the Preface to Francis I of France, published in 1536.[90] The Anabaptists rejected the authority of the magistrates, forbade Christians from participating in warfare, and swearing an oath. Although Calvin affirmed that "God forbids all Christians from killing," nonetheless he believed this rule only applies to private citizens. Conversely, when a private individual is acting in some government capacity that obliges killing, that person must fulfil their role in wielding the sword.[91] In so doing one is acting on God's behalf and under God's authority. However, magistrates must not exercise the authority of the sword out of emotional impulse and out of private interests.[92] Similarly the government should be wary of engaging in war arbitrarily. War should be a last resort.[93]

Calvin also responded to the Anabaptists in his exegesis of Romans 13. Here, he argued, "There are indeed always some tumultuous spirits who believe that the kingdom of Christ cannot be sufficiently elevated, unless all earthly powers be abolished, and that they cannot enjoy the liberty given by him, except they shake off every yoke of human subjection."[94] Calvin repeated the attack against the Anabaptists in various sections of the *Institutes*.[95] According to Calvin, Anabaptists misconstrued the meaning of Christian

---

35) notes that Müntzer's social revolution theology was inspired by the so-called "Zwickau prophets" namely, Niklaus Storch, Markus Stubner, and Thomas Drechsel, who "taught the slaying of the godless—identified as the rich and anyone in authority—and the abolition of a professional clergy and of officially imposed religion (the godly have no need of them since were under the guidance of the Spirit)." Motivated by the radical prophets, Müntzer organized an army to revolt against the ruling class and the clergy. He envisioned the Bohemian church as a "mirror to the whole world," the starting place of the new militant church. Urging the Bohemian church to take up the sword and defend the gospel, and remove "the rotten apples" (those with power and wealth), Müntzer mobilized an "eternal League of God" to achieve this stated purpose. Consequently, his followers followed him to their death. On 15 May 1525, Müntzer's forces were massacred at Frankenhausen. Over six thousand peasants were killed. Müntzer was captured and beheaded. For more on Müntzer and the Peasants' Revolt, see Hans-Jürgen, "Mystic with the Hammer;" Matheson, "Thomas Müntzer's Idea"; Janz, *Reformation Reader*, 162–167; Müntzer, *Collected Works*; Baylor, "Thomas Müntzer's 'Prague Manifesto'"; Baylor, *Revelation and Revolution*; Gritsch, *Reformer without a Church*; Gritsch, *Thomas Müntzer*; Hillerbrand, *Fellowship of Discontent*; Boer, *Political Grace*, 13–18.

90. Boer, *Political Grace*, 6.

91. Calvin, *Institutes*, IV.1.10. See, Wolterstorff, *Mighty and the Almighty*, 76–77.

92. Calvin, *Institutes*, IV.20.12.

93. Calvin, IV.20.12.

94. Calvin, *Commentary on Romans*, 19:477, (on Rom 13:1).

95. Calvin, *Institutes*, III.3.14; III.19.15; IV.1.10, 28; IV.20.7.

freedom by their assumption that it means independence from any form of civil authority or involvement in civil affairs. Calvin believed that true freedom constrains human conscience to the rule of God for the purpose of carrying out acts of charity and care for the neighbor.[96] True freedom, therefore, does not mean abrogation of authority nor does it entail libertine behavior.[97] Christians must behave responsibly knowing they are accountable to God. The next section examines the purpose and role of government according to Calvin.

The Purpose and Role of Government

Civil government plays significant roles. First it ensures that basic needs of humanity are met (i.e. that people "breathe, eat, drink, and are kept warm"[98]). Second, government ensures freedom of worship. It protects churches from attack while at the same time maintaining peace and tranquility in the society.[99] This protection of churches is conditional. Only churches that meet the definition of a true church (preaching of God's Word and administration of sacraments), are legitimate churches that the State must protect.[100] At the same time not all forms of governments, for example oppressive tyrannical regimes or terrorist regimes, can claim divine legitimacy.[101] Only governments that operate in line with the rights and well-being of its citizens, especially the disenfranchised and the poor, at the same time protecting the freedom of religion, operate with God's blessing.

---

96. See Calvin, Institutes, III.19.12. "But it is the part of a godly man to realize that free power in outward matters has been given him in order that he may be the more ready for all the duties of love."

97. Calvin, *Institutes*, III.19.9.

98. Calvin, IV.20.3

99. Calvin, IV.20.3.

100. Stevenson, ("Calvin and Political Issues," 175) notes that for Calvin, not all kinds of preaching meets the definition of preaching and also not all kinds of administration of sacraments are legitimate. It is only the preaching that affirms the key elements of God's Word such as "God is one; Christ is God and the Son of God; our salvation rests in God's mercy; and the like" and "administration of sacraments means the public performance of the biblically mandated ceremonies which signify God's forgiving and redeeming grace (namely baptism and the Lord's Supper (IV.14.22)."

101. In his commentary on Romans 13:1 Calvin, (*Commentary on Romans*, 19:479) writes, "For though tyrannies and unjust exercise of power, as they are full of disorder, are not an ordained government; yet the right of government is ordained by God for the wellbeing of mankind."

Calvin envisioned government as protectors of the disenfranchised and the poor. In his commentary on Jeremiah 7:5–7 he argued that judges must "render everyone his right, redress injuries, pronounce what was just and right when any contention arose," but most importantly, they must protect "strangers and orphans and widows" because they are "subject to many wrongs, as though they were exposed as a prey."[102] Calvin believed that God instituted the government for the sake of the poor: "whenever a right government is referred to, God mentions strangers and orphans and widows" because they are easily marginalized in "the public administration of justice."[103] Real integrity, according to Calvin, is to protect the weak and the poor and to render justice "without favor or hatred."[104]

Calvin asserted that people have a right to deliberate on the best form of government that would suit their particular circumstances.[105] Out of the three forms of government prominent at the time (monarchy, aristocracy, and democracy), Calvin preferred a blend between aristocracy and democracy.[106] Yet Calvin recognized that the best form of government is that which allows for collegiality. "Therefore, men's fault or failing causes it to be safer and more bearable for a number to exercise government, so that they may help one another, teach and admonish one another; and, if one asserts himself unfairly, there may be a number of censors and masters to restrain his willfulness."[107] Calvin's choice of plural governance as contrasted with monarchy, is tied to his belief that human beings are fallen, and thus without checks and balances, rulers are prone to domination and abuse of power.[108] Thus rule by numbers allows for co-operation, mutual admonition, and restriction of self-aggrandizement. Thus this is the reason why

---

102. Calvin, *Commentary on Jeremiah*, 9:367, (on Jer 7:5–7).

103. Calvin.

104. Calvin.

105. Calvin, *Institutes*, IV.20.8.

106. Calvin, IV.20.8. Hunt, ("Calvin's Theory," 64) asserts that Calvin's own experiences under the monarchical leader, Henry II in France and by Mary in England, persuaded him that monarchy is not the best form of government. Also, Calvin's "jealousy for the honour of God made him regard monarchial government as derogatory to the divine sovereignty."

107. Calvin, *Institutes*, IV.20.8.

108. "The fall from kingdom to tyranny is easy; but it is not much more difficult to fall from the rule of the best men to the faction of a few; yet it is easiest of all to fall from popular rule to sedition." (Calvin, *Institutes*, IV.20.8).

Calvin made use of the Little Council to hold meetings for the purposes of criticism and self-evaluation.[109]

Calvin saw in Micah 5:5 a divine mandate for the popular elections of rulers.[110] On this text, Calvin commented, "Hence he says, that though Assur should come to our land, and break through with such force and violence that we could not drive him out, we shall yet set up for ourselves shepherds and princes against him."[111] Then Calvin added, "In this especially consists the best condition of the people, when they can choose, by common consent, their own shepherds: for when any one by force usurps the supreme power; it is tyranny; and when men become kings by hereditary right, it seems not consistent with liberty."[112] Calvin took the word "shepherd" to mean political rulers. Thus it is clear that Calvin favored plural governance and one that comes about through voting and not through revolt. However, Calvin also believed that leaders must ascertain their power especially when people seek to revolt against authority. Even though people may choose their leaders, it is God who mandates civil governance and thus citizens must always honor those in leadership.[113] The next section examines Calvin's view on the duties of citizens towards civil authority.

Duties of Citizens towards Civil Authority

Citizens have two fundamental duties towards civil authority according to Calvin. The first is to respect the various civil officers. The reason for this respect is because the various officers are God's servants and the duties they do are not profane but holy "ministries." The officers are to be respected "as God-ordained officials." The citizens should hold rulers in high esteem and not see them as "necessary evil" because rulers are God's servants. Politics,

---

109. McNeil, "Introduction of Calvin's *Institutes (1559),*" 1493 (commenting on *Institutes,* IV.20.8).

110. Micah 5:5 says, "When the Assyrian shall come into our land, and when he shall tread in our palaces, then we shall raise [up] against him[, or on him,] seven shepherds, and eight principal men," (KJV).

111. Calvin, *Twelve Minor Prophets*, XIV:308, (on Mic 5:5).

112. Calvin, XIV:309–310, (on Mic 5:5).

113. Calvin, (*Twelve Minor Prophets*, XIV:310) comments, "When shall then set up for ourselves princes, says the Prophet; that is, the Lord will not only give breathing time to his Church, and will also cause that she may set up a fixed and a well-ordained government, and that by the common consent of all." Thus it is God who chooses the leaders through the process of popular elections.

for Calvin, is not a dirty enterprise, but a holy calling and ministry.[114] The second duty of a citizen is to obey rulers not on account of the rulers' own personality but on the basis of God's anointing on them. Thus Calvin rejected popular resistance against civil government because the varieties of governors and governments are instituted by God for the governance of people, and to resist them is to resist God.[115] "For if it seemed good to [God] to set kings over kingdoms, senates or municipal officers over free cities, it is our duty to show ourselves compliant and obedient to whomever he sets over the places where we live."[116] Calvin believed that a private citizen must not attempt to seize power from appointed rulers, for to do so is to induce anarchy.[117]

Calvin argued that the citizens show their obedience to those in power through "paying taxes, or by undertaking public offices and burdens, which pertain to the common defense, or by executing any other commands of theirs."[118] He also noted that even though those in authority may use the revenues collected "to meet the public expenses of their office" and "for the magnificence of their household," in accord "with the dignity of the authority they exercise," they are nonetheless prohibited from abusing their power and from overcharging and overburdening their citizens with taxes.[119] Calvin affirmed that the revenues collected from citizens "are not so much [the princes'] private chests as the treasuries of the entire people . . . which cannot be squandered or despoiled without manifest injustice."[120] Thus the leaders must be accountable in how they use public resources.

Calvin was careful to argue that obedience is due to both the just and the unjust magistrate except when the magistrate usurps God's divine authority.[121]

---

114. Bradstock, "Reformation," 73.

115. Calvin, *Institutes*, IV.20.23.

116. Calvin, IV.20.8.

117. Calvin, *Commentary on Romans*, 19:482.

118. Calvin, *Institutes*, IV.20.23.

119. Calvin, IV.20.12, 13.

120. Calvin, IV.20.13.

121. Calvin, IV.20.25, 2, 29, 31. In his *Commentary on First Peter*, 22:82–83, Calvin asserts:

Were any one again to object and say, that we ought not to obey princes who, as far as they can, pervert the holy ordinance of God, and thus become savage wild beasts, while magistrates ought to bear the image of God. My reply is this, that

Christian citizens must obey civil authority, even be willing to suffer under their leadership, as long as obedience to earthly rulers does not become disobedience to God the King of kings.[122] In his *Lectures on Daniel* (6:22), Calvin clarified why Christians should disobey unjust rulers who forbid the worship of God or lead people away from God: "[W]hen princes forbid the service and worship of God, when they command their subjects to pollute themselves with idolatry and want them to consent to and participate in all the abominations that are contrary to the service of God, they are not worthy to be regarded as princes or to have authority attributed to them."[123] Indeed Calvin observed that the reason he left France was because the leaders there curtailed "the truth of God, pure religion, and the doctrine of eternal salvation."[124] Thus by leaving, Calvin showed that one way of opposing unjust rulers is to seek refuge in a different country.[125]

In his commentary on Acts (5:29), Calvin repeated the same exception, "If a king, ruler, or magistrate, become so lofty that he diminishes the honor and authority of God, he becomes a mere man."[126] Even though private

---

government established by God ought to be so highly valued by us, as to honour even tyrants when in power . . . some kind of government, however deformed and corrupt it may be, is still better and more beneficial than anarchy.

122. As to willingness to suffer instead of rebelling against civil power, see *Institutes*, IV.20.31. As to the exception to the rule of obedience, see *Institutes*, IV.20.32. In his *Commentary on First Peter*, 22:86 (1 Pet 2:18), Calvin also speaks about obedience to masters. "For subjection due to men is not to be so far extended as to lessen the authority of God. Then servant are to be subjects to their masters, only as far as God permits, or as far as the altars, as they say." In this text, Calvin asserts that masters are accountable to God in how they treat their servants. The servants, however, must always obey their masters although Calvin admits that servants may be unfairly treated by their masters. Servants must seek recourse in God in such cases.

123. As cited in Wolterstorff, *Mighty and the Almighty*, 74.

124. Calvin, *On God and Political Duty*, 88.

125. The fact that Calvin thrived despite being away from his home country shows that exile affords an opportunity for Christians to question traditional assumptions about nationalism, allegiance to territorial boundaries, land, and so forth. As Daniel L. Smith-Christopher, (*Biblical Theology of Exile*, 8) argues, "exilic theology" or "diasporic theology," "challenges the virtual capitulation to the normative status of nationalism as the only viable context for Christian theology and Christian social existence." Thus Christians can still be faithful to God despite being dispossessed of their lands and countries. Several scholars have emphasized the significance of the exile/diasporic paradigm for informing or shaping Christian theology and practice. These scholars include, Beach, *Church in Exile*; Brueggemann, *Cadences of Home*; Brueggemann, *Deep Memory*; Frost, *Exiles*.

126. Wolterstorff, *Mighty and the Almighty*, 74.

individuals must always obey the rulers, Calvin believed that magistrates, by virtue of their office as "constitutional defenders of the people's freedom," have a right to inhibit monarchical absolutism or tyranny.[127] As example to the magistrates resisting evil rulers, Calvin cited the case of the ephors against the Spartan kings, the tribunes of the people against the Roman consuls, and the demarchs against the senate of the Athenians.[128] Calvin's letter to Francis I of France, urging him to be tolerant to Protestant Christians undergoing persecution within his jurisdiction, shows that Calvin believed that all rulers are not above the law and are thus subject to criticism from the standpoint of scriptural faith.[129]

Andrew Bradstock notes that Calvin's followers in subsequent centuries, received with enthusiasm, Calvin's conditional, albeit reluctant, authorization to resist or remove unjust rulers.[130] Calvin's dislike of absolute monarchy inspired Calvin's later followers to resist tyrannical authority. Where the monarchs were perceived to be unfair or unjust to their subjects, they were resisted, even overthrown, basing such actions on the scriptural grounds that Calvin prescribed. Thus the Wars of Religion was spearheaded by a Calvinist group; Calvinists, most notably, John Knox, were responsible for bringing the Reformation to Scotland despite opposition from a Catholic queen, and Oliver Cromwell, a puritan political leader who gained inspiration from Calvin's teachings, was responsible for deposing Charles I in 1649.[131] Thus rather than motivating aloofness and quietism, Calvin's sociopolitical thoughts inspired active participation in the affairs of the State. The next section retrieves the usefulness and limitations of Calvin's sociopolitical thought for the Kenyan context.

---

127. Calvin, *Institutes*, IV.20.31.
128. Calvin, IV.20.31.
129. McNeil, "Introduction," x.
130. Bradstock, "Reformation," 74–75.
131. Bradstock, 74–75.

Insights and Limitations of Calvin's Political Theology for the Kenyan Context

The following section retrieves insights and limitations of Calvin's political theology for the Kenyan context. The book proposes four insights from Calvin's political theology: inspiration for sociopolitical engagement, the basis for a prophetic critique of ethnic-based politics, basis for a prophetic critique of politics as eating, and inspiration for charity, compassion, and an ethic of work. The section begins with how Calvin's politics inspires sociopolitical engagement.

Inspiration for Sociopolitical Engagement

Wolterstorff notes that original Calvinism inspired sociopolitical engagement. He writes, "The emergence of original Calvinism represented a fundamental alteration in Christian sensibility, from the vision and practice of turning away from the social world in order to seek a closer union with God to the vision and practice of working to reform the social world in obedience to God."[132] Wolterstorff calls this kind of engagement "world-formative Christianity" contrasted with "avertive Christianity."[133] However, the active social engagement stifled after the First World War.

Hannah Kinoti, a Kenyan theologian, argues in her article titled "Evangelical Women and Politics in Africa" that, until the Lausanne conference in 1974, evangelicals around the world embraced an aloof posture in regard to social issues.[134] This lack of concern, according to her, was acute in Africa. She writes, "If evangelicals in general had mislaid their social conscience temporarily, African evangelicals had been non-starters. Whereas 18th century revivals had resulted in socio-political action in the West, revivals in Africa have stifled that spirit."[135] Drawing on the analysis of John Stott's *Issues Facing Christians Today* (1984), Kinoti attributes this non-involvement on several issues, which include the church's preoccupation with other-worldly concerns, overreaction against liberalism and the "social gospel" movement both assumed to be a danger to orthodox theology, and

---

132. Wolterstorff, *Until Justice*, 11.
133. Wolterstorff, 3.
134. Kinoti, "Evangelical Women and Politics," 7.
135. Kinoti, 7.

disenchantment on the past reform movements especially considering the damaging effects of the First World War.[136]

Kinoti argues that politics in Africa is depicted as a "worldly" affair, a dirty game, and Christians, especially the clergy, are told to stay away from it especially when they criticize the government.[137] Chapter 3 of this book shows explicitly that the clergy of mainline churches (i.e. Catholic, Presbyterian, Methodist, and Anglican), under the leadership of the NCCK, prior to multipartyism in Kenya, even when criticized or threatened, did not cede their ground. They continued to critique the State and to hold it accountable. Some clergymen were physically abused. Bishop Alexander Muge was assassinated. However, evangelicals, under the leadership of the Evangelical Fellowship of Kenya, sided with the government of the day.

Rather than staying away from political issues, as Ronald Sider shows in *The Scandal of Evangelical Politics*, Christians must be at the forefront of sociopolitical engagement.[138] Sider advocates for prayer, renewing and transforming culture, educating Christians to think biblically and wisely about politics, fostering a spirit of dialogue and civility in the congregation, educating the public on specific political issues, lobbying elected officials, promoting the election of specific candidates, and running for political office. As Calvin shows, these political issues that Sider mentions are not profane. The Kenyan clergy, therefore, should refuse to leave politics to the politicians.[139]

---

136. Kinoti, 7. See also Noelliste, "Exploring the Usefulness," 232.

137. Kinoti, "Evangelical Women and Politics," 8.

138. Sider, *Scandal of Evangelical Politics*.

139. A word of clarification on this statement is necessary. Historically, the Kenyan clergy are often told to leave politics to politicians (see chapter 7). What this means for the Kenyan politician is that the clergy must not criticize politicians but must focus on preaching God's Word. What Kenyan politicians fail to see is that God's Word speaks against injustice, corruption, dehumanization of people, and all other social ills. Thus, for the clergy to be true to their calling, they must speak the whole truth, which includes speaking truth to power. Thus, "not leaving politics to politicians" is not about campaigning for a particular candidate, promoting a specific political party or opinion, or using the authority of the office of pastor to win votes for oneself or for someone else. Pastors must be non-partisan especially when they speak from the authority of their office. But being non-partisan does not mean not speaking against social injustice or failing to express the Christian perspective on some social issues for example torture, abortion, the use of ethnicity to win votes, etc. Pastors must speak on issues that matter to the congregation. The major point of contention, especially in Kenya, is whether it is appropriate for pastors to join or lead a protest. Chapter 3 shows that several

Another issue in Calvin's political thought that aids the church in Kenya in its political endeavors is the value attached to systemic change. As Dieumème argues, Calvin believed that social action must go beyond mere social services if the needed social provision was to be addressed once and for all. Social action must embrace within its domain structural and corporate change.[140] Thus Calvin focused not only on temporary alleviation of needs, but on the elimination of the root causes. Calvin ensured that the Genevan church, through the ministry of deacons, cooperated with the city to serve the needs of the people and to effect institutional changes that would enhance better lives for the Genevan citizens and the refugees living there.[141] Calvin himself ensured the refugees were provided for, he was active in legislative reforms, was at the forefront of hospital reforms, and was instrumental in starting the Geneva Academy. Calvin reminds the clergy on the necessity of being students, not only of God's Word but of God's world. The clergy must be well-informed of current affairs and political issues. They must educate themselves and their congregations of responsible ways to engage politically without ceding their faithfulness to God's word. Thus Bishop Gitari's initiative of training the Anglican clergy in rural and urban development is an example of such pedagogical initiative. Several Bible colleges in Kenya are now teaching courses in politics, governance, development, and peace and conflict studies.[142]

---

clergy participated in street protests during the quest for multipartyism. It might have been appropriate at the time to participate in such protests but this is a very divisive issue especially in a culture that values public decorum for those who hold public offices (street protest in Kenya tend to become chaotic) and thus, contemporary clergy must weigh if it is proper for pastors to do so. Also, as shown in chapter 3, one of the reasons the church in Kenya lost its prophetic voice after 2002, is because some clergy, especially those who held important offices like the Secretary General of the NCCK, became coopted by the government. Others sought elective positions in governments while still serving as pastors (a few were bishops). This move was very detrimental to the church. I do not support the view that a pastor can run for political office while still serving full-time as a pastor.

140. Noelliste, "Exploring the Usefulness," 233.

141. Lee, "Calvin's Ministry in Geneva," 209–211.

142. When I went to Scott Theological College as a student from 2001–2005, these courses were not taught. I only took a course in Christian leadership. We were not prepared to tackle the various sociopolitical issues we were later to encounter in ministry.

Basis for a Prophetic Critique of Ethnic-Based Politics

Calvin's political theology helps critique the ethnicization of politics in Kenya. Ethnic-based politics is a reality in Kenya's scene. For many people, a politician's ascent to power means the entire tribe ascends to power. Ethnicization of politics is connected to corruption because for many politicians, the goal is to get rich quickly so that they can use the funds to cement their grasp on their ethnic communities. Consequently, leaders transfer their allegiance from nation to ethnic community.[143] The ethnic community pays back through allegiance to the politician, for example, by tolerating the politician's corruption. John Githongo, a former Permanent Secretary in the Office of the President in charge of Governance and Ethics, before being forced into exile when he revealed corrupt practices in the Kenyan Government, succinctly captures this mentality when he writes that for many Kenyans, "Corruption by someone of my ethnicity is tolerable so long as she or he shares it with me and our kith and kin."[144] Though Kenya is constitutionally, a multiparty democracy, ethnocracy dominates political governance.[145] Ethnocracy is a type of political governance in which the State machinery is arrogated by a particular ethnic community (or communities) to further their own interests, power, and resources at the expense of others. Accordingly, the ethnic community in power gets preferential treatment in hiring, issuance of government grants and scholarships, land title deeds, allocation of public funds, registration of businesses, and so on.[146]

Calvin's political theology speaks to the problem of ethnicization of politics through its emphasis on service to all humanity regardless of affiliations. Leaders must serve the interests of all people, not just their ethnic

---

143. Njogu, ("Prologue to Ethnic Diversity," xii) rightly observes, "Despite the fact that common citizenship as enshrined in nationalism assumes that all citizens are equal in the eyes of the State, the State in most Africa has tended to promote, protect or obstruct and frustrate ethnic interests through patronage."

144. Githongo, "Crossroads in the Fight," 7.

145. I agree with John Lonsdale, ("Moral and Political Argument," 91) that Kenya has the appearance of a democracy but it is not. Lonsdale writes, "Kenya's political culture is not democratic. It does, however, exhibit many of democracy's characteristics. It is privately grasping, publicly censorious, alert to the merest whisper of shifts in the bargains of power, resentful—perhaps envious—of privilege and its corruptions, but scarcely, as yet, fired and disciplined by the doctrine and practice of citizen equality."

146. Wamwere, *Towards Genocide*, 216–220.

communities. They must serve all without favor or hatred. Calvin's choice of plural form of governance rather than monarchy shows that Calvin would critique any form of governance that elevates a particular tribal leader to a status of a kingpin. Calvin believed that collegiality in leadership ensures checks and balances thus curtailing domination and abuse of power. Certainly, Calvin critiqued the use of money to buy or acquire power. For Calvin, leaders should be responsible to God and humanity in how they use their resources. This point is elaborated below.

Basis for a Prophetic Critique of Politics as Eating

Kenyan politicians and voters see politics as an opportunity to "eat" the "national cake."[147] President Uhuru Kenyatta recently re-affirmed the ideology of "eating" in a speech delivered during the funeral of a prominent Kenyan politician. Speaking in Swahili, the president told the Opposition team led by Raila Odinga, *Kumeza mate si kula nyama. Sasa nyinyi endeleeni kumezea mate, sisi tutaendelea kula nyama* ("Salivating does not mean you have eaten meat. Continue salivating as we eat meat").[148] The president was responding to Raila's criticism of the Jubilee Government. Arguably, the president's statement can be interpreted in many ways, but the common interpretation is that the opposition are not in power so they should let those in power enjoy "eating" in peace. Certainly, the president was not condoning corruption but his assumption that politics is "eating" is problematic. If there is such a thing as "eating the national cake," then it is all the Kenyan people who should eat, not just a select few.

Emmanuel Katongole observes that the term "corruption" does not capture very well the ideology of "eating the national cake" because the term "corruption," "often reflects a mere failure to approximate the rational-legal model of authority – a short-coming that might be addressed through the right ethical principles and legal safeguards."[149] However,

> Within this politics of the state as a "national cake" (to be shared), corruption is just another form of "eating." Even when,

---

147. On the ideology of "eating from the national cake," see, Tostensen et al., *Kenya's Hobbled Democracy*, 11; Sesi, "Ethnic Conflicts in Africa," 134; Wrong, *Our Turn to Eat.*

148. Citizen TV, "President Uhuru Kenyatta's Speech."

149. Katongole, *Sacrifice of Africa*, 80.

as happens every so often, the government answers to its own rhetoric of "anti-corruption" measures and sets up an anti-corruption unit, this too simply becomes another means of "eating." Those in charge of the "anti-corruption" committee are compensated with large stipends and allowances, simply to come up with a bogus report, which the government never does anything about. Thus the anti-corruption effort becomes just another vehicle of corruption.[150]

As Katongole asserts, the existence of an anti-corruption agency does not necessarily mean the government is willing to combat corruption. In Kenya, for example, although the major cases of corruption such as the Goldenberg Scandal; the Anglo-leasing Scandal; the Tokyo Embassy Property Purchase Scandal; the National Youth Service (NYS) Scandal; the National Health Insurance Fund (NHIF) Scandal; Standard Gauge Railway Tendering Scandal, and more recently, Afya House Scandal, among so many other cases, have been investigated or are currently being investigated by the Ethics and Anti-corruption Commission (EAC) – previously known as Kenya Anti-corruption Commission (KACC) – no influential person has been charged. The EAC, which does not have prosecution powers, has submitted various names to the Director of Public Prosecutions, but nothing substantial has happened.

The worldview popularly known as *mali ya umma*, a concept which literally means "public property" in Swahili, has helped perpetuate the ideology of "eating." *Mali ya umma* is the ideology that public property is up for grabs. In other words, *mali ya umma* is the ideology of "pilfering the public" that Jacqueline Klopp talks about in her article about land grabbing in Kenya.[151] According to Klopp, the problem of misuse of public property, especially land, in Kenya, dates back to the colonial era whereby colonialists grabbed the most fertile land for themselves rendering thousands of Africans poor.[152] Later on, when Kenya gained independence, Kenyan elites allegedly grabbed the most fertile parcels of land for themselves. For example, the families of

---

150. Katongole, 81.
151. Klopp, "Pilfering the Public."
152. Klopp, 15.

Kenyatta (Kenya's first president) and Moi (second president) are the richest land owners in Kenya. The closer one is to these families, the wealthier they become.

Mali ya umma informs the plundering of government coffers and vandalism of public property in Kenya. Because of this belief, State, civic, and other institutional officers amass wealth for themselves. It is surprising that Kenyans reward the corrupt by electing them to office.[153] Upon election, Kenyan leaders, and indeed most African leaders, accumulate wealth for themselves.[154] Patrick Lumumba, the former chairman of the Kenya Anti-Corruption Commission, offers a first-hand experience of corruption in Kenya with the following words written after his failure to win the Kamukunji parliamentary elections:

> As I traversed my Kamukunji Constituency and occasionally made forays in other constituencies in Coast, Western, Nairobi, Rift Valley, Central, Eastern, and Nyanza provinces I saw something that appears to be a national culture; the love for money which is sometimes demanded by menaces. I witnessed children, barely seven years, middle aged women, old men and women crying for money. In Western Province they called it *"shindu shititi"* (something small). In Central Province they asked for *"kindu kinini"* (something small), in Coast Province they asked for *"kitu kidogo"* (something small) . . . in some churches they called it *"special offerings,"* in some Muslim institutions they called it *"amana"* (gift). Kenyans desire to reap what they have not sown. Politicians capitalize on this

---

153. Lumumba, (*Call for Hygiene*, 45–46) explains:

If one cares to look at the recent history of many of the contestants in the 2007 elections (some of whom are now "Honourable" Members of Parliament), he will find lawyers who had been struck off the Roll of Advocates for embezzling clients' money, Engineers whose claim to fame is dubious performance of contracts, former civil servants whose businesses defy logic and many other individuals who cannot pass the integrity test, however low the bar is set. The truth is that the man or woman of integrity has the chance of a snowball in hell in the furnace that is the ethnicized and corruption riddled Kenyan politics.

154. Miller and Allen, (*Against all Hope*, 28), captures this extravagance when they write that "according to estimates from the United Nations Economic Commission, approximately U.S. $148 billion dollars is in secret bank accounts of African rulers. This represents about half of the $300 billion that Africa as a whole owes its foreign creditors."

cultural menace to buy votes. Thus Kenyans get the leaders they deserve.[155]

Indeed as Lumumba observes, corruption permeates every sector of the Kenyan economy. During an interview with a Dutch newspaper, NRC Handelsblad, former Chief Justice and President of the Supreme Court, Willy Mutunga, said that Kenya has become "a bandit economy" held captive by "mafia-like" cartels run by political bosses and corrupt business people.[156] During a speech for a governance and accountability conference held at State House Nairobi, on 18 October 2016, President Kenyatta seemed to acknowledge that Kenya is under the grip of corrupt cartels. The president said with frustration, "Corruption is frustrating me. The pressure is on me to do something about corruption but my hands are tied."[157] Thus theology must speak to the ideology of politics as eating.

Calvin's political theology speaks to the reality of corruption in Kenya. Wolterstorff asserts, "Calvin vigorously and unflinchingly denounced corruption in the church, tyranny in the polity, and inequitable wealth in the economy."[158] In his sermon on the Eighth Commandment, "you shall not steal" (Exod 20:15; Lev 19:11), Calvin emphasized God's judgment on those who steal.[159] To Calvin, God sees the intentions of the heart and defends the cause of the poor and the oppressed. Quoting Isaiah 1:23 ("Your rulers are rebels, companions of thieves; they all love bribes and chase after gifts. They do not defend the cause of the fatherless; the widow's case does not come before them"), Calvin condemned those who steal thinking no one is watching them; "it is imperative then that we case our eyes down, realizing that we shall benefit nothing, even though our thefts are excusable in the world's eyes, whether we cover or falsify them."[160] Elsewhere, Calvin argued that thieves, those who profit from the loss of others, and those who accrue

---

155. Lumumba, *Call for Hygiene*, 46.

156. Lindijer, "Kenya Has Become"; Lindijer, "Dit is de man die oorlog voert tegen de Afrikaanse Al Capones."

157. NTV Kenya, "Uhuru Rebukes Agencies."

158. Wolterstorff, *Hearing the Call*, 128.

159. Calvin, *Sermons on the Ten Commandments*, 187.

160. Calvin, 187.

wealth by illegal means will answer to God.[161] God is watching and will one day vindicate the oppressed.

Calvin affirmed that material possessions are a result of God's sovereign and distributive will. In other words, God is the giver of property. Human beings are stewards responsible to God. Even political leaders are accountable to God. Leaders must acquire power and property the right way. For Calvin, work is the only legitimate way of acquiring money and property.[162] Calvin also argued that management of earthly resources is a demonstration of Christian piety. Pious people embrace different priorities in life. They do not let wealth master their lives. They master wealth. Calvin argued that Christians should practice the "Saint Paul's Rule," which is "to learn how to be rich and poor, hungry and thirsty, as well as enjoy abundance."[163] Enjoyment of earthly wealth should go hand in hand with sobriety and charity.[164] Charity means treating others with respect. "This, then, is the rule of charity that everyone's rights should be safely preserved, and that none should do to another what he would not have done to himself."[165] Charity and compassion should be apparent in the treatment of the poor and the oppressed in the society.

Related to enjoyment, is Calvin's rejection of the Stoic and Augustinian ideal of apathy, which called for detachment from the world's concerns.[166] The Stoics warned against attachment to earthly wealth as well as open expression of grief. They detested human vulnerability. Calvin believed that the

---

161. Calvin, *Commentaries on the Four Last Books*, III:114, (on Deut 24:15).

162. Biéler, *Social Humanism of Calvin*, 43.

163. Calvin, *Sermons on the Ten Commandments*, 193.

164. Calvin, 199.

165. Calvin, *Commentaries on the Four Last Books*, III:110, (on Deut 20:15)

166. Calvin, *Institutes*, III.8.9, 11. Wolterstorff, (*Hearing the Call*, 119–122) argues that Augustine's apathy in the face of suffering shaped medieval theology and response to suffering. For Augustine and his predecessors, to be human is to be in search of happiness. Augustine followed the Platonic tradition in his belief that "one's love, one's *eros*, is the fundamental determinant of one's happiness . . . The cure is to detach one's love from such objects and to attach it to something immutable and indestructible. For Augustine, the only candidate was God." (116). Wolterstorff argues that according to Augustine, humans should "struggle to eliminate all attachments to things such that the disappearance or alteration of these things would cause us grief" (128). Calvin's theology was radically different from Augustine's. "We should not try to alter our created nature; we should honor it. To indignity, death, injustice, and a multitude of other evils in this life, grief is not only the normal but the appropriate response" (128).

Stoics set an ideal impossible for humans to attain because humans are beset by various problems and challenges and cannot be totally free from pain.[167] Calvin buttressed his criticism of the Stoic idealism through emphasizing Christ's suffering and response to it: "Our Lord and Master . . . groaned and wept both over his own and other's misfortunes. And he taught his disciples in the same way: 'The world,' he says, 'will rejoice; but you will be sorrowful and will weep' (John 16:20)."[168] Wolterstorff argues that the proper response to grief and suffering, according to Calvin, is to cultivate "the discipline of becoming patient in our suffering."[169] According to Calvin, Christ is the perfect exemplar of patient endurance in the face of suffering. Patience does not mean passive acceptance of evil but confronting evil through the gospel.[170] Indeed, Calvin himself responded to the injustices prevalent in Geneva at the time of his ministry by courageously condemning injustice and instituting various means of enabling human flourishing.

Yet Calvin's political theology has serious limitations. As already argued, his emphasis on the soul as the primary seat of the image of God and that the body was a prison house of the soul, is problematic for it results in an anthropology that demeans the body and consequently a spirituality that neglects embodiment.[171] In terms of his personality, Calvin is often viewed as an autocratic dictator.[172] Although social historians have dispelled this perception it still has potential to impede the reception of Calvin's views especially in Africa where people are often ruled by authoritarian leaders.[173]

---

167. Calvin, *Institutes*, III.8.10.

168. Calvin, *Institutes*, III.8.9 quoted in Wolterstorff, *Hearing the Call*, 121.

169. Wolterstorff, *Hearing the Call*, 121.

170. Wolterstorff, (*Hearing the Call*, 130) notes,

Calvinist patience, then, is the paradoxical, unstable combination of grieving over the pain and deprivation that come one's way as one lives a life incorporating struggle for the gospel and for justice, of thankfully allowing one's suffering to contribute to the "making" of one's soul, and of taking joy from being united through one's suffering more firmly with the Christ who cried out upon the cross and the God who is wounded by the world's wounds.

171. See chapter 4.

172. See chapter 4 section titled "A Reconstruction Theologian or a Dictator?."

173. For publications that dispel the view that Calvin was a tyrant, see McGrath, *Life of John Calvin*, 108–109; Monter, "Daily Life and the Reformed," 246; Benoit, "Pastoral Care," 65–66; Larson, *Calvin's Doctrine*, 4–5. These scholars argue that Calvin had no power in civil matters. Calvin was a pastor who was concerned about church order and discipline and had

Furthermore, when people hear Calvin, they think about the doctrine of double predestination and the Dutch Reformed Church and apartheid in South Africa. The Dutch Boers used Calvin's theology of predestination to segregate against the black race. Furthermore, as Noelliste argues, Calvin's theo-centric political theology may be used to "to justify the status quo, stem the tide of change, and impede the pursuit of freedom."[174] Noelliste cites several factors in Calvin's political theology. Foremost, Calvin's grounding of political legitimacy on God alone can be used to support politician's claim to political privilege and create a feeling of inviolability. Also, Calvin's claim that political powers are accountable to God alone can easily lead to political neglect and disregard of duty. Indeed, some politicians claim that God is the only one who can remove them from power. Furthermore, Calvin's emphasis that private citizens must always obey civil authority except in cases where the authorities usurp divine authority may easily lead to lack of political engagement. Finally, Calvin's granting of political legitimacy to any form of government regardless of how it came about, can destabilize the democratic process, encourage the employment of illegitimate means to acquire power, and threaten social harmony.[175]

However, while these points impede the applicability of Calvin's political thought, they also have a positive effect. First, Calvin's grounding of all civil authority on God liberates the political from the stigma of politics as inherently unholy and by so doing makes politics a vocation that Christians can pursue.[176] As Kinoti mentions, politics among many Christians in Kenya, is regarded as unholy and Christians are encouraged to stay away from it.[177] Some Christians heed the advice thus staying away from politics. Second, Calvin's emphasis on the purpose and roles of civil government shows that

---

a desire to reform Geneva through God's Word. Furthermore, social historians emphasize the roles of the Company of Pastors, the Consistory, and the Small Council in Geneva. Particularly, they emphasize that the Small Council alone had the power to decide on civil matters. Calvin was an employee of the Council and did not have authority on civil matters. Even the execution of Michael Servetus was decided solely by the Small Council, not Calvin.

174. Noelliste, "Exploring the Usefulness," 234.

175. Noelliste, 235.

176. Noelliste, 235.

177. Kinoti, "Evangelical Women and Politics," 8.

politics should serve the public, not private gain.[178] Third, Calvin's subordination of all temporal authority on God alone de-sacralizes power.

Kwame Bediako argues in his article titled, "De-sacralization and Democratization," that some African politicians absolutize political power basing on traditional ancestor-veneration frame of reference thus claiming "mystical credentials."[179] De Gruchy offers a similar sentiment when he offers a connection between the forms of governance practiced in pre-colonial African communities and those of today. He notes that pre-colonial African communities employed a type of political tradition, which was "'organically structured' akin to the organic type of society which characterized medieval Christendom."[180] He adds, "Organic societies are not democratic, but hierarchical, and authority is often sacralized. Traditionally, chiefs were imbued with transcendent legitimacy and made whatever important decisions were necessary."[181] Whereas Africans relished "a tradition of participation and consultation without which rulers had little legitimacy," de Gruchy adds, "many societies did not always function with such procedures," but were in fact, "oppressive, dictatorial, patriarchal, and, in some instances, imperialistic."[182] De Gruchy makes the connection, as Bediako does, between the past traditional African society with its sacralized notion of power and the modern African tendency towards one-party states and dictatorships.[183] He observes that a characteristic of organic societies with a sacralized notion of authority is that they are oftentimes intolerant to dissent and plurality.[184] The way forward, then, for African Christianity is, according to de Gruchy, to assist African communities to become democratic, through "retrieving communal participation, challenging hierarchical domination, affirming community, stressing the importance of interpersonal relations rather than possessive individualism, and promoting an integrative spirituality."[185]

---

178. Noelliste, "Exploring the Usefulness," 235.

179. Bediako, "De-sacralization and Democratization," 7.

180. de Gruchy, *Christianity and Democracy*, 189.

181. de Gruchy, 189–190.

182. de Gruchy, 190.

183. de Gruchy, 190.

184. de Gruchy, 190.

185. de Gruchy, 191.

Similarly, Bediako argues that "if African politics in the future is to be able to integrate a wider political pluralism and to manifest a greater tolerance of dissent," then it must embrace a de-sacralizing view of power rooted in the kingdom of God to which all the kingdoms of the world must submit.[186] According to Bediako all political power is derivative and delegated from God. Thus political power cannot be used impulsively without account-ability.[187] Bediako then adds, "The recognition that power truly belongs to God, rooted in the Christian theology of power as non-dominating, liberates politicians and rulers to be humans among fellow-humans, and ennobles politics and the business of government into the business of God and the service of God in the service of fellow-humans."[188] Although Bediako does not reference Calvin or neo-Calvinist scholars such as Abraham Kuyper, he is in agreement that power should be subjected to prophetic critique and must at all times be subordinated to the only absolute authority, Jesus Christ.

However, in a pluralistic society like Kenya what it means to subject power and culture to the Lordship of Christ is that this happens mainly through gentle persuasion rather than force. This posture is not just necessary because of pluralism. It is necessary because of the doctrine of sin and how God deals with his rebellious creatures. Andrew Walls argues that discipling a nation is a process that takes time and "involves Christ's entry into the nation's thought, the patterns of relationship within that nation, the way the society hangs together, the way decisions are made."[189] Therefore, as Richard J. Mouw argues, Abraham Kuyper's assertion (derived from Calvin's thought) that "There is no square inch of the entire creation about which Jesus Christ does not cry out, 'This is mine! This belongs to me!'" should not be construed to mean Christians should embrace a triumphalist spirit that believes "since Christ owns all those square inches of the creation, our mandate as Christians is to go forth and conquer them in his name!"[190] Rather, Christians must patiently participate in Christ's suffering. Although Christ has conquered sin,

---

186. Bediako, "De-sacralization and Democratization," 8.
187. Bediako, 9.
188. Bediako, 10.
189. Walls, *Missionary Movement*, 51.
190. Mouw, *Uncommon Decency*, 147–148.

many of those square inches are presently occupied by people with stinking, rotting flesh, by grieving parents, by frightened children – the abused, the abandoned, the persecuted and the desperately poor . . . our "claiming" those places means that we must go out to join [God] "in the distressing disguise" as he makes the agony of the suffering his very own.[191]

Thus, Christians effect the transformation of culture mainly through gentle persuasion. When Christians engage in prophetic critique of power they must do so in a humble way. More importantly, Christians must embody in word and deed the transformation that God has already effected in their lives. When Christians embody in word and deed what it means to be faithful followers of Christ, they show the world a different way of life and with time influence others to be followers of Christ and consequently embrace a different worldview from the prevailing worldview, for example, of ethnopolitical balkanization. Thus, Calvin's political theology that re-defines the meaning of power is beneficial for the African, particularly, the Kenyan context where politicians tend to abuse power. Calvin's political theology also has implications for charity, compassion, and work.

Inspires Charity and Compassion and an Ethic of Work

Calvin's political theology has particular relevance for acts of charity and compassion. For Calvin, Christian charity is rooted in God's love and provision and God's image in humanity. Nothing comes apart from God's will.[192] J. H. van Wyk asserts that according to Calvin, "Everything is from God and through God and to God."[193] God is the source of everything a believer has; believers are stewards.[194] Calvin argued that although human beings may prosper materially through dishonest means, such is against God's

---

191. Mouw, 154.

192. In the *Institutes*, III.7.4, Calvin asserted, "For thus we are instructed to remember that those talents which God has bestowed upon us are not our own goods but the free gifts of God; and any persons who become proud of them show their ungratefulness."

193. van Wyk, "Calvin on the Christian," 234.

194. Calvin, (*Institutes*, III.7.5), asserted, "We are the stewards of everything God has conferred on us by which we are able to help our neighbor, and are required to render account of our stewardship." On this point, Wyk, ("Calvin on the Christian," 240) observes, "In everything man is nothing but a *steward*, seeing that God is the absolute Possessor of all things."

will.[195] For Calvin, it is better to be poor than to obtain wealth through unscrupulous means.[196] Poverty is better than illegal prosperity because, for Calvin, poverty is a means in which a believer can draw closer to God. Bonnie Pattison asserts, "In Calvin's thought, poverty and affliction strip away all human securities and false assurances, drawing a person to rest upon divine promises alone, thereby allowing the Holy Spirit to work in their lives."[197] Calvin believed that the love of money and prosperity leads to actions that demean others.

Calvin also emphasized that God's love is the source and the pattern of Christian charity.[198] He maintained that human love is self-love but God's love is love for all. By patterning their lives after God's love, Christians are motivated to love without discriminating others.[199] In discussing the question "Who is our neighbor?" Calvin responded that the term "neighbor" extends beyond those in close relationships. "It is the common habit of mankind that the more closely men are bound together by the ties of kinship, of acquaintanceship, or of neighbourhood, the more responsibilities for one another they share."[200] However, he argued that Christian love should extend beyond close kin. "We ought to embrace the whole human race without exception in a single feeling of love; here there is no distinction between barbarian and Greek, worthy and unworthy, friend and enemy, since all should be contemplated in God, not in themselves."[201] Thus God is the source and the pattern of Christian love.

Additionally, God's image that all human beings possess is the foundation of Christian charity. In this note, Calvin wrote, "we are not to consider that men merit of themselves but to look upon the image of God in all men, to which we owe all honor and love."[202] He also added, "Therefore, whatever man you meet who needs your aid, you have no reason to refuse to help him" even if that person "is a stranger" or is "contemptible and worthless"

---

195. Calvin, *Institutes*, III.7.8.
196. Calvin, II.10.12; III.20.46.
197. Pattison, *Poverty in the Theology*, 193.
198. See Zachman, "'Deny Yourself,'" 473.
199. Calvin, *Institutes*, II.8.54.
200. Calvin, II.8.55.
201. Calvin, II.8.55.
202. Calvin, III.7.6.

or you think that "you owe nothing for any service of his" or is underserv-
ing of help.[203] A believer must practice forgiveness even to those who do
not deserve it. A believer must "remember not to consider [humanity's] evil
intention but to look upon the image of God in them, which cancels and
effaces their transgressions, and with its beauty and dignity allures us to
love and embrace them."[204] Reverencing all human beings as image bearers
does not mean, for Calvin, excusing their evil actions. Ultimately everyone
is accountable to God and will answer for every action committed.[205]

Considering that not all people would be willing to share their resources with the poor, Calvin affirmed the practice of money-lending. Though
Calvin's teaching on money-lending does not directly apply to the banking
sector, for Calvin rejected the possibility that someone can make money
solely by lending, nevertheless, the teaching applies directly to how the rich
treat the poor.[206] In his letter *De Usuris* ("On Usury"), Calvin approved usury
(lending at interest) so long as it is practiced in love, fairness, and justice
especially to the poor.[207] Calvin contended that money-lending should be
practiced not only with those who can repay but also those from whom no
hope of repayment is possible.[208] In other words, in Calvin's mind, creditors

---

203. Calvin, III.7.6.

204. Calvin, III.7.6. In his commentary on Matthew 5:43, Calvin, (*Harmony of the
Evangelists*, 17:304) asserts, "But the charity, which God requires in his law, looks not at
what a man has deserved, but extends itself to the unworthy, the wicked, and the ungrateful."

205. As already mentioned in chapter 6, Calvin believed in discipline, justice, and
human order. Although human beings are ultimately answerable to God, God also placed
various mechanisms of discipline and justice on earth. For Calvin, the magistrates and the
various ecclesiastical authorities, are the mechanism of fostering discipline, justice, and order.
The Consistory of Geneva adjudicated several civil and criminal cases, and ensured that order
and peace prevailed.

206. Schulze, "Calvin on Interest and Property," 223.

207. Calvin, "On Usury," 453–455. Also *Institutes*, III.19.9. For an explanation of
Calvin's view on usury, see, Sauer, *Faithful Ethics*, 175–226; Schulze, "Calvin on Interest
and Property," 217–228; Wyk, "Calvin on the Christian," 253–256.

208. Calvin, "On Usury," 453. Calvin presents other conditions for lending funds to
the poor:

> The first is that no one should take interest [usury] from the poor, and no one,
> destitute by virtue of indigence or some affliction or calamity, should be forced
> into it. The second exception is that whoever lends should not be so preoccupied
> with gain as to neglect his necessary duties, nor, wishing to protect his money,
> disdain his poor brothers. The third exception is that no principle be followed
> that is not in accord with natural equity, for everything should be examined in
> the light of Christ's precept: Do unto others as you would have them do unto

should not oppress borrowers by charging exorbitant interests.[209] Lenders should always remember to be fair to borrowers. They should not seek unjust profit at their expense. Helping the poor, not profiting, should be the motivation. The poor should be treated humanely.

Calvin also maintained that Christians must work for their income. André Biéler argues that according to Calvin, because work, "when rightly accomplished, [is] the very work of God by which God supports the life of his creatures," to "deprive man of work is truly a crime . . . equivalent to taking away his life."[210] Thus idleness is contrary to God's will. People must work for their upkeep. Idleness perpetuates dependency on other human beings, which God condemns. Calvin's message is relevant in Kenya, for Kenyan people love to receive free money from politicians.

Work gives the opportunity to employers to affirm the dignity and honor of their laborers.[211] Because laborers are created in God's image, they must be treated humanely, for example through a just compensation for the work done. Indeed Calvin affirms the dignity of workers in his commentary on Deuteronomy 24:15 where he asserted, "We must endeavor, as far as possible, that everyone should safely keep what he possesses, and that our neighbour's advantage should be promoted no less than our own. The sum is, that humanity is so to be cultivated that none should be oppressed, or

---

you. This precept is applicable every time. The fourth exception is that whoever borrows should make at least as much, if not more, than the amount borrowed. In the fifth place, we ought not to determine what is lawful by basing it on the common practice or in accordance with the iniquity of the world, but should base it on a principle derived from the word of God. In the sixth place, we ought not to consider only the private advantage of those with whom we deal but should keep in mind what is best for the common good . . . in the seventh place, one ought not to exceed the rate that a country's public laws allow. Although this may not always suffice, for such laws quite often permit what they are able to correct or repress. Therefore, one ought to prefer a principle of equity that can curtail abuse.

209. Before the new law (signed by the president on 24 August 2016) that caped interest loans to not more than four percentage points above the Central Bank's rate, currently at 10.5 percent, Kenyan banks were notorious for charging exorbitant interests. President Kenyatta acknowledged that Kenyans are frustrated with the banking sector. The interest rate had increased to 24 percent in some banks.

210. Biéler, *Social Humanism of Calvin*, 43, 45.

211. Biéler, 50–51.

suffer loss from default of payment." Thus the pay should foster the dignity of the worker.[212]

Employers should not treat workers as slaves, "or should be too illiberal and stingy towards them, since nothing can be more disgraceful than that, when they are in our service, they should not at least have enough to live upon frugally."[213] Calvin's emphasis on the dignity of workers has particular relevance for Kenya. Despite the government of Kenya's effort to harmonize salaries and thus to create parity, the Salaries and Remuneration Commission (SRC), admits that most Kenyan workers in the public sector are paid very little such that they cannot afford a decent life.[214] Yet Kenya's Members of Parliament are ranked the second-highest paid lawmakers in the world.[215]

Conclusion

This chapter established that Calvin's political theology is multifaceted and covers various issues relevant for the Kenyan context. Scholars differ in how they interpret the various issues in Calvin's political thought. Whereas many issues still need to be examined, the chapter showed that Calvin's politics speaks to the various issues in Kenya. Contrary to the politics of self-interest and corruption that prevail in Kenya, Calvin showed that politics is about the public good, not self-enrichment. Also, politicians must be accountable in how they acquire and use their wealth. They must serve the interests of the poor and the marginalized. The next three chapters examine and critique, from a Reformed perspective, the contributions of four Kenyan scholars in addressing the problem of ethnopolitical conflict in Kenya.

---

212. Calvin, *Commentaries on the Four Last Books*, III:111, (on Deut 20:15).

213. Calvin, III:114, (on Deut 20:15).

214. Kerandi, *Fair Play for Fair Pay*.

215. Herbeling, "Kenyan Legislators Emerge Second," Kenyan MPs earn more than US $15,000 a month (not considering other stipends they get), in a country where 42 percent of the population live below the poverty line.

CHAPTER 7

"A Hungry Stomach Has No Ears": The Political Theology of David Gitari and Henry Okullu as Theological Responses to Ethnopolitical Conflict in Kenya

This chapter examines and critiques the work of David Gitari and Henry Okullu. Gitari and Okullu were practical theologians, precisely pastoral scholars who served the Anglican Church of Kenya as bishops, being true to the African proverb "an hungry stomach has no ears," meaning, the church cannot feed the spiritual needs of the congregation and ignore their physical and social wellbeing. Thus, both bishops advocated for multipartyism, human rights, and the active involvement of the church in politics. They led street protests, preached fiery sermons against injustices in Kenya, issued several press statements, and wrote several publications criticizing and challenging the State over issues the bishops thought impaired Kenya's progress. As Sabar-Friedman observes, the Anglican Church during the time of Gitari and Okullu, rose "from a purely religious body into an extra-parliamentary political institution that sought to cater to the basic needs of large segments of Kenyan society."[1] Thus, this chapter examines the theological underpinnings of these two bishops' sociopolitical engagement and how that theology informs the quest for ethnopolitical cohesion in Kenya.

---

1. Sabar-Friedman, "'Politics' and 'Power,'" 448.

Bishop John Henry Okullu

John Henry Okullu was born between 1929 and 1934 in Ramba village, Asembo Location in Western Kenya. The date, month, and year are unknown since his parents were illiterate and did not record the details.[2] Okullu chose 1 September 1929 as his official date of birth for purposes of securing an insurance policy.[3] He began his career as a clerk for the East African Railway in Kampala, Uganda, before responding to God's call to the priesthood. He joined Bishop Tucker Theological College in Mukono, Uganda. He also studied at Virginia Theological Seminary (1963–1965). The Anglican Church ordained him deacon in December 1958. From 1958 to 1971 he worked as a journalist for several newspapers, namely *New Day* (Uganda), *Liverpool Daily* (UK), and *Target/Lengo* (NCCK's newspapers in Kenya and Tanzania).[4] He also preached in various churches and schools. Virginia Seminary awarded him an honorary Doctoral Degree in Divinity in 1974.

Okullu used his writing skills to advance his firm belief in justice and democracy. F. D. Maurice (1805–1872), an Anglican social theologian and a firm advocate of social justice, and one of the founders of Christian socialism in the UK, shaped and influenced Okullu's theology especially in regard to social criticism.[5] Okullu observes that Maurice's assertion that, "a churchman must be a politician" influenced his perception of a Christian's role in politics.[6] Okullu's journalistic and editorial skills were also instrumental in getting innovative articles and columns for the newspapers he worked for. He wrote several articles highly critical of social evils in Kenya. One such example is his critique of the proposed construction of KANU party headquarters in Nairobi. KANU had proposed to construct the building at

---

2. Okullu, *Quest for Justice*, 1.

3. Okullu, 2.

4. "Lengo" is the Swahili word for "Target." Until 1963, *Target/Lengo* was referred to as *Rock*. Okullu was the senior editor of both newspapers. The Christian Council of Kenya (CCK) later to become the National Christian Council of Kenya (NCCK) then later on National Council of Churches of Kenya (NCCK), together with the Christian Council of Tanzania established the African Venture Company Limited as an umbrella organization to produce Christian literature such as *Lengo* and *Target*.

5. Oluoch, *Christian Political Theology*, 50.

6. Okullu, *Quest for Justice*, 37.

a cost of 2.8 million Kenyan pounds.[7] Okullu argued that it was immoral for KANU to spend such amounts of money when thousands of people live in squalid conditions. The editorial provoked anger within government. The editor, John Schoefield, was fired and immediately replaced. Ironically, Okullu replaced him as editor.[8] Okullu worked as editor till 1971 when he resigned to become the first Kenyan Provost of the All Saints Cathedral, Nairobi. On 24 February 1974, Okullu became Bishop of the Maseno South Diocese of the Anglican Church of Kenya, a position he retained until 1994. He also served two terms as chairman of NCCK (1976–1978, 1988–1991), chairman of the National Ecumenical Civic Education Programme (1992), chairman of Friends of Democracy (1995), and as a member of the Central Committee of the World Council of Churches, and as president of the World Conference on Religion and Peace (African Region).[9]

Bishop Okullu is remembered for his sermons, which were mainly on the relevance of Christianity to social concerns. He said that his sermons "challenged corruption, land grabbing, tribalism in employment or educational opportunities, detention without trial, and authoritarianism."[10] Thus he preached sermons with such titles as, "Amos: Prophet of Justice," "Signs of the Times," "A Moment to Decide," "Why the Crisis?" "The Ideals We Stand For," "Mistakes of the KANU Government," "Democracy," and, "Detention Never Helps," among others.[11] He also preached at the memorial service for the late Alexander Muge, Bishop of Eldoret, who had died in a mysterious road accident.[12] Bishop Okullu died on 13 March 1999 at the age of seventy.

Okullu's Political Theology

The theological underpinnings of Okullu's sociopolitical engagement are laid down in his two books, *Church and Politics in East Africa* (1974) and *Church and State in Nation Building and Human Development* (1984). He also published a book on marriage titled, *Church and Marriage in East Africa* (1976), and an autobiography called *Quest for Justice* (1997). He also wrote

---

7. Okullu, 50.
8. Okullu, 50–51.
9. Oluoch, *Christian Political Theology*, xvii–xviii.
10. Okullu, *Quest for Justice*, 63.
11. Okullu, 151–160.
12. See the full sermon in Okullu, *Quest for Justice*, 156–160.

several essays and articles.[13] These books emerged out of Okullu's active involvement in Kenya's public affairs particularly in the area of social justice.

His political theology centered on the premise that the church must "assist in the definition, validation and articulation of just political, economic and social objectives."[14] His publications were an attempt to fulfil this goal.[15] For example, in *Church and Politics in East Africa*, Okullu sought to provide a Christian understanding on development, corruption, tribalism, church and State, democracy, crime and punishment, and the indigenization of the church.

In his discussion on the relationship between the church and the State, Okullu addressed several points. First, he discussed the origins and purposes of these two institutions. While the church owes its origin to Christ, God established the State to serve human society. Furthermore, each of these institutions serve two different purposes.

> The State is created to keep law and order in society. Without outward civil order, no society can exist at all. The Church, on the other hand, is instituted by God to bring the mind of God to bear upon total human life and to contribute to the buildings of value systems upon which a sound human society may be built.[16]

---

13. These include, Okullu, "Church-State Relations," 79–88; Okullu, "African Context," 30–33; Okullu, "Theological and Ethical Considerations," 97–112; Okullu, "Church, State," 25–37; and Okullu, "Render unto Caesar," 147–54.

14. Okullu, *Quest for Justice*, xv.

15. Indeed, it was urgent to provide a Christian political philosophy in Kenya at that time. In 1978, John Lonsdale et al., ("Emerging Pattern of Church," 267–284) argued that the churches of Kenya with the exception of the Roman Catholic Church, were yet, at the time, to possess a fully developed theology of secular power (267). The Evangelical churches, "in addition to its fundamentalist insistence on the strict authenticity of the Bible, has tended to place a strong, eschatological emphasis on individual salvation rather than social improvement in this world" (268). Thus, Okullu's work came at the right time for the church in Kenya.

16. Okullu, *Church and Politics*, 15–16. Okullu's assertion that the State and the church serve two purposes is similar to Luther's two-kingdoms theology in which the two kingdoms are distinct. John Witte, (*Law and Protestantism*, 5–6) provides a helpful summary of Luther's two-kingdoms view this way:

> God has ordained two kingdoms or realms in which humanity is destined to live, Luther argued: the earthly kingdom and the heavenly kingdom. The earthly kingdom is the realm of creation, of natural and civic life, where a person operates primarily by reason and law. The heavenly kingdom is the realm of redemption, of spiritual and eternal life, where a person operates primarily by faith and love. These

Second, Okullu asserted the doctrine of separation of church and State though, for him, this separation should not be seen to be an invitation to inactivity.[17] The church must be active in public affairs. For Okullu, church and State serve the common good. Thus both are distinct but inseparable elements of the total human experience. Furthermore, both institutions need each other if they are to fulfil their God-given mandate.[18] Okullu argued that the church must support those structures within government that enhance human flourishing such as democracy, human rights, accountability, multipartyism, fairness, and so on. Though these structures do not automatically guarantee flourishing, they provide an environment that enrich human life. On the other hand, the State should pay attention to the moral injunctions of the church.[19]

Okullu asserted that the Christian faith ought to affect every facet of a believer's life.[20] He notes that the reason why Christianity took such a long time to affect the social, cultural, and political life of African Christians is that the missionaries taught Africans that their primary goal was to win

---

two kingdoms embrace parallel forms of righteousness and justice, government and order, truth and knowledge. They interact and depend upon each other in a variety of ways. But these two kingdoms ultimately remain distinct. The earthly kingdom is distorted by sin, and governed by law. The heavenly kingdom is renewed by grace and guided by the Gospel. A Christian is a citizen of both kingdoms at once and invariably comes under the distinctive government of each. As a heavenly citizen, the Christian remains free in his or her conscience, called to live fully by the light of the Word of God. But as an earthly citizen, the Christian is bound by law, and called to obey the natural orders and offices of household, state and church that God has ordained and maintained for the governance of this earthly kingdom.

However, absent in Witte's summary is Luther's strong focus on the awareness of the tension between the devil and God. Oberman, (*Luther*), argues that Luther lived, did theology, and ministry within a worldview that took the supernatural world seriously. Oberman asserts that the experiential worldview between God and the devil that permeated medieval times shaped Luther's polemical engagement with his contenders. In Oberman's mind, Luther the man and his theology must be understood within his own context. Oberman notes that modern scholarship on Luther commits a serious intellectual mistake when it ignores the medieval worldview, especially the belief in satanic conflict with God's people. Oberman observes that "In all modern classroom and textbook treatments of Luther, the Devil is reduced to an abstraction: be he a figment of mind or time. Thus the Evil One, as a medieval remnant, can be exorcised from the core of Luther's experience, life, and thought" (4).

17. Okullu, *Quest for Justice*, xv.

18. Okullu, xv–vi.

19. Okullu, xv.

20. Okullu, *Church and Politics*, 2–3, 6.

souls, not to engage in mundane matters.[21] Okullu rejected this dualistic philosophy. He argued that the mission of the church was to develop the whole human person.[22] Indeed he wrote,

> I cannot think of theology except in the context of a hungry child crying for food, Ugandan refugees running away from Amin's tyranny, a coup d'état in Ethiopia, a parent in Kenya with two young children who have failed their examinations, a villager without water and proper sanitation, a beggar in the streets of Nairobi, the forest of buildings in Lagos, hunger and death in the Sahel . . . This to me is theology, this is Christianity.[23]

During a sermon delivered at the All Saints Cathedral in Nairobi on 7 November 1982 titled, "Amos: Prophetic of Justice," Okullu reminded the congregation about justice with the following words: "Just treatment of the poor is religion. A just distribution of Kenya's wealth, development, and job opportunities is true worship. As far as God is concerned, there is no other religion he will accept and recognize."[24] Thus Christianity must address the needs of the whole human being not just their souls.

In addition to being involved in public affairs, the church must critique social injustice and provide alternatives to it. The church must not sit back and watch when evil is committed. Okullu cited the example of the Roman Catholic Church in Germany during Hitler's regime. He observed that in failing to condemn the massacre of six million Jews, the Roman Catholic Church "bears eternally an indelible stigma."[25] Christians must also offer an alternative to the prevailing situation; "For Christians must not only criticize

---

21. Okullu, 3. Okullu (*Quest for Justice*, 16) also acknowledges that during his early days of ministry, he was indifferent to sociopolitical engagement because winning souls was his primary goal. He wrote, "I had heard of the big names like Kenyatta, Tom Mboya, Oginga Odinga, Milton Obote, Julius Nyerere, James Gichuru and Eliud Mathu. My heroes were however great preachers like William Nagenda, Eric Sabiti, later the first Anglican Archbishop of Uganda, Josiah Kinuka and Joe Church of Rwanda."

22. Okullu, *Church and Politics*, 4. See also Okullu, *Quest for Justice*, 37; Okullu, *Church and State*, 1–3; and Okullu, "Theological and Ethical Considerations," 108.

23. Okullu, *Church and State*, xiv–xv.

24. Okullu, *Quest for Justice*, 65–66.

25. Okullu, *Church and Politics*, 5.

and attack what is; more than that, they should propose what would be the Christian ideals for society."[26] Such ideals include love in place of hatred, hope in place of despair, courage in place of fear, humility in place of arrogance, and reconciliation in place of conflict.

Furthermore, Okullu argued that the church is called to be a prophet or watchdog of society. This prophetic role of the church is particularly needed in countries such as Kenya where civil societies were yet, at the time of Okullu's publications, to be independent of political influences.[27] Contrary to State interference, Okullu maintained, the church is not answerable to politicians but to God because the church is not "a praying department of government."[28] Okullu also added, "It is not the role of the Church to give divine and biblical support to philosophies whose motive is purely political, although they may be coined in biblical terms."[29] Okullu's statement here was a response to the co-option of church leaders. Okullu observed that though Moi came into power as an ardent Christian who seemed to support the church, Kenyans soon "realized that it [the Church] was being used to provide blanket support to push for a philosophy of government."[30] Instead of being co-opted to support politicians and their agendas, church leaders must hold the leaders accountable. They must question their excesses and expose their corruption.[31]

In response to the problem of tribalism in Kenya, Okullu argued that the church must transcend ethnic divides. He considered tribalism as "Africa's second devil."[32] For Okullu, tribal loyalties, in Africa, overrides Christian loyalties. According to Okullu, tribalism had affected every African Christian movement, church union, and denomination and even bishops were being

---

26. Okullu, 70.

27. Okullu, *Church and Politics*, 18. Elsewhere, Okullu, ("Church, State," 38) comments on the dangers of State interference of non-state organizations: "Politicization of people's organizations stifles development by making those institutions answerable to political masters, whose development philosophy may not necessarily be people oriented."

28. Okullu, "Church, State," 32.

29. Okullu, "Theological and Ethical Considerations," 110.

30. Okullu, "Render unto Caesar," 149.

31. Okullu (*Church and State*, 40) asserts that corruption is Kenya's biggest challenge; "nearing dangerous proportions" and "has become a way of life in Kenya."

32. Okullu, *Church and Politics*, 43. Corruption is the first "devil."

elected on the basis of their ethnicity.[33] Even members of the East African Revival, a movement considered a beacon of Christianity in East Africa comparable to the Keswick Movement in Europe, were guilty of tribalism.[34] Okullu acknowledged that tribalism in East Africa, especially in Kenya, was strongly tied to politics such that "Churches, which do not consider themselves politically strong fear that they would be swallowed up by those with strong political backing."[35]

However, Okullu argued that tribal identity was not wholly bad because tribal groupings are an extension of family systems and are an asset to nation building.[36] In addition, tribal identity may aid smaller communities to resist dominance by bigger communities who may consider themselves nobler than the rest because of their geography, natural resources within their disposal, being civilized earlier, political power, among other reasons.[37] Thus the problem is not ethnic identity but the misuse of ethnic identity for political reasons.

Okullu offered two theological responses to the problem of tribalism in Africa. The first response is "heroic faith," the kind of faith, which rises up against tribal identification.[38] He cited the example of courageous Christians in Kenya who stood up against tribal politics, some of them paying the ultimate price for their actions.[39] He also mentioned Jesus Christ, Paul, Peter, and historical leaders such as Martin Luther as excellent examples and motivators of heroic expressions of faith.[40] Okullu stood up against

---

33. Okullu, "Theological and Ethical Considerations," 111.

34. Okullu, *Church and Politics*, 43–44. The East African Revival began in 1920 in Rwanda through the work of Joe Church (1899–1989). It spread to Uganda, Tanzania, and Kenya during the 1930s and 40s. Okullu observes that after independence in 1963, the Brethren of the Revival (another term for the East African Revival movement), became embroiled in tribal differences as they sought to better themselves economically. For more on the East African Revival Movement, see, Church, *Quest for the Highest*; Makower, *Coming of the Rain*; Osborn, *Pioneers*.

35. Okullu, *Church and Politics*, 45.

36. Okullu, 45.

37. Okullu, 45–46.

38. Okullu, 51.

39. Okullu, 51.

40. Okullu, *Quest for Justice*, 123.

injustices in Kenya. Thus he modeled heroic faith.[41] He stood up against those who wanted him to become a tribal leader of the Luo people. One year to retirement from priesthood, the *Daily Nation* newspaper reported that Okullu had offered himself to lead the Luo. Okullu responded by saying, "Why, after 35 years as a priest, does the *Daily Nation* now want to reduce me to a tribal leader? I wish to state that, even if I join politics after my retirement next year, I will serve the Luo, the Kamba, the Kikuyu, the Kalenjin and the rest."[42] Okullu offered to serve all ethnic communities though he never really joined politics.

His other theological response to tribalism is identity in Christ constituting the brotherhood of all believers. Okullu asserted that the believer's allegiance should be on Christ, not on ethnic identities. He asserted, "Christians are a distinctive people no matter what their tribal background, no matter what material benefits they may derive: they are brothers, the children of one Father, of our Lord Jesus Christ who died that we might find peace with one another . . . (Eph 2:14–16)." Thus as brothers and sisters, Christians should live in peace with one another. His sermons reinforced this point. In a sermon preached at St Stephen's Cathedral in Kisumu Okullu denounced violence as a means of solving political differences.[43] The following is an excerpt from the sermon:

> Lastly, fellow country people, let us not fight each other. It is futile to disown a brother and sister because of the accidental place of her/his birth. We are brothers and sisters created by God, in God's image, and when things went wrong between him and Adam, he made a new plan. He sent his son, on a second rescue operation. Kenyans were first liberated through a liberation movement from the colonial powers, but we are now involved in second liberation from black colonialists.[44]

---

41. Okullu (*Quest for Justice*, 22) reflected on the dangers he encountered because of his critique of the powers that be: "My life has always been under threat like the lives of others like Archbishop Desmond Tutu ever since I took to the platform of justice and democracy. I know the risks involved and yet I cannot turn back. I have stood against injustice and dictatorship. I have preached freedom for all but political leaders were not happy with all these."

42. Weekly Review, "Okullu Ready for 1994," 3.

43. Oluoch, *Christian Political Theology*, 94.

44. Cited in Oluoch, 94.

In conclusion, Okullu played a significant role in the quest for ethnopolitical cohesion in Kenya. Particularly, his emphasis on social justice and a critique of the powers that be was a major contribution. Okullu himself was a tough critic of the government. He stood against human rights abuses. He advocated for multiparty democracy and governance. He was not alone for he worked with other theologians like David Gitari.

Archbishop David Mukuba Gitari

David Mukuba Gitari was born on 16 September 1937 in Kirinyaga County in the foothills of Mount Kenya. His parents were Samuel Mukuba and Jessie Njuku, both of them from two different ethnic communities, Samuel was a Kamba and Jessie a Gikuyu. Julius Gathogo observes that Samuel's marriage to Jessie reinforced the importance of diversity and ethnic coexistence in Kenya as both of them were married at a time when intertribal marriages were rare though not utterly impossible.[45] Samuel and Jessie Mukuba were devout Christians. Gitari recalls his Christian childhood with the following words, "My parents were so committed to the mission of the church that in our home compound there was a chapel and every day my father would ring the bell at 6.00am for morning prayers and again at 6.00pm for evening prayers. He would start the service whether or not there was a congregation in attendance."[46]

On 8 May 1955, Gitari gave his life to Jesus. He joyfully remembers this day: "how my heart was strangely warmed and filled with joy! I was liberated to render service and preach the Gospel to my fellow students. I continued faithful to the Lord in the face of opposition, strengthened by the presence of the Holy Spirit in me."[47] Although Gitari does not reference John Wesley, his conversion experience is similar to Wesley's description of his experience at the Alder's Gate. Gitari, being an Anglican theologian and especially a follower of the East Africa Revival Movement that traces its origin to the Keswick Revival Movement, is heir of the Wesleyan heritage. However, although Gitari is a spiritual heir of the revival movements, after attending

---

45. Gathogo, "Meddling on to 2008," 145.

46. Gitari, *Troubled but Not Destroyed*, 5.

47. Gitari, "Holy Spirit in Renewal," 594.

the Lausanne Congress on World Evangelization in 1974, he became a tough critic of the Revival Movement's focus on inward spirituality at the expense of social engagement.[48]

Gitari studied at the Royal College Nairobi (now the University of Nairobi) from 1959 to 1964. During these years, Gitari took keen interest in the politics of the day such as the clamor for independence and for the release of Jomo Kenyatta from prison.[49] He observed that he was present during the first Madaraka Day (Independence Day) celebration on 1 June 1963 when Kenya was granted internal self-government, and was also present at Uhuru Gardens when Kenya got full independence on 12 December 1963.[50] After his university studies, Gitari served as lay chaplain at the University of Nairobi as well as General Secretary of the Pan African Fellowship of Evangelical Students (PAFES) from 1966 to 1968.[51] From 1968 to 1971 he went to study theology at Tyndale Hall in Bristol, England.[52]

Upon his arrival from London, Gitari became the third General Secretary of the Bible Society of Kenya in September 1971 till December 1975.[53] In December 1972 the Anglican Church ordained him. In 1974, together with Henry Okullu,[54] Gitari attended the International Congress on World Evangelization held in Lausanne, Switzerland, which took place from 16 to 25 July 1974. The theme of the congress was "Let the Earth Hear His Voice."[55] More than 2,000 Christians representing 151 countries attended the meeting.[56] The Billy Graham Association convened the Congress while John Stott chaired the plenary session that drafted the Lausanne Covenant,

---

48. Gitari, "Church and Politics," 11; Gitari and Knighton, "On Being a Christian Leader," 251.

49. Gitari, *Troubled but Not Destroyed*, 17.

50. Gitari, 17.

51. Gitari, 18–19; Knighton, *Religion and Politics*, 146–147.

52. Gitari (*Troubled but Not Destroyed*, 31) observes that he was "the fourth Anglican Kenyan to obtain a University degree in Theology after Dr John Mbiti, the Revd Thomas Kalume (who became a Member of Parliament) and the Revd Henry Okullu (who at that time was the Editor of Target Newspaper)."

53. Gitari (*Troubled but Not Destroyed*, 29) writes of his success as Secretary General: "During my tenure, Kenya sold more Scripture in proportion to its population than any other society in Africa."

54. Okullu, *Quest for Justice*, 88.

55. For the proceedings of the congress, see Douglas, *Let the Earth Hear His Voice*.

56. Gitari, *Troubled but Not Destroyed*, 27.

a document that provides a theological framework for evangelical social responsibility.[57] Mark Noll asserts, "If Graham provided the spark, publicity, and funding that made Lausanne possible, Stott contributed depth, cultural sensitivity, and effective mediation."[58] Gitari admits that this meeting opened his eyes to understand the relationship between the gospel and social action, thereby he returned home motivated to implement the Lausanne Covenant's resolutions on Christian social responsibility.[59]

Twelve months after Lausanne, Gitari was elected the first bishop of Mount Kenya East diocese and on 20 July 1975, at the age of thirty-seven, he was consecrated and enthroned.[60] He served until 1 July 1990 when the diocese of Mount Kenya East was subdivided into the dioceses of Embu and Kirinyaga. Gitari moved to Kirinyaga diocese therefore becoming the first bishop of Kirinyaga (1990–1996).[61] In November 1997, the Anglican Church consecrated and enthroned him the third Primate and Archbishop of the Anglican Church of Kenya and Bishop of the Diocese of Nairobi. He served until his retirement in 2002.

Bishop Gitari also served four terms as chairman of NCCK, between 1978 and 1984. These years were significant in Kenya's history. President Jomo Kenyatta, Kenya's founding father, died in office on 22 August 1978. His death opened a period of intense succession struggles. Daniel arap Moi, Kenyatta's deputy, won the 1979 elections. In June of 1982 Parliament

---

57. The other key contributors of the Lausanne Covenant include Carl F. Henry, George Hoffman, Billy Graham (North Americans), René Padilla, Samuel Escobar (Latin Americans), and Orlando Costas (Latin American American). The Lausanne Covenant was signed by 2,100 out of the 2,500 attendees. Steers (Steer, *Basic Christian*, 162) points out that the main reason why the four-hundred delegates did not sign the document was because of a clause in the Covenant that stated, "Those of us who live in affluent circumstances accept our duty to develop a simple lifestyle in order to contribute more generously to both relief and evangelism." This was a highly-debated statement because some delegates did not think they could make such a commitment. Ruth Graham, the wife of Billy Graham, did not sign the document too. She felt that taking care of her five children hinders her from a commitment to frugality that the document seems to call for. John Stott, a single man with no children to take care, made the commitment. This could be the reason why Stott chose to donate almost all of his earnings towards the growth of the church in the Majority World. I am a beneficiary of Stott's Langham Partnership program, which provides funds to scholars from the Majority World for their PhD studies.

58. Noll, *Turning Points*, 289–300.

59. Gitari, *Troubled but Not Destroyed*, 27–28, 40.

60. Gitari, 29.

61. Gitari, 56.

declared Kenya a *de jure* one-party state and in August of the same year there was an unsuccessful coup attempt at President Moi. The coup attempt changed President Moi significantly. He became indifferent to the opposition and those with divergent views. People who spoke against his regime were detained without trial, others were forced to seek refuge abroad. Gitari escaped an assassination attempt against his life in April 1989.[62]

During this time, Gitari became a vocal critic of Moi's leadership. He used the pulpit to attack Moi's policies especially his one-party system and rigging in elections.[63] In addition to his fiery sermons, Gitari published several books namely, *God with Us* (1980), *Witnessing to the Living God in Africa* (1987), *Let the Bishop Speak* (1988), *In Season and out of Season: Sermons to a Nation* (1996), and *Responsible Church Leadership* (2005). He also wrote an autobiography titled, *Troubled But Not Destroyed* (posthumously published in 2014). He also wrote several journal articles and essays.[64] The next section examines Gitari's sociopolitical involvement beginning with his mode (method) of public engagement, model (theoretical framework) of public engagement and then the theological justifications for his public engagement.

The Mode of Gitari's Public Engagement

Expository preaching was Gitari's primary mode (method) of public engagement.[65] He believed in expository preaching delivered mainly through stories and analogies and applied directly to recent political events in Kenya such as the introduction of multiparty democracy, the queue system for voting,

---

62. Gitari, "You are in the World," 229.

63. KANU adopted *mlolongo* (queuing system for elections) on 20 August 1986. Gitari, ("Church and Politics," 15) observes that massive rigging of elections characterised this voting system: "At one of the polling stations we witnessed daylight rigging when a candidate who had only five people behind was declared the winner against his opponent who had six hundred and sixteen people behind him. Such rigging was witnessed in a number of other polling stations and was influenced by top KANU leadership in the district."

64. These include Gitari, "Christian Perspective," 210–222; Gitari, "Church and Politics," 7–17; Gitari, "Church and Nationhood," 7–17; Gitari, "Evangelization and Culture," 101–121; Gitari, "Mission of the Church," 25–42; and Gitari, "Church's Witness," 119–140, among others.

65. Selected sermons of Bishop Gitari are found in his two books, *In Season and Out of Season*, and *Let the Bishop Speak*. The later also contains excerpts from Kenyan newspapers of the government's reactions to Gitari's sermons.

or to specific cases of corruption and violence.[66] He stated, "I have always confined myself to the Word of God, expounding it faithfully and systematically and applying the same to the prevailing political position."[67] The Old Testament, Jesus's teachings and ministry, and the Sermon on the Mount were his favorite texts for his preaching on sociopolitical issues. For example, in 1987 he preached on Matthew 9:35–38 ("And Jesus went about all the cities and villages, teaching in their synagogues and preaching the gospel of the kingdom, and healing every disease and every infirmity" [RSV]) to challenge Kenyan preachers to focus on both the spiritual and social needs of the people.[68] On another occasion, he preached from Jeremiah 1:4–8 and 7:1–8 urging preachers to "tear down" "idols of our times" such as money, lies, physical strength, security, and power, and to facilitate true worship.[69] On another occasion, the story of Daniel as Prime Minister designate of the Persian Empire in Daniel chapter 6, served as a reminder to Kenya's civil servants to serve God and God's people without fear because "the truth is always triumphant."[70] Similarly, the story of Naboth's vineyard, usurped by King Ahab, the evil king (1 Kgs 21:1–29), "urges us to seek to know our fundamental human rights and to defend those rights at whatever cost."[71] Gitari also added "the story also serves as a warning to all land grabbers, whoever they may be."[72]

Gitari mentioned John Stott as a great inspiration to him in expository preaching.[73] The primary thrust of Stott's theology of preaching is that the Word of God must convict and shape the preacher before they can preach from it.[74] Furthermore Stott believed that true preaching is biblical preaching; "we do not occupy the pulpit in order to preach ourselves."[75] For Stott,

---

66. Gitari and Knighton, "On Being a Christian Leader," 247–248; Freston, *Evangelicals and Politics*, 150; Knighton, *Religion and Politics*, 149–151.

67. Gitari, "Church and Politics," 13.

68. Gitari, *Let the Bishop Speak*, 11–19.

69. Gitari, 24–32.

70. Gitari, 35–41.

71. Gitari, *In Season and Out*, 105.

72. Gitari, 105.

73. Gitari, *Troubled but Not Destroyed*, 23. Biographies of John Stott are Dudley-Smith's *John Stott: A Global Ministry*; and Steer's, *Basic Christian: The Inside Story of John Stott*.

74. Stott, *Between Two Worlds*, 92.

75. Stott, *Living Church*, 98.

"all Christian preaching is expository preaching."[76] Stott defined preaching this way, "To preach is to open up the inspired text with such faithfulness and sensitivity that God's voice is heard and God's people obey it."[77] Stott affirmed that the preacher performs a double role – staying true to the biblical text and staying true to the contemporary world.[78] This double role is what Stott termed as "double listening," where a preacher has to bridge the gap between the text of scripture and the context (the world) of the audience.[79] He added,

> We have to struggle to understand the rapidly changing world in which we live. We have to listen to its many discordant voices, the cries and the sighs of the oppressed. We need to listen to the questions of the questioner and the loneliness of those who have lost the way. We need to feel the disorientation and despair of the world around us . . . So this is our double obligation.[80]

Following Stott's model, Gitari emphasized that preaching must be holistic. "We are not only going to preach for people to be saved but we are going to respond to needs for their entire well-being."[81] The reason for this holistic understanding of ministry is that a human being is a psychosomatic unit (body and soul) in one unit and the two cannot be separated.[82] Thus for Gitari, every sermon must be relevant to the contemporary situation. Thus "bringing God's word to bear on our contemporary situation is part of what is meant by a prophetic ministry."[83] As to Gitari's own political engagement he stated, "For my part, there was not a Sunday that went by that I did not preach against the one-party system and the evils of the political establishment."[84] Gitari critiqued Kenyan preachers who did not believe

---

76. Stott, *Between Two Worlds*, 125.
77. Stott, *Contemporary Christian*, 208.
78. Stott, *Living Church*, 98.
79. Stott, *Between Two Worlds*, 143.
80. Stott, "Biblical Preaching," 122–123.
81. Gitari and Knighton, "On Being a Christian Leader," 253.
82. Gitari and Knighton, 257; Gitari, *Troubled but Not Destroyed*, 41.
83. Gitari, *Let the Bishop Speak*, xi.
84. Crouch, *Vision of Christian Mission*, 95.

in political involvement. He argued that such preachers misunderstood the mission of the church as well as the meaning of political engagement; aloofness is also a political action.[85]

Gitari also argued that a preacher should spend quality time preparing their sermon and praying that the Holy Spirit would use the sermon to build others.[86] He emphasized that preachers must acquire the necessary theological and biblical training so that they can proclaim the Word of God "powerfully, intellectually and fearlessly."[87] As an Archbishop, Gitari invested resources of the Anglican Church to found and support various theological schools for the training of Anglican priests.[88] These theological schools such as St Andrews College of Theology and Development had a department of development and social services. Gitari believed that by training priests in both theology and development, they would be able to minister the holistic gospel.[89] Indeed, for Gitari, the pulpit provides a platform for preachers to achieve various goals: "The pulpit can be used to touch people's hearts so that they are born again or transformed. The pulpit can be used to educate the people on matters of their health, good farming, water etc. The pulpit can also be used to bring changes in a nation."[90] The next section examines the theological foundations of Gitari's sociopolitical engagement.

Gitari's Model of Public Engagement

Constructive dialogue was Gitari's model (theoretical framework) of public engagement. Gitari argued that there are four possible attitudes to the powers and states with which it coexists: enthusiastic support, passive ignoring, constructive dialogue, or outright opposition.[91] According to Gitari, enthusiastic support is naive acceptance of the intention and goals of the State.[92] Churches that follow this model, mainly those who enjoy a privileged position with the powers that be, support the State at all times and are mostly

---

85. Gitari, "Church and Politics," 7.
86. Gitari, *Troubled but Not Destroyed*, 313.
87. Gitari, 315.
88. Gitari, 44–54.
89. Gitari, "Mission of the Church," 34.
90. Gitari, "Bishop as Leader," 14.
91. Gitari, "Church's Witness," 119.
92. Gitari, 119.

mute to the injustice of the State. The Africa Inland Church as well as the Redeemed Gospel Church in Kenya adopted this posture because of their close relationship with the ruling regime.

Passive ignoring is silence or aloofness in relation to public affairs. The brethren of the East African Revival Movement, followed this model. The assumption of this group of Christians is that politics is a dirty game and must be left to politicians. The main role of the church is to pray and evangelize. These group of Christians, according to Gitari, were quick to praise the government for giving them freedom of worship. Gitari critiques this view arguing that freedom comes from God not politicians; "What the state is supposed to do is to guarantee that freedom."[93]

Constructive dialogue, also known as "critical, constructive and creative participation" is the model of active engagement in the affairs of the society.[94] In this model, the church participates constructively in national affairs. According to Gitari, constructive dialogue is two-pronged. On the one hand the church should work with the government whenever the government upholds standards of justice and righteousness that God requires, and on the other hand, the church must criticize the government courageously when it departs from those standards.[95] Gitari used an analogy of fire to illustrate this model,

> Our relationship with powers that be should be like our relationship with fire. If you go too close to fire you get burnt, and if you go too far away you will freeze. Hence, stay in a strategic place so that you can be of help. You can support the authority, but when they become corrupt you can criticize fearlessly.[96]

In other words, Christian leaders should avoid being too close to politicians so that they can maintain their credibility yet they should not be too far from them so that they can still be able to advice and critique them.

Outright opposition or resistance of the powers of the State is the fourth model of public engagement. Gitari argues that when the governing

---

93. Gitari, 125.

94. Gitari ("Church's Witness," 126) notes that his model can also be referred to as "critical, constructive and creative participation."

95. Gitari, "Mission of the Church," 39; Gitari, "Church's Witness," 134–137.

96. Gitari, "You are in the World," 229.

authorities can no longer be called "servants of God for the good of the citizens" (Rom 13:1–2), then the church is obligated to boldly oppose and even resist it.[97] Gitari's assertion that political leaders are such through leadership, is closely similar to Calvin's argument that political leaders forfeit the authority of their office if they rule unjustly. This assertion was derived from medieval political thought especially Isidore of Seville who argued that if a king becomes a tyrant he forfeits respect for his office. Gitari also emphasized that if the church fails to challenge injustice, it sanctions it. Thus for Gitari, silence was not an option. Having briefly highlighted Gitari's model of public engagement, the chapter now examines the theological foundations for his views.

The Theological Basis for Gitari's Political Engagement

Gitari rooted his political theology in three doctrines. The first is the doctrines of creation and humanity. The second is the doctrine of incarnation. The third is the doctrine of the kingdom of God. The doctrine of creation and humanity shows God's active involvement in the world and creating human beings in God's image. The doctrine of the incarnation shows God's ongoing presence and participation in human affairs through Jesus Christ. Even more than mere participation, Jesus's presence in the world was a political statement. The doctrine of the kingdom of God is about the active presence of God in the world affairs. The kingdom is not just about future events; it is both realized and future. To believe in the future coming kingdom is to work for the ideals of that kingdom here and now.

The Doctrines of Creation and Humanity

Gitari argued that the doctrine of creation reinforces the idea that God not only creates but sustains his creation, while the doctrine of humanity as bearers of God's image reinforces the sanctity of human life.[98] He argued that Genesis 1:3 portrays God as the one who "lets be." This "letting be" is God's conferral of being on those he creates such that the creatures God creates participate in God's creativity.[99] Gitari emphasized that humanity's

---

97. Gitari, "Church's Witness," 131.

98. Gitari, "Church and Politics," 8; Gitari, "Sanctity of Human Life," 21–22.

99. Gitari, "Church and Politics," 8; Gitari, "You are in the World," 220.

participation in God's creativity is directly linked to their creation in the image of God. "Humankind was created in God's image so that they could cooperate with God not only in 'letting be' but also in caring for what God has created."[100] Gitari argued that dominion should not be interpreted as abuse of creation but as responsible stewardship of it. Good stewardship is an acknowledgment that human beings do not own the earth; the earth belong to God (Ps 24:1). Furthermore, dominion is the responsibility of all human beings, men and women together. Also, dominion of God's world is not a responsibility of politicians alone.[101] In fact, for Gitari, it is disastrous to leave this responsibility to politicians alone: "Politicians left on their own have sometimes made decisions that have devastated creation, and their actions have demonstrated the reality of the doctrine of the fall."[102]

Gitari also argued that the doctrine of the image of God affirms the intrinsic dignity of humanity. Quoting from the Lausanne Covenant, Gitari affirmed that "every human being has an intrinsic dignity for which he should be honoured and respected, not exploited or eliminated."[103] This affirmation, according to Gitari, means murder is not only illegal but against God's teaching. Gitari maintained that affirming the creation of humanity in God's image has significant relevance in Kenya. First, it challenges preachers not to abandon public affairs to politicians alone because the welfare of humanity should not depend on a few individuals. Second, it challenges the Kenyan government to preserve the sanctity of human life by doing all it takes to stop ethnic clashes, road accidents, and violence in cities and rural areas.[104]

According to Gitari, the government had participated in the cover up of assassinations of popular politicians such as J. M. Kariuki, Gama Pinto, Tom Mboya, and Robert Ouko.[105] Following the assassination of J. M. Kariuki in

---

100. Gitari, "Church and Politics," 8.

101. Gitari, 8.

102. Gitari, "You are in the World," 220.

103. Gitari, "Sanctity of Human Life," 21.

104. Gitari, 21.

105. Gitari and Knighton, "On Being a Christian Leader," 253; Gitari, "Sanctity of Human Life," 22; Gitari, "You are in the World," 227–229.

March of 1975,[106] which sparked nation-wide unrest, the NCCK requested
Gitari to give six live talk shows on the state-owned Voice of Kenya (VOK)
now renamed Kenya Broadcasting Corporation (KBC), just five minutes
before the morning seven o'clock news.[107] The programme, called "Lift up
your hearts," expounded the first stanza of the national anthem, which runs,

> O God of all creation,
> Bless this our Land and nation
> Justice be our shield and defender
> May we dwell in unity
> Peace and liberty
> Plenty be found within our borders.

Each morning Gitari explained each verse of the anthem from a biblical
perspective.[108] "My main purpose was really to teach the sanctity of human
life, that God has created us in his image and the greatest offence we can
do to him is to take away innocent blood."[109] Gitari likened the powerful
persons in authority to Cain who killed his brother Abel.

> When Cain murdered his brother Abel, God asked him,
> "Where is Abel your brother?" And Cain answered: "I do not
> know. Am I my brother's keeper?" And God said to Cain,
> "What have you done Cain? The voice of your brother's blood
> is crying to me from the ground and now you are cursed" . . .
> Today God is asking Kenyans, "Where is your brother J. M.
> Kariuki?" And those who assassinated him or planned his as-
> sassination are saying, "Am I my brother's keeper?"[110]

---

106. His full name is Josiah Mathenge Kariuki but well known in Kenya as J. M.
Kariuki or simply J. M. He was the Member of Parliament for Nyandarua North. He actively
participated in the freedom struggle for Kenya's independence. When Kenyatta came to
power after Independence in 1963, J. M. started critiquing his policies and holding him
accountable. J. M. was assassinated in March 1975. His badly burned body was discovered
in Ngong Hills south of Nairobi city.

107. Gitari, *Troubled but Not Destroyed*, 33.

108. The entire sermon is recorded in *In Season and Out of Season* (13–21)

109. Gitari and Knighton, "On Being a Christian Leader," 253.

110. Gitari, *In Season and Out*, 19.

After the sermons, the Minister of Information summoned Gitari to his office to explain what he meant by his Abel-Cain analogy. The minister told Gitari that the sermons were very disturbing as they seem to implicate the government in the murder of J. M. Kariuki. Unshaken, Gitari responded to him and the seven men seated with him that if the sermons were disturbing, then they had served their purpose as the gospel of Jesus Christ brings discomfort to sinners.[111] Furthermore, Gitari told each one of them, "Every human being is created in the image of God and has sanctity for which they should be served and not be exploited or eliminated" upon which the minister told him to continue preaching.[112] Gitari also argued that the doctrine of the divine image affirms that humans are social creatures (Gen 2:18) and must live peacefully with one another.[113] The next section examines the doctrine of the incarnation according to Gitari.

The Doctrine of Incarnation

Gitari defined the doctrine of incarnation as "the perception that Jesus 'emptied himself' and chose to 'become flesh' and to live among us, thus identifying with humanity."[114] For Gitari this doctrine compels Christian social action. He cited John 1:14, Philippians 2:6–8, and Hebrews 1:1–2, to support his assertion. He argued that the prologue to the gospel of John attests the reality of Jesus's presence among humanity, "a truly human being who mingled with people, and felt such human emotions as hunger, sorrow, anger, pity etc."[115] For Gitari, the Logos who existed before the world was created became human without losing the qualities of the Logos in any way. Furthermore, Jesus revealed his divinity not so much by mighty acts but by compassion, love, and humble service.[116]

In addition, Gitari argued, Jesus's incarnational living was a political statement. For Gitari, the living God "emptied himself" and chose to "become flesh" and "to live among us," thus identifying himself with humanity.[117] "By

---

111. Gitari, *Troubled but Not Destroyed*, 33; Gitari, *In Season and Out*, 13–21.

112. Gitari, *Troubled but Not Destroyed*, 34.

113. Gitari, "Church and Politics," 8.

114. Gitari, 10.

115. Gitari, 9.

116. Gitari, 9.

117. Gitari, "Evangelization and Culture," 118.

going where people were [referring to Matt 9:35], he was able to see with his own eyes the plight of the people and to make statements, which the politicians of the day would have considered highly political and provocative."[118] Gitari claimed that the poor whom Jesus ministered to were not only those who were spiritually poor but also those who were economically and socially disenfranchised by the structures of the society.[119] Jesus's model calls for Christian social engagement in the world. Christians can never claim to follow Christ and yet at the same time be aloof to the world's concerns and problems. Thus in response to Kenyan politicians who argue that Kenyan preachers should stay away from politics, Gitari commented, "To tell us not to be involved in the welfare of our country is virtually to tell us not to follow the example of Jesus Christ."[120]

Gitari's category of involvement surpasses preaching and evangelization. It is an invitation to proclaim the gospel "not from a distance but rather by penetrating communities and cultures, cities and villages so that we can see for ourselves the harassment and helplessness of God's people and then stand in solidarity with them even if that means taking a political stand, which brings hope to humanity."[121] Participation in humanitarian efforts such as providing shelters for internally displaced persons, starting development programs in areas of health, agriculture, water, education, AIDS awareness, and provision of other social services, is an important way for the church to exercise its incarnational presence in the society.[122] However, Gitari stressed that the role of the church should not stop at humanitarian activities, for to do so is to pauperize and degrade its recipients. Going beyond humanitarian efforts means questioning the root cause of the problem and to seek ways and means of solving the problem. Questioning injustice is taking political action.[123]

---

118. Gitari, "Church and Politics," 10.

119. Gitari, *Troubled but Not Destroyed*, 41.

120. Gitari, "Church and Politics," 10.

121. Gitari, 10.

122. Gitari, "Sanctity of Human Life," 21. See also Gitari and Knighton, "On Being a Christian Leader," 250–251.

123. Gitari, "Mission of the Church," 37.

In his charge delivered during his enthronement as Archbishop, Gitari affirmed that Kenyan churches must always ask why Kenya is the way it is, even if asking that question disturbs the powers that be. He noted that those in authority applaud when the church actively participates in the provision of humanitarian activities, "But the moment we ask what is the root cause of poverty, ignorance, disease and death, some politicians will tell us to keep away from politics and confine ourselves to purely spiritual matters."[124] Thus

> If asking "Why are there so many road accidents in Kenya?" is a political question, then we as church leaders will ask that question many a time and will persistently sensitize our government to regularly repair the roads and bridges, fill in the potholes, urge the traffic police to stop receiving bribes from drivers of unroadworthy vehicles, for these are some of the causes of carnage and loss of lives on our roads.[125]

Therefore, the church must speak against social injustice at all times, especially when everything seems fine. Gitari remembers that upon the advent of multiparty era in 1991, the church kept quiet. "We have been quiet in recent months because those people who should be allowed to speak are now speaking. But the Church must not keep quiet. We must not assume all is well."[126] Gitari's caution to the church should have been repeated in 2002 when the church lost its vision because of its silence. The church thought it had won the battle because Moi had finally retired from power. The silence of the church damaged the church's credibility.

The Doctrine of the Kingdom of God

The doctrine of the kingdom of God is linked to the doctrine of incarnation because "it demonstrates how the incarnate Son of God got deeply involved in the affairs of the world be they economic, political, social, or spiritual."[127] Gitari believed that the theme of the kingdom of God was central to Jesus's ministry on earth. Rather than envision the kingdom as a future expectation, Gitari stressed that the kingdom had dawned on earth in the person

---

124. Gitari, "Sanctity of Human Life," 21.

125. Gitari, 21.

126. Crouch, *Vision of Christian Mission*, 97.

127. Gitari, "Church and Politics," 10.

and work of Jesus Christ. Every healing action Jesus did was a fulfilment of the kingdom of God, a foretaste of the realities of the kingdom.[128] Thus, for Gitari, eschatology is not just about future events; it is both realized and future. To believe in the future coming kingdom is to work for the ideals of that kingdom here and now.

Gitari's theology of the kingdom is also linked to his theology of conversion. He asserted that the doctrine of the kingdom affirms that when people receive Christ they are born into God's kingdom and should work towards propagating the ideals of that kingdom here on earth. He writes, "To be converted to Christ means to give one's allegiance to the Kingdom, to enter into God's purposes for the world expressed in the language of the Kingdom."[129] Thus Gitari emphasizes that contrary to the theology of the brethren of the East Africa Revival of which he was a part of at one point, conversion should not be "inward looking" but wholistic.[130] The Revival emphasized inward spiritual disciplines, confession of sin to one another, pursuit of personal holiness, speaking the truth in love, and detachment from politics. Gitari observes that the followers of the Revival did not participate in politics beyond voting because to them "politics was a dirty game."[131] These Christians were "so concerned with their own individual souls that they show no concern for the corrupt and sinful world around them, except to invite sinners to come out of the 'sinking ship' and join 'the lifeboat' of the brethren."[132]

Gitari also argued that participation in the kingdom of God also means not leaving politics to politicians alone because to do so is to perpetuate the belief that "the purpose of religion is to prepare people for the future not the present."[133] On the contrary, the Kingdom of God as well as conversion is about concrete historical realities, publicly representing God in actual situations on earth as prophets or watchdogs of the society.[134] Furthermore,

---

128. Gitari, 11.

129. Gitari, 11.

130. Gitari, 11; Gitari and Knighton, "On Being a Christian Leader," 251.

131. Gitari and Knighton, "On Being a Christian Leader," 251.

132. Gitari, "You are in the World," 218.

133. Gitari, "Church and Politics," 11.

134. Gitari, 11.

to represent the Kingdom of God on earth is to pray the Lord's Prayer, "Your Kingdom Come, Your will be done on earth as it is in heaven (Matt. 6.10–11)."[135] Gitari maintained that to pray "Your Kingdom come" in Kenya is to ask and work for the end to:

> [1] rigging of National elections, which has made unpopular politicians find their way to parliament where they now sing a litany of Praise for the government and no longer represent the wishes of the people; [2] expulsion of people from the only political party we have thus filling people with fear of expressing different views except those of the establishment; [3] detention of people without trial thus denying the victims of detention opportunity to defend their innocency; [4] destruction of shanties of poor people in the city of Nairobi thus rendering them homeless without providing them with alternative adequate shelter; [5] corruption, which has made some people amass wealth at the expense of others; [6] threats against those dissatisfied with the one party and who now wish legal steps to be taken to return Kenya to a multi-party democracy as it was at the time of Independence; [7] threats against church leaders who wish to preach the implications of inauguration of God's Kingdom by Jesus and its effects on the present day secular society.[136]

Gitari also argued that to pray "Your Kingdom Come" is to espouse a different identity, a Christ-like identity, an identity that cares for the poor and the hurting in the society, an identity that lives differently in a world of violence.[137] This identity should also transcend ethnic biases. "It is absurd to view the world exclusively through the narrow prism of tribal ethnicity."[138] Gitari also argued that commitment to justice has to accompany prayer. "We have to cooperate with God in bringing about a just, united, peaceful and

---

135. Gitari, 12.
136. Gitari, 12, (numbering added).
137. Gitari, 12.
138. Gitari, "Sanctity of Human Life," 22.

liberated nation."[139] The church should model this kind of commitment by being salt and light of the world.

Peace (*shalom*) is another key issue in Gitari's doctrine of the Kingdom. He defines *shalom* as "the state of things, which comes when God's will is being done."[140] Citing Isaiah 32:16–17 and Isaiah 48:18, Gitari maintained that there is no true *shalom* where justice, righteousness, and God's will are hindered.[141] "Injustice is the great cause of strife among men; but when justice is done, the cause of peace is served."[142] Thus by putting justice before peace, Gitari offered a biblically centered critique of President Moi's *nyayo* (the Swahili word for "footsteps") philosophy. When Moi took over from Kenyatta in 1978, he told the nation that he was going to follow Kenyatta's footsteps (*nyayo*). Thus he started popularizing the term to the extent that Kenyans nicknamed him *Nyayo*. With time, *nyayo* became the official philosophy of Moi's government, and to avoid the word becoming an empty slogan, the Attorney General declared *nyayo* a protected word, summarized with a biblical slogan of "peace, love, and unity." But instead of promoting these biblical virtues, *nyayo* became an intolerant political philosophy.[143]

Furthermore, Moi's call to follow Kenyatta was problematic not only because nobody understood what exactly he meant by it, but also because it was wrong to follow the footsteps of another human being who is prone to error; human beings are called to follow the *nyayo* of Jesus Christ and only of those who are following Christ's *nyayo*.[144] Furthermore, Christians are true *nyayo* followers only if they promote these biblical virtues, not because they follow a human being. "If *Nyayo* philosophy stands for peace, love and unity, I would like to state that regardless of where they classify you, you remain a true *Nyayo* follower, if you are working for peace in the spirit of love by struggling against all kinds of injustice."[145] Thereby Gitari avoided the cheapening of "peace, love, and unity" as characteristic of Moi's government

---

139. Gitari, *Let the Bishop Speak*, 32.

140. Gitari, *In Season and Out*, 46.

141. Gitari, "Church's Witness," 129.

142. Gitari, *In Season and Out*, 46.

143. Gitari, "Church's Witness," 129.

144. Gitari and Benson, *Witnessing to the Living God*, 128–129.

145. Gitari, *In Season and Out*, 89.

of espousing them yet at the same time curtailing their prevalence in Kenya for as Gitari asserts, during Moi's regime, "Kenya was neither peaceful nor loving, and there was no unity."[146] Similarly, Samuel Kobia, another prominent Kenyan theologian and ecumenist, argues that the *nyayo* philosophy was a mere "sloganeering meant to appeal to cultures of affection and a weak conscience."[147] He added that it was under the emblem of political love that politicians manipulated ethnicities to their advantage; it was in the name of peace that the police committed brutal acts against the people; and it was in the name of unity that politicians clung to power at all cost.[148]

Okullu, Gitari, and Calvin

Okullu and Gitari emphasized the use of the pulpit to address different social issues in their day. The two were pastor-theologians like Calvin. Their main goal was preaching and ministering in the local church, not teaching in the academia. None of them taught fulltime in the seminary or the university. They served the Anglican Church as pastors then as bishops (Gitari became an archbishop). However, none of them references Calvin in their publications. Okullu draws from F. D. Maurice while Gitari draws from John Stott. However, their political theology has a lot in common to Calvin's political theology.

Foremost, they do not advocate for a complete separation of church and State. They recognize that church and State are separate institutions but should not be antithetical to each other. Okullu and Gitari emphasized that the State must serve the common good and the church must hold the State accountable. Even though they do not reference the historic two-kingdom theology, they however, make similar conclusions. Okullu argued that though both kingdoms owe their origin in God, both serve two distinct purposes. The spiritual kingdom serve spiritual needs of people while the political kingdom enhance law and order thus ensuring human flourishing. In this regard, Okullu's political theology was closer to Luther's two-kingdom doctrine. However, whereas Luther believed the kingdoms are completely

---

146. Gitari "You Are in the World," 228.
147. Kobia, *Courage to Hope*, 47.
148. Kobia, 47.

distinct and parallel and may not mix, Okullu believed the two kingdoms, although distinct, may mix. Thus politics and church can mix. For Gitari, though both kingdoms owe their origin in God and are distinct, both are united by a common interest, which is service to God for God's glory. Thus Gitari's political theology was closer to Calvin's. Overall, the three rejected the belief that politics was a dirty game.

Okullu and Gitari, like Calvin, emphasized that the two kingdoms are not at variance. The emphasis on the un-antithetical nature of both spiritual and political kingdoms allowed them freedom to emphasize Christian participation in secular matters. Conversely, as Calvin rejected the Anabaptist's zeal to escape the world, Okullu and Gitari similarly rejected the Kenyan evangelicals' insistence on complete separation of church and State and the East African Revival Movement's insistence on prioritizing salvation of souls over social action. Their criticism of the Revival follower's stance on politics took a lot of courage because both of them were at one time members of the Revival. Thus Okullu and Gitari's soteriology exceeded individual focus. Salvation is wholistic. Furthermore, they refused, as Calvin did, to separate the world into two domains (spiritual and secular). Instead, they argued that concern for the world is faithful Christian discipleship.

As Calvin claimed, social issues are matters of spiritual concern (contrary to VanDrunen's argument explained earlier). Similarly, Okullu believed that everyday realities such as "preventing the soil from being washed away into the lake and seas, or destroying wildlife, rivers and lakes for quick gains" are much matters of salvation as other ecclesial-specific issues.[149] Also present in the theologies of Okullu and Gitari is the emphasis on the presence of the kingdom of God over the entire world including the redemption of the wider culture. The presence of the kingdom of Christ in the world invigorates the church's social action. To be a Christian is to exhibit and to spread the kingdom of God in the world thus saturating the entire world with the presence of God.

Okullu and Gitari, like Calvin, advocated complete autonomy of the church in overseeing its own affairs. Like Calvin, they insisted on complete freedom of the church. This is contrary to Luther who insisted that the

---

149. Okullu, "Theological and Ethical Considerations," 108.

church must utilize the power of the State to advance its course. Furthermore, Okullu and Gitari, like Calvin, called for obedience to the governing authorities but left the door wide open to resistance of those in power. Both Okullu and Gitari preferred democracy as the best form of governance while Calvin preferred a blend between aristocracy and democracy. All rejected tyranny of any kind in political governance. Calvin rejected monarchical form of governance while Okullu and Gitari rejected a one-party system of government. While Okullu was quick to support multiparty democracy, Gitari was willing to support one-party politics until he recognized that the system hindered Kenya's progress and should be replaced by another system.

Like Calvin, the two bishops emphasized the need for systemic change, compassion, justice, and accountability. They also condemned ethnic-based politics, corruption, and violence. Okullu's emphasis on "heroic faith" is similar in some ways to Calvin's emphasis on total commitment to Christ regardless of the cost. Indeed both bishops suffered because of their actions. Okullu was at one point a political exile in Uganda. Gitari survived an assassination attempt. Interestingly, Calvin too was a refugee most of his life. Like Calvin, Okullu and Gitari were instrumental in founding schools for the training of the clergy and laity not only in Bible and theology but also on development and social justice. In the area of development, Okullu and Gitari emphasized holistic development. They countered Western theories of development, which espoused notions of individualism, progressivism, and human self-sufficiency in the quest for material freedom and economic development. Okullu, Gitari, and Calvin accentuated the ideals of human dignity, fulfilment, and social justice for the poor in their theories of development.[150] They recognized that although humans have a role in their development, that role should not exclude belief in God. The primary loyalty is to God, not material wealth. The next chapter focus primarily in a theology of development from Kenya.

---

150. Okullu, *Church and State*, 102; Oluoch, *Christian Political Theology*, 101. For Calvin's view of human development, especially on money, wealth, and property, see Biéler, *Social Humanism of Calvin*, 30–42; Singer, "Calvin and the Social Order," 228.

Conclusion

This chapter has argued that Gitari and Okullu signify an active political engagement in Kenya. Both clerics represent different approaches to sociopolitical engagement. Okullu worked from the basis of justice and democracy and rarely exegete scripture to buttress his arguments while Gitari's approach embody evangelical biblical hermeneutics similar to that of John Stott and Calvin. As already shown, Okullu utilized his journalistic skills to avow a social theology centered on the concept of justice while Gitari began his prophetic sermons with an exposition of a biblical text then courageously applied the sermon to the prevailing sociopolitical situation in Kenya. The chapter has also shown how their theology addressed the challenge of ethnic based violence in Kenya. It is clear that they publicly condemned it through pulpit ministry and several publications including press statements. The next chapter examines the contribution of Jesse Mugambi's African Theology of Reconstruction (ATOR) to ethnopolitical cohesion in Kenya.

CHAPTER 8

Jesse Mugambi's Theology of Reconstruction as a Theological Response to Ethnopolitical Conflict in Kenya

This chapter focuses on the work of Jesse Mugambi, a notable Kenyan theologian who advanced a theology called African Theology of Reconstruction (ATOR). Mugambi is the pioneer and the key proponent of ATOR.[1] Charles Villa-Vicencio from South Africa, Valentin Dedji from Benin (West Africa), and Kä Mana from Congo (Central Africa), are the other theologians of reconstruction. The basic thesis of Mugambi's reconstruction theology is that the biblical narrative of Nehemiah's reconstruction of the wall of Jerusalem provides the theological paradigm for the reconstruction and the social transformation of Africa after colonialism, apartheid, and the Cold War. Reconstruction theology challenges the church in Africa to actively promote human rights, social justice, peace, and reconciliation in the midst of the atrocities bedeviling the African continent. It also challenges the African people in general to be proactive in combating all that hinders human development and to work towards a better Africa. ATOR is "characterized by calls for rebuilding, renaissance, renewal, development and rebirth."[2] Since ethnopolitical conflict in Kenya is closely related to poverty, which makes many Kenyan people accept handouts from politicians resulting in easy

---

1. Gathogo ("Black Theology of South Africa," 328) observes that Mugambi is the "the undisputed founder of theology of reconstruction in Africa."
2. Gathogo, "Genesis, Methodologies, and Concerns," 26–27.

manipulation of ethnicities for the politician's selfish ends, it is imperative to examine how an emphasis on development and reconstruction might assist in the quest for a theology of ethnopolitical cohesion in Kenya.

A Brief Biography of Jesse Mugambi

Mugambi's full name is Jesse Ndwiga Kanyua Mugambi, born 6 February 1947 at Kiangoci in Embu District in the Eastern County of Kenya. J. N. K. Mugambi, for that is how his name appears in his publications, is the Distinguished Professor of Religious Studies at the University of Nairobi from which he attained his BA in Education (1974), MA in Philosophy and Religious Studies (1977), and PhD in Philosophy and Religious Studies (1983).[3] John Mbiti, "the father of contemporary African theology," mentored Mugambi but while Mbiti left Kenya to pursue life in Switzerland from where he teaches and writes, Mugambi has always worked in Nairobi except for the occasional sabbatical breaks, conferences, and brief teaching opportunities in various schools abroad.[4]

Mugambi has been Guest Professor at Christian Theological Seminary, Indianapolis (USA), Union Theological Seminary (USA), Rice University (USA), Emmanuel College Toronto (Canada), University of South Africa, Lund University (Sweden), University of Helsinki (Finland), and University of Copenhagen (Denmark).[5] Mugambi is an Anglican theologian. His specialty includes religion, ecology, applied ethics, education, and communication policy. In addition to teaching, Mugambi has served as the Theology Secretary for Africa for the World Student Christian Fellowship (1974–1976), a member of the Faith and Order Commission of the World Council of Churches (1974–1984); a member of the WCC Sub-Unit of Church and Society (1984–1994); a founding member of the Ecumenical Association of Third World Theologians (EATWOT); the Senior Consultant

---

3. Gathogo, "Jesse Mugambi's Pedigree," 184.

4. In conversation with the author on 5 July 2016 at St Paul's University, Limuru, Kenya, Mugambi acknowledged that Mbiti played a significant role in his career as a scholar. Mugambi said that Mbiti facilitated and enabled the publication of Mugambi's earliest works. Furthermore, he considers Mbiti a mentor and a role model.

5. Gathogo, "Jesse Mugambi's Pedigree," 178–187; Dedji, *Reconstruction and Renewal*, 88.

for Development and Research at the All Africa Conference of Churches (1994–1997); and since 1994, he has been a member of the WCC Working Group on Climate Change. He is also a member of the Kenya National Academy of Sciences (KNAS) since 1994, and in 2010 the President of Kenya conferred him the National Honor of the Order of Elder of the Burning Spear (EBS), the second-highest commendation that the President can bestow upon a civilian. Mugambi has published more than forty books (as author, co-author, editor, and co-editor) and at least a hundred articles.[6]

A few books are specifically on the subject of Christian reconstruction. These include, *The Church of Africa: Towards a Theology of Reconstruction* co-authored with Jose Chipenda, Andrew Karamaga, and C. K. Omari (1990), *From Liberation to Reconstruction: African Christian Theology after the Cold War* (1995), *Christian Theology and Social Reconstruction* (2003), and *The Church and Reconstruction of Africa: Theological Considerations* (1997). This chapter focuses on these select books and other publications relevant to his theology of reconstruction. Before examining Mugambi's reconstruction theology, the chapter now briefly examines the roots of African theology of reconstruction.

The Roots of African Theology of Reconstruction

ATOR is different from the Christian Reconstructionism (Theonomy) of Rousas John Rushdoony (1916–2001) of the United States of America.[7] Theonomy advocated the restoration of the Old Testament laws especially the Mosaic penal sanctions in the social, political, and cultural reconstruction of the American society.[8] Rather than drawing inspiration from Reconstructionism, ATOR drew from the process of *perestroika*, a term denoting the restructuring of the Soviet Union's political and economic structures under Mikhail Gorbachev in the late 1980s.[9] The contribution of

---

6. Dedji, *Reconstruction and Renewal*, 88; Heaney, *Historical to Critical*, 4–5.

7. For a detailed explanation of Christian Reconstructionism, see, Rushdoony, *Institutes of Biblical Law*.

8. North and DeMar, *Christian Reconstructionism*, 85.

9. Villa-Vicencio (*Theology of Reconstruction*, 241) asserts that *perestroika* denotes "building within the shell of an old society step by step." The best way to reconstruct old societies is through a democratically elected government. Governments must gain the support of the people as long as it is working in the interest of the electorate.

perestroika to African reconstruction theology is twofold. First, Gorbachev's reconstruction agenda, which inadvertently led to the break up of the USSR, helped to popularize the notion of "reconstruction" as a viable political idea in Africa.[10] Second, Gorbachev's reconstruction of his country inspired African scholars to encourage the African people to engage in the reconstruction of Africa.[11] Reconstruction theology also drew inspiration from Pan-Africanism and African Renaissance.

Kwame Nkrumah of Ghana was the leading proponent of Pan-Africanism.[12] His major publications on Pan-Africanism include *Consciencism: Philosophy and Ideology for Decolonization and Development* (1964) and *I Speak of Freedom: A Statement of African Ideology* (1961).[13] Ali Mazrui observes that Nkrumah's Pan-Africanist ideologies had roots in American politics, grassroots initiatives, and the writings of Afro-American scholars such as Marcus Garvey, William DuBois, and George Padmore, and Aimé Césaire from the West Indies.[14] Aimé Césaire was the first to coin the term "Négritude," a term, which gained popularity in the works of Léopold Sédar Senghor, a Pan-Africanist poet and politician from Senegal.[15] Pan-Africanism as an ideology, emphasizes the belief that the progress and development of Africa

---

10. Maluleke, "Half a Century," journal article, 22.

11. Villa-Vicencio, *Theology of Reconstruction*, 3.

12. Other Pan-Africanists include Jomo Kenyatta (Kenya), Gamal Abdul Naser (Egypt), Ahmed Sékou Touré (Guinea), Julius Nyerere (Tanzania), and Muammar Gaddafi (Libya).

13. Nkrumah, *I Speak of Freedom*; Nkrumah, *Consciencism*. Though Nkrumah advanced Pan-Africanism in Africa, the ideology had already taken root in the United States and Europe. Flanya, ("Recourse to History," 5–6), summarizes the various Pan-African Congresses since 1919. The first Pan-African Congress occurred in 1919 convened by J. E. B. Du Bois leading to the formation of the Pan-African Association, fifty-seven delegates representing fifteen countries attended the Congress. The second Congress, attended by 113 delegates, happened concurrently in London, Paris, and Brussels in 1921. The conveners demanded the end of colonial rule and racial discrimination. The third Congress occurred in London and Lisbon in 1923. The fourth Congress was held in New York in 1927. The fifth Congress was held in Manchester, UK, in 1945 under the leadership of George Padmore and Kwame Nkrumah. According to Flanya, ("Recourse to History," 5–6), it was the Manchester conference in particular that "galvanized the leaders of African Independence Movements and contributed immensely towards the eventual liberation of many African countries from the yoke of colonialism." According to Mugambi (*From Liberation*, 38), the Manchester Congress "declared that no African country could consider itself free until all the countries in the continent were liberated from colonialism."

14. Mazrui, *Towards Pax Africana*, 51–61.

15. Senghor, (*Prose and Poetry*, 96) defines "Négritude" as "the awareness, defence and development of African cultural values . . . It is the awareness by a particular social

as a continent and Africans as a people wherever they live, greatly depends on African identity and unity. Thus, Africans in Africa and the diaspora, embracing their roots as African people, must come together to conquer marginalization, racism, and exploitation.[16] Due to this "collective self-reliance" ideology, the Organization of African Unity (OAU), now called African Union (AU) since 2001, was constituted on 25 May 1963, in Addis Ababa, Ethiopia, "to promote unity and development; defend the sovereignty and territorial integrity of members; to promote unity and cooperation among all African states and to bring an end to colonialism."[17]

Similar to Pan-Africanism, African Renaissance is the concept that African people can achieve cultural, scientific, and economic development without having to rely on external tutelage. It furthers authentic African art, music, language, cultures, and customs as necessary for achieving African renewal.[18] Cheikh Anta Diop, a Senegalese scholar, and Thabo Mbeki, a South African politician (president from 1999 to 2008), popularized African Renaissance.[19] In an address delivered at the University of Havana, Cuba, on 27 March 2001, titled, "The African Renaissance: Africans Defining Themselves," Mbeki described what African Renaissance stood for:

> The last decade of the 20th century prepared the conditions for us to claim the 21st century as the African Century, that must be characterized by the all-around advance and development of the African continent, during which, through its own efforts and in the context of a new internationalism, it must catch up with those described today as developed.[20]

However, more than merely borrowing from these African movements, reconstruction theology, as Farisani observes, "is the specifically theological

---

group of people of its own situation in the world, and the expression of it by means of the concrete image."

16. See Nkrumah, *I Speak of Freedom*, 133.

17. African Union, "Pan-Africanism," 1–2.

18. African Union, 2.

19. Cheikh Diop's Pan-Africanist ideas centered on the revival of indigenous languages as necessary for an African renaissance comes out in his book titled, *Towards the African Renaissance* while Thabo Mbeki's vision is found in his several speeches published in *Africa: The Time Has Come* and, *Africa: Define Yourself*.

20. Mbeki, *Africa: Define Yourself*, 75–76.

articulation of Pan-Africanism and African Renaissance."[21] Thus reconstruction theology provides the biblical and theological basis for the projects of Pan-Africanism and African Renaissance.[22] Having examined the roots of reconstruction theology, the next section discusses Mugambi's call to shift from liberation to reconstruction theology.

From Liberation to Reconstruction: The Thesis and Methods of ATOR

ATOR gained prominence after the All African Conference of Churches (AACC) meeting held on 30 March 1990 at Nairobi, Kenya, convened under the leadership of Archbishop Desmond Tutu, the then President of the AACC, and Jose B. Chipenda the then General Secretary. This event occurred at a time of critical importance in Africa. Earlier, between 1984 and 1986, African scholars had convened under the auspices of the United Nations University to deliberate on alternative futures for the continent of Africa. Two books emerged out of this initiative. The first is titled, *Hope Born out of Despair: Managing the African Crisis* (1988) and the other is,

---

21. Farisani, "Transformation and Renewal," 63.

22. Not all African theologians celebrate Pan-Africanism and African Renaissance. Katongole ("African Renaissance," 207–219) argues that they perpetuate a liberal capitalistic vision (209). According to him, these initiatives are "declared from the tenth floor of some air-conditioned offices in New York, London or Cape Town" and mean very little to the ordinary people in rural villages in Africa (209). According to him, these top-down narratives cover up the real intentions of the big multi-nationals and organizations such as the World Bank, IMF, WTO, which is to perpetuate Africa's dependency on them while legitimating their relevance in Africa by using "highly selective sociology of statistics" (210). Furthermore, according to Katongole, such narratives and dreams result in warped values such as individualism, competitiveness, greed, consumerism, and exclusion. Though Katongole's warning is valid in so many ways, nevertheless his wholesale rejection of these movements is problematic. His assumption that these two ideologies and movements did not have real impact on the lives of ordinary people except to perpetuate a capitalistic outlook is overstated. As a person who grew up in rural Kenya, I have seen first-hand the real impact of, for example, rural electrification projects funded by the World Bank. In rural and urban areas where thousands languish in poverty, people are longing for what would truly make a difference in their lives, and if this difference comes from such initiatives as Pan-Africanism or African Renaissance, or such-like initiatives, then they are a welcome "gift" and must be used for the betterment of Africa and the African people. The church should support and encourage such initiatives of development and progress. Where a political system supports human flourishing and the cause of justice and development, it is prudent to support and even work within it than advocating an alternative expression. John Mbiti also rejects Pan-Africanism as an insufficient ideology to meet the needs of the Africa people (See chapter 9).

Beyond Hunger in Africa: Conventional Wisdom and an African Vision (1990).[23] These books influenced and shaped the prevailing conversation at the time, inspiring African people to rethink the destiny of Africa.[24]

Another formative event is the release of Nelson Mandela from prison on 11 February 1990 after twenty-seven years of incarceration, heralding a new era in South Africa and culminating in the collapse of apartheid. Another factor is the African National Congress (ANC) forums and deliberations on a document called Reconstruction and Development Programme (RDP). This document later became, in modified version, the ANC's manifesto in 1994 when ANC took over the leadership of South Africa under Nelson Mandela.[25] Also, at the time, most African countries had attained independence with Namibia attaining its own on 21 March 1990, and most African countries were moving from one-party dictatorship to multiparty democracy. Furthermore, in the 1990s, according to the Center for Global Development, several African countries were "putting behind them the conflict, stagnation, and dictatorships of the past."[26] Thus as Brigalia Bam observes, African theologians were asking themselves what next?[27]

The next step came from Professor Mugambi who gave the keynote address at the AACC meeting titled, "The Future of the Church and the Church of the Future in Africa."[28] He argued for a paradigm shift from the Exodus motif of liberation to the Ezra-Nehemiah motif of reconstruction, with reconstruction as the resultant theological axiom.[29] He defines "paradigm" as "the main framework for theory and practice within a cultural context."[30] Prior to this conference and the subsequent emphasis on reconstruction theology, inculturation theology (indigenization/contextualization) and African liberation theology were dominant theologies in Africa. It is necessary to offer a quick explanation of theologies.

---

23. Odhiambo, ed., *Hope Born Out of Despair*; Achebe et al., *Beyond Hunger*.

24. See, Mugambi, *From Liberation*, 83–85.

25. Vellem, "Ideology and Spirituality," 548.

26. Radelet, *Emerging Africa*, 1.

27. Bam, "Foreword," xi.

28. This essay appears in Chipenda et al., *Church of Africa*, 29–50, and it also appears in Mugambi, *From Liberation*, as chapter 10.

29. Mugambi, *From Liberation*, 5.

30. Mugambi, "Theology of Reconstruction," 140.

Inculturation is an approach in missions/evangelization of witnessing to a culture from within.[31] As a theology, mainly in Roman Catholic circles, it argues that the gospel has to be "incarnated" in human cultures, into the lives of converts, and must be expressed in the converts' own unique ways in order for it to be relevant. Contextualization, the process of relating the Christian message to the convert's sociocultural context, is the Protestant equivalent of inculturation. Inculturation (contextualization) seeks ways Christianity is compatible with culture, including the salvific relationship between pre-Christian cultures and Christianity, and ways Christianity might be expressed in the receiver's own cultural forms.[32] This expression must in-

---

31. Ukpong, "Christology and Inculturation," 40.

32. The relationship between Christianity and African pre-Christian traditions or precisely, African Traditional Religion (ATR); African culture and African religion are intertwined and inseparable; was, and still is, a major issue of debate among African theologians of different theological persuasions. Richard Gehman, (*African Traditional Religion*, 396–402), provides three approaches on this issue: continuity, discontinuity, and continuity-discontinuity. Continuity is the belief that Christianity and African Traditional Religion are expressions of God's revelation. However, Christianity is the final and the superior means of revelation (396). This view is rooted in several theological bases. First, there is only one God who reveals himself to every people groups on earth at different times and in different ways. Bolaji Idowu (*Olódùmarè*, 31) asserts,

> surely God is One, not many, and that to the one God belongs the earth and all its fullness. It is this God, therefore, Who reveals Himself to every people on earth and Whom they have apprehended according to the degree of their spiritual perception, expressing their knowledge of Him, if not as trained philosophers or educated theologians, certainly as those who have had some practical experience of Him.

For Idowu, the God missionaries introduced to Nigerians is the same God Nigerians worshipped in the past before the missionaries showed up (Idowu, *Olódùmarè*, 31). Thus all the people of the earth have some knowledge of God because God reveals Himself to them. Potentially, this view leads to universalism since all divine revelations are valid. Consequently, all religions worship the same God, and all religious expressions are salvific as they lead to the same God. John Mbiti (*African Religions and Philosophy*, 277) provides a Christological basis for the continuity perspective, which counters this universalism. He asserts that African pre-Christian traditions constitute a *praeparatio evangelica* but only Christianity offers the way to the "ultimate Identity, Foundation and Source of security" (277). Jesus Christ is humanity's ultimate identity. For Mbiti, Jesus fulfils and completes African traditional religiosity (277). Furthermore, Mbiti, as Ukpong observes, asserts that since Jesus existed before Abraham (John 8:58), it is accurate to assert that Christ was already present in African pre-Christian religious and cultural heritage prior to the proclamation of the gospel, "and since Jesus is one with the Father (John 10:30) and Africans do worship God, Jesus has actually been worshiped without a name" (Ukpong, "Christology and Inculturation," 43). The second approach is discontinuity. Discontinuity sees a total disconnect between ATR and Christianity. Akin to Justin Martyr's "What has Athens to do with Jerusalem?" or Karl Barth's "The Revelation of God is the Abolition of Religion," or Dietrich Westermann's advice to missionaries that "giving the new [Gospel] means taking away the old [traditional cultures]" (Westermann,

clude the "three-self" principles of mission: self-governing, self-propagating, and self-supporting. However, Mugambi observes that though incultura-tion theology incarnated the Christian faith into cultural forms of African converts, it was nonetheless a "one-way" theology because the faith being incarnated reflected the foreign culture of the missionaries more than the receiver's culture.[33] Thus as argued below, Mugambi advocates indigenization of the gospel that truly reflects the cultural patterns of the African people including the use of vernacular languages.[34] Thus his project of indigeniza-tion or contextualization is a form of self-theologizing (the "fourth self" of missions)[35] or theological reflection from within the African cultural context.

Liberation theology in Africa is of two varieties: South African Black Theology contending mainly against racial segregation (apartheid) and African liberation theology (including African women's theology) in the independent part of Africa, which emphasized wholistic liberation or

---

Africa and Christianity, 2), this view sees no salvific possibility in ATR. Most missionaries to Africa assumed pre-Christian Africa was a religious "tabula rasa," a clean slate ready for impartation of the Christian faith. According to Bediako, ("Roots of African Theology," 58) this mentality assumed Africa's pre-Christian heritage had nothing meaningful to offer Christianity and it was wrong. The third approach is Continuity/Discontinuity. This approach sees meaningful points of contact between Christianity and African traditional heritage yet also highlights various points of disconnect between them. I subscribe to this third view because it pays attention to the importance of cultural heritage yet understands that it is not the most important definitive characteristic of a believer. Our allegiance is to Christ not our cultural past. Being uprooted from our cultural heritage is not a precondition for accepting and following Christ.

33. Mugambi, "Fresh Look," 356; Mugambi, "Missionary Presence," 172. Ela (*My Faith,* xiv), a Roman Catholic theologian from Cameroon, makes a similar observation when he asks, "Who should undertake the fundamental task of inculturation?" then he answers: "Surely the initiative must not be left to men and women who have come from elsewhere, sometimes themselves disoriented by different cultural origins, education and background" (xiv). Ela continues to argue that if indeed African Christians themselves should handle the task of inculturation in Africa, then African theologians must be equipped (trained) to theologically respond to questions and concerns of African Christians (xiv). This training should be an ongoing process because culture is dynamic and thus questions keep changing (xv). Like Mugambi, Ela believes that the relevance of contemporary African Christianity largely depends on how African Christians critically reflect on and respond to "the structures or strategies of exploitation and impoverishment against which Africans have always struggled" (xvii).

34. For more on this point, see, Mugambi, "Missionary Presence," 172. Lamin Sanneh, (*Translating the Message,* 88–156), provides a more elaborate historical analysis of the role of vernacular in the appropriation of the gospel.

35. Paul Hiebert, (*Anthropological Insights,* 193–224) proposed self-theologizing as the "fourth self" principle of missions.

liberation from anything that dehumanizes God's people.[36] The aim of liberation theology is to address two primary questions: "What does it mean to be a Christian in a context of oppression?" and "What is the relevance of the Christian faith to life in a society where there is terrible injustice and exploitation?"[37] In African liberation theology, the African people were analogically identified with the Israelites who needed to be liberated from the Egyptian bondage (referring to colonialism, apartheid, and neo-colonialism) and led to Canaan, the land of freedom and prosperity (referring to the anticipated freedom) by "Moses" (Africa's nationalist leaders, scholars, or theologians).[38] These theologies, especially liberation theology in its various strands, were dominant in Africa until 1990 when Mugambi called for a paradigm shift.

During the AACC meeting, Mugambi argued that inculturation and liberation have been taken as the most basic ideas for African Christian theology far too long. On this point Mugambi writes, "Christian theology in Africa, particularly during the 1960s and 1970s, emphasized very much the theme of liberation as Exodus from colonial bondage, without highlighting the transformative and reconstructive dimensions. The exodus motif was so dominant that there were hardly any other biblical texts that could be associated with African Christian theology."[39] But since the African context has changed in recent years from colonialism and apartheid to independence and freedom, Mugambi argued, the change necessitated a shift of gears.[40] The "New World Order,"[41] for Mugambi, is an important historical moment that challenges African theology to shift gears from the Exodus motif to

---

36. Wholistic liberation was the main focus of the EATWOT meeting in Dar es Salaam, Tanzania, in August 1976.

37. Padilla, "Liberation Theology," 427.

38. Mugambi, *From Liberation*, 165. Also Ela's *African Cry*, chapter 3, "An African Reading of Exodus."

39. Mugambi, *From Liberation*, 39.

40. Mugambi, "Social Reconstruction," 2. See also Mugambi, *Christian Theology*, 128; Gathogo, "Survey of African Theology," 125; Mugambi, *From Liberation*, 40.

41. The term "New World Order," as used in ATOR, denotes the end of colonialism, apartheid, and the Cold War. In the post-9/11 world, this term has gained a new meaning. President George W. Bush used it to signify the dawn of terrorism in the world. For Bush, countries such as Iraq, Afghanistan, and Palestine represent "the axis of evil" and with direct involvement of the US military, Bush hoped to rid the world of terrorism.

other viable motifs such as "the Exilic motif (Jeremiah), the Deuteronomic motif (Josiah), the Restorative motif (Isaiah 61:4), the Reconstructive motif (Haggai and Nehemiah), and so on."[42] Of these motifs, Mugambi preferred the motif of reconstruction as found in the book of Nehemiah.[43] The book, of course, notes Mugambi, should be "read critically, taking into consideration all hermeneutical, exegetical, theological and ethical limitations associated with the reconstruction project of Nehemiah."[44] It is questionable whether or not Mugambi himself reads Nehemiah critically. In addition to Nehemiah, Mugambi foregrounds his reconstruction theology on Christ's mission and preaching, for example that Christ came to set the captives free and to initiate the kingdom of God on earth (Luke 4:18–19). Also, he highlights albeit very briefly that the Sermon on the Mount and the writings of Paul provide the biblical grounding for reconstruction theology.[45]

In addition to the Bible, other resources for reconstruction theology include social sciences, philosophy, creative writing, biology, and physical sciences.[46] It must also involve a critical reading and analysis of "alternative social structures, symbols, rituals, myths and interpretations of Africa's social reality by Africans themselves . . . "[47] Furthermore, reconstruction should transcend denominational divides, "considering that the task of social reconstruction after the Cold War cannot be restricted to any religious or denominational confines."[48] Thus in addition to being multidisciplinary it must also be ecumenical. The resultant theology would have the following qualities:

> This theology should be reconstructive rather than destructive; inclusive rather than exclusive; proactive rather than reactive; complementary rather than competitive; integrative rather than disintegrative; programme-driven rather than project-driven;

---

42. Mugambi, *From Liberation*, 39.

43. Specifically, Mugambi, (*From Liberation*, 166) observes, "The central biblical text for African Christian theology in the 21st century will perhaps, be the Book of Nehemiah, rather than the Book of Exodus."

44. Mugambi, *From Liberation*, 166.

45. Mugambi, "Theology of Reconstruction," 147–148.

46. Mugambi, *From Liberation*, 40.

47. Mugambi, 40.

48. Mugambi, 2.

people-centred rather than institution-centred; deed-oriented rather than word-oriented; participatory rather than autocratic; regenerative rather than degenerative; future-sensitive rather than past-sensitive; co-operative rather than confrontational; consultative rather than impositional.[49]

Mugambi avers that reconstruction has four levels: personal, cultural, ecclesial, and socio-economic. The next section examines these four levels.

Personal Reconstruction

According to Mugambi, the process of social-political reconstruction begins with personal or individual reconstruction; an individual must "continually reconstruct oneself in readiness for the tasks and challenges ahead."[50] He argues that according to Jesus's teachings in the New Testament, change must first occur within the motives and intentions of people. He references several New Testament writings, which include Luke 18:9–14, Matthew 23:1–13 and Luke 12–13. From the Luke 18:9–14 text, Mugambi argues that the confession of the Publican and the pride of the Pharisee are contrasts intended to highlight the appropriate disposition necessary for social change to occur.[51] He also cites three hymns, "Amazing Grace," "Take My Life and Let it Be," and "Just as I am," to show the significant role of spiritual transformation. He concludes, "These hymns are reminders that the key to social transformation is appropriate disposition of the individual members of the community concerned, especially its leaders."[52] Furthermore believers must conform their lives to the teachings of Jesus especially the Sermon on the Mount. The Sermon according to Mugambi, is a concise outline of reconstructive theology.[53] Though Mugambi does not elaborate further on this point, he clearly believes in personal transformation as a necessity for the reconstruction of Africa.

---

49. Mugambi, xv.
50. Katongole, *African Theology Today*, 203; Mugambi, *From Liberation*, 15.
51. Mugambi, "Liberation to Reconstruction," 203.
52. Mugambi, 204.
53. Mugambi, "Theology of Reconstruction," 147.

Cultural Reconstruction

According to Mugambi culture is the next element of reconstruction. He defines culture as "the cumulative product of people's activities in all aspects of life, in their endeavor to cope with their social and natural environment."[54] He identifies politics, economics, ethics, aesthetics, and religion as components of culture. Also, the present cultural manifestations of consumerism, globalization, and secularism, must be incorporated into the discussion of culture in Africa. African cultural and religious heritage, Mugambi argues, should never be limited to primordial worldviews for it goes beyond that.[55] He argues that reforms must occur in all the components of culture. Without reconstruction of these elements, chaos and unrest might occur.[56] Mugambi goes ahead to explain how the various components of culture need reconstruction. First, economics focuses on reconstruction in matters of management of resources. Second, politics deals with reconstruction in the management of social influence and must include democracy, fairness, and sharing of power. He rejects the political system of winner-loser and advocates for winner-winner, in which all contestants participate in the future reconstruction of their countries having learned from their past mistakes.[57] Third, moral reconstruction concentrates on reconstruction in matters of values in the society. Fourth, aesthetics deals with the sense of proportion and balance in all aspects of life. Fifth religion provides the worldview and perception that shapes goals and aspirations of people. Religion too needs reconstruction as explained below.[58]

Furthermore, Mugambi argues that cultural reconstruction must touch on ways people are evangelized. Evangelism and missions, he argues, is not about uprooting people from their cultural and religious heritage, but about embedding the gospel into their cultural and religious identity.[59] Mugambi offers a scathing attack on the past and current Euro-American missionary enterprise for its failure to respect the cultural identity of African converts.

---

54. Mugambi, "Liberation to Reconstruction," 204.

55. Mugambi, "Fresh Look," 353.

56. Katongole, *African Theology Today*, 204; Mugambi, *From Liberation*, 16–17.

57. Mugambi, *From Liberation*, viii–ix.

58. Mugambi, 17.

59. Mugambi, "Fresh Look," 359.

Missionaries to Africa, he maintains, adopted a superiority mentality and derided African culture and heritage. Rather than learn and adopt the cultures of the converts, the missionaries demanded the converts to learn and adopt their cultures. Thus, according to Mugambi the modern Christian missionary initiative has assumed, in general, that the culture and ethics of the missionary is "Christian" and "good," whereas that of the prospective converts is "non-Christian" and "evil."[60] According to Mugambi, such an attitude amounts to "imperial expansionism."[61] Indeed, for Mugambi, the conduct of the missionaries was not always distinguishable from that of the imperial colonialists who came to Africa with a mindset of civilizing the "primitive," "dark," and "undeveloped" continent.[62] He adds, "Generally, African converts were expected to adopt the new 'Christian' way of life, without necessarily being taught that this new 'way' was a product of a particular denominational interpretation and expression, developed in the context of particular Western cultural backgrounds."[63]

In contrast, Mugambi emphasizes that the current African Christians should be given a chance to express their faith in a characteristically African outlook "in rituals, symbols, vestments, music, liturgy, architecture, metaphors, and theological emphases."[64] Thus conversion should provide the convert the courage and possibility of affirming their own cultural identity. He asks this crucial question, "If the missionary enterprise is unable to offer exemplary applications of the Gospel in all cases, how can future converts be expected to establish model Christian communities in their own local environments?"[65] This contextualization, for Mugambi, is the acid test for the durability of Christianity in Africa.[66]

Ecclesial Reconstruction

Mugambi also argues that the church needs reconstruction. Of the various components of culture shown above, religion is the leading component.

---

60. Mugambi, "Problem of Teaching," 14.
61. Mugambi, 14.
62. Mugambi, *God, Humanity and Nature*, 19; Mugambi, *From Liberation*, 94.
63. Mugambi, *African Heritage*, 42.
64. Mugambi, *From Liberation*, 43.
65. Mugambi, 96.
66. Mugambi, 43.

Religion shapes and forms worldview. Religion is "that pillar of culture, which provides the presupposed world-view and the basic principles for the organization of society."[67] Since Africans are "notoriously religious,"[68] Mugambi argues, the way forward is not to remove them from their religiosity but to ground them in the gospel of Jesus Christ and to allow them to express their faith in their own religious and cultural ways. Mugambi also argues that ecclesial reconstruction should include reconstruction in the management of resources, financial policies, pastoral care, human resource development, research, family education, service, and witness.[69] He argues that the church in Africa should position itself to address the challenges that emerge because of the influence of globalization, capitalism, technology, and other modern inventions because these forms of progress will push the church to the periphery of society and the church must be prepared to assert itself when it is no longer the dominant voice in society.[70]

Mugambi defines theology as "the systematic articulation of human response to revelation within a particular situation and context."[71] Thus theology, for him, is always contextual. Theologians have to reflect theologically within their own cultural contexts. They must respond to relevant questions coming out of those contexts. Such questions include: "What is the meaning of Church in our context? Should we maintain the ecclesiastical structures we have inherited from other cultures? If so, with what justification? Who do we say Jesus is? How do we relate the teaching of Jesus about God to the African religious heritage?" and many other contextual questions.[72] Mugambi also reiterates that theological reflection does not always have to be done in academic settings; people may theologize without having to write anything.[73]

Mugambi also argues for Christian unity, which should transcend the unity of one denomination to include unity between Catholics and Protestants and unity between different ethnic communities.[74] He laments

---

67. Mugambi, "Social Reconstruction," 19.
68. A statement attributed to Mbiti, *African Religions and Philosophy*, 1.
69. Mugambi, *From Liberation*, 17.
70. Mugambi, "Social Reconstruction," 22–23.
71. Mugambi, *From Liberation*, 19.
72. Mugambi, 25.
73. Mugambi, 20.
74. Mugambi, 203.

that Euro-American missionaries bequeathed the African church with highly fragmented denominations. This fragmentation, for him, is analogous to "tribalism" in Africa. "Not surprisingly, therefore, the Euro-American missionary enterprise in Africa has endeavoured to 'de-tribalize' and 'civilize' African converts, while denominationalizing them into new 'denominational tribes.'"[75] These "denominational tribes" complicates the church's quest for ethnic cohesion in Africa. Thus Mugambi argues that the new generation of African Christians should find ways of transcending denominationalism and other sectarian divisions. The church in Africa must bear a witness in words and deed. It must be agents of reconciliation between the various ethnic communities of Africa.[76] The church must support the needs of refugees and displaced persons living in Africa.[77] But even more important, the church must be a catalyst of "long-term programme[s] for conflict-resolution within and between denominations and also in the context of national and international conflicts."[78] This is another acid test of the credibility and contextual relevance of Christianity in Africa.

Socio-economic Reconstruction

Socio-economic reconstruction focuses on the reconstruction of economics and helping initiate poverty alleviation in Africa. While acknowledging the active role of churches, organizations, and individuals in relief and emergency programs, the most crucial challenge, for Mugambi, is for the church in Africa is to "discern the *causes* and *contexts* which generate these crises."[79] Such crises include "economic crisis, debt crisis, population crisis, technological crisis, knowledge crisis, and so on."[80] Mugambi laments that it is indeed ironical that a continent, which stretches through the equator and, which contains all the climates and vegetations of the world, should also have the greatest food deficit in the world.[81] According to Mugambi the main causes of food deficit in Africa is social instability as well as weak

---

75. Mugambi, 174.
76. Mugambi, 174–175.
77. Mugambi, 176.
78. Mugambi, 177.
79. Mugambi, 72.
80. Mugambi, 162.
81. Mugambi, 86.

infrastructure, which African leaders have created.[82] He also blames "external conditionalities" such as weapons from the West, for Africa's underdevelopment.[83] The way forward out of this debacle is to reconsider Africa's social structure, to reform them and make them more efficient and productive.[84] He proposes "alternative strategies" out of Africa's economic crisis, which include "self-reliant programmes for food production, preservation and storage, education on the international economy, strengthening and stabilizing of local and national marketing infrastructures, and so on."[85]

Mugambi also emphasizes that Africa's economic freedom depends on Africa's freedom from fatalism and negativity. For Mugambi, Africa has something significant to contribute to the world. Africa "should be internationally viewed not as a dumping ground for obsolete technologies and a laboratory for untested ones, but as a creative and innovative participant in the re-configuration of the world."[86] For Mugambi, this reorientation of Africa's image is a theological task that calls for a total rejection of all the dehumanizing imaginings of the African people. African Christians should forge a positive self-image and reject the old colonial images of Africa as the "sleeping question mark" or Africa as the "dark continent."[87]

Support and Critique of Mugambi's Reconstruction Theology

Mugambi's reconstruction theology gained support from several leading African theologians such as Brigalia Bam, Charles Villa-Vicencio, and Kä Mana. In a Foreword to *Being the Church in South Africa* (1995), Bam, a theologian from South Africa, notes that the collapse of apartheid in South Africa and the defeat of colonialism by many African countries by the early 1990s when Mugambi called for a paradigm shift, necessitated a re-evaluation of African Christian engagement as well as African Christian

---

82. Mugambi, 86.
83. Mugambi, 164.
84. Mugambi, 161.
85. Mugambi, 156.
86. Mugambi, "Social Reconstruction," 24.
87. Mugambi, *From Liberation*, 49.

theology. She writes, "At first there seemed to be a stunned silence throughout the Church. Next came the inevitable question - what now? Resistance
was no longer sufficient. We were obliged to ask how we could best share
in rebuilding the nation. The new context demanded a new message."[88] The
new message Bam talks about is reconstruction. She contends that the way
forward for the South African Council of Churches (SACC) is to participate
in the process of reconstruction of their nation. She reiterates the direction
SACC ought to take considering the new context in which resistance is
no longer desirable. The way forward for SACC is to support government
programs that enrich the lives of people. The church must not sit on the side
lines but must participate; "We need to learn what it means theologically
and in praxis to address the problems of the political economy, education,
housing, health care and a host of related problems."[89] Bam adds, "To turn
away from this opportunity is surely to deny the call of the gospel to feed the
hungry, minister to the poor and heal those who cry out for the liberating
power of Christ. We *must* be part of the nation-building process."[90]

In his *A Theology of Reconstruction* (1992), Villa-Vicencio, also from South
Africa, like Mugambi, argues that Africa, after colonialism and apartheid,
needs reconstruction. For him, this reconstruction is a shift from liberation
(resistance) to nation building (a theology of home-coming and nation
building).[91] Villa-Vicencio asserts that the current realities in South Africa
require more than resistance or saying "No." The church must now engage in
the difficult task of saying "yes" to the unfolding process of national reconstruction.[92] Unlike Mugambi who clearly rejects liberation theology in favor
of reconstruction, Villa-Vicencio admits that his reconstruction theology is

---

88. Bam, "Foreword," xi.

89. Bam, xii.

90. Bam, xi.

91. Villa-Vicencio, *Theology of Reconstruction*, 32. Elsewhere he writes,

Today South Africa stands on the brink of a new society, if only in the sense that
a new phase in the history of struggle has begun. Reconstruction is anticipated
at a number of different levels, and the time is overdue to identify the essential
characteristics of a theology of nation-building. It could have implications for
what it means to be the church in other parts of the world (37).

92. Villa-Vicencio, *Theology of Reconstruction*, 7.

a new kind of liberating theology, precisely liberatory theology.[93] Indeed, it can be argued that even Mugambi's reconstruction theology is also a kind of liberating theology. Liberation paradigm dominated his earlier work leading up to the publication of his *African Christian Theology: An Introduction* in 1989. Here, Mugambi embraces both the spiritual and physical dimensions of salvation; "the good news of Jesus is relevant to the material, social, political, and psychological needs of those for whom Jesus came to the world, the poor and exploited; the captives; the physically disabled and the mentally depressed."[94] However, he abandoned the liberation paradigm in favor of reconstruction as already argued above.

Like Mugambi, Villa-Vicencio sees in scripture powerful resources for reconstruction theology. Thus, with the help of the Bible as well as other resources from social sciences, law, economics, and other disciplines, reconstruction theology should advocate for economic justice and empowerment of the poor.[95] It must aid in turning people away from greed, domination, and exploitation while nurturing human rights and freedom.[96] However, Villa-Vicencio, like Mugambi, does not engage in thorough exegesis of scripture to support his reconstruction theology.[97] Villa-Vicencio also argues that theology should not be used to legitimate the status quo or any form of political ideology, nor should it be a tool in the hands of politicians and political empires.[98] Thus like Mugambi's reconstruction theology, Villa-Vicencio's reconstruction theology has a strong emphasis on critiques of

---

93. Villa-Vicencio, 13, 29. He is also open to learn from the past theological contributions (38). Villa-Vicencio ("Liberation Theology," 184–196) offers an elaborate explanation of liberation theology.

94. Mugambi, *African Christian Theology*, 97.

95. Villa-Vicencio, *Theology of Reconstruction*, 2.

96. Villa-Vicencio, 2, 5.

97. This lack of exegetical work could be attributed to Villa-Vicencio's methodology of targeting a wider readership. Thus he (*Theology of Reconstruction*, 3) acknowledges that his work is "unambiguously inter-disciplinary" and "It is written at the nexus of theological, political, economic, philosophical and legal debate, with a focus on human rights in a struggle for the creation of a more equitable and just society. There is an implicit theology operative in even within the non-theological sections of the book." Besides, Villa-Vicencio is not a biblical scholar.

98. Villa-Vicencio, *Theology of Reconstruction*, 22–23.

sociopolitical structures.[99] He also emphasizes that for reconstruction theology to be relevant politically, it must aid the church and the community in the process of producing tangible proposals to deal with the complex day-to-day problems.[100] For the church, this process must include translation of the values of the gospel into tangible practices. Thus both Mugambi and Villa-Vicencio's reconstruction theology are contextual and praxis-oriented.[101] The church's significant contribution to the world, according to Villa-Vicencio, is its production of utopic visions of a new society on earth. "If the Church loses that vision, allowing that the prevailing order at any given time is essentially all that can be hoped for, it neglects an essential eschatological contribution to society."[102]

Likewise, Kä Mana supports the shift to reconstruction but argues that deconstruction must precede reconstruction.[103] Africa must deconstruct in order to reconstruct. Imagination is the major area of deconstruction that must happen if Africans are to re-invent a new future for themselves. The major problem with the African continent according to Kä Mana is fatalistic attitudes or the subtle realities of alienation and powerlessness, which cripple or hinder Africa's well-being, progress, and development.[104] What is at stake in conquering these realities and introducing a different way of being,

---

99. Villa-Vicencio (*Theology of Reconstruction*, 40) advocates for social analysis, defined as

> the separating of the different components of a policy or political programme, with a view to uncovering its true intent and actual consequence. It involves uncovering the causes of suffering and exploitation in society, as well as identifying the signs of new birth that reside within the community as a basis for both confronting the State and encouraging programmes of hope and renewal.

100. Villa-Vicencio, *Theology of Reconstruction*, 38.

101. This praxis nature of theology is clear in Villa-Vicencio's statement hereby quoted:

> If an agenda of nation-building does not take the church beyond debate into the actual process of shaping the character of society, the church will again have failed to demonstrate that its pronouncements on social justice ought in any way to be taken seriously by those whose concern it is to reconstruct society in the wake of the devastation left behind by dying and dead societies of corruption. (*Theology of Reconstruction*, 40).

102. Villa-Vicencio, *Theology of Reconstruction*, 30.

103. His publications on reconstruction include, Kä Mana, *Christians and Churches*; Kä Mana, *Théologie africaine pour temps de crise*; Kä Mana, *Foi chrétienne, crise africaine et reconstruction de l'Afrique*.

104. Kä Mana, *Christians and Churches*, 20–21.

according to Kä Mana, is for Africans to embrace hope rooted in the life and story of Jesus the Christ. So instead of blaming Western countries and Euro-American missionary enterprises for the problems bedeviling Africa as Mugambi does, Kä Mana argues that Africans should reconsider their social *imaginaire*[105] and by so doing re-invent Africa's destiny because it is in the very imagination of the people that a new future is made possible.[106] Kä Mana also emphasizes that it is Christ who makes this new future possible by opening new possibilities for the African people and generating for them a new vision of what it means to be human in a broken world.[107] Thus for Kä Mana Jesus Christ is the enabler of reconstruction "a catalyst for changing a life, a lever for raising the future, a ferment for bringing in a new society and a solution to the ultimate questions about death and the world beyond."[108] Jesus as Christ and savior enables the orientation of ethics of true being causing the African people to value others and to be available to others.[109] Christ, for Kä Mana, enables a new imagination and possibilities. "Christ is the one who saves us from our insignificance, inconsistency and loss of value."[110] He adds, "Proclaiming God and humanizing humans, [Christ] launches Africa on the path of reconstruction, building a new society."[111] While Mugambi grapples with the possibility of utilizing Africa's ancestral resources to define a future for Africa,[112] Kä Mana has no place for such, equating them to "sterile monuments," which provide some form of escapism from the realities of the present.[113] Even here, Kä Mana subjects ancestral history to the lordship of Christ; Christ "is the yardstick by which we perceive our ancestors in their view of humanity . . . the measure

---

105. Dedji ("Ethical Redemption," 254) explains that the French word *imaginaire* is common in Kä Mana's argument and it "relates more closely to certain patterns of ideas than to facts" and it denotes "patterns of thought or the 'inner drive' motivating [a community's] behaviour in specific circumstances."

106. Kä Mana, *Christians and Churches*, 17.

107. Kä Mana, 54.

108. Kä Mana, 2.

109. Kä Mana, 34.

110. Kä Mana, 35.

111. Kä Mana, 35.

112. Mugambi, *From Liberation*, 88.

113. Kä Mana, *Christians and Churches*, 65.

of humanity against which we measure all human cultures in their claim to build a society of 'shared happiness.'"[114]

While Kä Mana, Villa-Vicencio, and Brigalia Bam supported the shift to reconstruction theology, Musa Dube strongly critiqued it. She argued that as a post-colonial feminist theologian, she strongly believes that liberation theology provides a better framework for the quest for the freedom of women from oppression. "As women in various cultures and religions, our liberation and rights are hardly guaranteed. It is within the parameters of the struggle for liberation that we are able to call and ask for our rights and for reconstructive efforts that embrace and affirm women and men."[115] In an email message to Julius Gathogo, a Kenyan theologian who wrote his book on Mugambi's reconstruction theology, Dube said that she disagreed with Mugambi as he "naively responded joyfully to the collapse of the Berlin Wall and saw globalisation as ushering in a new time, a fair time, where all can walk, act, see and think freely."[116] But according to Dube, Mugambi's work "remains quite blind to the superstructure of patriarchy, which must be deconstructed in order to reconstruct."[117] Indeed, Mugambi does not pay much attention to gender issues in his major publication on reconstruction. For example, though he has fourteen chapters in his *From Liberation to*

---

114. Kä Mana, 67.

115. Dube, "Jesse Mugambi," 4.

116. As cited in Gathogo, "Jesse Mugambi's Pedigree," 175. Mugambi's optimism was widely held by political and intellectual leaders at the time. See for example, Fukuyama, *The End of History and the Last Man* in which he was optimistic that the end of Communism in eastern Europe, and the triumph of liberal democratic capitalism, was the beginning point of a new world order. For Fukuyama, human history had been moving towards liberal democracy. The end of the Cold War signaled the apex of human ideological evolution. De Gruchy (*Christianity and Democracy*, 231–232) asserts that "Unlike Fukuyama's scheme of things, the end of history does not mean boredom, nor does it mean the universal homogenization of culture, nor does it require Nietzschean 'will-to-power' and human aggression to get the cycle of history moving again. The reign of God means *shalom*—it opens up the future for justice, peace, and the restoration of the integrity of creation." Practically, the failure of liberal democracies in most African countries casts doubt on Fukuyama's thesis. By assuming that humans had reached the apex of their ideological evolution, Fukuyama assumed Western democracy had to be exported to other nations. However, African nations must address African problems through forms of governance that grow from within the African context (See, de Gruchy, *Christianity and Democracy*, 188–192). However, since the world is now a global village, African nations must also critically integrate forms of governance, values, and institutions that emerge from other parts of the world.

117. As cited in Gathogo, "Jesse Mugambi's Pedigree," 175.

Reconstruction none address gender inequality though it is a serious problem in Africa. Thus Dube's critique seems less about reconstruction itself than that Mugambi did not address gender issues. Feminist concerns should be included within a reconstruction political theology.

Similarly, Valentin Dedji, Wilson Niwagilia, and Tinyiko Maluleke critique Mugambi's claim that "the end of the old order is the beginning of the New Order."[118] They assert that this assertion is problematic as far as Mugambi believes "the New Order" is free from "systems of oppression" such as "colonialism, racism, and ideological propaganda."[119] It is apparent that Mugambi holds to such a belief, for he writes, "the stance of Reconstruction presupposes that the struggle is already won, and the effort is directed towards building the new society."[120] These scholars argue that such a belief offers false hope to the people of Africa because Africa can never be said to be truly free of these "systems of oppression."[121] For the common rural and urban poor of Africa, nothing much has changed. African politicians and power brokers have replaced the old colonial masters and in many African countries, ethnicity, nepotism, xenophobia, and sexism, have replaced apartheid. Similarly, Niwagilia reinforces this situation with the following words: "The 'Exodus to Freedom' has turned to be an exodus to bewilderment; honey and milk have turned to be hunger and poverty, harmony, peace, joy and prosperity turned to be agony, killings and hatred. Many have been left in the wilderness to die as refugees and misplaced people."[122] These authors are correct.

A quick look at Africa's politics reveal that the African people are still oppressed. Consider for example the February 2016 general elections in Uganda where President Yoweri Museveni, a man highly praised many years ago as a pan-Africanist or "Uganda's Moses,"[123] did all he could to curtail

118. See Mugambi, *From Liberation*, xv.

119. Mugambi, "Social Reconstruction," 2. See also Mugambi, *Christian Theology*, 128; Gathogo, "Survey of African Theology ," 125.

120. Mugambi, *Christian Theology*, 74.

121. Maluleke, "Half a Century," in *The Church and Reconstruction of Africa*, 107. See also Dedji, *Reconstruction and Renewal*, 75.

122. Niwagilia, "Our Struggle," 171.

123. Mugambi, ("Theology of Reconstruction," 144), observes that the first generation of Africa's leaders were invariably likened to Moses because of their role in liberating Africa

the election process including sanctioning raiding of the opposition head-quarters and arrest of the opposition leader only a day before the national polls.[124] Likewise, it was the rigidity of President Mwai Kibaki and Raila Odinga of Kenya, which precipitated the 2007 post-election violence leading to the loss of lives. Africa lags behind in progress and development because of leadership problems and thus it is difficult to imagine reconstruction of Africa without liberation.

Several authors see Mugambi's choice of Ezra-Nehemiah as problematic. Masiiwa Gunda argues that Nehemiah's sole leadership is problematic for solving the problem of power centered on one individual in Africa.[125] Just like the Moses figure was problematic in liberation theology, for African leaders were likened to Moses thus producing authoritarian leaders who were not willing to share power, so also the figure of Nehemiah as the sole leader in the reconstruction of Israel, is problematic.[126] Gunda argues that reconstruction theology should pay attention to the dangers of legitimizing authoritarian leadership by using scripture. Similarly, Musa Dube argues that the Ezra-Nehemiah texts not only legitimizes colonialism and neocolonialism, they are also oppressive to the rights of women.[127] She adds, "the leader of the community in the reconstruction is male and he calls for what I can call some form of 'ethnic cleansing.' Ezra-Nehemiah urges all Israelite men who had married foreign women to divorce them, and they do."[128] Dube's goal in her publications is to redefine biblical reading so that it does not

---

from colonialism

124. Museveni came to power on 26 January 1986 when his National Resistance Army (NRA) toppled Milton Obote. He became a darling of the West and Africa as he restored peace and stability to the war-torn country. During this time, Museveni delivered nationalist speeches throughout Africa and abroad and wrote several essays. These have been condensed into a book titled, Museveni, *What is Africa's Problem?* However, Museveni, has abused his presidential powers. He has been in power for more than three decades. His recent manipulation of the electoral process resulted in post-election violence in several parts of the country. Robert Mugabe, the President of Zimbabwe is another example of Pan-Africanists turned dictator. One wonders whether the project of Pan-Africanism and African Renaissance has totally failed Africa.

125. Gunda, "African Theology of Reconstruction," 89.

126. Gunda, 91.

127. Dube, "Jesse Mugambi," 13.

128. Dube, 13.

"continue to endorse the colonizing of any nation or people."[129] Dube believes that the Bible is a culturally bound book used to support imperialism, to rob Africans of their land, dignity and power, and a proper reading of the bible will prevent the endorsement of these ills.[130] Likewise, Farisani critiques Mugambi for not paying attention to ideology behind the Ezra-Nehemiah texts, "an ideology, which is biased in favour of the returned exiles, but biased against the *am haaretz* [the Jews who did not go into Babylonian exile but stayed in Palestine, the people of the land]."[131] Farisani notes that by excluding the *am haaretz* in the reconstruction project (Ezra 4:3; Nehemiah 2:20), the returned exiles fostered marginalization, hatred, and enmity between themselves and the *am haaretz*.[132] Such an ideology, Farisani argues, is very problematic for ethnic cohesion in Africa. Thus "if reconstruction theology has to contribute to the resolution of ethnic conflicts in Africa, it has to take into account the voices of all groups within such a conflict."[133] The next section examines the contribution of ATOR to ethnic cohesion.

Contribution of Mugambi's Reconstruction Theology to the Quest for Ethnic Cohesion

As seen above, Mugambi's reconstruction theology has implication for sociopolitical cohesion in Kenya. First of all, Mugambi and other reconstruction theologians such as Villa-Vicencio, must be applauded for their quest to rebuild Africa through theological reflection. They must be commended for not abandoning the work of reconstruction to social scientists, NGOs, politicians, and civil societies. They believe that theology is a significant contributor to the reconstruction of Africa. However, considering that most of their publications came out in the 1990s, it is important to constantly review and analyze their success in actually providing a vision for Africa, especially in regard to ethnopolitical cohesion. As already shown, ethnic conflict is a major impediment to the destiny of many African nations. How then does

---

129. Dube, "Rereading the Bible," 61.

130. Dube, *Postcolonial Feminist Interpretation*, 15–17.

131. Farisani, "Use of Ezra-Nehemiah," 34.

132. Farisani, 41.

133. Farisani, 45.

Mugambi's reconstruction address the challenge of ethnic conflict in Africa as a whole and specifically in Kenya?

It is true that ethnic conflict in Kenya is closely tied to control of resources especially the presidency. The closer a community is to the center of power, the more likely it is to access and/or to control national resources. Thus generating more wealth becomes an economic agenda of those in power thus leading to corruption by those in power and oppression and manipulation of communities who are not close to power. When those who are oppressed are finally in power, they in turn oppress or suppress others as Mugambi observes, "when liberation has been achieved, there is always the temptation of former slaves to become oppressors themselves."[134] Thus there is a need for reconstruction to pay attention to these forms of oppression and manipulation or otherwise the quest for economic empowerment fails to free Africa from these systems of oppression.

Another issue in Mugambi's reconstruction theology is his downplaying of inculturation and liberation theologies.[135] Mugambi discarded liberation and inculturation theologies in favor of reconstruction. However, it was necessary to build on these previous theologies instead of discarding them. Indeed, as Robert Schreiter argues, reconstruction is "a different kind of liberation theology."[136] By rejecting these theologies, however, Mugambi's reconstruction theology deprives itself of drawing from them. Leonardo Boff, a key proponent of liberation theology, notes that the books of Ezra and Nehemiah inspired the people of Central America in their quest for social reconstruction because the books "portray the efforts at restoring the people of God after the critical period of Babylonian captivity."[137] Boff shows that it is possible to develop a theology of reconstruction without rejecting liberation theology.

---

134. Mugambi, *Christian Theology*, 25.

135. Mugambi (*From Liberation*, 165) writes, "For most African countries, that metaphor has been applied for too long, and perhaps should have been replaced at the time of the declaration of African republics during decolonization. However, it is not too late." Elsewhere Mugambi ("Social Reconstruction," 20–21) writes, "For this purpose, the Exodus motif is inappropriate and inadequate."

136. Schreiter, *New Catholicity*, 110.

137. Boff, *Introducing Liberation Theology*, 35.

Indeed, in several African countries, it is impossible to reconstruct without liberation. For a true reconstruction to have effect, it must have some elements of liberation. Countries not only need constructors like Nehemiah, in some cases, they also need liberators and agitators like Moses. Some structures have to be destroyed, pulled out, or flattened, before reconstruction can begin. Kenya still needs people such as Archbishop Gitari and Bishop Okullu who were brave enough to question and interrupt the rhetoric of ethnic hatred and to make possible a genuine democratic process that acknowledged the contribution of different parties not just one individual. If indeed the major task of liberation theology is to say "no" to all forms of oppression as Villa-Vicencio asserts, then liberation is always part of the prophetic ministry of the church.[138] The church should always say "no" to "systems of oppression" including all forms of exclusion. Furthermore, Kenya is yet to free itself from corrupt politicians who amass wealth for themselves and use all means to stay in power, including exploiting ethnicity for selfish reasons. How would Kenya reconstruct when it still needs to liberate itself?

In general, ATOR is relevant for ethnic cohesion but it must expand its arguments to incorporate liberation theology and capitalize on other biblical themes especially the creation of humanity in the image of God and the "reconstruction" of believers in the image of Christ. Thus to rise above marginalization and exclusion, reconstruction theology must read Nehemiah from the lenses of creation in the image of God and recreation of humanity in God's image in Christ. This is because the doctrine of the image of God (properly interpreted) leaves no room for marginalization and exclusion while at the same time providing room for reconstruction or transformation of sinful humanity.[139] Furthermore, in the image of God humans are called to serve God, and not to serve idols of our times such as individualism, materialism, and consumerism. Arguably, seeking national material prosperity may in some ways be an affirmation of the idols of our

---

138. Villa-Vicencio, *Theology of Reconstruction*, 1.

139. "Properly interpreted" because not all interpretations of the image of God lead to human flourishing. Hall's *Imaging God*, for example, shows that some readings of the image of God have contributed to the ecological crisis and Reynold's *Vulnerable Communion*, shows that some interpretations of the image of God have led to the dehumanizing of people with disabilities.

time. Thus Christian theology of reconstruction must continually define what constitutes human flourishing.

Mugambi and Calvin

Mugambi's political reconstruction theology has similarities and differences to Calvin's political theology. Mugambi's theology came at a time when Africa was gaining momentum in political liberation and progress. There was a lot of optimism in the "African dream" as proposed and advocated by Pan-Africanists. In the wake of the African optimism, Mugambi argued that the liberation motif was no longer sufficient for Africa's future. He preferred reconstruction. His reconstruction project advocates for a critical analysis of social structures.

Although Mugambi bases his reconstruction theology on scripture, he also draws from social sciences and other disciplines. Thus, his project is multidisciplinary. Calvin's project of reforming Geneva was mainly centered on God's Word. Like Calvin, Mugambi emphasizes personal spiritual re-construction as the beginning point of societal reconstruction (though his treatment of the subject is minimal in his major book on reconstruction theology). Unlike Calvin, Mugambi does not deal widely on the devastating effects of the fall on humanity. This lack of hermatiological focus reflects in his assumption, for example, that the end of colonialism, apartheid, and the Cold War, presupposes the end of "systems of oppression" and the beginning of a new world order. This assumption downplays the gravity of evil in the world. Calvin, on the other hand, emphasizes the total vitiation of human powers by sin. Thus, whereas Mugambi is optimistic of human achievements and progress, Calvin is pessimistic.

Although Mugambi does not use the Reformed language of "culture making," he believes that reconstruction of Africa must include cultural reconstruction. Precisely, Mugambi stresses cultural transformation and engagement. He also advocates for systemic change when he talks about socio-economic reconstruction. Additionally, Mugambi acknowledges that part of the problem bedeviling Africa is an anthropology that dehumanizes the African people. Thus a way out of Africa's crisis is to redefine what it means to be human in Africa. As this study has shown, redefinition of what it means to be human in Kenya must begin with and take the doctrine of the image of God seriously. Another key issue in Calvin's political theology that can enrich Mugambi's reconstruction political theology is the emphasis on the lordship of Jesus Christ over every facet of life (a key emphasis of Reformed theology). ATOR must emphasize Christ as the liberator and reconstructor of the African people.[140] This is not to say that Mugambi does not assert the role of Christ in reconstruction, but that his emphasis lie more in programs of reform, institutional change, and Africa's traditional heritage.

Conclusion

This chapter examined Mugambi's reconstruction theology and its relevance in addressing the challenge of ethnopolitical conflict in Kenya. It shows that ATOR is developmental in approach and addresses poverty, underdevelopment, and other ills in Africa. The chapter also examined the various supports and criticism of ATOR showing that Mugambi provides a brief explanation of personal/spiritual reconstruction but chooses to devote more attention to social and political reconstruction. The next chapter examines the contribution of John Samuel Mbiti's theologies of identity, culture, and community to ethnopolitical cohesion in Kenya.

---

140. See Kä Mana's reconstruction theology for example.

John Mbiti's Theologies of Identity, Culture, and Community as Theological Responses to Ethnopolitical Conflict in Kenya

This chapter examines John Mbiti's views of identity, culture, and community and their relevance for a theology of ethnopolitical cohesion in Kenya. Ethnopolitical conflict in Kenya is strongly tied, not only to politics, but also to identity, culture, and community.[1] A people's beliefs, values, and shared historical experiences influence their self-identity and their response to and relationship with other communities and may mobilize an identity that excludes outsiders especially those from other ethnic communities.[2] If not checked, these markers fan animosity between groups, which may

---

1. Mbiti is the major figure of reference in respect to these three themes.

2. Jack David Eller ties culture to ethnicity and ethnicity to conflict in his *From Culture to Ethnicity to Conflict*. Eller argues that communities end up in conflict not primarily because of their ethnic backgrounds but because of cultural conditioning (4). For him, ethnicity is a product of tradition, values, and a people's way of life. When a community chooses a certain way of life to influence them, or when they choose to embrace a certain narrative or construct over another, different reactions (including violent reactions) to other communities ensue. Thus for him, culture is transformed to ethnicity and ethnicity is transformed to conflict. This is indeed the nature of Kenya's ethnopolitical conflict as Ruth Wangeci Ndung'u, ("Socialization and Violence," 110–125) argues. Ndung'u argues that Kenyans "have been socialized into violence through multifaceted ideas and practices; politics, economics and culture all have something to do with this socialization" (111). Ndung'u also shows the role language plays in ethnic socialization. She asserts, "If a violent culture is institutionalized through linguistic choices in a group, community or nation the individuals, groups, communities and nations may be obligated to enforce it and thus promote misunderstanding, intolerance and lack of appreciation of diversity" (112). She proves the various ways cultural practices have been used to propagate a culture of negative ethnicity in Kenya.

result in conflict. This chapter has four parts: (1) a brief biographical information about Mbiti; (2) Mbiti's theology of identity situated within the African quest for selfhood and identity; (3) Mbiti's theology of culture; and (4) Mbiti's theology of community anchored in the African indigenous religion and culture.[3] This chapter argues that although Mbiti develops a comprehensive account of ethnic identity, culture, and community, he pays minimal attention to their connection with ethnopolitical conflict. His aim, as one of the pioneers of the study of African indigenous religious heritage, is to provide a positive appraisal of Africa's indigenous heritage (traditional beliefs, concepts, and practices) vis-à-vis the Christian faith.[4] Thus this chapter argues that Mbiti, although making an important contribution to indigenous African theology, offers little on the contemporary critical issue of ethnopolitical conflict.

A Brief Biography of John Samuel Mbiti

John Samuel Mbiti was born in Mulango, Ukambani, Kenya, on 30 November 1931. He was educated at Makerere University College, Uganda, which at the time was a constituent college of the University of London. He earned a degree in English and Geography. After that he joined Barrington College in New England, USA, to study theology. Afterwards, he returned to Kenya to teach at a teacher's college for two years after which he left to teach African Christianity at Selly Oak Colleges in Birmingham, UK. He proceeded to Cambridge University to pursue doctoral studies in New Testament, which he completed in 1963. It was at Cambridge that Mbiti met his wife Verena Siegenthaler, who, at the time, was studying English. They were married in Switzerland. Upon graduating from Cambridge, Mbiti taught religion, theology, and New Testament studies at his Alma Mater, Makerere University, for ten years (1964–1974) rising in rank to professor and Head of the Department of Religious Studies. Thereafter he moved to Switzerland where he served, from 1974 to 1980, as the Director of

---

3. Mbiti ("Man in African Religion," 55) defines "African Religion" as "the indigenous religious system and life of African peoples, [which] developed gradually, without particular founders, systematic doctrines, or written scriptures."

4. Bediako, ("John Mbiti's Contribution," 386) observes that Mbiti's writings had the desired effect of "rehabilitating Africa's rich cultural heritage and religious consciousness."

and professor at the Ecumenical Institute Bossey, an institute of the World Council of Churches and an affiliate of the University of Geneva; he extended the influence of the institute beyond Europe and America.[5] Afterwards, he served as Parish Minister for the Reformed Church of Bern in Burgdorf from 1981 to 1996 while at the same time serving as part-time professor of Missions and Extra-European Theology at the University of Bern. Mbiti has since retired from ministerial service but continues to teach as Professor Emeritus at the University of Bern.[6]

Mbiti has taught at several universities around the world including Harvard, Princeton, and Union Theological Seminary.[7] He is a recipient of three honorary degrees: Barrington (Gordon) College (1973), the University of Lausanne, Switzerland (1991), and General Theological Seminary in New York (1997). Oxford University Press published his PhD thesis titled, "Christian Eschatology in Relation to Evangelisation of Tribal Africa," as *New Testament Eschatology in an African Background: A Study of the Encounter between New Testament Theology and African Traditional Concepts* in 1971. His other notable writings are *Poems of Nature and Faith* (1969); *African Religions and Philosophy* (1969); *Concepts of God in Africa* (1970); *The Crisis of Mission in Africa* (1971); *Love and Marriage in Africa* (1973); *The Prayers of African Religion* (1975); *Introduction to African Religion* (1975); *Bible and Theology in African Christianity* (1986) among others. He has also edited more than fifteen books and published more than four hundred journal articles. He is hailed as "the father of modern African (Anglophone) theology,"[8] "the father of contemporary African theology,"[9] "the most productive African scholar in theology in our time,"[10] "the leading African theologian,"[11] "a pioneer in the systematic analysis of traditional African religious concepts,"[12] and a

---

5. Olupona, "Biographical Sketch," 6.

6. Mbiti, "Foreword in Theological Education," xv; Olupona, "Biographical Sketch," 1–2; Heaney, *Historical to Critical*, 4–5; Kinney, "Theology of John Mbiti," 65–68.

7. Mbiti, "John Mbiti," 4.

8. Heaney, *Historical to Critical*, 3. The emphasis on "Anglophone" (English speaking Africa) distinguishes his contributions from those from "Francophone" (French speaking Africa).

9. Perkinson, "John S. Mbiti," 455.

10. Olupona, "Biographical Sketch," 7.

11. Hastings, *History of African Christianity*, 232.

12. Kinney, "Theology of John Mbiti," 65.

man with "the weightiest bibliography among modern African theologians."[13] Furthermore, McVeigh Malcolm observes that Mbiti, along with others, exerted "a function for Africa equivalent to that of Barth, Tillich, Niebuhr, and Rahner in Europe and North America."[14]

Mbiti is a strong proponent of African theology deeply established in the African heritage, culture, and religiosity. His major aim, throughout his varied publications, is to assert a form of Christianity that is "indigenous," "traditional," and "African," for it is only that form of Christianity that "holds the greatest potentialities of meeting the dilemmas and challenges of modern Africa."[15] Therefore he delineates an African Christianity rooted in the African traditional milieu.[16] He believes that the African traditional heritage was a *praeparatio evangelica* (preparation for the gospel) in the sense that it provided a ready seedbed, "more than anything else," for Christianity to take root in Africa.[17] He firmly believes that Christ fulfills all human cultures. African cultures are not exempted.[18] "Without African religiosity whatever its defects might be, Christianity would have taken much longer to be understood and accommodated by African peoples."[19] He also notes, "It is this preparedness that has undergirded the spreading of the gospel like wildfire among African societies, which had hitherto followed and practiced traditional religion."[20]

---

13. Bediako, "John Mbiti's Contribution," 367.

14. Malcolm, "Sources," 2–3.

15. Mbiti, *African Religions and Philosophy*, 1st ed., 271. In "Christianity and African Culture," 390, Mbiti observes, "The only lasting form of Christianity in this continent is that which results from a serious encounter of the Gospel with the indigenous African culture when the people voluntarily accept by faith the Gospel of Jesus Christ."

16. Bediako ("John Mbiti's Contribution," 367) asserts that though Mbiti critiques the Euro-American missionary enterprise for its failure to foster a form of Christianity rooted in the African heritage, "nevertheless, the subject of missionary errors and misconceptions concerning African religious life figures less prominently in Mbiti's work than in the writings of some other African theologians." Bediako observation is true. See for example Jesse Mugambi's theology of reconstruction, which is laden with heavy critiques of mission Christianity. For a more detailed study of the comparison of the critique of mission Christianity in the theological writings of Mugambi and Mbiti, see Heaney, *Historical to Critical*, 31–50.

17. Mbiti, "African Indigenous Culture," 79–95. See also Mbiti, *Introduction to African Religion*, 190.

18. Bediako, "John Mbiti's Contribution," 373.

19. Mbiti, "African Indigenous Culture," 86.

20. Mbiti, "Encounter of Christian Faith," 819.

This emphasis on African Christianity rooted in the African roots falls within the long scholarly and lived tradition of the search for an authentic African identity. This tradition sought freedom from negative images of the Euro-American missionaries, anthropologists, and colonialists who demeaned the African people and their cultures. African nationalists such as Kwame Nkrumah of Ghana, Patrice Lumumba of Congo, Julius Nyerere of Tanzania, Jomo Kenyatta of Kenya, Léopold Sédar Senghor of Senegal, and Afro-American theologians and secular intellectuals as well as scholars from the West Indies, participated in this search for meaning and identity. The following section explains the concept of identity in Mbiti as located within the quest for identity among African theologians and secular intellectuals.

The Identity Question of Africa

Identity, a person's or a community's self-definition and self-understanding, is a major point of discussion among African theologians and secular intellectuals.[21] Communal or social nature of life is what defines African identity. The need for a definition of what it means to be African in Africa (and the African diaspora) arose out of the various contexts of life in Africa: the challenge of the missionary enterprise, the colonial experience especially the colonialists' ethnocentric attitudes toward Africans, the formation of new governments after the colonialists left (between 1954 and 1994), the post-colonial land resettlement programs, which uprooted some people from their ancestral lands (for example the case of the Sabaot in Mount Elgon in Kenya); the reality of apartheid in South Africa, the challenges of modernization and globalization, rural to urban migrations, the embrace of foreign languages (English, French, Arabic, and Portuguese) at the expense of indigenous languages, the loss of tradition, and the various challenges of poverty and diseases that ravage the continent of Africa.[22] African secular

---

21. Appiah, "Quest of African Identity," 55; Lowery, "Identity and Ecclesiology," 12–13.

22. Mazrui, (*African Condition*, 68) states, "Christianity, Western liberal democracy, urbanization, Western capitalism, the rules of Western science and the rules of Western art have jointly exerted an unparalleled influence on the emergence of personalized identity in Africa." Similarly, Tiénou, ("Right to Difference," 25) states, "The Africans' search for their past is the result of a reaction to Western domination and domestication." As to the missionary factor and its influence on African Christian identity, Tiénou ("Right to Difference," 31) observes, "Wittingly or unwittingly, missions in Africa contributed to the making of the

intellectuals sought to define what it means to be an African in the same way African theologians sought to define what it means to be an African and an African Christian.[23] As African intellectuals sought to generate authentic Africanness in the midst of demeaning experiences, African theologians sought to achieve this quest and more.[24] African theologians grasp identity as a theological matter, which has serious implications for Christian life.[25] Consequently an apologetic of African identity characterizes African scholarship both Christian and secular.

Simon Kofi Appiah identifies three reasons for the identity crisis in Africa.[26] The first is "cultural amnesia," or "a crisis of communal (cultural) memory," which he defines as the loss of authentic cultural roots because of the uprooting of the African people from their backgrounds.[27] Second, the loss of the "mythical and historical narratives" of the African people. Narrative, according to Appiah, is more than the organized sequence of words; "It also contains interactive silence, emotions, feelings, desires, unexpressed thoughts that establish connections to the past and to the present, movements of the body and of the mind."[28] For Appiah, narrative is what defines communal life of a people group. Any loss or distortion of narrative results in loss of identity.[29] Third is the loss of "narrative ethics," which results in "social dysfunction."[30] Elsewhere, Appiah argues that African Christian

---

Black man into the White man. That is why the quest for African theology is also a quest for selfhood and emancipation."

23. Maluleke, ("Identity and Integrity," 31) observes that for African theologians, "The question therefore is not merely what it means to be an African Christian convert, but what it means to be an African, period."

24. Simon Appiah, (*Africanness*, 6) explains that the term "Africanness" is best described as "the desire for authenticity and the struggle to redress the state of alienation that resulted from the historical experiences of cultural domination, slavery and colonialism in Africa. In this sense, Africanness directs our attention to the complex web of issues involved in the African struggle for the rehabilitation and integral liberation of Africans, as basic topics of African theology."

25. Tiénou, "Right to Difference," 31; Bediako, *Theology and Identity*, 6, 31–33; Ferdinando, "Christian Identity," 121.

26. Appiah, "Quest of African Identity," 57–58.

27. Appiah, 57; Appiah, *Africanness*, 55. Ilo, (*Church and Development*, 114) calls this crisis, a crisis of "homelessness."

28. Appiah, *Africanness*, 53–54.

29. Appiah, "Quest of African Identity," 57.

30. Appiah, 58.

ethics has to take seriously the African indigenous moral traditions if it is to have a lasting impact on the African people.[31] Similarly, Stan Chu Ilo identifies two factors for the identity crisis in Africa. The first is historical factors, "which have created the political structures of African nations, and continue to influence African economy, social integration or social disloca-tion in most of these countries."[32] The second is cultural factors, "which touches on identity, worldview, status, equality, gender issues, family life and traditions, the social capital, the common good, and the bases for liv-ing and working together among various ethnic nationalities and diverse cultural and religious communities in Africa."[33] For Ilo these factors have created a serious crisis in Africa.

In addition to debating the roots of the identity crisis, African intellectu-als have also questioned the legitimacy of the term "Africa." Questions such as "Did 'Africa' refer to a province, a people with a particular skin color, or an entire continent? And would the people categorized have claimed that a unity or similarity existed between them?" characterized the discussion.[34] Valentin Mudimbe, in his study of sixth-century Latin nomenclature, argues that the term "African," "is the equivalent of *Afer*, as substantive as well as adjective, and simply designates any person from the continent regardless of his or her color. It literally translates *Africanus*."[35] He continues to assert that for the Romans, "Africa" referred to one of their provinces and "Africans," "'the *Afri* or *Africani*, its inhabitants.'"[36] Whereas the Latins referred to Africa as *Afer* and the inhabitants as *Africanus*, the Greeks referred to *Africa* as *Ethiopia* (*Aithiops*), the land inhabited by darker skinned, black peoples who live south of the Sahara desert.[37] They came to this conclusion because *Aithiops* literally means "a face burned by the sun."[38] It was this later associa-tion of "Africa" with skin color that gave birth to racism and other forms of disparagement of the African people. Kombo notes that this negative

---

31. Appiah, *Africanness*, 6.
32. Ilo, *Church and Development*, 114.
33. Ilo, 114.
34. Lowery, "Identity and Ecclesiology," 22.
35. Mudimbe, *Idea of Africa*, 26.
36. Mudimbe, 26.
37. Mudimbe, 27; Kombo, *Doctrine of God*, 1.
38. Kombo, *Doctrine of God*, 1.

perception began at the time of the European exploration. "The European favored *Nigritia* (from Latin *Niger*) as the name for the continent and called the inhabitants *Nigriti*."[39] Kombo, following Philip Curtin's argument in *The Image of Africa*, argues that though the original meaning of the terms *Nigritia* and *Nigriti* was equivalent to *Aithiops* as Mudimbe explains, with European exploration, the terms were used in a negative sense to distinguish Europeans as civilized and progressive, from Africans deemed primitive and savage.[40]

Along with Mudimbe and Kombo, Emmanuel Katongole agrees that "Africa was to a large extent the way it was (is) imagined by Europe, with concepts like 'chaos,' 'tribe,' and 'primitive' integral to that imagination – if only as a way to confirm the European imagination of Europe as civilized and developed."[41] Katongole asserts that a new future for Africa involves cultural deconstruction and interruption of these definitions of Africa. For him, this quest for definition is an ecclesiological task. In characteristic Hauerwasian language, Katongole asserts, "the gospel does not have a social message (from which to draw implications), but that the gospel *is* a social message."[42] This ecclesiological task calls for concrete physical embodiment

---

39. Kombo, 1.

40. Kombo, 1–2. Other scholars have a similar perspective as Kombo's. See, Curtin, *Image of Africa*, 28–57; Tiénou, "Right to Difference," 26–27. Similarly, Appiah (*Africanness*, 51–53) argues that with an ethnocentric approach, European anthropologists and missiologists treated African cultures as "experimental specimen" of research for understanding primitive cultures. They believed that the European culture was too intellectually developed to derive any meaningful conclusions about the genesis of human beings and their cultures; thus they needed to study more "primitive" cultures such as the African culture. This cultural superiority is clearly clear in Lucy Mair's study of the Baganda people of Uganda. Mair, (*African People*, 3) states: "Christian missionaries have set their faces against all the patently 'uncivilized' aspects of native culture, whether or not they were strictly forbidden by the Scriptures: they have opposed polygamy, slavery, the payment of bride-price, initiation ceremonies, dancing, wailing at funerals . . . as all being repugnant to a civilization in which mechanical warfare was a recognized institution" (3). Mair's judgment of Christian mission shows that missionaries approached the African cultures with a lot of suspicion and prejudicial judgments. The missionaries used their own Western cultures as the benchmark or the standard for marking or judging the African cultures.

41. Katongole, *Sacrifice of Africa*, 8.

42. Katongole, *Sacrifice of Africa*, 195. Other scholars have asserted the active role of the church as a place where social imagination is formed thus resulting in "alternative" social practices. These scholars include Stanley Hauerwas, (*A Community of Character*); David Fitch, (*The End of Evangelicalism?*); Graham Ward, (*The Politics of Discipleship*); Jürgen Moltmann, (*God for a Secular Society*); William T. Cavanaugh, (*Theopolitical Imagination*). The arguments of these scholars are varied but they agree that the church is called to interrogate narratives and ideologies of the world and to foster an alternative social imagination; "imagination"

of godly values in communities, which God's people inhabit. "The search for an alternative history takes place at the grassroots in communities of faith and in the ordinary realities of everyday life."[43]

As Katongole observes, Africans have to counter the negative characterization of their continent. These negative imaginings give birth to fatalistic and destructive attitudes among the people. Read Hollis, writing in 1864, provides the grim picture of the African continent at the time:

> Africa is a land of the most singular contrasts. Nowhere else do such extremes meet – fertility and barrenness – beauty and deformity – civilization and barbarism – light and darkness – human elevation and human depression. Though one of the earliest known, and the earliest civilized quarters of the globe, yet Africa has remained for the last three thousand years the least known, and the least civilized; sometimes the most blessed, but generally the most cursed of any part of the world.[44]

Such negative perceptions of Africa have yielded sentiments such as "the dark continent," "the neglected continent," "the land of shadow and mystery," "the land of atrocities," "an ailing continent," "the traumatized continent," "a black hole," "the continent of churches and coffins," among other negative

---

in this case being more than thoughts but includes practices. These scholars emphasize that the church effects its influence by way of weakness not power. They emphasize the resultant community formed to continue the work of Christ on earth, and that this community, the church, looks forward to the expected new creation where all humanity, including all powers of the world, will be ultimately subjected to the lordship of Christ. Meanwhile, the church lives out a distinctive way of life enabled by the cross and resurrection in the midst of the world's brokenness. For them, the church does not need to prove itself to the world, for that is to acquiesce to worldly standards. Rather the church exercises their influence marginally and powerlessly. Exilic orientation is a powerful way the church ought to exist in this time and age. In this regard, the first task of the church is to be the church. To live right in a broken world is the calling of the church. Living right in a broken world, includes, first and foremost questioning of social-political presumptions that drive societies, and then engendering an alternative way of being human, an alternative rooted in the story of God's love for the world. This theological outlook also advocate for the transformation of societies. They emphasize that transformation is a gift from God. Communities are transformed upon their reception of God's gift of life. Those who receive the gift become, together, the new community that slowly and marginally, effect new and powerful radical changes to the world that God so dearly loves. Thus this group of theologians do not speak of "the role of the church in politics" but the church as a political community (an alternative *polis*).

43. Katongole, *Sacrifice of Africa*, 109.
44. Hollis, *Negro Problem Solved*, 14.

images.[45] Professor Ali Mazrui, in his Reith Lectures delivered in 1979 at the BBC and published as *The African Condition: A Political Diagnosis* (1980), spoke of the "six paradoxes of the African predicament."[46] These paradoxes are humiliation, habitation, acculturation, fragmentation, retardation, and location.[47]

Alongside this discussion on the crisis of identity and the definition of Africa and Africans, is the question of whether it is possible to speak of an African unity. For example, do we speak of African traditional religion or African traditional religions? Is it African theology or African theologies? Is it African Christianity or African Christianities? Is there a collective African culture? There are two schools of thought on this issue.

The pluralist view avers that African cultures differ in significant ways and thus it is not possible to speak of "Africa" except in a reductionist way.[48] Kwame Anthony Appiah, Tinyiko Sam Maluleke, and V. Y. Mudimbe hold to this view. Appiah argues that there is no collective African culture, no "common stock of cultural knowledge," but several African cultures and identities.[49] Thus for Appiah pan-Africanism is an illusion that offers deceptive hope to the African people. Maluleke is of the same opinion. He observes, "It is important to be conscious of the vastness, divisions, affinities, and diversities of Africa. To that extent, there is some truth in the

---

45. Hollis, 13; Katongole, *Sacrifice of Africa*, 29; Adeyemo, *Is Africa Cursed?*, 2, 9–18.

46. Mazrui, *African Condition*.

47. Mazrui, (*African Condition*, xv–xvi) explains these paradoxes as follows:

The first is *the paradox of habitation*. Africa is the earliest habitat of man, but is in a sense the last to become truly habitable. Secondly, we have the paradox of humiliation. Africans are not necessarily the most brutalized of peoples, but they are almost certainly the most humiliated in modern history. Thirdly, there is *the paradox of acculturation*. African societies are not the closest culturally to the western world, but they have been undergoing the most rapid pace of westernization witnessed this century. Fourthly, we have *the paradox of fragmentation*. Africa is by no means the smallest of the continents physically, but it is almost definitely the most fragmented politically. Fifthly, we must bear witness to the *paradox of retardation*. Africa is not the poorest of the regions of the world, but after Antarctica it may well be technically the most retarded and least developed. And finally we return to the *basic paradox of location*. Africa is the most centrally located of all continents on the globe physically, but again after Antarctica it is probably the most peripheral politically. (Emphasis original).

48. Kombo, *Doctrine of God*, 3.

49. Appiah, *In my Father's House*, 80.

suggestion that 'Africa' does not exist 'as such,' but rather to the extent that people articulate a shape and form for the Africa they desire."[50] Maluleke's aim is to avoid generalizations, which Mbiti is accused of doing.[51] Mudimbe likewise rejects cultural unity, writing, "Idowu's postulations or Mulago's Africanity, as a 'common factor' of African cultures and religious beliefs, are just hypotheses . . . Mbiti's theory of the cultural unity of the continent as a foundation for the coherence of African religions and philosophy is supported by nothing except his own subjectivity."[52] However, to accuse Mbiti and other proponents of African unity of engaging in simplistic generalizations is to misconstrue their methodology. Mbiti's detailed study of East African societies draws him to apply the study to other communities of Africa with similar beliefs. Other African scholars of African religion often draw similar conclusions about African religion as Mbiti does. Being a pioneer in the study of African religion, Mbiti legitimized his generalizing methodology the following way:

> In this study [referring to *African Religions and Philosophy*] I have emphasized the unity of African religions and philosophy in order to give an overall picture of their situation. This approach does not give room for the treatment in-depth of individual religions and philosophical systems of different African peoples . . . I have therefore chosen to highlight both similarities and differences considering the African picture as a whole. For this reason, I have drawn examples from all over Africa, both making general observations and giving detailed illustrations.[53]

---

50. Maluleke, "Half a Century," journal article, 7.

51. Maluleke, 11.

52. Mudimbe, *Invention of Africa*, 79.

53. Mbiti, *African Religions and Philosophy*, 1st ed., xii. Mbiti's *Concepts of God in Africa*, also a pioneer piece of work on this subject, bears similar methodology. Mbiti argues that his work contains "practically all the information I could find in writing and otherwise, on African reflection about God." He claims to have gathered this information from over two hundred and seventy different peoples (tribes) (xii). See also Mbiti, "Encounter of Christian Faith," 817, where Mbiti claims he studied more than three hundred "tribes" in his quest to understand the concept of God in Africa. With such a magnitude of study, it is therefore, legitimate to make generalized conclusions about African cultures in regard to their beliefs about God.

The cultural unity view affirms a possibility of religious, linguistic, and cultural unity of Africa. Léopold Sédar Senghor, Placid Tempels, Alexis Kagame, Kwame Nkrumah, Cheikh Anta Diop, John Mbiti, Bolaji Idowu, Mercy Oduyoye, and James Kombo are proponents of cultural unity.[54] These scholars identify Africa's shared cosmology, Africa's valuing of social relationships, and Africa's shared history of slave trade and colonialism as threads that unify the continent. Tite Tiénou observes that these proponents of African cultural unity aimed "to restore the Black person and the primitive into full human dignity" especially their right to think and to think differently.[55] Thus these writers rejects the definitions of Africa based on race choosing instead the shared worldview.[56] For example, though Kombo accepts the fundamental unity of Africa, he rejects the stereotypical images of Africa as a suffering continent and he also rejects the definition of *African* in terms of shared slavery and colonialism, asserting, "There is more to Africa than pauperization and the Western domination of Africa."[57]

This book aligns with this second perception of Africa. Particularly, it affirms the unity and diversity of the African peoples. It notes that though African cultures, languages, and ethnic identities differ in substantial ways, as Mbiti notes, it is possible to provide common themes and patterns, which unify the African people especially those who live south of the Sahara.[58] At least three themes unify the African people. The first is socio-linguistic. There are four major racial categories in Africa: Bantu, Hamites, Semites, and the Nilotes. Africans belonging to each racial cluster and living across the African continent share many linguistic, cultural, and religious similarities so that it is possible to say they are united culturally and linguistically. Furthermore, other aspects of culture and identity sweep across the different racial clusters. Second, community (relationality) and the holistic view of

---

54. Senghor, *Nationhood*; Tempels, *Bantu Philosophy*; Kagame, *La philosophie bàntu*; Nkrumah, *Consciencism*; Idowu, *Towards an Indigenous Church*; Oduyoye, "Christianity and African Culture"; Kombo, *Doctrine of God*.

55. Tiénou, "Right to Difference," 29.

56. Lowery, "Identity and Ecclesiology," 29; Kombo, *Doctrine of God*, chapter 7.

57. Kombo, *Doctrine of God*, 3n8.

58. Mbiti (*African Religions and Philosophy*, 99–100) notes that Sub-Saharan Africa alone has over 3,000 distinct ethnic societies that speak over 2,100 languages. Though of course, as Mbiti observes, this "blessing of diversity" has become a curse. He writes, "This great number of languages is often one of the sources of difficulties in modern nationhood" (100).

life cut across most Sub-Saharan African cultures.[59] This cultural value for community and holistic view of life transcends death. Ancestors and the recently deceased (the living dead) are implored to assist in overcoming the complexities of life.[60] Third, the aspirations and desires of the African people unite them. Like all people of the world, Africans long for freedom from oppression and poverty. These longings are the same everywhere, even in the much-developed South Africa. Fourth, African communities have the same conceptual framework unique to them. Mugambi explains this framework as "characteristically based on physical experimental perception rather than on mystical contemplation."[61] Rather than contemplating on metaphysical issues, Africans contemplate on their everyday experiences and practices. This kind of conceptual framework is called ethnophilosophy. Samuel Imbo explains this perception of reality:

> The core of ethnophilosophy is its function as a descriptive anthropology. In contrast to a discursive, analytical philosophy, ethnophilosophy treats as philosophy the indigenous cosmologies, the traditional beliefs such as those about supernatural beings and magic. Beliefs, myths, and cosmology are believed to be interwoven into the complex ritual practices that are the manifestation of philosophy. Though unwritten and systematized, the rituals and systems of believe nevertheless form an intricate web that guides the people in making sense of their lives. Though the description of the rituals and beliefs, the cosmology and the religious worldview of the people can be reconstructed.[62]

---

59. Mugambi, (*God, Humanity, Nature*, 22) argues that relationality as opposed to mystical and metaphysical concerns was and still is the concern of most African peoples. Similarly, M. W. Makgoba (*Mokoko*, 197–198) notes that Africans are unified by their common beliefs and cherished values such as "hospitality, friendliness, the consensus and common framework-seeking principle, ubuntu, and the emphasis on community rather than on the individual. These features typically underpin the variations of African culture and identity everywhere. The existence of African identity is not in doubt."

60. Mbiti was the first person to coin the term the "living-dead," meaning, "the departed who are still remembered personally by someone in their family." See Mbiti, *Concepts of God*, 179.

61. Mugambi, *God, Humanity, Nature*, 25. See also Kombo, *Doctrine of God*, 141–161.

62. Imbo, Introduction to *African Philosophy*, 55.

Thus the source of ethnophilosophy is the everyday experiences and practices of people. Orality rather than written languages is the main means of communication of thoughts and values. The fact that Africans communicate their thoughts orally rather than in writing does not infer intellectual inferiority.[63] John Mbiti is a reputed African ethnophilosopher along with Placid Tempels, Alexis Kagame, and others. Mbiti asserts that African philosophy is found in "religion, proverbs, oral traditions, ethics and morals."[64] These cultural elements depict, for Mbiti, the way adherents understand and express their beliefs and practices. Thus it is not possible to understand a people's past and present without considering these cultural manifestations and ways of thought. That is why Mbiti focuses a lot of his research work in Africa's past heritage. The next section examines Mbiti's concept of African indigenous identity.

Mbiti's Concept of the Indigenous African Identity

Mbiti's understanding of African identity is derived from and rooted in Africa's traditional heritage. In chapter 20 of his *African Religions and Philosophy*, "The Search for New Values, Identity and Security," Mbiti critiques and rejects several ideological proposals such as Négritude, African Personality, African Unity, and Pan-Africanism as all insufficient to meet the needs of indigenous African people.[65] Though he appraises them for contributing interesting ideas about the search for meaning in Africa, he says about them, "All these political ideologies and economic attempts point to a progress being made in Africa. But it is a progress in search; it lacks concreteness, historical roots, and a clear and practical goal, at least for the individual to be able to find in it a sense of direction worthy of personal identification and dedication."[66] One particular weakness of these ideologies, according to Mbiti, is their inability to permeate into every department of life as religion is able to. For Mbiti,

> Only religion is fully sensitive to the dignity of man as an
> individual, person and creature who has both physical and

---

63. See Kombo, *Doctrine of God*, 141–142.

64. Mbiti, *African Religions and Philosophy*, 2.

65. Mbiti, *African Religions and Philosophy*, 2nd ed., 260–265.

66. Mbiti, *African Religions and Philosophy*, 271.

spiritual dimensions. It is only religion which embraces and grants an equal place for every member of humanity, whether he is an idiot or philosopher, slave or student, beggar or ruler. It provides a common denominator for all in origin, experience and destiny. It is only religion which contains the area and tools for everyone to search for and fathom the depths of his being. These depths involve a redefinition of not only "who I am," but also who or what is "my brother," "my neighbour," "the universe" and the whole of existence.[67]

Therefore instead of rooting his concept of identity on these ideologies, Mbiti roots identity in indigenous-religious heritage. He argues that this traditional heritage is religious and bears a holistic outlook to all of reality. In traditional life, there is no dichotomy between the sacred and the secular, between the natural world and the supernatural world, between the spiritual world and the material world.[68] This outlook defines all reality from a religious perspective. Mbiti asserts,

Whenever the African is, there is his religion: he carries it to the fields where he is sowing seeds or harvesting a new crop; he takes it with him to the beer party or to attend a funeral ceremony; and if he is educated, he takes religion with him to the examination room at school or in the university; if he is a politician he takes it to the house of parliament.[69]

This means that indigenous Africans interpret reality from a religious perspective and also understand their identity to be tied to this religious orientation. In other words, indigenous Africans do not interpret their identity from a secular perspective, neither do they interpret it from an ideological perspective.[70] Because religion is part of their worldview it forms a core part

---

67. Mbiti, 274.

68. Mbiti, *African Religions and Philosophy*, 2nd ed., 2.

69. Mbiti, 2. Mbiti (*Bible and Theology*, 101) observes that in traditional life, "Religious beliefs belong to life, they are part of life, like fetching water from the river, breathing air, using fire for cooking, and so on." Thus there is no compartmentalization of life and its events.

70. However, Marxism gained ground in some African countries like Tanzania and Ghana through the works of Pan-Africanist scholars and liberators such as Kwame Nkrumah and Julius Nyerere. Though prominent and appealing to the ruling elites, these ideologies are not accepted as African ideologies but foreign. This is the reason why even after reading

of their identity. Mbiti observes that though modern changes (urbanization, migration, technology) have undermined this outlook in significant ways, religion remains intact among the African people.[71] In a time of crisis and desperation like sickness, death, and catastrophes, and also in moments of joy and celebration like birth, wedding, or communal events, religion comes to the surface.[72]

Mbiti also writes about "the five-fold categories of African ontology" in which God, spirits, humanity, animals and plants, and the inanimate world coexist in an unbreakable "unity, so that to break up that unity is to destroy one or more of these modes of existence, and to destroy one of them is in effect to destroy them all."[73] This indigenous ontology is part of the identity of the African people. God is the power that holds all these categories together.[74] Therefore, even though African traditional anthropology is anthropocentric, for everything, including God, exists for the sake of human beings,[75] it is nonetheless a theological (theocentric) anthropology because for the African there is no existence apart from God.[76] Mbiti argues that though African peoples have a strong notion of God, God is not the center of everything; instead, humans are.[77] Being at the center, however, humans are not masters of the universe because the world is complex and cannot be completely mastered.[78] There is, thus, an acknowledgment of things that are beyond human comprehension. This incomprehensible nature of the world challenges the African people to place their fate in the hands of the Supreme

---

Marx, Julius Nyerere of Tanzania proposed African socialism, *ujamaa* (familyhood) as the better ideology.

71. Mbiti, *African Religions and Philosophy*, 1st ed., 263.

72. Mbiti, 275.

73. Mbiti, 16.

74. Idowu, (*African Traditional Religion*, 104) believes that God means everything for the African peoples; if God does not exist, for an African, all things would breakdown.

75. See Mbiti, *Concepts of God*, 219; Mbiti, *African Religions and Philosophy*, 1st ed., 92; Kapolyo, *Human Condition*, 19.

76. See for example the myths of creation and original state of humanity in Mbiti, *Concepts of God*, 161–170. All these myths show that God is the origin and the sustainer of human life. Furthermore, Mbiti (*Concepts of God*, 219) shows that relationship between God and humans utilitarian and not purely spiritual; practical not mystical. Africans do not seek after God for God's spiritual satisfaction, but for what God can give them.

77. Mbiti, *African Religions and Philosophy*, 2nd ed., 92.

78. Mbiti, *Introduction to African Religion*, 39.

Being. Thus as Mbiti observes, "When everything else within man's abilities fails to cope with misfortune, the people say, 'Leave it to God.'"[79]

There is indeed a strong belief about God among African communities. Mbiti argues that Africans take the belief about God for granted.[80] For example, the Ashanti people of Ghana say, "No one shows a child the Supreme Being," meaning, knowledge about God is acquired at an early age.[81] If Africans have always had a strong sense of the divine, then oversees missionaries, for Mbiti, did not bring God to Africa. God brought the missionaries to Africa because God has always been present in Africa.[82] The missionaries only brought knowledge about Jesus Christ to Africa. Even here, Mbiti argues that Jesus had to be introduced to the African people in the language they understood, including using the names of the God who was and is already known in Africa.[83] Furthermore, he asserts that for Christianity to have a lasting impact in Africa, it has to meet the African people on the plane of their traditional religiosity especially their holistic view of life.[84] Thus it would be disastrous for Christianity to propagate a form of faith limited only to Sundays. The Christian faith should saturate the whole person and the whole life of African Christians or otherwise they will revert back to the negative aspects of their indigenous cultures especially in times of fear or crisis.[85] Propagating the "whole" gospel is the formation of Christian identity. This identity must claim "the whole person and the whole cosmos as the property of Christ."[86] Mbiti believes that it is Jesus, and only Jesus, "who deserves to be the goal and standard for individuals and mankind" because Jesus is the "external, absolute and timeless denominator" who shapes and transforms humanity.[87] In this regard, Christianity has the

---

79. Mbiti, *Concepts of God*, 244.

80. Mbiti, *African Religions and Philosophy*, 29.

81. Mbiti, *Bible and Theology*, 101.

82. Mbiti, 11; Mbiti, "Encounter of Christian Faith," 818.

83. Mbiti, "Encounter of Christian Faith," 818.

84. Mbiti, "Christianity and Traditional Religions," 147.

85. Mbiti, *African Religions and Philosophy*, 2nd ed., 3; Mbiti, "Christianity and Traditional Religions," 147; Mbiti, "Christianity and Culture," 276; Mbiti, "African Indigenous Culture," 87.

86. Mbiti, *African Religions and Philosophy*, 1st ed., 267.

87. Mbiti, 277.

responsibility of pointing and transposing people to this "ultimate Identity, Foundation, and Source of security."[88]

Mbiti also argues that though Africans value individual identity, corporate identity surpasses individual identity.[89] Even in religious matters, traditional religious beliefs are corporately held because the community is the sole custodian of these beliefs. It is the role of the individual to automatically accept them and to assent to them by virtue of being a member of the wider community.[90] In this view, there is no private faith. A people's religious beliefs animate their actions and what they do stems from their beliefs; belief and action are intertwined.[91] Everyone is born into a particular religious community and becomes part of that community through participation in the beliefs, rituals, festivals, rites of that community.[92] These beliefs and practices are not written anywhere but handed over from one generation to the next and exist in the heart of the individual; "each [individual] is himself a living creed of his own religion. Where the individual is, there is his religion, for he is a religious being. It is this that makes Africans so religious: religion is in their whole system of being."[93] Elsewhere, Mbiti writes,

> African peoples have no creeds to recite: their creeds are within them, in their blood and in their hearts. They have a body of beliefs about God, but this is not formulated into single creeds that can be recited. Their beliefs are expressed through concepts of God, attitudes towards him, and the various acts of worship. Furthermore, they are collective, communal, or corporate beliefs, held by groups or communities. The individual "believes" what other members of the corporate society "believe," and he "believes" because others "believe."[94]

There was no such a thing as conversion to another community's beliefs and practices, since these are unique to a particular ethnic community. Thus,

---

88. Mbiti, 277.

89. Mbiti, "Man in African Religion," 61–65.

90. Mbiti, *Bible and Theology*, 101.

91. Mbiti, *African Religions and Philosophy*, 2nd ed., 4.

92. Mbiti, 2.

93. Mbiti, 3.

94. Mbiti, *Concepts of God*, 218.

"Traditional religions have no missionaries to propagate them; and one individual does not preach his religion to another."[95] Nor can a person apostate from the religion of his or her community, "to do so is to be severed from his roots, his foundation, his context of security, his kinships and the entire group of those who make him aware of his own existence."[96] Also, African traditional religion does not have founders and reformers though it may have reputed religious leaders, heroes, and heroines.[97] Even though Mbiti is right in this observation of traditional belief, he fails to point in what ways this belief impacts the church's outreach and missions. Could this outlook be the reason why African churches are mainly ethnic churches? How, for example, will an African Christian surpass this attitude of not witnessing his or her community's beliefs to a person of another ethnic community? Could African Christians be embracing the church as "my own/our own" ethnic enclaves such that the church (for example denominations) are now the new tribe?

Mbiti presents the African indigenous identity as corporate identity but it is clear that he does not identify how this identity shapes the African Christians' beliefs and relationships to each other. To address the problem of ethnic conflict then, one has to reform this ethnic communal identity by emphasizing the ecclesial identity formed through a relationship with Christ. Mbiti hints on this identity but does not expand on it. Though he points that by its very nature the church is a communal body, and that in this community, the old identities of ethnicity do not matter more than the new identity in Christ, Mbiti fails to account for why Africa is a continent that has experienced a lot of ethnic conflict. Why is it that even within the church ethnicity matter more than anything else? What is it in African people's worldview that drives them to pay allegiance to their communities instead of Christ? Why it is that Christians (including the clergy) in Kenya find it difficult to accept each other as one in Christ just because they come from different ethnicities? These questions cast doubt to Mbiti's assertion that religion is fundamental to African identity. Is ethnicity the fundamental identity?

---

95. Mbiti, *African Religions and Philosophy*, 2nd ed., 4.

96. Mbiti, 2.

97. Mbiti, 4.

Mbiti's brief focus on Christocentric identity as the ultimate identity calls for more elaboration. Mbiti mentions this form of identity but does not expand on it. In fact he briefly acknowledges that the search for identity in Africa is an ecclesial search "and in the light of the scriptures."[98] This search, for Mbiti, should lead people to Christ because "To be the Church is to project the very image of God in Christ Jesus."[99] This focus on the image of God in Christ offers greater prospect for addressing the problem of ethnocentrism in Africa, not only because it addresses the role of the individual, a weak aspect in African worldview, but also because it stresses the radical discontinuity between Christian identity and cultural identity, also a weak aspect in the writings of some African theologians. Radical discontinuity between Christian identity and cultural identity is needed especially in situations where culture is in opposition to the gospel. Without Christocentric identity, Christianity propagates ethnic identities. The following examines Mbiti's theology of culture.

Mbiti's Theology of Culture

To Mbiti, culture, which he defines as a pattern of behavior and understanding in response to human environment, is expressed in three ways, "in physical forms (such as agriculture, the arts, technology etc.), in interhuman relations (such as institutions, laws, customs, etc.) and in the forms of reflection on the total reality of life (such as language, philosophy, religion, spiritual values, world views, the riddle of life-birth-death, etc.)."[100] It is this third expression, which motivates Mbiti's insistence that Africans have a right to understand, to articulate, to practice, and to propagate the Christian faith in their own unique ways. Thus he writes, "the Gospel has been, and should continue to be, proclaimed within the melodies of our African culture, through words of our one thousand languages, through the vibrant tunes of our ten thousand musical instruments, through the joyous rhythm of our bodies and the solemn symbols of our artists."[101] Furthermore,

---

98. Mbiti, *Bible and Theology*, 234.

99. Mbiti, 234.

100. Mbiti, "Christianity and Culture," 273; Mbiti, "African Indigenous Culture," 79; Mbiti, "Christianity and African Culture," 387.

101. Mbiti, "Christianity and Culture," 275.

Mbiti emphasizes that culture is dynamic not static; "it is always in a process of renewal, change, decay, interaction and modification."[102] Thus Christian engagement to culture should also be multiform and dynamic. There is no single way to engage culture.

Mbiti maintains a clear distinction between the gospel and culture. He argues that the gospel comes from God and is eternal and unchanging while culture is a creation of human beings and is temporal and changing. While the gospel is distinct from culture and it transverses culture and no culture can monopolize or imprison it, it has to be expressed in a particular cultural context using symbols, languages, and means of a particular culture.[103] He argues that though Christianity is the outcome of the message of Christ, it depends on culture to be proclaimed and embraced. Mbiti wrote, "We can add nothing to the Gospel for this is an eternal gift of God; but Christianity is always a beggar seeking food and drink, cover and shelter from the cultures it encounters in its never-ending journeys and wanderings."[104] Once the gospel is welcomed, it judges, saves, transforms, and exorcises the "demons" of cultures.[105] Thus though the gospel must be appropriated in cultural forms, not all cultural forms are of benefit to the gospel. Christians must be critical and vigilant to exorcise, eliminate, avoid, and if possible destroy, detrimental cultural elements, grounding their critical judgment on the gospel.[106]

According to Mbiti, the process of cultural analysis involves three things. The first is examining those issues that overlap with Christianity and that may aid in rooting the faith in receiving cultures.[107] The second is examining issues in the traditional past, which clearly falls outside the Christian tradition and which have to be abandoned. The third is the area of uncertainty, which does not necessarily injure or interfere with the Christian faith. This third element calls for ongoing critical engagement and discernment. But

---

102. Mbiti, "African Indigenous Culture," 79.

103. Mbiti, "Christianity and Culture," 275; Mbiti, "Christianity and African Culture," 388; Mbiti, "Introduction to the Colloquium," 22–23.

104. Mbiti, "Christianity and Traditional Religions," 155. See also Mbiti, "African Indigenous Culture," 79; and Mbiti, "Christianity and Culture," 281.

105. Mbiti, "Christianity and Culture," 281.

106. Mbiti, 279. Mbiti, *Bible and Theology*, 19; Mbiti, "Christianity and African Culture," 394.

107. Mbiti, "Christianity and Traditional Religions," 148–149.

of greater importance is for Christians to generate God-glorifying cultures in local settings.[108] This process of creating cultures is a mark of spiritual maturity. When Christians generate God-glorifying cultures, they will be able to counteract, even to overcome, the evil demands of culture.

Indeed Mbiti accentuates that Christians should pay unwavering allegiance to Christ in their relationship to culture. Christians must always remember that their allegiance is to Christ not their cultural or ethnic identities, and ultimately "confessing Christ" means journeying from culture to Christ.[109] For Mbiti, this pilgrimage from culture to Christ is important because culture always subjugates or molds people into cultural identities, which contrasts or obscures Christian identity.[110] Therefore, for Mbiti, the goal of preaching and accepting the gospel in Africa is to transpose allegiance from tribal (and other forms of allegiances) to the Lord Jesus Christ. If this is the case, then, the process of transposition should bear on the entire life of the African people. Allegiance to Christ must supplant other allegiances. However, faithfulness to Christ does not mean that a person is uprooted from his or her own culture. Christians must be enabled to follow Christ from within their cultural environments. The following provides Mbiti's theology of community.

---

108. Mbiti, "Christianity and Culture," 280.

109. Mbiti, 283. Similarly, Andrew Walls (*The Missionary Movement*, 3–15) speaks of this "pilgrimage" nature of Christianity in relationship to culture. He argues that there are two opposing tendencies within Christianity, "indigenizing principle" and the "pilgrim principle." In his estimation, both these realities have to exist in creative tension. The former speaks of the gospel as transcending all cultural environments accepting people from different backgrounds; the gospel does not dislocate people from their environments, identities, and history but saves and transforms them from within their backgrounds. Consequently, though the gospel is universal (transcends culture), the gospel is also particular (can only be communicated within a particular cultural milieu). The later speaks of the gospel as antithetical to human identities. The gospel is a destabilizing or an alienating element of all cultures. The gospel "whispers" to a believer that he or she "has no abiding city and warns him [or her] that to be faithful to Christ will put him [or her] out of step with his [or her] society" (8). The transient nature of human identities means that every Christian has a dual citizenship, but the identity in Christ inspires an unwavering loyalty that exceeds ethnic and all other forms of loyalties. Thus, Christians should always pay attention to whom they pay their allegiance to, whether it is Christ or cultural identities.

110. Mbiti, "Introduction to the Colloquium," 24; Mbiti, "Confessing Christ Today," 10.

Mbiti's Theology of Community

Mbiti establishes his ecclesiology in the context of the African indigenous heritage, an heritage, which "lay a great emphasis on communal welfare, values, concerns and kinship, both horizontally and vertically (to include the departed)."[111] He argues that the African life is centered on community. He captures this communal orientation with the now famous dictum, "I am, because we are; and since we are, therefore I am."[112] For Mbiti, community manifests itself with reference to blood and marital kinship, land, tribal affiliation, clan roots, ritual celebrations, rites of passage and death, and shared oppression and suffering.[113] Community has both vertical and horizontal dimensions. The vertical aspect is the people's relationship with their Supreme Being and the spirit world. The horizontal dimension includes relationship between individuals, clans, sub-clan, individual families, the larger tribe, the departed, and the unborn.[114] Death does not destroy community but animates it.[115] One is related to the visible community, but also vital relationships are to be maintained with the invisible world. Furthermore, community also includes harmony with the non-human world (animals, objects, rivers, and so on) because ideally, in the African worldview, nature is "sacred" and human beings have a priestly relationship with it.[116]

Mbiti asserts that by its very nature the church is a communal body. This ecclesial communal orientation has parallels with African traditional

---

111. Mbiti, "African Indigenous Culture," 86.

112. Mbiti, *African Religions and Philosophy*, 2nd ed., 106. There are several words, which capture well this emphasis on community in Africa. The words popularly used include, *ubuntu/umunthu/botho* (South Africa) or *utu/umundu/ujamaa* (East Africa). Of these words *ubuntu* is the most common. Bishop Desmond Tutu of South Africa popularized the term *ubuntu* when he used it to construct a theology of racial reconciliation (See Tutu, *No Future*, 31).

113. Mbiti, "Bible in African Culture," 36; Mbiti, *Bible and Theology*, 171; Mbiti, "Man in African Religion," 59.

114. Mbiti, "Bible in African Culture," 36; Mbiti, "Hearts cannot be Lent," 6–7; Mbiti, *Bible and Theology*, 171–172.

115. Mbiti, *NT Eschatology*, 127–139.

116. Mbiti, "An African Answer," 89. See also Mbiti, "Bible in African Culture," 36; Mbiti, "Hearts cannot be Lent," 6–7; Mbiti, *Bible and Theology*, 171–172. Elsewhere Mbiti, ("Man in African Religion," 65), opines, "African Religion recognizes clearly that, if man abuses nature, in return nature will strike back at him. In this case man is not a master over nature to treat it as he wishes. Instead, man is the priest towards nature soliciting its kindness and expressing respect towards it."

life in which kinship ties and the extended family are of prime significance. From this outlook, the "Church is the Christian family, in which all are related to one another through faith and baptism in Jesus Christ."[117] In this community, the new identity in Christ supersedes the old allegiances of ethnicity, clans, and so forth. However, this new identity in Christ does not imply replacement or obliteration of ethnic identities but a fulfilment of them in such a way that it satisfies the longings, aspirations, and search for meaning expressed before. Thus in Christ, old identities still exist but do not matter more than the new identity in Christ but are in fact clarified in Christ. Therefore, the church is the center of existence from which the African people are formed as the community of God.

For Mbiti, this communal nature of African life has implications on how the gospel has to reach the African people. The gospel must redeem the African people from within their cultures not apart from them.[118] In addition, the gospel must be propagated in the context of the African corporate community life. From this perspective even conversion should not be seen as being limited to the individual believer. "While conversion follow personal decisions, we have to take note also of the corporate aspect of conversion in the African situation. The process of conversion involves other people: family, friends, and community."[119] Thus the gospel should not sever the African people from their communal (including ethnic) identities but should facilitate the transfer of allegiances to Christ. Thus in Christ ethnicities are not destroyed but redeemed. However, Mbiti does not say how Christians should deal with the problem of ethnicity within their congregations. It is a reality that most churches in Kenya are divided along ethnic lines. Mbiti is correct that conversion is often envisaged as a corporate event but it is problematic when it is only limited to a particular corporate identity (one's ethnic community). How will Kenyan Christians see their conversion as a new identity in Christ, an identity that transcends tribal affiliations?

Mbiti also recognizes the relationship between religion (Christianity) and state. In his *Bible and Theology in African Christianity* he mentions

---

117. Mbiti, *Introduction to African Religion*, 190.
118. Mbiti, *African Religions and Philosophy*, 1st ed., 237.
119. Mbiti, *Bible and Theology*, 230.

this role within his discussion of mission outreach in African theology.[120] In this discussion, he rejects the "sharp dichotomy between Church and State, which has tended to be emphasized from overseas" arguing that this dichotomization is foreign and harmful.[121] He believes that the gospel should impact all areas of life and if the State is sympathetic to the church then the church should partner with it for the betterment of all. This partnership may include even receiving funds and legal help from the State for the benefit of advancing Christianity. He offers a practical and a theological reason for this attitude. The practical reason, for him, is that in most Sub-Saharan African countries, Christians constitute the majority and they pay taxes to the State and some of them hold government positions. What would be wrong, he asks, for these Christian leaders to use their influence in advancing Christianity? His theological reason is his belief that "the kingdom of God is fundamentally a politico-theological concept, and God's mission is essentially a politico-theological mission."[122]

Mbiti is correct that the church should partner with the State and governments in advancing human good. However, Mbiti's assertion that the church in African may receive funds from the State is problematic. Mbiti asks, "Is Africa bold enough to engage in Christian mission with an attitude that is open to embrace, utilize and benefit from opportunities that may be available from the institution of the state?" In Kenya, where Mbiti comes from, several churches embraced this attitude but in the process lost its prophetic ministry because they fell prey to politician's manipulative tactics. As chapter 3 shows, historically, the state in Kenya manipulated the church to gain or to sustain votes from church members. Also, historically in Kenya, the state co-opted the church and its leaders in order to suppress criticisms.

He particularly addresses the theme of peace and reconciliation in his speech delivered at Princeton Theological Seminary and published in the Princeton Seminary Bulletin of 1999.[123] Here, he seeks to answer the question, "what does African Religion say about 'peace and reconciliation'"?[124]

---

120. Mbiti, 220–222.
121. Mbiti, 221.
122. Mbiti, 221.
123. Mbiti, "Hearts cannot be Lent."
124. Mbiti, 2.

Mbiti begins by studying the prayers for peace and reconciliation from select African communities. He concludes that in these prayers, God is acknowledged as the giver and the sustainer of peace. Also, peace has both communal and personal dimensions, is familial and clan-oriented, and also extends to nature, the unborn, and even the spiritual world, especially with the recently deceased.[125] Mbiti also covers the symbolic ritual measures that enact peace and reconciliation. Such rituals, which are religious, are performed in the following order: laying down of the weapons of warfare, presentation of animal sacrifices for repentance and restitution as well as for protection from harm, followed by rituals of sharing of food, prayers to God, and finally pronouncing of formal curses to those who break the peace accord.[126] Mbiti also observes that African communities enacted covenants to cement the new relationships. Such covenants were performed either directly to the Supreme Being or to the Earth. They included marriages, agreements, adoption of children, mutual exchanging of personal blood, sharing of property, eating and drinking together (especially eating from the same plate and drinking from the same cup), and so on.[127]

In this article, Mbiti does not specifically address how the African church has incorporated these indigenous methods of obtaining peace and reconciliation to foster the same within their congregations and their communities though elsewhere he writes that the church should participate in "cultivating reconciliation, harmony, peace and security with and within oneself, the community, the nation and the universe."[128] Mbiti believes that in the search after peace and reconciliation "the two religions [ATR and Christianity] speak a largely common language and undergird each other" and the message of Jesus Christ "does not contravene the efforts of [African] traditional religion."[129] Indeed both religions desire peace and reconciliation but do they really speak the same language? Isn't the peace that comes from Christianity of a superior kind than the peace of traditional religions? If both are the same then there is no purpose of introducing Africa to "the peace of God which

---

125. Mbiti, 5–7.
126. Mbiti, 7–9.
127. Mbiti, 9–11.
128. Mbiti, *African Religions and Philosophy*, 1st ed., 274.
129. Mbiti, "Hearts Cannot be Lent," 12.

transcends all understanding." Indeed the church should utilize resources from indigenous culture but the message of peace and reconciliation from the church surpasses that of the indigenous culture. Also, by saying that the message of Jesus "does not contravene the efforts of [African] traditional religion" is also problematic for it can limit the role of Christ in contravening and reforming culture. Indeed, some cultural elements need contravention. Also, more than merely fostering peace and reconciliation in communities, Christians in Africa should embody peace and reconciliation in their lives. The church must show the broken world what it means to live in peace with one another.

Mbiti and Calvin

John Mbiti's theology focuses on identity, culture, and community. These themes have consequential importance to ethnopolitical cohesion. A people's perception of their identity, their culture, and their community may contribute to how they perceive and relate with other communities. Mbiti's effort in African theology is to explain the place of Africa's socio-religious past in the growth and development of African Christianity. Mbiti's focus on identity shows the ongoing need for an anthropology that frees people from the various forms of dehumanization. African Christianity should counter the negative imaginings of their people, which have resulted in fatalistic and destructive attitudes. The aim of Mbiti's emphasis on African identity is to restore the full dignity of all the African people. However, he rejects political ideologies such as pan-Africanism as not helpful for offering an anthropology that frees the people of Africa. For Mbiti, only religion can offer human dignity because religion permeates to the deepest human longings. Thus both Mbiti and Calvin offer theocentric anthropology.

Mbiti, like Calvin, advocates for a Christian faith that is holistic (affecting every facet of life), because for Mbiti, African culture is holistic. Like Calvin, the Christian faith should claim "the whole person and the whole cosmos as the property of Christ." Mbiti also focuses on communal identity, which he believes is a key aspect of African identity. He asserts that to live is to be with others. Thus his communal view coheres with relational anthropologies, including Calvin's emphasis on the image of God as communion, not only with God but with fellow humanity. Furthermore, Mbiti writes about culture, including the fallen nature of culture. He emphasizes like Calvin does, that Christianity critiques and transforms culture. Mbiti emphasizes the temporal nature of culture even to the point where he says that culture has no eschatology to offer. Thus Mbiti diminishes the eschatological redemption of culture (a key emphasis of the Reformed tradition). Of greater importance for Mbiti is that the gospel must be transmitted in the vernacular. In terms of his political views, Mbiti rejects the sharp dichotomy between church and State and advocates for mutual partnership between them.

Conclusion

This chapter has established that the themes of identity, culture, and community are prominent in John Mbiti's several books and articles. However, even though these themes are significant to the salience and prominence of ethnic conflict in Kenya, Mbiti rarely addresses this connection. However, Mbiti's main contribution to the quest for ethnic cohesion in Kenya and other African countries lies in his extrapolation of these three themes showing that there is no true cohesion of African communities, which ignores Africa's heritage and identity, African focus on community, and African cultures. All these themes must be examined in the light of scripture and theology. For example, with regard to Africa's heritage and identity, more focus need to be placed on Christian identity, which supersedes cultural, especially, ethnic identities. Mbiti hints that the image of God is the ultimate basis for Christian identity. As shown in chapter 4, it is because human beings are created in the image of God that gives them dignity and respect.

Similarly, in regard to community, it is important to expound on the meaning of community, expanding it beyond "tribal" and familial/kinship community, which is the main way "community" is understood in Africa while at the same time emphasizing the role of the individual person in the community. Furthermore, there is a need to scrutinize the character, meaning, and formation of communal identity among God's people (the church) and how this identity grows out of ethnic/cultural identities as well as differs or contrasts with these identities.

CHAPTER 10

Conclusion, Limitations, and Further Research

The burden of this book has been to present a contextual theological response to the problem of ethnopolitical violence in Kenya. The thesis of the study is that *the search for ethnic cohesion in Kenya is a theological task that calls for a new theological anthropology and politics*. To achieve this purpose, the book introduced in chapter 2, the history of ethnopolitical violence in Kenya from the colonial era to the contemporary period. The chapter argued that the roots of ethnopolitical violence in Kenya can be traced back to the colonial era. In addition, post-colonial Kenyan governments have failed to rise above ethnic-based and political divisions such that Kenya is now divided along ethnic and political lines. The chapter also showed that ethnopolitical conflict in an ongoing reality in Kenya. Kenya is going to the polls in August 2017 and there is concern already, among many stakeholders and the international community, that politicians are dividing the Kenyan people along ethnic lines. It is a repeat of 2007/2008 ethnopolitical conflict once again. Before the mayhem of 2007/2008, politicians stirred up ethnic hatred through hate speech. Sadly, politicians are repeating the same mistakes again.

Chapter 3 presented the successes and failings of Kenyan churches in addressing the problem of ethnopolitical conflict. The chapter showed that despite the successes of the church in Kenya prior to the multi-party era (1991 and afterwards), the church in Kenya is still struggling to overcome ethnocentrism in the church and therefore because of this failure, the church has not been able to be a light to the Kenyan society in how to rise above ethnic and political divisions.

Chapters 4 to 6 presented a constructive theology of ethnopolitical co-hesion based on a study of John Calvin's theology of the divine image, the Christian life, and political theology respectively. The premise of studying the three theological themes is guided by the thesis of the book: *the search for ethnic cohesion in Kenya is a theological task that calls for a new theological anthropology and politics.* The aim of the three chapters was to show that Calvin's theology as presented in his *Institutes of the Christian Religion* (1559 edition) and biblical commentaries, although written five hundred years ago, still speaks for today's churches, especially in Kenya.

The initial introductory sections of chapter 4 demonstrated that nothing much has been written about Calvin's theology for Reformed churches in Kenya. Therefore it is paramount to resource Calvin for Kenyan churches. Obviously not everything in Calvin's thought and ministry practice is use-ful for today. One particular element of Calvin's legacy that must not be carried forward to today's churches is his intolerance to dissent, although scholars differ on whether actually Calvin was intolerant to, for example, Michael Servetus. However, that Calvin sanctioned Servetus' execution is a dark indelible stain on his legacy. However, the dark stain on Calvin's legacy notwithstanding, Calvin left a rich theological legacy that can be informative and transformative for churches in Kenya. Calvin's theology inspired various projects of reforms in the West. Calvinist scholarship has been intense and rigorous especially in the West and in South Africa, and therefore, there is a need to study Calvin in Kenya. A study of Calvin will show Reformed churches in Kenya that the history of their denominations is further and richer than what missionaries bequeathed them. Kenyan churches must trace their roots, not only to the Reformation, but even further, to the ancient church. Therefore, the Christian past has rich theological resources, which can help churches in Kenya to regain their theological and prophetic voice in the context of various sociopolitical realities.

Chapters 7 to 9 presented theological responses of four Kenyan scholars: David Mukuba Gitari, John Henry Okullu, Jesse Mugambi, and John Mbiti. These authors are representative of (prospective) theological responses to ethnopolitical conflict. Their theologies are "prospective" for addressing ethnopolitical conflict in Kenya. A need exists to examine how the theologies of these Kenyan theologians address or fail to address ethnopolitical issues in Kenya.

Gitari and Okullu address ethnopolitical conflict mainly through the pulpit, street protests, and through the media. Mugambi speaks to the reality of ethnopolitical conflict through his emphasis on reconstruction while Mbiti through his emphasis on culture, identity, and community (although he rarely actually writes about ethnopolitical conflict). Mugambi's concern is social development while Mbiti's concern is an apologetic of Africa's socioreligious heritage. Overall, the chapters showed that although these notable theologians teach and write on topics that are of consequential importance to ethnopolitical conflict, rarely do they delineate a theology of ethnopolitical cohesion. It is important to note that all the four Kenyan scholars studied are Anglican theologians. Thus they are not Reformed theologians but they are "the giants" of Kenyan theology, arguably of African theology; definitely Mbiti and Mugambi are pacesetters in their particular areas of research.

Limitations of the Book

A project of any kind has to limit itself to certain parameters. Some of the limitations could have been avoided if the author had more time and resources. The study was limited to the *Institutes* (1559) and biblical commentaries. Considering that the *Institutes* and commentaries represent a small portion of Calvin's works, the book would have benefited by drawing from more sources such as treatises, letters, sermons, and other writings. Indeed, the author is aware of this lack, in his work, and hopes to retrieve these sources for future research projects. In addition, because the author chose Anglican theologians as major interlocutors, there is a need to study Reformed theology as written by Reformed theologians in Kenya.[1] One particular voice the author hoped to study but was not able to, is Timothy Njoya, a retired Presbyterian minister.[2] Njoya has published a book on democracy, on human

---

1. The writer had a lot of difficulty accessing publications by Reformed theologians from Kenya. Beyond the books written, (which the writer was not able to access), Reformed theologians have not published much. Leading theologians in Kenya are Catholics and Anglicans. Their books are also easily accessible in Canada.

2. See chapter 3 for Timothy Njoya's role in sociopolitical engagement in Kenya.

dignity, and one, which is a collection of his sermons.[3] However, the books were not readily accessible. Another limitation was difficulty in retrieving materials from the offices of NCCK and EFK.

Further Research and Engaging
Non-Christian Audiences

As already shown, the book barely scratched the surface of Calvin's theological works. The author hopes to delve deeper into other areas of Calvin's theology in future research work. Since as already demonstrated, the shape of Reformed theology in Kenya has not been studied in depth, this means that there is a lot of work to be done. Thus it is not really possible to tell whether Calvin's views have influenced Kenyan churches in substantial ways.

This book proposed a theology of ethnopolitical cohesions from a specific ecclesial tradition. The main challenge going forward is how to transition from this ecclesio-theological perspective (Reformed) to a public theology that speaks to the wider public sphere. This is admittedly a major challenge that calls for discernment as there is no single way to engage culture. Of prime importance is for Reformed churches (and Reformed theologians) in Kenya to embrace a posture that is not adversarial or combative for that would be detrimental to sociopolitical engagement. As already mentioned, the African worldview is pluralistic and is not antagonistic to religion. What this means for the Kenyan context is that a Reformed political theology must find a way of dialoging with a society that is already pluralistic. This can be achieved through respect for others' opinions and views. Achieving the transformation of Kenya without the use of combative means is the whole thrust of this project. Kenyan Christians, as they respond to God's gift of grace in their lives, are enabled to live lives that truly reflect the meaning of love and neighborliness in a society that is characterized by ethnic hatred and political divisions. When Christians view their responsibility of social engagement as not merely an activity they do but a way of life, then they do not need to be combative in their approach to culture.

---

3. Njoya, *Divine Tag on Democracy*; Njoya, *Human Dignity and National Identity*; Njoya, *Out of Silence*.

Christians in Kenya must embrace a worldview that views everything as within God's reign for there is no sphere of life that God does not touch. The embrace of this conviction, however, does not mean that Christians should impose their views on others; Christians should be civil in their engagement with culture.[4] Christian conviction also means that Christians participate at the various levels of the public. This must include voting, advocacy, serving in public office, and supporting grassroot initiatives that enrich lives. All these activities can be achieved through co-operation with other like-minded individuals. Christian civility also entails thinking about the use of Christian language in conversation with non-Christians. The African context already has important resources that can nourish Christian-non-Christian conversations. The language of *ubuntu* for example can supplement the language of *imago Dei* when Christians are talking with non-Christians. However, Christians should also point out ways the context is deficient and how Christianity addresses that deficiency. Finally, it is important for Reformed theologians in Kenya and elsewhere to be in conversation with other like-minded individuals who do not subscribe to the Reformed views. Conversations (or at least resourcing each other) is an important element of a mature theological commitment. Each ecclesial tradition has something meaningful to offer. This book engaged in such an endeavor through resourcing Anglican theologians. Such engagements are beneficial for sociopolitical engagement in Kenya, a multiplex society.

---

4. Mouw, *Uncommon Decency*, 12; Bacote, *Political Disciple*, 57.

Response to Reinhold Niebhur's
Moral Man and Immoral Society

It is important to respond to Reinhold Niebuhr's, *Moral Man and Immoral Society*, which espouses a divergent position. Niebuhr critiqued ethical moralists who believed that advanced intelligence and genuine religious morality lead to societal (political) morality. For Niebuhr, these individuals downplay the "brutal character of the behavior of all human collectives, and the power of self-interest and collective egoism in all inter-group relations" (xx). Niebuhr argues that rationality and religiously inspired goodwill cannot help advance collective morality and foster social cohesion because of the power of human selfishness and egoism. The way forward is to balance justice and injustice, coercion and peace. For him, social cohesion, justice, and peace comes through coercion and political force because societies are always in a state of war. For Niebuhr, the goal is not to create ideal societies free from coercion for this is not possible, but one in which coercion is free from violence (22). Niebuhr highlighted important issues. He showed what is humanly possible. His emphasis that reason alone does not help human beings to live peacefully with one another although it may aid them to be aware of the needs of others, is crucial. He also pointed to the failure of religion of obscuring morality in its emphasis on divine-human relationship (69). He also offers various examples of the instances when the church maintained the status quo even when the church was quite conscious of the conflict between the status quo and the church's own ideals (76). However, some issues in Niebuhr's argument are problematic.

Foremost, Niebuhr's contention that religion has the capacity only to influence individual morality but not collective morality (i.e. politics) is problematic for it limits the work of God to Christians. For Niebuhr, religion does not have the resources to foster sociopolitical cohesion of communities. He limited the influence of religion to an individual's relationship with God as well as to intimate religious communities, not societies/groups. He defined religion as "a sense of the absolute" (52) and that this sense of the absolute fosters an otherworldly orientation, a social indifferentism, as well as quietism, defeatism, and sentimentality (70). But religion need not result in these postures. Christianity has been responsible for setting up schools, hospitals, human rights agencies, and other transforming initiatives. It was the church that rose up against the unjust social structures in the society. Niebuhr acknowledged that the inability of the church to foster a public presence results from "a too consistent God-world, spirit-body dualism" (78). But what of an alternative understanding of the relationship between humans and God?

What happens when the church exemplifies a different way of being? Another point of disagreement with Niebuhr's thesis is his ecclesiology in which the focus is on an individual person. This argument could derail the role of the church as community that must engage in public witness. Writing about the cross, Niebuhr argued, "The devotion of Christianity to the cross is an unconscious glorification of the individual moral ideal. The cross is the symbol of love triumphant in its own integrity, but not triumphant in the world and society" (82). This assertion seems to limit the work of the cross to individual believers not the wider world. However, the resurrection of Jesus affirmed the power of God's active presence in the world, for it was God who resurrected Jesus from the dead thus affirming the continued work of God even in the moment of the supposed defeat. Niebuhr accuses religion of defeatism and yet his assumption that society is in a state of perpetual warfare and that this warfare has no justifiable remedy, is alarming. He asks, "If social cohesion is impossible without coercion, and coercion is impossible without the creation of social injustice, and the destruction of injustice is impossible without the use of further coercion, are we not in an endless cycle of social conflict?" (231).

Niebuhr had a high view of the human condition but a low view of the remedy of this condition. Even though believers are unable to establish the kingdom of God through reasoning or moral conversion, they are, a

leavening influence in the world, to work for the ideals of God's kingdom and through that active participation make the world a better place.
Christians recognize that the world they live in is not the new Jerusalem.
Nevertheless, the world is God's world. Thus the world is not fundamentally evil; it has a divine purpose. It is God's world. To say that the world is
perpetually in an irremediable state of war is to resign God's world to the
forces of darkness.

Bibliography

Abdullahi, Ahmednasir M. "Ethnic Clashes, Displaced Persons, and the Potential for Refugee Creation in Kenya: A Forbidding Forecast." *International Journal of Refugee Law* 9, no. 2 (1997): 196–206.

Achebe, Chinua, Göran Hydén, Christopher Magadza, and Achola P. Okeyo. *Beyond Hunger in Africa: Conventional Wisdom and an African Vision.* Nairobi: Heinemann, 1990.

Ackerman, John. *Listening to God: Spiritual Formation in Congregations.* Bethesda, MD: Alban Institute, 2001.

Adeyemo, Tokunboh. *Is Africa Cursed? A Vision for the Radical Transformation of an Ailing Continent.* Revised ed. Nairobi: WordAlive, 2009.

African Union. "Pan-Africanism and African Renaissance." *AU Echo* (2013): 1–10.

Allen, John W. *A History of Political Thought in the Sixteenth Century.* 3rd ed. London: Methuen, 1951.

Anderson, David M. *Histories of the Hanged: Britain's Dirty War in Kenya and the End of the Empire.* London: Weidefeld and Nicolson, 2005.

———. "'Yours in Struggle for Majimbo:' Nationalism and the Party Politics of Decolonization in Kenya, 1955-1964." *Journal of Contemporary History* 40, no. 3 (2005): 547–564.

Appiah, Kwame Anthony. *In My Father's House: Africa in the Philosophy of Culture.* London: Methuen, 1992.

Appiah, Simon Kofi. *Africanness Inculturation Ethics: In Search of the Subject of an Inculturated Christian Ethics.* Frankfurt: Peter Lang, 2000.

———. "The Quest of African Identity." *Exchange* 32, no. 1 (2003): 54–65.

Aquinas, Thomas, St. *Summa Theologica.* Translated by The Fathers of the English Dominican Province. Vol 20. London: Burns, Oates & Washbourne, 1922.

Atieno, Winnie. "Counties Turn Down Medics on Ethnic Grounds." *Daily Nation,* June 13, 2015.

Augustine, Saint. *The City of God.* Translated by Marcus Dods. Modern Library Classics. New York: Modern Library, 2000.

———. *The Trinity*. Translated by Charles Dollen. Boston: Daughters of St. Paul, 1965.

Bacote, Vincent. *The Political Disciple: A Theology of Public Life*. Ordinary Theology Series. Grand Rapids: Zondervan, 2015.

Bainton, Roland Herbert. *The Travail of Religious Liberty: Nine Biographical Studies*. London: Lutterworth, 1953.

Balke, Willem. *Calvin and the Anabaptist Radicals*. Translated by W. J. Heynen. Grand Rapids, MI: Eerdmans, 1981.

Bam, Brigalia. "Foreword." In *Being the Church in South Africa Today*, edited by Barney Pityana and Charles Villa-Vicencio, xi–xii. Johannesburg: South African Council of Churches, 1995.

Barth, Christoph. *God with Us: A Theological Introduction to the Old Testament*. Edited by Geoffrey William Bromiley. Grand Rapids, MI: Eerdmans, 1991.

Barth, Karl. *Church Dogmatics*. Vol. 4, part 2. Edited by Geoffrey William Bromiley. Edinburgh: T & T Clark, 1958.

Battenhouse, Roy W. "The Doctrine of Man in Calvin and in Renaissance Platonism." *Journal of the History of Ideas* 9, no. 4 (1948): 447–471.

Baur, John. *2000 Years of Christianity in Africa: An African History*. Nairobi: Paulines, 1994.

Bax, Douglas S. *A Different Gospel: A Critique of the Theology Behind Apartheid*. Johannesburg: Presbyterian Church of South Africa, 1979.

Baylor, Michael G. *Revelation and Revolution: Basic Writings of Thomas Müntzer*. Bethlehem: Lehigh University Press, 1993.

———. "Thomas Müntzer's 'Prague Manifesto.'" *Mennonite Quarterly Review* 63 (1989): 30–57.

BBC. "Kenyatta Arrested in Security Raid." *BBC News*, 21 October 1952. http://news.bbc.co.uk/onthisday/hi/dates/stories/october/21/newsid_3754000/3754366.stm.

Beach, Lee. *The Church in Exile: Living in Hope after Christendom*. Downers Grove, IL: IVP Academic, 2015.

Bediako, Kwame. "De-sacralization and Democratization: Some Theological Reflections on the Role of Christianity in Nation-Building in Modern Africa." *Transformation* 12, no. 1 (1995): 5–11.

———. "John Mbiti's Contribution to African Theology." In *Religious Plurality in Africa: Essays in Honour of John S. Mbiti*, edited by Jacob K. Olupona, Sulayman S. Nyang, 367–390. Berlin: Walter Mouton de Gruyter, 1993.

———. "The Roots of African Theology." *International Bulletin of Missionary Research* 13, no. 2 (1989): 58–62.

———. *Theology and Identity: The Impact of Culture upon Christian Thought in the Second Century and in Modern Africa*. Oxford: Regnum, 1999.

Bell, Theo. "Man is a Microcosmos: Adam and Eve in Luther's *Lectures on Genesis* (1535–1545)." *Concordia Theological Quarterly* 69, no. 2 (2005): 159–184.

Benedetto, Robert and Donald K. McKim. *Historical Dictionary of the Reformed Churches*. 2nd ed. Lanham: Scarecrow, 2009.

Benoit, Jean-Daniel. "Pastoral Care of the Prophet." In *John Calvin Contemporary Prophet, A Symposium*, edited by Jacob Tunis Hoogstra, 51–67. Grand Rapids, MI: Baker, 1959.

Berkouwer, G. C. *Man: The Image of God*. Grand Rapids, MI: Eerdmans, 1962.

Berman, Bruce and John Lonsdale. "Nationalism in Colonial and Post-Colonial Africa." In *The Oxford Handbook of the History of Nationalism*, edited by John Breuilly, 308–317. Oxford: Oxford University Press, 2013.

———. *Unhappy Valley: Conflict in Kenya and Africa*. London: James Currey, 1992.

Bevans, Stephen. *Models of Contextual Theology*. Maryknoll, NY: Orbis Books, 1992.

Biéler, André. *The Social Humanism of Calvin*. Richmond, VA: John Knox, 1964.

Blocher, Henri. "Calvin's Theological Anthropology." In *John Calvin and Evangelical Theology: Legacy and Prospect*, edited by Sung Wook Chung, 66–84. Louisville, KY: Westminster John Knox, 2009.

Blomberg, Craig L. "'True Righteousness and Holiness': The Image of God in the New Testament." In *The Image of God in an Image Driven Age: Explorations in Theological Anthropology*, edited by Beth Felker Jones and Jeffrey W. Barbeau, 66–87. Downers Grove: IVP Academic, 2016.

Boer, Roland. *Political Grace: The Revolutionary Theology of John Calvin*. Louisville, KY: Westminster John Knox, 2009.

Boesak, Allan Aubrey. *Black and Reformed: Apartheid, Liberation, and the Calvinist Tradition*. Maryknoll, NY: Orbis Books, 1984.

Boettner, Loraine. *The Reformed Doctrine of Predestination*. Grand Rapids: Eerdmans, 1941.

Boff, Leonardo, and Clodovis Boff. *Introducing Liberation Theology*. Liberation and Theology Series. London: Burns & Oates, 1987.

Bolt, John. "The Background and Context of Van Ruler's Theocentric (Theocratic) Vision and its Relevance for North America." In *Calvinist Trinitarianism and Theocentric Politics: Essays Toward a Public Theology*, edited by Arnold van Ruler and John Bolt, ix–xliv. Toronto Studies in Theology. Lewiston, NY: Edwin Mellen, 1989.

Bonhoeffer, Dietrich. *Life Together: The Classic Exploration of Faith in Community*. Translated by John W. Doberstein. New York: HarperSanFrancisco, 1954.

Borneman, Adam. "'All Things Turned Upside Down' – Calvin on Slavery." *Political Theology Today*, n.d. http://www.politicaltheology.com/blog/all-things-turned-upside-down-calvin-on-slavery/.

———. "Presbyterians, Civil Rights, and the Spirituality of the Church: A Brief Historical Survey." *Political Theology Today*, n.d. http://www. politicaltheology.com/blog/presbyterians-civil-rights-and-the-spirituality-of-the-church-a-brief-historical-survey/.

Bornkamm, Heinrich. *Luther's Doctrine of the Two Kingdoms in the Context of His Theology*. Translated by Karl H. Hertz. Philadelphia: Fortress, 1966.

Bosch, David Jacobus. *Transforming Mission: Paradigm Shifts in Theology of Mission*. Maryknoll, NY: Orbis Books, 1991.

Botha, Elaine M. "Christian-National: Authentic, Ideological or Secularized Nationalism?" In *Our Reformational Tradition: A Rich Heritage and Lasting Vocation*, edited by B. J. van der Walt, 470–509. Silverton: Potchefstroom University for Higher Education, 1984.

Boulton, Matthew Myer. *Life in God: John Calvin, Practical Formation, and the Future of Protestant Theology*. Grand Rapids, MI: Eerdmans, 2011.

Bouwsma, William James. *John Calvin: A Sixteenth-Century Portrait*. New York: Oxford University Press, 1988.

Bradstock, Andrew. "The Reformation." In *The Blackwell Companion to Political Theology*, edited by Peter Scott and William T. Cavanaugh, 62–75. Malden, MA: Blackwell, 2004.

Branch, Daniel. *Kenya: Between Hope and Despair*. New Haven: Yale University Press, 2011.

Bratt, James, ed. *Abraham Kuyper: A Centennial Reader*. Grand Rapids: Eerdmans, 1998.

Bretherton, Luke. *Christianity and Contemporary Politics: The Conditions and Possibilities of Faithful Witness*. Chichester, UK: Wiley-Blackwell, 2010.

Brueggemann, Walter. *Cadences of Home: Preaching among Exiles*. Louisville, KY: Westminster John Knox, 1997.

———. *Deep Memory, Exuberant Hope: Contested Truth in a Post-Christian World*. Minneapolis, MN: Fortress, 2000.

Brunner, Emil. *The Christian Doctrine of Creation and Redemption*. Translated by Olive Wyon. Philadelphia: Westminster, 1952.

Bujo, Bénézet. *Foundations of an African Ethic: Beyond the Universal Claims of Western Morality*. New York: Crossroad, 2001.

Burgess, Elaine M. "The Resurgence of Ethnicity: Myth or Reality?" *Ethnic and Racial Studies* 1, no. 3 (1978): 265–285.

Burns, Lanier. "From Ordered Soul to Corrupted Nature: Calvin's View of Sin." In *John Calvin and Evangelical Theology: Legacy and Prospect*, edited by Sung Wook Chung, 85–106. Colorado Springs: Paternoster, 2009.

Cairns, David. *The Image of God in Man*. London: SCM, 1953.

Calvin, John. *Calvin's Commentary on Seneca's De Clementia*. Translated by Ford Lewis Battles and Andre Malan Hugo. Leiden: Brill, 1969.

———. *Commentaries on the Book of Joshua*. Translated by Henry Beveridge. 500th Anniversary ed. Grand Rapids, MI: Baker Books, 2009.

———. *Commentaries on the Book of the Prophet Jeremiah and the Lamentations*. Translated by John Owen. 500th Anniversary ed. Grand Rapids: Baker Books, 2009.

———. *Commentary on the Epistle of Paul the Apostle to the Corinthians*. Translated by John Pringle. 500th Anniversary ed. Grand Rapids: Baker Books, 2009.

———. *Commentaries on the Epistle of Paul the Apostle to the Hebrews*. Translated by John Owen. Grand Rapids: Christian Classics Ethereal Library, n.d. http://www.ccel.org/ccel/calvin/calcom44.titlepage.html?highlight=commentaries,on,the,epistle,of,paul,apostle,to,hebrews#highlight.

———. *Commentaries on the Epistle of Paul the Apostle to the Romans*. Translated by John Owen. 500th Anniversary ed. Grand Rapids: Baker Books, 2009.

———. *Commentaries on the Epistles of Paul to the Galatians and Ephesians*. Translated by William Pringle. 500th Anniversary ed. Grand Rapids: Baker Books, 2009.

———. *Commentaries on the First Book of Moses Called Genesis*. Translated by John King. 23 vols. 500th Anniversary ed. Grand Rapids: Baker Books, 2009.

———. *Commentaries on the First Epistle of Peter*. Translated by John Owen. 500th Anniversary ed. Grand Rapids: Baker Books, 2009.

———. *Commentaries on the Four Last Books of Moses Arranged in the Form of Harmony*. Translated by Charles William Bingham. 500th Anniversary ed. Grand Rapids: Baker Books, 2009.

———. *Commentaries on the Twelve Minor Prophets*. Translated by John Owen. 500th Anniversary ed. Grand Rapids: Baker Books, 2009.

———. *Commentary on a Harmony of the Evangelists: Matthew, Mark, and Luke*. Translated by John Pringle. 500th Anniversary ed. Grand Rapids: Baker Books, 2009.

———. *Commentary on Isaiah*. Translated by William Pringle. Grand Rapids: Christian Classics Ethereal Library, (n.d.), http://www.ccel.org/ccel/calvin/commentary,on,isaiah#highlight.

———. *Commentary on Psalms*. Translated by James Anderson. Grand Rapids: Christian Classics Ethereal Library, n.d., https://www.ccel.org/ccel/calvin/calcom08.i.html.

———. *Golden Booklet of the True Christian Life*. Translated by Henry J. Van Andel. Grand Rapids: Baker Books, 2004.

———. *Institutes of the Christian Religion*. Edited by John T. McNeil. Translated by Ford Lewis Battles. 2 vols. Library of Christian Classics. Philadelphia: Westminster, 1960.

———. *Letters of John Calvin*. Translated by Jules Bonnet. New York: B. Franklin, 1973.

———. *On God and Political Duty*. Edited by John T. McNeil. New York: Macmillan, 1950.

———. On the Christian Life: Selections from the Institutes, Commentaries, and Tracts. Edited by John T. McNeil. Indianapolis: Liberal Arts, 1957.

———. "On Usury." In *From Christ to the World: Introductory Readings in Christian Ethics*, edited by Wayne G. Boulton, 453–455. Grand Rapids, MI: Eerdmans, 1994.

———. *A Reflection Book: Introduction to the Writings of John Calvin*. Translated by Hugh T. Kerr. New York: Association, 1960.

———. *Sermons on the Ten Commandments*. Translated by Benjamin Farley. Grand Rapids: Baker Books, 1980.

———. *Treatises against the Anabaptists and against the Libertines*. Translated by Benjamin Farley. Grand Rapids: Baker Academic, 1982.

Cantle, Ted. *Community Cohesion: A New Framework for Race and Diversity*. Basingstoke, UK: Palgrave Macmillan, 2005.

Cavanaugh, William T. *Migrations of the Holy: God, State, and the Political Meaning of the Church*. Grand Rapids: Eerdmans, 2011.

———. Theopolitical Imagination: Christian Practices of Space and Time. London: T & T Clark, 2002.

Chacha, B. K. "Pastors or Bastards? The Dynamics of Religion and Politics in the 2007 General Elections in Kenya." In *Tensions and Reversals in Democaractic Transitions*, edited by K. Kanyinga and D. Okello, 101–135. Nairobi: Society for International Development, 2010.

Charry, Ellen T. "Sacramental Ecclesiology." In *The Community of the Word: Toward an Evangelical Ecclesiology*, edited by Mark Husbands and Daniel J. Treier, 201–216. Downers Grove, IL: InterVarsity Press, 2005.

Chege, Michael. "Ethnic Pluralism and National Governance in Africa: A Survey." In *Ethnic Diversity in Eastern Africa: Opportunities and Challenges*, edited by Kimani Njogu, Kabiri Ngeta, and Mary Wanjau, 3–17. Nairobi: Twaweza Communications, 2010.

Cheluget, L. K. *Nyanza Province Annual Report, 1972*. Provincial Commissioner's Annual Report. Nyanza, 1972.

Chemorion, Diphus C., and Esther Mombo, and C. B. Peter, eds. *Contested Space: Ethnicity and Religion in Kenya*. Limuru, Kenya: Zapf Chancery, 2013.

Chenevière, Marc. "Did Calvin Advocate Theocracy?" In *Calvin's Thought on Economic and Social Issues and the Relationship of Church and State*, edited by Richard C. Gamble, 108–116. Articles on Calvin and Calvinism 11. New York: Garland, 1992.

Chipenda, José B., Andre Karamaga, H. N. K. Mugambi, and C. K. Omari, eds. *The Church of Africa: Towards a Theology of Reconstruction*. Nairobi: All Africa Conference of Churches, 1991.

Chung, Sung Wook. "Taking up Our Cross: Calvin's Cross Theology of Sanctification." In *John Calvin and Evangelical Theology: Legacy and Prospect*, edited by Sung Wook Chung, 163–180. Colorado Springs: Paternoster, 2009.

Church, Joe E. *Quest for the Highest: An Autobiographical Account of the East African Revival*. Exeter: Paternoster, 1981.

Citizen TV. "President Uhuru Kenyatta's Speech at Ntimama Funeral." Nairobi: Citizen TV, 2016. https://www.youtube.com/watch?v=CdzeKjaxwrY.

———. "Western Kenya Intrigues." Video. Nairobi: Citizen TV, 2016.

Clines, David J. A. *On the Way to the Postmodern: Old Testament Essays*. 2 vols. Journal for the Study of the Old Testament, Supplemental Series 293. Sheffield: Sheffield Academic, 1998.

———. "The Image of God in Man." *Tyndale Bulletin* 19 (1968): 53–103.

Collinson, Patrick. *The Reformation*. London: Weidenfeld and Nicholson, 2003.

Colonial Report. *Masai Move, 1911*. Kenya National Archives, n.d.

Coredo, Julius. "Kenyans Can Replace Tribal Bigotry with National Values." *Daily Nation*, 12 June, 2015. https://www.nation.co.ke/oped/letters/Kenyans-can-replace-tribal-bigotry-with-national-values/440806-2749826-p4ut44/index.html.

Cortez, Marc. *Christological Anthropology in Historical Perspective: Ancient and Contemporary Approaches to Theological Anthropology*. Grand Rapids: Zondervan, 2016.

———. *Theological Anthropology: A Guide for the Perplexed*. New York: T & T Clark, 2010.

Crouch, Andy. *Culture Making: Recovering Our Creative Calling*. Downers Grove: InterVarsity Press, 2008.

Crouch, Margaret. *A Vision of Christian Mission: Reflections on the Great Commission in Kenya*. Nairobi: NCCK, 1993.

Curtin, Philip D. *The Image of Africa: British Ideas and Action*. Madison: University of Wisconsin Press, 1964.

Cyprian. *De Unitate Ecclesiae*. Translated by Edward Henry Blakeney. London: Society for Promoting Christian Knowledge, 1928.

Daily Nation. "Clergymen Own Up to Partisan Role in Post-Election Chaos." 23 August 2008, https://www.nation.co.ke/news/1056-462380-koien2z/index.html.

———. "Did Church Leaders Fail Kenyans?" 28 January, 2008.

———. "These Leaders Must Not Be Allowed to Destroy Our Country with Hatred." 5 November, 2015.

———. "When the Shepherds Lead their Flocks Astray." 15 February, 2008.

de Gruchy, John W. *Christianity and Democracy: A Theology for a Just World Order*. Cambridge Studies in Ideology and Religion. Cambridge: Cambridge University Press, 1995.

———. *John Calvin: Christian Humanist and Evangelical Reformer*. Eugene, OR: Cascade, 2013.

———. *Liberating Reformed Theology: A South African Contribution to an Ecumenical Debate*. Grand Rapids: Eerdmans, 1991.

Dedji, Valentin. "The Ethical Redemption of African Imaginaire: Kä Mana's Theology of Reconstruction." *Journal of Religion in Africa* 31, no. 3 (2001): 254–274.

———. *Reconstruction and Renewal in African Christian Theology*. Nairobi: Acton, 2003.

Demmers, Jolle. *Theories of Violent Conflict: An Introduction*. London: Routledge, 2017.

Dieleman, Kyle J. "Body and Resurrection in Calvin's Commentaries." In *Anthropological Reformations: Anthropology in the Era of Reformation*, edited by Anna Eusterschulte and Hannah Wälzholz, 157–164. Göttingen: Vandenhoeck & Ruprecht, 2015.

Diop, Cheikh Anta. *Towards the African Renaissance: Essays in African Culture and Development*. Translated by Egbuna P. Modum. London: Karnak House, 1996.

District Commissioner's Office. "District Commissioner's Office Mumias." Kenya National Archives, 1909.

———. *Handing Over Report: North Kavirondo District*. Kisumu: District Commissioner's Office, 1909. Kenya National Archives.

Dooyeweerd, Herman. *Roots of Western Culture*. Toronto: Wedge, 1979.

Douglas, J. D. *Let the Earth Hear His Voice: International Congress on World Evangelization, Lausanne, Switzerland*. Minneapolis: Worldwide, 1975.

Douglass, Jane Dempsey. "Calvin's Relation to Social and Economic Order." In *Calvin's Thought on Economic and Social Issues and the Relationship of Church and State*, edited by Richard C. Gamble, 127–133. Articles on Calvin and Calvinism 11. New York: Garland, 1992.

———. "The Image of God in Humanity: A Comparison of Calvin's Teaching in 1536 and 1559." In *In Honor of John Calvin: Papers from the 1986 International Calvin Symposium*, edited by E. J. Furcha, 174–203. Montreal: McGill University Press, 1986.

———. *Women, Freedom, and Calvin*. Philadelphia: Westminster, 1985.

Dowey, Edward A. *The Knowledge of God in Calvin's Theology*. New York: Columbia University Press, 1952.

Drever, Matthew D. "Redeeming Creation: *Creatio ex nihilo* and the *Imago Dei* in Augustine." *International Journal of Systematic Theology* 15, no. 2 (2013): 135–153.

Dube, Musa W. "Jesse Mugambi Is Calling Us to Move From Liberation to Reconstruction! A Postcolonial Feminist Response." 1–16. Unpublished paper presented at the University of South Africa, September 21, 2002.

———, ed. *Other Ways of Reading: African Women and the Bible.* Atlanta: Society of Biblical Literature, 2001.

———. *Postcolonial Feminist Interpretation of the Bible.* St. Louis: Chalice, 2000.

———. "Rereading the Bible: Biblical Hermeneutics and Social Justice." In *African Theology Today*, edited by Emmanuel Katongole, 57–68. African Theology Today Series. Scranton, PA: University of Scranton Press, 2002.

Dudley-Smith, Timothy. *John Stott: A Global Ministry.* Downers Grove: InterVarsity Press, 2001.

Durant, Will. *The Reformation: A History of European Civilization from Wyclif to Calvin.* The Story of Civilization: Part VI. New York: Simon and Schuster, 1957.

Durrani, Shiraz. *Kimathi: Mau Mau's First Prime Minister of Kenya.* Middlex, UK: Vita Books, 1986.

Dyrness, William A. "Spaces for an Evangelical Ecclesiology." In *The Community of the Word: Toward an Evangelical Ecclesiology*, edited by Mark Husbands and Daniel J. Treier, 251–272. Downers Grove: InterVarsity Press, 2005.

Edgar, T. L. "KPF Convict No. 503/60 Muiluli s/o Mreanga. High Court Criminal Sessions Case No. 78 of 1952. Ref. your PR/KPF.503/60/10 dated the 9 November, 1960," n.d., Kenya National Archives.

Ela, Jean-March. *My Faith as an African.* Maryknoll, NY: Orbis, 1988.

Elkins, Caroline. *Imperial Reckoning: The Untold Story of Britain's Gulag in Kenya.* New York: Henry Holt, 2005.

Eller, Jack David. *From Culture to Ethnicity to Conflict: An Anthropological Perspective on International Ethnic Conflict.* Ann Arbor, MI: University of Michigan Press, 1999.

Engel, Mary Potter. *John Calvin's Perspectival Anthropology.* Atlanta: Scholars, 1988.

Evans, Eifion. "John Calvin: Theologian of the Holy Spirit." *Reformation & Revival* 10, no. 4 (Fall 2001): 83–104.

Ezigbo, Victor I. *Re-imagining African Christologies: Conversing with the Interpretations and Appropriations of Jesus Christ in African Christianity.* Eugene, OR: Pickwick, 2010.

Faber, Jelle. *Essays in Reformed Doctrine.* Neerlandia, AB: Inheritance, 1990.

Fairbairn, Donald. *Life in the Trinity: An Introduction to Theology with the Help of the Church Father.* Downers Grove: IVP Academic, 2009.

Falola, Toyin, and Hetty Ter Haar, eds. *Narrating War and Peace in Africa*. Rochester: University of Rochester Press, 2010.

Farisani, Elelwani. "The Use of Ezra-Nehemiah in a Quest for an African Theology of Reconstruction." *Journal of Theology for Southern Africa* 116 (July 2003): 27–50.

———. "Transformation and Renewal in Contemporary Africa (Rom. 12:1–2)." In *Text and Context in New Testament Hermeneutics*, edited J. N. K. Mugambi and Johanness A. Smit, 56–82. Nairobi: Acton, 2004.

Ferdinando, Keith. "Christian Identity in the African Context: Reflections on Kwame Bediako's Theology and Identity." *Journal of the Evangelical Theological Society* 50, no. 1 (2007): 121–143.

Finch, Jeffrey. "Irenaeus on the Christological Basis of Human Divinization." In *Theosis: Deification in Christian Theology*, vol. 1, edited by Stephen Filan and Vladimir Kharlamov, 86–103. Cambridge: James Clarke, 2006.

Finlayson, John. "Kenya: Mau Mau Uprising, 1952–1956." In *World Terrorism: An Encyclopedia of Political Violence from Ancient Times to the Post-9/11 Era*, vol. 2, edited by James Ciment, 322–323. Armonk, NY: M. E. Sharpe, 2011.

Fitch, David E. *The End of Evangelicalism? Discerning a New Faithfulness for Mission, Toward an Evangelical Political Theology*. Eugene, OR: Cascade, 2011.

Flanya, Seth Kwaku. "Recourse to History: Reviving the Return-to-Africa Initiative." *AU Echo* 5 (2013): 1–11.

Fowler, Stuart. "The Persistent Dualism in Calvin's Thought." In *Our Reformational Tradition: A Rich Heritage and Lasting Vocation*, edited by B. J. van der Walt, 339–352. Silverton: Potchefstroom University for Higher Education, 1984.

Freston, Paul. *Evangelicals and Politics in Asia, Africa and Latin America*. Cambridge, UK: Cambridge University Press, 2001.

Friedman, Robert. "The Doctrine of the Two Kingdoms." In *The Recovery of the Anabaptist Vision: A Sixtieth Anniversary Tribute to Harold S. Bender*, edited by Guy F. Hershberger, 105–118. Scottdale, PA: Herald, 1957.

Frost, Michael. *Exiles: Living Missionally in a Post-Christian Culture*. Peabody, MA: Hendrickson, 2006.

Frostin, Per. *Luther's Two Kingdoms Doctrine: A Critical Study*. Lund, Sweden: University of Lund Press, 1994.

Fuellenbach, John. *Church: Community for the Kingdom*. Maryknoll, NY: Orbis Books, 2002.

Fukuyama, Francis. *The End of History and the Last Man*. New York: Free Press, 1992.

Gachamba, Chege wa. "Gitari Tells Off Churches Group." *Daily Nation*, 7 May 2001.

Gaitho, Macharia. "We Do Ourselves a Disservice When We Deify Politicians Who Can Only Use Us." *Daily Nation*, 5 January 2016. https://www. nation.co.ke/oped/opinion/-We-do-ourselves-a-disservice-when-we-idolize-politicians/440808-3021368-su8frbz/index.html.

Gatabaki, Njehu. "Peace: Interview of the Most Rev. Manasses Kuria." *Finance*, October 1991.

Gathogo, Julius Mutugi. *African Hospitality from a Missiological Perspective*. Saarbrücken: LAP Lambert, 2011.

———. "African Hospitality: Is it Compatible with the Ideal Christ's Hospitality?" *Svensk Missionstidskrift* 94 (2006): 23–53.

———. "African Philosophy as Expressed in the Concepts of Hospitality and Ubuntu." *Journal for Theology for Southern Africa* 130 (March 2008): 39–53.

———. "Black Theology of South Africa: Is This the Hour of Paradigm Shift?" *Black Theology* 5, no. 3 (2007): 327–354.

———. "Genesis, Methodologies, and Concerns of African Theology of Reconstruction." *Theologia Viatorum: Journal of Religion and Theology in Africa* 32, no. 1 (2008): 23–62.

———. "Jesse Mugambi's Pedigree: Formative Factors." *Studia Historiae Ecclesiasticae* 32, no. 2 (2006): 173–205.

———. "Meddling on to 2008: Is There Any Relevance for Gitari's Model in the Aftermath of Ethnic Violence?" In *Religion and Politics in Kenya: Essays in Honor of a Meddlesome Priest*, edited by Ben Knighton, 143–154. New York: Palgrave Macmillan, 2009.

———. "Reading John Calvin in the African context: Any Relevance for the Social Reconstruction of Africa?" *Studia Historiae Ecclesiasticae* 35, no. 2 (2009): 219–235.

Gehman, Richard J. *African Traditional Religion in Biblical Perspective*. Revised ed. Nairobi: East African Educational Publishers, 2005.

———. "The Spreading Vineyard: The Growth of the Africa Inland Church, Kenya, from 1945 Onwards." Wheaton, IL: Oasis International, 2017.

———. "A Survey of African Theology of Reconstruction." *Swedish Missiological Themes* 95, no. 2 (2007): 123–148.

Gekara, Emeka Mayaka. "Cardinal Njue's Leadership Faces Litmus Test as Catholic Church Voices Differ." *Daily Nation*, 15 May 2009. https://www. nation.co.ke/news/1056-598696-k3gswwz/index.html.

———. "Religious Leaders Regain their Voice." *Daily Nation*, 21 March 2009. https://www.nation.co.ke/news/politics/1064-549286-7rk7lnz/index. html.

Gerrish, Brian A. "The Mirror of God's Goodness: Man in the Theology of Calvin." *Concordia Theological Quarterly* 45, no. 3 (1981): 211–222.

Getui, Mary N., and Peter Kanyandogo, eds. *From Violence to Peace: A Challenge for African Christianity*. African Christianity Series. Nairobi: Acton, 2003.

Gibelini, Rosino, ed. *Paths of African Theology*. Maryknoll: Orbis Books, 1994.

Gifford, Paul. *Christianity, Politics and Public Life in Kenya*. London: Hurst, 2009.

Gitari, David M. "The Bishop as Leader and Teacher." *Transformation* 15, no. 2 (1998): 12–15.

———. "A Christian Perspective on Nation Building." *Evangelical Fellowship in the Anglican Communion* 47 (1996): 210–222.

———. "Church and Nationhood in a Changing World." In *Church and Nationhood*, edited by Lionel Holmes, 21–28. New Delhi: Statesman Press, 1978.

———. "Church and Politics in Kenya." *Transformation* 8, no. 3 (1991): 7–17.

———. "The Church's Witness to the Living God in Seeking Just Political, Social and Economic Structures in Contemporary Africa." In *Witnessing to the Living God in Africa: Findings and Papers of Inaugural Meeting of Africa Theological Fraternity*, edited by David M. Gitari and G. P. Benson, 119–140. Nairobi: Uzima, 1987.

———. "Evangelization and Culture." In *Proclaiming Christ in Christ's Way: Studies in Integral Mission*, edited by Vinay Samuel and Albrecht Hauser, 101–121. Oxford: Regnum, 2007.

———. "The Holy Spirit in Renewal." In *Facing the Challenges: The Message of PACLA*, edited by Michael Cassidy and Luc Verlinden, 580–598. Kisumu: Evangel, 1978.

———. *In Season and Out of Season: Sermons to a Nation*. Carlisle, UK: Regnum, 1996.

———. *Let the Bishop Speak*. Nairobi: Uzima, 1988.

———. "Mission of the Church in East Africa." In *Crossroads Are for Meeting: Essays on the Mission and Common Life of the Church in a Global Society*, edited by Philips Turner, 25–42. Sewanee, TN: SPCK, 1986.

———. "The Sanctity of Human Life: Priority for Africa." *Transformation* 14, no. 3 (1997): 19–23.

———. *Troubled but Not Destroyed: The Autobiography of Archbishop David Gitari*. McLean, VA: Isaac, 2014.

———. "'You Are in the World but Not of It.'" In *Christian Political Witness*, edited by George Kalantzis and Gregory W. Lee, 214–231. Wheaton Theology Conference. Downers Grove: InterVarsity Press, 2014.

Gitari, David, and G. P. Benson, eds. *Witnessing to the Living God in Africa: Findings and Papers of Inaugural Meeting of Africa Theological Fraternity.* Nairobi: Uzima, 1987.

Gitari, David, and Ben Knighton. "On Being a Christian Leader: Story Contesting Power in Kenya." *Transformation* 18, no. 4 (2001): 247–262.

Githongo, John. "Crossroads in the Fight against Corruption." TI-UK Annual Anti-Corruption Lecture presented at the Transparency International UK, One Mile Square of the City of London, 2012. http://www.transparency.org.uk/publications/2012-anti-corruption-lecture-john-githongo/.

Godfrey, Robert W. *John Calvin: Pilgrim and Pastor.* Wheaton, IL: Crossway, 2009.

Goheen, Michael W., and Craig G. Bartholomew. *Living at the Crossroads: An Introduction to Christian Worldview.* Grand Rapids: Baker Academic, 2008.

Gona, George, and Mbugua wa-Mungai, eds. *(Re)membering Kenya: Identity, Culture and Freedom.* Nairobi: Twaweza Communications, 2010.

Government of Kenya. *Kenya Land Commission Evidence.* Vol. 1. Nairobi: Government Printers, 1932

———. *Kenya Land Commission Evidence.* Vol. 2. Nairobi: Government Printers, 1933.

———. *Kenya Land Commission Evidence.* Vol. 3. Nairobi: Government Printers, 1934.

———. Report of the Commission of Inquiry into the Illegal/Irregular Allocation of Public Land (Ndung'u Report). Nairobi: Government Printers, 2004.

———. Report of the Commission of Inquiry into the Post-Election Violence (Waki Report). Nairobi: Government Printers, 2008.

———. Report of the Judicial Commission Appointed to Inquire into Tribal Clashes in Kenya (Akiwumi Report). Nairobi: Government Printers, 2001.

———. Report of the Parliamentary Select Committee to Investigate Ethnic Clashes in Western and other Parts of Kenya. Nairobi: Government Printers, 1992.

Grabill, Stephen John. *Rediscovering the Natural Law in Reformed Theological Ethics.* Emory University Studies in Law and Religion. Grand Rapids: Eerdmans, 2006.

Great Britain Colonial Office. *Colonial Report: The Colony and Protectorate of Kenya for the Year 1949.* London: His Majesty's Stationery Office, 1949.

Greef, Wulfert De. "Calvin's Writings." In *The Cambridge Companion to John Calvin,* 41–57. Cambridge: Cambridge University Press, 2004.

Grenz, Stanley J. *The Social God and the Relational Self: A Trinitarian Theology of the Imago Dei.* Louisville, KY: Westminster John Knox, 2001.

———. *Theology for the Community of God.* Grand Rapids: Eerdmans, 2000.

Gritsch, Eric W. *Reformer without a Church: The Life and Thought of Thomas Müntzer*. Philadelphia: Fortress, 1967.

———. *Thomas Müntzer: A Tragedy of Errors*. Minneapolis: Fortress, 1989.

Guder, Darrell L. "The Church as Missional Community." In *The Community of the Word: Toward and Evangelical Ecclesiology*, edited by Mark Husbands and Daniel J. Treier, 114–128. Downers Grove: InterVarsity Press, 2005.

Gunda, Masiiwa Ragies. "African Theology of Reconstruction: The Painful Realities and Practical Options!" *Exchange* 38, no. 2 (2009): 84–102.

Gunton, Colin E. *Christ and Creation*. Carlisle, UK: Paternoster, 1992.

Gunton, Colin E., and Daniel W. Hardy, eds. *On Being the Church: Essays on the Christian Community*. Edinburgh: T & T Clark, 1989.

Gushee, David P. *The Sacredness of Human Life: Why an Ancient Biblical Vision is Key to the World's Future*. Grand Rapids: Eerdmans, 2013.

Hall, Douglas John. *Imaging God: Dominion as Stewardship*. Grand Rapids: Eerdmans, 1986.

Hallet, Adrian. "The Theology of John Calvin: The Christians Conflict with the Flesh." *Churchman* 105, no. 2 (1991): 1–44.

Hancock, Ralph C. *Calvin and the Foundations of Modern Politics*. Ithaca, NY: Cornell University Press, 1989.

Hankela, Elina. *Ubuntu, Migration, and Ministry: Being Human in a Johannesburg Church*. Leiden: Brill, 2014.

Hans-Jürgen, Goertz. "Mystic with the Hammer: Thomas Müntzer's Theological Basis for Revolution." *Mennonite Quarterly Review* 50 (April 1976): 83–113.

Harper, Brad and Paul Louis Metzger. *Exploring Ecclesiology: An Evangelical and Ecumenical Introduction*. Grand Rapids: Brazos, 2009.

Hart, Darryl. *Calvinism: A History*. New Haven: Yale University Press, 2013.

Hastings, Adrian. *A History of African Christianity*. Cambridge: Cambridge University Press, 1979.

Hauerwas, Stanley. *A Community of Character: Toward a Constructive Christian Social Ethic*. Notre Dame, IN: University of Notre Dame Press, 1981.

Healy, Nicholas M. *Church, World, and the Christian life: Practical-Prophetic Ecclesiology*. Cambridge: Cambridge University Press, 2000.

Heaney, Robert S. *From Historical to Critical Post-Colonial Theology: The Contribution of John S. Mbiti and Jesse N. K. Mugambi*. Eugene, OR: Pickwick, 2015.

Helm, Paul. *Calvin: A Guide for the Perplexed*. Guides for the Perplexed. London: T & T Clark, 2008.

Hempstone, Smith. *Rogue Ambassador: An African Memoir*. Sewanee, TN: University of the South Press, 1997.

Her Majesty's Stationery Office. *Colonial Reports, Kenya 1954*. London: Her Majesty's Stationery Office, 1954.

Herbeling, David. "Kenyan Legislators Emerge Second in Global Pay Ranking." *Business Daily*, 23 July 2013. Available online, http://www. businessdailyafrica.com/Kenya-MPs-come-second-in-global-salary-ranking-/539546-1924534-pr4uvf/index.html.

Herbert, David. *Creating Community Cohesion: Religion, Media and Multiculturalism*. Basingstoke, UK: Palgrave Macmillan, 2013.

Hester, David C. "The Sanctified Life in the Body of Christ: A Presbyterian Form of Christian Community." In *Community Formation in the Early Church and the Church Today*, edited by Richard N. Longenecker, 194–212. Peabody, MA: Hendrickson, 2002.

Hiagbe, Komi Ahiatroga. *Reconciled to Reconcile: An African View of John Calvin's Doctrine of Salvation*. Frankfurt: Peter Lang, 2007.

Hiebert, Paul G. *Anthropological Insights for Missionaries*. Grand Rapids: Baker Books, 1985.

Hillerbrand, Hans J. *A Fellowship of Discontent*. New York: Harper & Row, 1967.

Hinga, Teresia M. "African Feminist Theologies, the Global Village, and the Imperative of Solidarity Across Borders: The Case of the Circle of Concerned African Women Theologians." *Journal of Feminist Studies in Religion* 18, no. 1 (2002): 79–86.

Hoekema, Anthony A. *Created in God's Image*. Grand Rapids: Eerdmans, 1986.

Holcomb, Justin. "Two Major Streams of Reformed Theology." *The Gospel Coalition*, 24 September 2012. https://www.thegospelcoalition.org/article/two-major-streams-of-reformed-theology.

Holmes, Arthur F. "Concept of Natural Law." *Christian Scholar's Review* 2 (1972): 195–208.

———. "Human Variables and Natural Law." In *God and the Good: Essays in Honor of Henry Stob*, edited by Clifton J. Orlebeke and Lewis B. Smedes, 63–79. Grand Rapids: Eerdmans, 1975.

Hoogerwerf, Steven D. "Ecclesiology and Christian Nurture in the Theology of John Calvin: A Study of the Church's Instrumental Role in Nurturing Christian Life." In *Church Divinity 1989/1990*, edited by John H. Morgan, 44–71. Church Divinity Monograph Series. Bristol, IN: Wyndham Hall, 1990.

Hornsby, Charles. *Kenya: A History since Independence*. New York: I. B. Tauris, 2012.

Horowitz, Donald L. *Ethnic Groups in Conflict*. Berkeley: University of California Press, 1985.

Houle, Carrol. "Empowering the Victims." In *From Violence to Peace: A Challenge for African Christianity*, edited by Mary N. Getui and Peter Kanyandogo, 164–185. African Christianity Series. Nairobi: Acton, 2003.

Huff, Peter A. "Calvin and the Beasts: Animals in John Calvin's Theological Discourse." *Journal of the Evangelical Theological Society* 42, no. 1 (March 1999): 67–75.

Hughes, Lotte. *Moving the Maasai: A Colonial Misadventure.* London: Palgrave Macmillan, 2006.

Hughes, Philip Edgcumbe. "The Pen of the Prophet." In *John Calvin Contemporary Prophet, A Symposium*, edited by Jacob Tunis Hoogstra, 71–94. Grand Rapids: Baker, 1959.

Human Rights Watch. *"All the Men Have Gone": War Crimes in Kenya's Mt. Elgon Conflict.* New York: Human Rights Watch, 2007.

———. *Divide and Rule: State-sponsored Violence in Kenya.* New York: Africa Watch, 1993. https://www.hrw.org/reports/1993/kenya1193.pdf.

———. *"High Stakes: Political Violence and the 2013 Elections in Kenya." Human Rights Watch*, 7 February 2013. https://www.hrw.org/report/2013/02/07/high-stakes/political-violence-and-2013-elections-kenya#4ab8e3.

———. *Playing the Communal Card: Communal Violence and Human Rights.* New York: Human Rights Watch, 1995.

———. *Playing with Fire: Weapons Proliferation, Political Violence, and Human Rights in Kenya.* New York: Human Rights Watch, 2002. https://www.hrw.org/reports/2002/kenya/Kenya0502.pdf.

———. *Turning Pebbles: Evading Accountability for Post-Election Violence in Kenya.* USA, 2011. https://www.hrw.org/report/2011/12/09/turning-pebbles/evading-accountability-post-election-violence-kenya#.

Hunt, Carew R. N. "Calvin's Theory of Church and State." In *Calvin's Thought on Economic and Social Issues and the Relationship of Church and State*, edited by Richard C. Gamble, 2–18. Articles on Calvin and Calvinism 11. New York: Garland, 1992.

Huntingford, G. W. B. *Nandi: Work and Culture.* London: His Majesty's Stationery Office, 1950.

———. *The Nandi: The People's of Kenya.* Nairobi: Njia Kuu, 1944.

Idowu, Bolaji E. *African Traditional Religion: A Definition.* London: SCM, 1973.

———. *Olódùmarè: God in Yoruba Belief.* New York: Praeger, 1963.

———. *Towards an Indigenous Church.* London: Oxford University Press, 1965.

Ilo, Stan Chu. *The Church and Development in Africa: Aid and Development from the Perspective of Catholic Social Ethics.* Eugene, OR: Pickwick, 2011.

Imbo, Samuel Oluoch. *An Introduction to African Philosophy.* New York: Rowman and Littlefield, 1998.

Institute for Education in Democracy. *Report on the 1997 General Elections in Kenya.* Nairobi: Institute for Education in Democracy, Catholic Justice and Peace Commission, National Council of Churches of Kenya, 1998.

Intermediate Technology Development Group (ITDG). *Conflict in Northern Kenya: A Focus on Internally Displaced*. Nairobi: ITDG, 2003.

Janz, Dennis R. *A Reformation Reader: Primary Texts with Introductions*. 2nd ed. Minneapolis: Fortress, 2008.

Jeong, Koo Jeon. "Calvin and the Two Kingdoms: Calvin's Political Philosophy in Light of Contemporary Discussion." *WTJ* 72, no. 2 (2010): 299–320.

Juma, Erick. "Crack Whip on Hate Mongers." *People Daily*, 21 January 2016.

Kagame, Alexis. *La philosophie bǎntu-rwandaise de l'Etre*. New York: Johnson, 1966.

Kagwanja, Peter Mwangi. "Courting Genocide: Populism, Ethno-Nationalism and the Informalisation of Violence in Kenya's 2008 Post-Election Crisis." *Journal of Contemporary African Studies* 27, no. 3 (2009): 365–387.

Kagwanja, Peter Mwangi, and Roger Southall. "Introduction: Kenya – A Democracy in Retreat?" In *Kenya's Uncertain Democracy: The Electoral Crisis of 2008*, edited by Peter Mwangi Kagwanja and Roger Southall, 1–19. London: Routledge, 2010.

Kairos Theologians (Group). *The Kairos Document: Challenge to the Church: A Theological Comment on the Political Crisis in South Africa*. Grand Rapids: Eerdmans, 1986.

Kalu, Ogbu U. "Daughters of Ethiopia: Constructing A Feminist Discourse in Ebony Strokes." In *African Women, Religion, and Health: Essays in Honor of Mercy Amba Ewudziwa Oduyoye*, edited by Isabel Apawo Phiri and Sarojini Nadar, 261–274. Maryknoll, NY: Orbis, 2006.

Kamaara, Eunice. "Towards Christian National Identity in Africa: A Historical Perspective to the Challenge of Ethnicity to the Church in Kenya." *Studies in World Christianity* 16, no. 2 (2010): 126–144.

Kanyandogo, Peter. "Who Is My Neighbour? A Christian Response to Refugees and the Displaced in Africa." In *Moral and Ethical Issues in African Christianity: Explorative Essays in Moral Theology*, edited by J. N. K. Mugambi and Anne Nasimiyu-Wasike, 171–184. Nairobi: Acton, 2003.

Kanyinga, Karuti and Duncan Okello. "Contradictions of Transition to Democracy in Fragmented Societies." In *Tensions and Reversals in Democratic Transitions: The Kenya 2007 General Elections*, edited by Karuti Kanyinga and Duncan Okello, 1–32. Nairobi: Society for International Development, 2010.

Kanyoro, Musimbi. "African Women's Quest for Justice: A Review of African Women's Theology." *The Pacific Journal of Theology* 15 (1996): 77–88.

———. "Engendered Communal Theology: African Women's Contribution to Theology in the Twenty-First Century." In *Hope Abundant: Third World and Indigenous Women's Theology*, edited by Kwok Pui-Ian, 19–35. Maryknoll, NY: Orbis, 2010.

————. *Introducing Feminist Cultural Hermeneutics: An African Perspective*. New York: Sheffield Academic, 2002.

Kapolyo, Joe M. *The Human Condition: Christian Perspective Through African Eyes*. Carlisle, UK: Langham Global Library, 2013.

Karega-Munene. "Production of Ethnic Identity in Kenya." In *Ethnic Diversity in Eastern Africa: Opportunities and Challenges*, edited by Kimani Njogu, Kabiri Ngeta and Mary Wanjau, 41–54. Nairobi: Twaweza, 2010.

Kärkkäinen, Veli-Matti. *An Introduction to Ecclesiology: Ecumenical, Historical and Global Perspectives*. Downers Grove: IVP Academic, 2002.

Kasfir, Nelson. *The Shrinking Political Arena: Participation and Ethnicity in African Politics with a Case Study of Uganda*. Berkeley: University of California Press, 1976.

Katongole, Emmanuel. "African Renaissance and the Challenge of Narrative Theology in Africa." In *African Theology Today*, edited by Emmanuel Katongole, 207–219. African Theology Today Series. Scranton, PA: University of Scranton Press, 2002.

————, ed. *African Theology Today*. African Theology Today Series. Scranton, PA: University of Scranton Press, 2002.

————. *The Sacrifice of Africa: A Political Theology for Africa*. Grand Rapids: Eerdmans, 2011.

Keddie, Gordon J. "Calvin on Civil Government." In *Calvin's Thought on Economic and Social Issues and the Relationship of Church and State*, edited by Richard C. Gamble, 43–55. Articles on Calvin and Calvinism 11. New York: Garland, 1992.

Keesecker, William F. "John Calvin's Mirror." *Theology Today* 17, no. 3 (1960): 288–289.

Keller, Edmond J. *Identity, Citizenship, and Political Conflict in Africa*. Bloomington: Indiana University Press, 2014.

Kenya Human Rights Commission. *Killing the Vote: State Sponsored Violence and Flawed Elections in Kenya*. Nairobi: KHRC, 1998.

Kenya News Agency. "Prime Minister's Statement on Republican Constitution." *Kenya News Agency*, 1964. Kenya National Archives.

Kerandi, Divine Dian. *Fair Play for Fair Pay: Kenya's Public Service Job Evaluation*. Nairobi: Salaries and Remuneration Commission, 2016. http://www.src.go.ke/index.php/media-centre/video-gallery.

Kerich, Amos. "Livestock, Land Feuds Spark Narok Violence." *The Star*, 28 December 2015. http://www.the-star.co.ke/news/2015/12/28/livestock-land-feuds-spark-narok-violence_c1266236.

Khadiagala, Gilbert M. "Forty Days and Nights of Peacemaking in Kenya." *Journal of African Elections* 7, no. 2 (2008): 4–32.

Khasandi-Telewa, Vicky. "'She Worships at the Kikuyu Church:' The Influence of Scottish Missionaries on Language in Worship and Education among African Christians." In *Africa in Scotland, Scotland in Africa: Historical Legacies and Contemporary Hybridities*, edited by Afe Adogame and Andrew Lawrence, 287–306. Leiden: Brill, 2014.

Kilner, John F. *Dignity and Destiny: Humanity in the Image of God*. Grand Rapids: Eerdmans, 2015.

Kim, Yosep. *The Identity and the Life of the Church: John Calvin's Ecclesiology in the Perspective of His Anthropology*. Princeton Theological Monographs. Eugene, OR: Pickwick, 2014.

Kingdon, Robert M., ed. *Transition and Revolution: Problems and Issues of European Renaissance and Reformation History*. Minneapolis: Burgess, 1974.

Kinney, John W. "The Theology of John Mbiti: His Sources, Norms, and Method." *Occasional Bulletin* 3, no. 2 (1979): 65–67.

Kinoti, Hannah W. "Evangelical Women and Politics in Africa." *Transformation* 11, no. 4 (1994): 6–10.

Kipkorir, Benjamin E. *People of the Rift Valley*. Kenya's People Series. Nigeria: Evans Brothers, 1978.

Kipkorir, Benjamin E., and Frederick Burkewood Welbourn. *The Marakwet of Kenya: A Preliminary Study*. Nairobi: East African Publishers, 2008.

Kirwan, Michael. *Political Theology: An Introduction*. Minneapolis: Fortress, 2009.

Klopp, Jacqueline M. "Can Moral Ethnicity Trump Political Tribalism? The Struggle for Land and Nation in Kenya." *African Studies* 61, no. 2 (2002): 269–294.

———. "Pilfering the Public: The Problem of Land Grabbing in Contemporary Kenya." *Africa Today* 47, no. 1 (Winter 2000): 7–26.

———. "Kenya's Internally Displaced: Managing Civil Conflict in Democratic Transitions." In *East Africa and the Horn: Confronting Challenges to Good Governance*, edited by Dorina Akosua Oduraa Bekoe, 59–80. Boulder, CO: Lynne Rienner, 2006.

———. "The NCCK and the Struggle Against 'Ethnic Clashes' in Kenya." In *Religion and Politics in Kenya: Essays in Honor of a Meddlesome Priest*, edited by Ben Knighton, 183–199. New York: Palgrave Macmillan, 2009.

Knighton, Ben, ed. *Religion and Politics in Kenya: Essays in Honor of a Meddlesome Priest*. New York: Palgrave Macmillan, 2009.

Kobia, Samuel. *The Courage to Hope: The Roots for a New Vision and the Calling of the Church in Africa*. Geneva: World Council of Churches, 2003.

Kombo, James Henry Owino. *The Doctrine of God in African Christian Thought: The Holy Trinity, Theological Hermeneutics and the African Intellectual Culture*. Leiden: Brill, 2007.

Kroon, Marijn de. *The Honour of God and Human Salvation: A Contribution to an Understanding of Calvin's Theology According to his Institutes*. Edinburgh: T & T Clark, 2001.

Kuyper, Abraham. *Lectures on Calvinism: Six Lectures Delivered at Princeton University, 1898*. Peabody, MA: Hendrickson, 2008.

Lambert, Thomas A., and Isabella M. Watt, eds. *Registers of the Consistory of Geneva in the Time of Calvin: Volume 1: 1542–1544*. Translated by Wallace M. McDonald. Grand Rapids: Eerdmans, 2000.

Larson, Mark J. *Calvin's Doctrine of the State: A Reformed Doctrine and Its American Trajectory, The Revolutionary War, and the Founding of the Republic*. Eugene, OR: Wipf & Stock, 2009.

Lategan, Laetus O. K. "The Significance of Calvin's Anthropology for Preaching on Ethical Themes." *Hervormde Teologiese Studies* 54, no. 1/2 (1998): 143–152.

Lee, Jung-Sook. "Calvin's Ministry in Geneva: Theology and Practice." In *John Calvin and Evangelical Theology: Legacy and Prospect*, edited by Sung Wook Chung, 199–218. Louisville, KY: Westminster John Knox, 2009.

Leith, John H. *An Introduction to the Reformed Tradition: A Way of Being the Christian Community*. Atlanta: John Knox, 1977.

———. "Calvin's Doctrine of the Proclamation of the Word and its Significance for Today in the Light of Recent Research." *Review & Expositor* 86, no. 1 (1989): 29–44.

———. *John Calvin's Doctrine of the Christian Life*. Louisville, KY: Westminster, 1989.

LenkaBula, Puleng. "Beyond Anthropocentricity: Botho/Ubuntu and the Quest for Economic and Ecological Justice in Africa." *Religion and Theology* 15, no. 3/4 (2008): 375–394.

Leys, Colin. *Underdevelopment in Kenya*. London: Heinemann, 1975.

Lindberg, Carter. *The European Reformations*. Cambridge, MA: Blackwell, 1996.

Lindijer, Koert. "Dit is de man die oorlog voert tegen de Afrikaanse Al Capones," 2015. http://www.nrc.nl/nieuws/2015/12/29/oorlog-tegen-de-afrikaanse-al-capones-1572450-a495583.

———. "Kenya Has Become a 'Bandit Economy.'" *African Arguments*, 11 January 2016. https://africanarguments.org/2016/01/11/kenya-has-become-a-bandit-economy-says-chief-justice-willy-mutunga/.

Lonsdale, John. "The Conquest State of Kenya, 1895–1905." In *Unhappy Valley: Conflict in Kenya and Africa*, edited by Bruce Berman and John Lonsdale, 13–44. London: James Currey, 1992.

———. "Moral and Political Argument in Kenya." In *Ethnicity and Democracy in Africa*, edited by Bruce Berman, Dickson Eyoh, and Will Kymlicka, 73–95. Oxford: James Currey, 2004.

Lonsdale, John, Stanley Booth-Clibbon, and Andrew Hake. "The Emerging Pattern of Church and State Co-operation in Kenya." In *Christianity in Independent Africa*, edited by Edward W. Fasholé-Luke, 267–284. Bloomington: Indiana University Press, 1978.

Lowery, Stephanie A. "Identity and Ecclesiology: Their Relationship among Select African Theologians." PhD diss., Wheaton College, 2015.

Loyd, F. A. *Nyanza Province Annual Report 1957*. Provincial Commissioner's Annual Report. Kisumu: Provincial Offices Kisumu, 1960. Kenya National Archives.

Lumumba, Patrick. *A Call for Hygiene in Kenyan Politics*. Nairobi: MvuleAfrica, 2008.

———. "Electoral Justice: The Antidote for Post Election Violence in Kenya." In *Defining Moments: Reflections on Citizenship, Violence, and the 2007 General Elections in Kenya*, edited by Kimani Njogu, 147–167. Nairobi: Twaweza Communications, 2011.

Luther, Martin. *Luther's Works*. Philadelphia: Concordia, 1960.

———. *Luther's Works*. Edited by Walther I. Brandt. Philadelphia: Muhlenberg, 1962.

Lynch, Gabrielle. *I Say to You: Ethnic Politics and the Kalenjin in Kenya*. Chicago: University of Chicago Press, 2011.

Mair, Lucy Philip. *An African People in the Twentieth Century*. London: Routledge, 1934.

Makgoba, M. W. *Mokoko, the Makgoba Affair: A Reflection on Transformation*. Florida Hills: Vivlia, 1997.

Makower, Katherine. *The Coming of the Rain: The Life of Dr. Joe Church; A Personal Account of Revival in Rwanda*. Carlisle, UK: Paternoster, 1999.

Malcolm, McVeigh J. "Sources for an African Christian Theology." *Presence* 5, no. 3 (1972): 2–3.

Maloba, Wanyabari O. *Mau Mau and Kenya: An Analysis of a Peasant Revolt*. Nairobi: East African Educational Publishers, 1994.

Maluleke, Tinyiko Sam. "Half a Century of African Christian Theologies." In *The Church and Reconstruction of Africa: Theological Considerations*, edited by J. N. K. Mugambi, 84–114. Nairobi: All Africa Conference of Churches, 1997.

———. "Half a Century of African Christian Theologies: Elements of the Emerging Agenda for the Twenty-First Century." *Journal of Theology for Southern Africa* 99 (1997): 4–23.

———. "Identity and Integrity in African Theology: A Critical Analysis." *Religion and Theology* 8, no. 1/2 (2001): 26–41.

Mana, Kä. *Christians and Churches of Africa: Salvation in Christ and Building a New African Society*. Theology in Africa series. Maryknoll, NY: Orbis, 2004.

———. *Foi chrétienne, crise africaine et reconstruction de l'Afrique: sens et enjeux des théologies africaines contemporaine.* Nairobi: CETA, 1992.

———. *Théologie africaine pour temps de crise: Christianisme et reconstruction de l'Afrique. Chrétiens en liberté.* Paris: Karthala, 1993.

Manickam, J. A. "Race, Racism, and Ethnicity." In *Global Dictionary of Theology: A Resource for the Worldwide Church*, edited by William A. Dyrness and Veli-Matti Kärkkäinen, 718–724. Downers Grove: IVP Academic, 2008.

Marshall, Howard I. "Being Human: Made in the Image of God." *Stone-Campbell Journal* 4, no. 1 (2001): 47–67.

Masenya, Madipoane. "Reading the Bible the Bosadi (Womanhood) Way." *Bulletin for Contextual Theology in Southern Africa and Africa* 4, no. 2 (1997): 15–16.

Mathenge, Oliver. "Clerics Push for 'Faster Healing.'" *Daily Nation*, 29 June 2009. https://www.nation.co.ke/news/1056-617072-joc8fhz/index.html.

Matheson, Peter. "Thomas Müntzer's Idea of an Audience." *History* 76, no. 247 (1991) 185–196.

Mazrui, Ali Al'Amin. *The African Condition: A Political Diagnosis.* Reith Lectures. London: Heinemann, 1980.

———. *Towards Pax Africana: A Study of Ideology and Ambition.* Chicago: University of Chicago Press, 1967.

Mbeki, Thabo. *Africa: Define Yourself.* Cape Town: Tafelberg, 2002.

———. *Africa: The Time Has Come.* Cape Town: Tafelberg, 1998.

Mbiti, John S. "An African Answer." In *Why Did God Make Me?*, edited by Hans Küng and Jürgen Moltmann, 88–90. New York: Seabury, 1978.

———. "African Indigenous Culture in Relation to Evangelism and Church Development." In *The Gospel and Frontier Peoples*, edited by Pierce R. Beaver, 79–95. Pasadena: William Carey Library, 1973.

———. *African Religions and Philosophy.* London: Heinemann, 1969.

———. *African Religions and Philosophy.* 2nd ed. London: Heinemann, 1989.

———. *Bible and Theology in African Christianity.* Oxford: Oxford University Press, 1986.

———. "The Bible in African Culture." In *Paths of African Theology*, edited by Rosino Gibelini, 27–39. Maryknoll, NY: Orbis, 1994.

———. "Christianity and African Culture." In *Border Regions of Faith: An Anthology of Religion and Social Change*, Kenneth Aman, 387–399. Maryknoll, NY: Orbis, 1987.

———. "Christianity and Culture in Africa." In *Facing the Challenges: The Message of PACLA*, edited by Michael Cassidy and Luc Verlinden, 272–283. Kisumu: Evangel, 1978.

———. "Christianity and Traditional Religions in Africa." In *Crucial Issues in Missions Tomorrow*, edited by Donald McGavran, 144–158. Chicago: Moody, 1972.

———. *Concepts of God in Africa*. New York: Praeger, 1970.

———. "Confessing Christ Today." In *Confessing Christ in Different Cultures*, edited by John S. Mbiti, 7–21. Celigny: Ecumenical Institute Bossey, 1977.

———. "The Encounter of Christian Faith and African Religion." *The Christian Century* 97 (1980): 817–820.

———. "Foreword in Theological Education." In *Handbook of Theological Education*, edited by Dietrich Werner, xv–xvii. Regnum Studies in Global Christianity. Oxford: Regnum, 2013.

———. "'Hearts Cannot be Lent!' In Search of Peace and Reconciliation in African Traditional Society." *Princeton Seminary Bulletin* 20, no. 1 (1999): 1–12.

———. *Introduction to African Religion*. London: Heinemann, 1975.

———. "Introduction to the Colloquium." In *Confessing Christ in Different Cultures*, edited by John S. Mbiti, 22–25. Celigny: Ecumenical Institute Bossey, 1977.

———. "John Mbiti: A Quiet Quest for Peace." *Inspire* (Winter/Spring 1998): 4.

———. "Man in African Religion." In *Africa and the West: The Legacies of Empire*, edited by Isaac James Mowoe and Richard Bjornson, 55–67. New York: Greenwood, 1986.

———. *New Testament Eschatology in an African Background*. London: Oxford University Press, 1972.

McGrath, Alister E. *A Life of John Calvin: A Study in the Shaping of Western Culture*. Oxford, UK: Blackwell, 1990.

———. *Reformation Thought: An Introduction*. Oxford: Basil Blackwell, 1993.

———. *Theology: The Basic Readings*. 2nd ed. West Sussex, UK: Wiley-Blackwell, 2012.

McIlhenny, Ryan C. "Christian Witness as Redeemed Culture." In *Kingdoms Apart: Engaging the Two Kingdoms Perspective*, edited by Ryan C. McIlhenny, 251–276. Philipsburg, NJ: P & R Publishing, 2012.

———. "Introduction: In Defense of Neo-Calvinism." In *Kingdoms Apart: Engaging the Two Kingdoms Perspective*, edited by Ryan C. McIlhenny, xvii–xl. Philipsburg, NJ: P&R Publishing, 2012.

Mckee, Robert Guy. "Lynchings in Modern Kenya and Inequitable Access to Basic Resources: A Major Human Rights Scandal and One Contributing Cause." *GIAL Special Electronic Publications*, 2013. Available online, www.gial.edu/documents/McKee_Lynchings.pdf.

McLeod, Frederick G. *The Image of God in the Antiochene Tradition*. Washington, DC: Catholic University of America Press, 1999.

McNeil, John T. "Introduction." In *On God and Political Duty*, edited by John T. McNeil, viii–ix. New York: Macmillan, 1950.

Middleton, Richard J. "The Liberating Image? Interpreting the Imago Dei in Context." *Christian Scholar's Review* 24, no. 1 (1994): 8–25.

———. *The Liberating Image: The Imago Dei in Genesis 1*. Grand Rapids: Brazos, 2005.

Miller, Darrow and Scott Allen. *Against All Hope: Hope for Africa*. Nairobi: Samaritan Strategy Africa Working Group, 2005.

Milner, Benjamin Charles. *Calvin's Doctrine of the Church*. Studies in the History of Christian Thought. Leiden: Brill, 1970.

Mohr, Adam. *Enchanted Calvinism: Labor Migration, Afflicting Spirits, and Christian Therapy in the Presbyterian Church of Ghana*. Rochester, NY: Boydell & Brewer, 2013.

Moltmann, Jürgen. *God for a Secular Society: The Public Relevance of Theology*. Minneapolis: Fortress, 1999.

Monter, William E. "Daily Life and the Reformed Church." In *The Reformation*, edited by Pierre Chaunu, 244–252. New York: St. Martin's, 1990.

Mouw, Richard J. *Uncommon Decency: Christian Civility in an Uncivil World*. Downers Grove: InterVarsity Press, 1992.

Moynihan, Daniel P. *Pandemonium: Ethnicity and International Politics*. Oxford: Oxford University Press, 1993.

Mudimbe, V. Y. *The Idea of Africa*. African Systems of Thought. Bloomington, IN: Indiana University Press, 1994.

———. *The Invention of Africa: Gnosis, Philosophy, and the Order of Knowledge*. African Systems of Thought. Bloomington, IN: Indiana University Press, 1988.

Mueller, William A. *Church and State in Luther and Calvin*. Nashville, TN: Broadman, 1954.

Mugambi, J. N. K. *African Christian Theology: An Introduction*. Nairobi: Heinemann, 1989.

———. *The African Heritage and Contemporary Christianity*. Nairobi: Longman, 1989.

———. *Christian Theology and Social Reconstruction*. Nairobi: Acton, 2003.

———. "A Fresh Look at Evangelism in Africa." In *The Study of Evangelism: Exploring a Missional Practice of the Church*, edited by Paul Wesley Chilcote and Laceye C. Warner, 352–373. Grand Rapids: Eerdmans, 2008.

———. "From Liberation to Reconstruction." In *African Theology Today*, edited by Emmanuel Katongole, 189–206. Scranton, PA: University of Scranton Press, 2002.

———. *From Liberation to Reconstruction: African Christian Theology after the Cold War*. Nairobi: East African Educational Publishers, 1995.

———. *God, Humanity and Nature in Relation to Justice and Peace*. Geneva: World Council of Churches, 1987.

———. "Missionary Presence in Interreligious Encounters and Relationships." *Studies in World Christianity* 19, no. 2 (2013): 162–186.

———. "The Problem of Teaching Ethics in African Christianity." In *Moral and Ethical Issues in African Christianity: Exploratory Essays in Moral Theology*, edited by J. N. K. Mugambi and Anne Nasimiyu-Wasike, 11–28. African Christianity Series. Nairobi: Acton, 2003.

———. "Social Reconstruction of Africa." In *The Church and Reconstruction of Africa: Theological Considerations*, edited by J. N. K. Mugambi, 1–25. Nairobi: All Africa Conference of Churches, 1997.

———. "Theology of Reconstruction." In *African Theology on the Way: Current Conversations*, edited by Diane B. Stinton, 139–149. London: SPCK, 2010.

Mugambi, J. N. K., and Anne Nasimiyu-Wasike, eds. *Moral and Ethical Issues in African Christianity: Exploratory Essays in Moral Theology*. 3rd ed. African Christianity Series. Nairobi: Acton, 2003.

Mugivane, Fred. "Not Ready for Democracy." *The Weekly Review*, 4 July 1997.

Muigai, Githu. "Jomo Kenyatta and the Ethno-Nationalist State in Kenya." In *Ethnicity and Democracy in Africa*, edited by Bruce Berman, Dickson Eyoh, and Will Kymlicka, 200–217. Oxford: James Currey, 2004.

Müntzer, Thomas. *Collected Works of Thomas Müntzer*. Edited by Peter Matheson. Edinburgh: T & T Clark, 1988.

Murgor, C. C. *Nyanza Province Annual Report 1966*. Provincial Commissioner's Annual Report. Nyanza Province, 1966. Kenya National Archives.

Murunga, Edwin. "We Must Let Peace Prevail in 2016; but We Must Let Democracy To Also Thrive." *Daily Nation*, 2 January 2016.

———. "We Must Rise Above Tribal Pettiness and Address the National Question." *Daily Nation*, 19 June 2015.

Musana, Paddy, ed. *Peacebuilding in Africa: Exploring the Role of the Churches*. The Ecumenical Symposium of Eastern Africa Theologians 6. Nairobi: Paulines, 2013.

Museveni, Yoweri. *What is Africa's Problem?* Kampala: NRM, 1992.

Mutai, Birgen. "A House Divided." *The Weekly Review*, 11 December 1992.

Mwase, Isaac T., and Eunice Kamaara, eds. *Theologies of Liberation and Reconstruction*. Essays in Honour of Professor J. N. K. Mugambi. Nairobi: Acton, 2012.

Mwaura, Philomena Njeri. "Human Identity and the Gospel of Reconciliation: Agenda for Mission Studies and Praxis in the 21st century." *Mission Studies* 26, no. 1 (2009): 17–30.

Naphy, William G. *Calvin and the Consolidation of the Genevan Reformation*. Manchester: Manchester University Press, 1994.

Nasimiyu-Wasike, Anne. "Moral and Religious Implications for the Kenyan 2007 Post-Election Violence: The Role of the Church in National Healing." In *Peacebuilding in Africa: Exploring the Role of the Churches*, edited by Paddy Musana, 120–128. Nairobi: Paulines, 2013.

Nason, Vundi. "Ethnic Violence in Kenya Between 2007 and 2008: A Sociological Analysis and Response." In *Contested Space: Ethnicity and Religion in Kenya*, edited by Diphus C. Chemorion, Esther Mombo, and C. B. Peter, 99–113. Limuru, Kenya: Zapf Chancery, 2013.

National Cohesion and Integration Commission. *Building a Cohesive Kenyan Society: The NCIC Experience*. Nairobi: National Cohesion and Integration Commission, 2013. This can be accessed at: http://www.cohesion.or.ke/index.php/resources/downloads.

———. *The Status of Social Cohesion in Kenya, 2013*. Nairobi: National Cohesion and Integration Commission, 2013. This can be accessed at: http://www.cohesion.or.ke/index.php/resources/downloads.

National Council of Churhces of Kenya. *A Kairos for Kenya: NCCK Reflection on the KANU Review Committee Report and KANU Special Delegates' Conference Resolutions on it*. Nairobi: NCCK, 1991.

National Council of Churches of Kenya Executive Committee. "Hope for Kenya," 13 February 2008. https://rescuekenya.wordpress.com/2008/02/21/ncck-executive-committee-press-statement-13-feb-2008/.

Ndung'u, Nahashon. "Land and Violence in Kenya." In *From Violence to Peace: A Challenge for African Christianity*, edited by Mary N. Getui and Peter Kanyandogo, 57–69. African Christianity Series. Nairobi: Acton, 2003.

Ndung'u, Ruth Wangeci. "Socialization and Violence: Ideas and Practices in Kenya." In *(Re)membering Kenya: Identity, Culture and Freedom*, edited by George Gona and Mbugua Mungai, 110–125. Nairobi: Twaweza Communications, 2010.

Neuhaus, Richard John. *The Naked Public Square: Religion and Democracy in America*. Grand Rapids, MI: Eerdmans, 1984.

Ngaruiya, David K. "The Multifaceted Genesis of the 2007–2008 Postelection Violence in Kenya." In *Communities of Faith in Africa and the African Diaspora*, edited by Casely B. Essamuah, David K. Ngaruiya, and Tite Tiénou, 82–89. Eugene, OR: Pickwick, 2013.

Ngesa, Mildred. "House of God Divided but it Can Still Help Nurture Hope." *Daily Nation*, 13 March 2008.

Ngotho, Kamau. "The Day Democracy Visited and Stayed." *Daily Nation*, 7 July 2000. Available online, https://www.nation.co.ke/news/1056-364948-l8jm51z/index.html.

Ng'weshemi, Andrea M. *Rediscovering the Human: The Quest for a Christo-Theological Anthropology in Africa*. Studies in Biblical Literature. New York: Peter Lang, 2002.

Ngwiri, Magesha. "Where Are We Headed if Tribe is the Only Factor in Getting a Public Job?" *Daily Nation*, 12 June 2015. Available online, https://www.nation.co.ke/oped/opinion/Where-are-we-headed-if-tribe-is-the-only-factor-/440808-2749870-olw72nz/index.html.

———. "Why Kenyans Have Little Faith in Kaparo's Pledge to Fight Hate-Mongers." *Daily Nation*, 26 June 2015. Available online, https://www.nation.co.ke/oped/opinion/Francis-Ole-Kaparo-NNCIC-Peace-Kenya/440808-2766520-5p9e0u/index.html.

Niebuhr, Richard H. *Christ and Culture*. New York: Harper & Brothers, 1951.

———. *Christianity and Power Politics*. New York: Scribner's Sons, 1940.

———. *Moral Man and Immoral Society: A Study in Ethics and Politics*. New York: Scribner's Sons, 1932.

———. *The Nature and Destiny of Man: A Christian Interpretation*. Gifford Lectures. New York: Scribner's Sons, 1948.

Niesel, Wilhelm. *The Theology of Calvin*. Translated by Harold Knight. Philadelphia: Westminster, 1956.

Niwagilia, Wilson. "Our Struggle for Justice, Peace and Integrity of Creation: Quest for a Theology of Reconstruction in Africa." In *The Church and Reconstruction of Africa: Theological Considerations*, edited by J. N. K. Mugambi, 163–179. Nairobi: All Africa Conference of Churches, 1997.

Njogu, Kimani. *Defining Moments: Reflections on Citizenship, Violence, and the 2007 General Elections in Kenya*. Nairobi: Twaweza Communications, 2011.

———, ed. *Healing the Wound: Personal Narratives about the 2007 Post-Election Violence in Kenya*. Nairobi: Twaweza Communications, 2009.

———. "A Prologue to Ethnic Diversity in Eastern Africa." In *Ethnic Diversity in Eastern Africa: Opportunities and Challenges*, edited by Kimani Njogu, Kabiri Ngeta, and Mary Wanjau, vii–xvii. Nairobi: Twaweza Communications, 2010.

Njoroge, Nyambura J. "A New Way of Facilitating Leadership: Lessons from African Women Theologians." *Missiology* 33, no. 1 (2005): 29–46.

Njoya, Timothy M. *The Divine Tag on Democracy*. Yaounde, Cameroon: CLE-CIPCRE, 2003.

———. *Human Dignity and National Identity*. Nairobi: Jemisik, 1987.

———. *Out of Silence: A Collection of Sermons*. Nairobi: Beyond, 1987.

Nkrumah, Kwame. *Consciencism: Philosophy and Ideology for Decolonization and Development with Particular Reference to the African Revolution*. London: Heinemann, 1964.

———. *I Speak of Freedom: A Statement of African Ideology*. New York: Praeger, 1961.

Nnoli, Okwudiba. *Ethnic Conflicts in Africa*. Dakar, Senegal: Codesria, 1998.

Noelliste, Dieumème. "Exploring the Usefulness of Calvin's Socio-Political Ethics for the Majority World." In *John Calvin and Evangelical Theology: Legacy and Prospect*, edited by Sung Wook Chung, 219–241. Louisville, KY: Westminster John Knox, 2009.

Noll, Mark A. *Turning Points: Decisive Moments in the History of Christianity*. 3rd ed. Grand Rapids: Baker Academic, 2012.

North, Gary, and Gary DeMar. *Christian Reconstructionism: What It Is, What It Isn't*. Tyler, Texas: Institute for Christian Economics, 1991.

Norwegian Refugee Council. *Internally Displaced People: A Global Survey*. London: Earthscan, 2002.

———. *"Kenya: Speedy Reform Needed to Deal with Past Injustices and Prevent Future Displacement."* Geneva, Switzerland: Internal Displacement Monitoring Center, 2010. Available online, https://reliefweb.int/report/kenya/kenya-speedy-reform-needed-deal-past-injustices-and-prevent-future-displacement.

Nothwehr, Dawn M. *That They May Be One: Catholic Social Teaching on Racism, Tribalism, and Xenophobia*. Maryknoll, NY: Orbis Books, 2008.

Nouwen, Henri J. M. *Reaching Out: The Three Movements of the Spiritual Life*. Garden City, NY: Image, 1986.

NTV Kenya. "Uhuru Rebukes Agencies Over Anti-Graft Fight." *NTV Kenya*, 2016. Accessed 17 November 2017, https://www.youtube.com/watch?v=WgEFC2Gl2CY&t=125s.

Nyarora, Henry, and Duncan Ageta. "Ruto Preaches Unity as Survey Reveals Fear of Political Violence." *Daily Nation*, 13 June 2015.

Nyatete, Elias Mokua. "Political Bishops Betraying the People." *The East African Standard*, 23 January 2008.

Nyaundi, Nehemiah. "Walking the Slippery Road: A Possible Paradigm for De-Tribalization of the Christian Community in Kenya." In *Contested Space: Ethnicity and Religion in Kenya*, edited by Diphus C. Chemorion, Esther Mobo, and C. B. Peter, 115–129. Limuru, Kenya: Zapf Chancery, 2013.

Obeng, Emmanuel Adow. "Religious Dimensions of Refugee Suffering." In *From Violence to Peace: A Challenge for African Christianity*, edited by Mary N. Getui and Peter Kanyandogo, 121–133. African Christianity Series. Nairobi: Acton, 2003.

Oberman, Heiko A. *Luther: Man Between God and the Devil*. Translated by Eileen Walliser-Schwarzbart. New York: DoubleDay, 1982.

Ochieng, Philip. "Will Kenyans Ever Manage to Outgrow the Negative Aspects of Tribalism?" *Daily Nation*, 3 January 2016. https://www.nation.co.ke/

oped/opinion/Will-Kenyans-ever-manage-to-outgrow-tribalism/440808-3019396-p0yucsz/index.html.

Ochieng, William, ed. *A Modern History of Kenya 1895–1980*. Nairobi: Evans Brothers, 1989.

Odhiambo, E. S. Atieno. "Hegemonic Enterprises and Instrumentalities of Survival: Ethnicity and Democracy in Kenya." In *Ethnicity and Democracy in Africa*, edited by Bruce Berman, Dickson Eyoh, and Will Kymlicka, 167–182. Oxford: James Currey, 2004.

Odhiambo, Thomas R., ed. *Hope Born Out of Despair: Managing the African Crisis*. Nairobi: Heinemann, 1988.

O'Donovan, Oliver. *The Desire of the Nations: Rediscovering the Roots of Political Theology*. Cambridge: Cambridge University Press, 1996.

Oduyoye, Mercy Amba. "The African Family as a Symbol of Ecumenism." *Ecumenical Review* 43, no. 4 (1991): 465–478.

———. "A Critique of John Mbiti's View of Love and Marriage in Africa." In *Religious Plurality in Africa: Essays in Honour of John S. Mbiti*, edited by Jacob K. Olupona and Sulayman S. Nyang, 341–365. Berlin: Walter Mouton de Gruyter, 1993.

———. "Christianity and African Culture." *International Review of Mission* 84, no. 332/333 (1995): 77–90.

———. "Feminist Theology in an African Perspective." In *Paths of African Theology*, edited by Rosino Gibelini, 166–181. London: SCM, 1994.

———. *Hearing and Knowing: Theological Reflections on Christianity in Africa*. Maryknoll, NY: Orbis Books, 1986.

———. *Introducing African Women's Theology*. Cleveland, OH: Pilgrim, 2001.

Ogola, G. "No Longer the Beacon of Morality." *The East African Standard*, 15 September 2006.

Ogot, Bethwell. *Kenyans, Who Are We? Reflections on the Meaning of National Identity and Nationalism*. Kisumu: Anyange, 2012.

Ogutu, E. "Kenyan 'Prophets' Who Won No Respect." *The East African Standard*, 5 March 2008.

Okesson, Gregg A. "Sacred and Secular Currents for Theological Education in Africa." *Africa Journal of Evangelical Theology* 26, no. 1 (2007): 39–64.

Okullu, Henry. "The African Context and Its Issues." In *Facing the Challenges: The Message of PACLA*, edited by Michael Cassidy and Luc Verlinden, 30–33. Kisumu: Evangel, 1978.

———. *Church and Politics in East Africa*. Nairobi: Uzima, 1974.

———. *Church and State in Nation Building and Human Development*. Nairobi: Uzima, 1984.

————. "Church, State and Society in East Africa." In *30 Years of Independence in Africa: The Lost Decades*, edited by Peter Anyang Nyong'o, 25–37. Nairobi: African Association of Political Science, 1992.

————. "Church-State Relations: The African Situation." In *Church and State: Opening a New Ecumenical Discussion*, edited by World Council of Churches, 79–88. Faith and Order Paper 85. Geneva: World Council of Churches, 1978.

————. *Quest for Justice: An Autobiography of Bishop Henry Okullu*. Kisumu: Shalom, 1997.

————. "Render unto Caesar." In *A Vision of Christian Mission: Reflections on the Great Commission in Kenya*, edited by Margaret Crouch, 147–154. Nairobi: NCCK, 1993.

————. "Some Theological and Ethical Considerations in African Context." In *An African Call for Life: Contribution to the World Council of Churches Sixth Assembly Theme "Jesus Christ: The Life of the World,"* edited by Masamba M. Mpolo, Reginald Stober, and Evelyn V. Appiah, 97–112. Geneva: World Council of Churches, 1983.

Oloo, Adam. "The Church is Not Our Voice Anymore." *The East African Standard*, 5 November 2006.

————. "Party Mobilization and Membership." In *Tensions and Reversals in Democratic Transitions: The Kenya 2007 General Elections*, edited by Karuti Kanyinga and Duncan Okello, 31–59. Nairobi: Society for International Development, 2010.

Oluoch, Jemima Atieno. *The Christian Political Theology of Dr. John Henry Okullu*. Nairobi: Uzima, 2006.

Olupona, Jacob K. "A Biographical Sketch." In *Religious Plurality in Africa: Essays in Honor of John Mbiti*, edited by Jacob K. Olupona and Sulayman S. Nyang, 1–9. Berlin: Walter Mouton de Gruyter, 1993.

Omulokoli, Watson. "Foundational History of the Africa Inland Church, 1895-1903." *Africa Journal of Evangelical Theology* 14, no. 2 (1995): 45–54.

Onyango, Dennis. "Church's Worrying Slide to Silence." *The East African Standard*, 27 January 2008.

Opanga, Kwendo. "Kenya Badly in Need of New Leaders." *Daily Nation*, 18 October 2008. https://www.nation.co.ke/oped/opinion/440808-481580-h6f79iz/index.html.

Oriang, Lucy. "Heal Yourself first, Dear Clerics." *Daily Nation*, 8 September 2006. https://www.nation.co.ke/oped/1192-143138-l8t3v2/index.html.

Osanjo, Tom. "How Clergy Took Battle to Grim." *Daily Nation*, 23 March 2008. Available online https://www.nation.co.ke/news/1056-229794-lu03arz/index.html.

Osborn, H. H. *Pioneers in the East African Revival.* Winchester, UK: Apologia, 2000.

Osborne, Myles. *Ethnicity and Empire in Kenya: Loyalty and Martial Race Among the Kamba.* New York: Cambridge University Press, 2014.

Otieno, Nicholas. *Beyond the Silence of Death: The Life and Theology of Bishop Alexander Muge.* Nairobi: NCCK, 1993.

Oyeniyi, Bukola Adeyemi. "The 'Glocalization' of Terrorism in Post-Colonial Africa." In *Africa after Fifty Years: Retrospections and Reflections*, edited by Toyin Falola, Maurice Nyamanga Amutabi and Sylvester Gundona, 240–270. Trenton: Africa World Press, 2013.

Oyugi, Walter. "Ethnic Politics in Kenya." In *Ethnic Conflicts in Africa*, edited by Okwudiba Nnoli, 287–309. Dakar, Senegal: Codesria, 1998.

Padilla, René C. "Liberation Theology." In *Facing the Challenges: The Messages of PACLA*, edited by Michael Cassidy and Luc Verlinden, 420–428. Kisumu, Kenya: Evangel, 1978.

Parker, T. H. L. *Calvin's Doctrine of the Knowledge of God.* 2nd ed. Edinburgh: Oliver & Boyd, 1969.

———. *Calvin's Preaching.* Louisville, KY: Westminster John Knox, 1992.

Parsitau, Damaris Seleina. "From Prophetic Voices to Lack of Voice: Christian Churches in Kenya and the Dynamics of Voice and Voicelessness in a Multi-Religious Space." *Studia Historiae Ecclesiasticae* 38 (2012): 243–268.

———. "Pentecostalising the Church of Scotland? The Presbyterian Church of East Africa (PCEA) and the Pentecostal Challenge in Kenya." In *Africa in Scotland, Scotland in Africa: Historical Legacies and Contemporary Hybridities*, edited by Afe Adogame and Andrew Lawrence, 228–250. Leiden: Brill, 2014.

Partee, Charles. *Calvin and Classical Philosophy.* Leiden: Brill, 1977.

———. "Calvin's Central Dogma Again." *The Sixteenth Century Journal* 18, no. 2 (1987) 191–200.

Patel, Preeti. "Multiparty Politics in Kenya." *Revista Ciencia Politica 21* (2001): 154–173.

Pattison, Bonnie L. *Poverty in the Theology of John Calvin.* Eugene, OR: Wipf & Stock, 2006.

Pears, Angie. *Doing Contextual Theology.* New York: Routledge, 2010.

Pearse, Meic. *The Great Restoration: The Religious Radicals of the 16th and 17th Centuries.* Carlisle, UK: Paternoster, 1998.

Perkinson, James W. "John S. Mbiti." In *Empire and The Christian Tradition*, edited by Pui-Ian Kwok, Don H. Compier, and Joerg Rieger, 455–469. Minneapolis: Fortress, 2007.

Peterson, Eugene H. *Christ Plays in Ten Thousand Places: A Conversation in Spiritual Theology.* Grand Rapids: Eerdmans, 2005.

Plantinga, Cornelius, Jr. *Engaging God's World: A Christian Vision of Faith, Learning, and Living*. Grand Rapids: Eerdmans, 2002.

Poythress, Vern S. *The Lordship of Christ: Serving Our Savior All of the Time, In All of Life, with All of Our Heart*. Wheaton: Crossway, 2016.

Prins, Richard. "The Image of God in Adam and the Restoration of Man in Jesus Christ: A Study in Calvin." *Scottish Journal of Theology* 25, no. 1 (1972): 32–44.

Provincial Commissioner's Report. *Boundaries General*. Provincial Commissioner's Report. Nandi Native Reserve. Kisumu, 1910. 5/1550. Kenya National Archives.

Radelet, Steven. "*Emerging Africa: How 17 Countries Are Leading the Way.*" *Center for Global Development*, 2010. http://www.cgdev.org/doc/full_text/ EmergingAfrica/Radelet_EmergingAfrica.html.

Ramsey, Paul. *Basic Christian Ethics*. New York: Scribner's Sons, 1950.

Rasmussen, Steven D. H. "What Are We Going to Do about Them?" In *Contested Space: Ethnicity and Religion in Kenya*, edited by Diphus C. Chemorion, Esther Mombo, and C. B. Peter, 201–215. Limuru, Kenya: Zapf Chancery, 2013.

Ray, Benjamin C. *African Religions: Symbol, Ritual, and Community*. Englewood Cliffs, NJ: Prentice-Hall, 1976.

Read, Hollis. *The Negro Problem Solved; or, Africa as She was, as She Is, and as She Shall Be: Her Curse and Her Cure*. New York: A. A. Constantine, 1864.

Reynolds, Thomas E. *Vulnerable Communion: A Theology of Disability and Hospitality*. Grand Rapids: Brazos, 2008.

Royce, Josiah. *The Problem of Christianity*. Chicago: University of Chicago Press, 1968.

Rushdoony, Rousas John. *The Institutes of Biblical Law: A Chalcedon Study*. Nutley, NJ: P & R Publishing, 1973.

Sabar-Friedman, Galia. "'Politics' and 'Power' in the Kenyan Public Discourse and Recent Events: The Church of the Province of Kenya (CPK)." *Canadian Journal of African Studies* 29, no. 3 (1995): 429–453.

Sanneh, Lamin. *Translating the Message: The Missionary Impact of Culture*. 2nd ed. American Society of Missiology Series 13. Maryknoll, NY: Orbis Books, 2009.

Sauer, James B. *Faithful Ethics According to John Calvin: The Teachability of the Heart*. Lewiston, KY: Edwin Mellen, 1997.

Sayagie, George. "Fear Grips Village after Militia Attack Leaves Two Dead." *Daily Nation*, 24 December 2015. http://www.nation.co.ke/counties/Fear-grips-village-after-militia-attack-leaves-two-dead/-/1107872/3009096/-/7vgquv/-/index.html.

———. "Narok Violence Forces Hundreds to Spend Christmas Night in the Cold." *Daily Nation*, 27 December 2015. http://www.nation.co.ke/news/Hundreds-of-families-displaced-in-ongoing-Narok-clashes/-/1056/3010532/-/aqniqoz/-/index.html.

Schaff, Philip. *History of the Christian Church*. Vol. 8. Grand Rapids, MI: Eerdmans, 1979.

Schreiner, Susan E. "Calvin's Use of Natural Law." In *A Preserving Grace: Protestants, Catholics, and Natural Law*, edited by Michael Cromartie, 51–76. Washington, DC: Eerdmans, 1997.

———. *The Theater of His Glory: Nature and the Natural Order in the Thought of John Calvin*. Studies in the Study of Historical Theology 3. Durham, NC: Labyrinth, 1991.

Schreiter, Robert J. *Constructing Local Theologies*. Maryknoll, NY: Orbis Books, 2007.

———. *The New Catholicity: Theology Between the Global and the Local*. Maryknoll, NY: Orbis Books, 1999.

Schulze, L. F. "Calvin on Interest and Property: Some Aspects of His Socio-Economic View." In *Our Reformational Tradition: A Rich Heritage and Lasting Vocation*, edited by B. J. van der Walt, 217–230. Silverton: Potchefstroom University for Higher Education, 1984.

Schwöbel, Christoph. "Human Being as Relational Being: Twelve Theses for a Christian Anthropology." In *Persons Divine and Human: King's College Essays in Theological Anthropology*, edited by Christoph Schwöbel and Colin E. Gunton, 141–170. Edinburgh: T & T Clark, 1991.

Scott, Peter, and William T. Cavanaugh, eds. *The Blackwell Companion to Political Theology*. Malden, MA: Blackwell, 2004.

Sekoh-Ochieng, Jacinta. "Musyimi Clears Air Over Team Selection." *Daily Nation*, 29 April 2001. https://www.nation.co.ke/news/1056-342656-l9t5vjz/index.html.

Selderhuis, Herman J., ed. *The Calvin Handbook*. Translated by Henry J. Baron, Judith J. Guder, Randi H, Lundell, and Gerrit W. Sheeres. Grand Rapids: Eerdmans, 2009.

Senghor, Léopold Sédar. *Nationhood and the African Road to Socialism*. African Political Leaders. Paris: Présence Africaine, 1962.

———. *Prose and Poetry*. Translated by John Reed and Clive Wake. London: Oxford University Press, 1965.

Sesi, Stephen Mutuku. "Ethnic Conflicts in Africa: The Case of Land Clashes." In *Contested Space: Ethnicity and Religion in Kenya*, edited by Diphus C. Chemorion, Esther Mombo, and C. B. Peter, 131–151. Limuru, Kenya: Zapf Chancery, 2013.

———. "Ethnic Realities and the Church in Kenya." In *African Missiology: Contribution of Contemporary Thought*, edited by Caleb Chul-Soo Kim, 25–39. Nairobi: Uzima, 2009.

Shults, F. LeRon. *Reforming Theological Anthropology: After the Philosophical Turn to Relationality*. Grand Rapids: Eerdmans, 2003.

Sider, Ronald J. *The Scandal of Evangelical Politics: Why are Christians Missing the Chance to Really Change the World?* Grand Rapids: Baker Books, 2008.

Singer, Gregg C. "Calvin and the Social Order or Calvin as a Social and Economic Statesman." In *Calvin's Thought on Economic and Social Issues and the Relationship of Church and State*, edited by Richard C. Gamble, 143–157. Articles on Calvin and Calvinism 11. New York: Garland, 1992.

Smith, James K. A. *Desiring the Kingdom: Worship, Worldview, and Cultural Formation*. Cultural Liturgies. Grand Rapids: Baker Academic, 2009.

———. *Imagining the Kingdom: How Worship Works*. Cultural Liturgies. Grand Rapids: Baker Academic, 2013.

———. "Reforming Public Theology: Two Kingdoms, or Two Cities?" *Calvin Theological Journal* 47 (2012): 122–137.

———. *You Are What You Love: The Spiritual Power of Habit*. Grand Rapids: Brazos, 2016.

Smith-Christopher, Daniel L. *A Biblical Theology of Exile*. Overtures to Biblical Theology. Minneapolis: Fortress, 2003.

Snyder, Howard A., and Joel Scandrett. *Salvation Means Creation Healed: The Ecology of Sin and Grace; Overcoming the Divorce between Earth and Heaven*. Eugene, OR: Cascade, 2011.

Sparks, Kenton L. *Ethnicity and Identity in Israel: Prolegomena to the Study of Ethnic Sentiments and Their Expression in the Hebrew Bible*. Winona Lake, IN: Eisenbrauns, 1998.

Spykman, Gordon J. "Sphere-Sovereignty in Calvin and the Calvinist Tradition." In *Exploring the Heritage of John Calvin*, edited by David E. Holwerda, 163–208. Grand Rapids: Baker Books, 1976.

Steer, Roger. *Basic Christian: The Inside Story of John Stott*. Downers Grove: IVP, 2009.

Steinmetz, David Curtis. *Calvin in Context*. New York: Oxford University Press, 1995.

Stevenson, William R. "Calvin and Political Issues." In *The Cambridge Companion to John Calvin*, edited by Donald K. McKim, 173–187. Cambridge: Cambridge University Press, 2004.

Stocker, H. G. "Calvin and Ethics." In *John Calvin Contemporary Prophet, A Symposium*, edited by Jacob Tunis Hoogstra, 127–147. Grand Rapids: Baker Books, 1959.

Stott, John R. W. *Between Two Worlds: The Art of Preaching in the Twentieth Century*. Grand Rapids: Eerdmans, 1982.

———. *The Contemporary Christian: Applying God's Word to Today's World*. Downers Grove: InterVarsity, 1992.

———. "Biblical Preaching in the Modern World." In *The Folly of Preaching: Models and Methods*, edited by Michael P. Knowles, 113–126. Grand Rapids: Eerdmans, 2007.

———. *The Living Church: Convictions of a Lifelong Pastor*. Downers Grove: IVP, 2007.

Studebaker, Steven M. "Creation Care as 'Keeping in Step with the Spirit.'" In *A Liberating Spirit: Pentecostals and Social Action in North America*, edited by Michael Wilkinson and Steven M. Studebaker, 248–263. Pentecostals, Peacemaking, and Social Justice Series. Eugene, OR: Pickwick, 2010.

———. *From Pentecost to the Triune God: A Pentecostal Trinitarian Theology*. Pentecostal Manifestos. Grand Rapids: Eerdmans, 2012.

———. "Servants of Christ, Servants of Caesar: A Theology for Life in Post-Christian America." In *The Globalization of Christianity: Implications for Christian Ministry and Theology*, edited by Gordon L. Heath and Steven M. Studebaker, 52–68. Eugene, OR: Pickwick, 2014.

Swanepoel, J. "Calvin as a Letter-Writer." In *Our Reformational Tradition: A Rich Heritage and Lasting Vocation*, edited by B. J. van der Walt, 279–299. Silverton: Potchefstroom University for Higher Education, 1984.

Tachin, Philip. "Humanity in the Image of God: Towards Ethnic Unity in Africa." *African Journal of Evangelical Theology* 33, no. 1 (2014): 67–82.

Tarus, David, and Julius Mutugi Gathogo. "Conquering Africa's Second Devil: Ecclesiastical Role in Combating Ethnic Bigotry." *Online Journal of African Affairs* 5 (2016): 8–15.

Tarus, Richard A. "Sales of Lands in Rift Valley," 1962. Kenya National Archives.

Tempels, Placide. *Bantu Philosophy*. Paris: Présence Africaine, 1959.

Templin, J. Alton. "The Individual and Society in the Thought of Calvin." *Calvin Theological Journal* 23, no. 2 (1988): 161–177.

The East African Standard. "Church Embedded Long Before Elections." 15 *February 2008*.

The Nairobi Law Monthly. "The Nandi Clashes." November, 1991.

The Weekly Review. "A Blessing for the Mothers." 27 March 1992.

———. "A Call to End the Violence: Excerpts from a Statement by Catholic Bishops on the Security Situation in Laikipia and Njoro." 30 *January 1998*.

———. "The Church Factor: The NCCK Tries to Unite the Opposition Parties." 19 *June* 1992.

———. "Clerics Kick Up Storm." 5 January 1990.

———. "A Controversial Churchman." 29 March 1985.

———. "Dangerous Development." 22 *August* 1997.

———. "A Dissenting Patriot." 4 *May* 1990.

———. "Election Controversy Deepens." 30 April 1993.

———. "Ethnic Strife." 20 March 1992.

———. "Ethnic Violence: Attempts at Reconciliation." 15 January 1993.

———. "Ethnicity in the CPK." 12 November 1993.

———. "Ford's Response to the Government Statement: Kanu Has Perpetrated Wanton Murder." 29 May 1992.

———. "Fresh Outbreak of Violence." 17 April 1992.

———. "The Government Statement on Ethnic Clashes: It's Ford That Has Incited the Violence." 29 May 1992.

———. "A Heated Debate." 4 May 1990.

———. "Katakwans to Do It Their Way." 2 February 1990.

———. "Lawlessness Must End." 24 January 1992.

———. "Likoni Mystery." 22 August 1997.

———. "The Luhya Dilemma." 14 May 1993.

———. "The Luhya Factor." 30 April 1993.

———. "Moving into the Political Arena." 27 March 1992.

———. "Mt. Elgon: Ethnic Rivalries Come to the Fore." 23 October 1992.

———. "A New American Assertiveness." 4 May 1990.

———. "A New Angle to the Strife." 10 April 1992.

———. "New Radicalism in Pastoral Letter," 14 February 1992.

———. "Njoya at It Again." 12 January 1990.

———. "Of Clergymen and Tribalism." 11 December 1992.

———. "Oh, Not Again!" 30 January 1998.

———. "Okullu Ready for 1994." 7 January 1994.

———. "Okullu's Volley: Bishop Calls for Multi-Party System." 4 May 1990.

———. "Onslaught on Kalenjin Leaders." 15 May 1992.

———. "The Outspoken Clergyman." 7 January 1994.

———. "A Partisan Role in Politics." 22 May 1992.

———. "People Have Lost Confidence in You." 8 May 1992.

———. "Playing the Tribal Card." 8 January 1998.

———. "A Poor Pastoral Strategy." 25 March 1994.

———. "The Question of Opposition." 12 January 1990.

———. "The Queue-Voting Furore." 4 May 1990.

———. "The Reality of Ethnic Politics." 8 January 1993.

———. "A Report on Ethnic Violence." 19 June 1992.

———. "Self-Appointed Honest Broker." 19 June 1992.

———. "A Severe Dressing Down for the President." 8 May 1992.

———. "Show of Force." 11 July 1997.

———. "Stop This Heinous Atrocity." 1 May 1992.

———. "A Stormy Enthronement." 17 January 1992.

———. "The Spectre of Majimboism." 8 August 1997.

———. "Strike! And the Luhya Factor Rumbles in the Background." 7 May 1993.

———. "A Strike for Freedom." 6 March 1992.

———. "The Tribal Factor in Elections." 31 October 1997.

———. "Tribal Trouble in Laikipia." 23 January 1998.

———. "Troubled Areas Relatively Calm." 3 April 1992.

———. "Turmoil in Bungoma District." 14 April 1992.

———. "United by a Common Cause." 15 May 1992.

———. "Violation of Secrecy and Trust." 15 May 1992.

———. "Volatile Politics." 18 July 1997.

Thuku, Wahome. "Churches in Threat of Merger." *Daily Nation*, 27 April, 2001. https://www.nation.co.ke/news/1056-342806-l9t4g2z/index.html.

Tiénou, Tite. "The Right to Difference: The Common Roots of African Theology and African Philosophy." *Africa Journal of Evangelical Theology* 9, no. 1 (1990): 24–34.

Torrance, Thomas F. *Calvin's Doctrine of Man*. London: Lutterworth, 1949.

———. *Kingdom and Church: A Study in the Theology of the Reformation*. London: Oliver & Boyd, 1956.

———. *The Hermeneutics of John Calvin*. Edinburgh: Scottish Academic, 1988.

Tostensen, Arne, Bård-Anders Andreassen, and Kjetil Tronvoll. *Kenya's Hobbled Democracy Revisited: The 1997 General Elections in Retrospect and Prospect*. Human Rights Report. Oslo: Norwegian Institute of Human Rights, 1998.

Troeltsch, Ernst. *The Social Teaching of the Christian Churches*. Translated by Olive Wyon. New York: Macmillan, 1931.

Truth, Justice, and Reconciliation Commission. *The Report of the Truth Justice and Reconciliation Commission: Volume 1*. Truth, Justice, and Reconciliation Commission. Nairobi: TJRC, 2013. www.tjrckenya.org.

———. *The Report of the Truth Justice and Reconciliation Commission: Volume II A*. Truth, Justice, and Reconciliation Commission. Nairobi: TJRC, 2013. www.tjrckenya.org.

———. *The Report of the Truth Justice and Reconciliation Commission: Volume II B*. Truth, Justice, and Reconciliation Commission. Nairobi: TJRC, 2013. www.tjrckenya.org.

———. *The Report of the Truth Justice and Reconciliation Commission: Volume II C*. Truth, Justice, and Reconciliation Commission. Nairobi: TJRC, 2013. www.tjrckenya.org.

———. *The Report of the Truth, Justice and Reconciliation Commission: Volume III*. Truth, Justice, and Reconciliation Commission. Nairobi: TJRC, 2013. www.tjrckenya.org.

———. *The Report of the Truth, Justice and Reconciliation Commission: Volume III*. Truth, Justice, and Reconciliation Commission. Nairobi: TJRC, 2013. https://www.kenya-today.com/wp-content/uploads/2013/05/TJRC_report_Volume_3.pdf.

Tuininga, Matthew J. "Calvin as Two Kingdoms Theologian: In Theology, In Church, and In State." In *Anthropological Reformations: Anthropology in the Era of Reformation*, edited by Anna Eusterschulte and Hannah Wälzholz, 393–401. Göttingen: Vandenhoeck & Ruprecht, 2015.

———. "Good News for the Poor: An Analysis of Calvin's Concept of Poor Relief and the Diaconate in Light of his Two Kingdoms Paradigm." *Calvin Theological Journal* 49, no. 2 (2014): 221–247.

Tutu, Desmond. *No Future Without Forgiveness*. New York: DoubleDay, 1999.

Ukpong, Justin S. "Christology and Inculturation: A New Testament Perspective." In *Paths of African Theology*, edited by Rosino Gibelini, 40–61. Maryknoll, NY: Orbis Books, 1994.

United Nations Office for the Coordination of Humanitarian Affairs. *Affected Populations in the Horn of Africa Region*. Nairobi: OCHA Regional Office, 2004. Available online, https://reliefweb.int/sites/reliefweb.int/files/resources/A2E3E9A02187E938C1256D160040E553-ocha-hor-31mar.pdf.

US Government Printing Office. *The Political Crisis in Kenya: A Call for Justice and Peaceful Resolution: Hearing Before the Subcommittee on Africa and Global Health of the Committee on Foreign Affairs, House of Representatives, One Hundred Tenth Congress, Second Session, February 6, 2008*. Washington: US Government Printing Office, 2008. http://purl.access.gpo.gov/GPO/LPS106659.

Vähäkangas, Auli. "African Feminist Contributions to Missiological Anthropology." *Mission Studies* 28, no. 2 (2011): 170–185.

Van Es, Rowland. "Hosting a Stranger: Insights from the Old Testament." In *Contested Space: Ethnicity and Religion in Kenya*, edited by Diphus C. Chemorion, Esther Mombo, C. B. Peter, 37–52. Limuru, Kenya: Zapf Chancery, 2013.

van der Walt, J. L. "The School That Calvin Established in 1559." In *Our Reformational Tradition: A Rich Heritage and Lasting Vocation*, edited by B. J. van der Walt, 300–338. Silverton: Potchefstroom University for Higher Education, 1984.

VanDrunen, David. *Biblical Case for Natural Law*. Studies in Christian Social Ethics and Economics. Grand Rapids: Acton Institute, 2006.

———. *Living in God's Two Kingdoms: A Biblical Vision for Christianity and Culture*. Wheaton: Crossway, 2010.

———. *Natural Law and the Two Kingdoms: A Study in the Development of Reformed Social Thought*. Grand Rapids: Eerdmans, 2010.

———. "The Two Kingdoms Doctrine and the Relationship of Church and State in the Early Reformed Tradition." *Journal of Church and State* 49, no. 4 (2007): 743–763.

Vanier, Jean. *Community and Growth: Our Pilgrimage Together*. Toronto: Griffin, 1979.

Vatican Radio. "Kenya Bishops Call for Unity as Country Awaits Pope Francis," 11 November 2015. Available online, http://www.radiovaticana.va/Afr_bulletin/15_11_11.html#Art_1186124.

Vellem, V. S. "Ideology and Spirituality: A Critique of Villa Vicencio's Project of Reconstruction." *Scriptura* 105 (2010): 547–558.

Villa-Vicencio, Charles. *A Theology of Reconstruction: Nation-Building and Human Rights*. Cambridge Studies in Ideology and Religion. New York: Cambridge University Press, 1992.

———. "Liberation Theology." In *Doing Theology in Context: South African Perspective*, edited by John de Gruchy and Charles Villa-Vicencio, 184–196. Theology and Praxis 1. Maryknoll, NY: Orbis Books, 1994.

Vliet, Jason Van. *Children of God: The Imago Dei in John Calvin and His Context*. Reformed Historical Theology. Göttingen: Vandenhoeck & Ruprecht, 2009.

Volf, Miroslav. *After Our Likeness: The Church as the Image of the Trinity*. Grand Rapids: Eerdmans, 1998.

———. *Exclusion and Embrace: A Theological Exploration of Identity, Otherness, and Reconciliation*. Nashville: Abingdon, 1996.

Vorster, Jakobus Marthinus. "Calvin and Human Dignity." *In die Skriflig* 44, no. 1 (2010): 197–213.

Wafula, Linet, and Gloria Kagonya. "Mudavadi Tours Counties in Hunt for Votes." *Sunday Nation*, 13 December 2015. https://www.nation.co.ke/news/Mudavadi-tours-counties-in-hunt-for-votes/1056-2994124-hhbaedz/index.html.

Wallace, Ronald S. *Calvin, Geneva, and the Reformation: A Study of Calvin as a Social Reformer, Churchman, Pastor and Theologian*. Edinburgh: Scottish Academic, 1988.

———. *Calvin's Doctrine of the Christian Life*. Edinburgh: Oliver and Boyd, 1959.

Walls, Andrew F. *The Missionary Movement in Christian History: Studies in the Transmission of Faith*. Maryknoll, NY: Orbis Books, 1996.

Walsh, Brian, and Richard J. Middleton. *The Transforming Vision: Shaping a Christian World View*. Downers Grove: InterVarsity Press, 1984.

Walters, Gwyn. "The Doctrine of the Holy Spirit in John Calvin." PhD diss., University of Edinburgh, 1949.

Wamanji, Erick. "Ethnicity and the Church Comes of Age." *The East African Standard*, 27 February 2008.

Wamwere, Koigi wa. *Towards Genocide in Kenya: The Curse of Negative Ethnicity*. Nairobi: MvuleAfrica, 2008.

Ward, Graham. *The Politics of Discipleship: Becoming Postmaterial Citizens*. Grand Rapids: Baker Academic, 2009.

Warfield, B. B. *Calvin as a Theologian and Calvinism Today*. London: Evangelical Press, 1970.

Waruta, D. W. "Tribalism as a Moral Problem in Contemporary Africa." In *Moral and Ethical Issues in African Christianity: Exploratory Essays in Moral Theology*, edited by J. N. K. Mugambi and Anne Nasimiyu-Wasike, 119–135. Nairobi: Acton, 2003.

Webster, John. *Word and Church: Essays in Christian Dogmatics*. Edinburgh: T & T Clark, 2001.

Wendel, François. *Calvin: The Origins and Development of his Religious Thought*. Translated by Philip Mairet. London: Collins, 1950.

Westermann, Claus. *Genesis 1-11: A Commentary*. Translated by John J. Scullion. Minneapolis: Augsburg, 1984.

Westermann, Dietrich. *Africa and Christianity*. Duff Lectures. London: Oxford University Press, 1937.

Willis, Edward David. *Calvin's Catholic Christology: The Function of the So-called Extra Calvinisticum in Calvin's Theology*. Studies in Medieval and Reformation Thought. Leiden: Brill, 1967.

Witte, John. *Law and Protestantism: The Legal Teachings of the Lutheran Reformation*. Cambridge: Cambridge University Press, 2002.

———. *The Reformation of Rights: Law, Religion, and Human Rights in Early Modern Calvinism*. Cambridge: Cambridge University Press, 2007.

Wolters, Al. *Creation Regained: Biblical Basics for a Reformational Worldview*. Grand Rapids: Eerdmans, 2005.

Wolterstorff, Nicholas. *Hearing the Call: Liturgy, Justice, Church, and World*. Edited by Mark R. Gornik and Gregory Thompson. Grand Rapids: Eerdmans, 2011.

———. *The Mighty and the Almighty: An Essay in Political Theology*. Cambridge, UK: Cambridge University Press, 2012.

———. *Until Justice and Peace Embrace*. Grand Rapids: Eerdmans, 1983.

Wright, Christopher J. H. *The Mission of God's People: A Biblical Theology of the Church's Mission*. Grand Rapids: Zondervan, 2010.

Wright, N. T. *Surprised by Hope: Rethinking Heaven, the Resurrection, and the Mission of the Church*. New York: HarperOne, 2008.

Wright, William. *Martin Luther's Understanding of God's Two Kingdoms: A Response to the Challenge of Skepticism*. Texts and Studies in Reformation and Post-Reformation Thought. Grand Rapids: Baker Academic, 2010.

Wrong, Michela. *It's Our Turn to Eat: The Story of a Kenyan Whistle-Blower*. New York: HarperOne, 2009.

van Wyk, J. H. "Calvin on the Christian Life." In *Our Reformational Tradition: A Rich Heritage and Lasting Vocation*, edited by B. J. van der Walt, 231–278. Silverton: Potchefstroom University for Higher Education, 1984.

Yong, Amos. *In the Days of Caesar: Pentecostalism and Political Theology*. The Cadbury Lectures 2009; Sacra Doctrina: Christian Theology for a Postmodern Age Series. Grand Rapids: Eerdmans, 2010.

———. *The Missiological Spirit: Christian Mission Theology for the Third Millennium Global Context*. Eugene, OR: Cascade, 2014.

Zachman, Randall C. "'Deny Yourself and Take up Your Cross': John Calvin on the Christian life." *International Journal of Systematic Theology* 11, no. 4 (2009): 466–482.

———. *Image and Word in the Theology of John Calvin*. Indiana: University of Notre Dame Press, 2007.

———. "Jesus Christ as the Image of God in Calvin's Theology." *Calvin Theological Journal* 25, no. 1 (1990): 45–62.

———. *John Calvin as Teacher, Pastor, and Theologian: The Shape of His Writings and Thought*. Grand Rapids: Baker Academic, 2006.

Index of Subjects

A

Africa Inland Church 72, 94, 95, 217
Africa Inland Mission 65, 94
African identity 235, 265, 266, 273, 274, 279, 287
African liberation theology 237, 239
African political theology 2
African Renaissance 234–236, 254
African Theology of Reconstruction 29, 230, 231
Akamba. *See* Kamba
Akiwumi Commission 12, 26
All Saints Cathedral 69, 203, 206
Anglican Church of Kenya 201, 203, 212

B

Billy Graham Association 211
Black Theology 239
Bomas Draft 81, 82

C

Calvin's political theology 15, 27, 28, 158, 159, 183, 186, 190, 192, 196, 200, 258, 290
Church Missionary Society 65, 94
Church Province of Kenya (CPK) 66, 69, 72, 78, 87, 330, 334
Circle of the Concerned African Women Theologians 8, 15
cohesion 2, 4, 81, 86, 152, 173, 295

common grace 163, 167, 168, 173
community cohesion 3, 4
Crown Lands Ordinance 37

D

democracy 9, 66, 70, 71, 87, 178, 186, 202, 204, 205, 229, 230, 243, 252
Dorobo 39, 43, 44

E

EAK. *See* Evangelical Alliance of Kenya
East Africa Revival 210, 224
Electoral Commission of Kenya 61
Embu 33, 42, 50–52, 54, 65, 72, 81, 212, 232
ethnic
   cleansing 47, 58, 60, 128, 254
   cohesion 2, 53, 66, 77, 246, 255, 257, 288
   communities 2, 3, 5, 6, 10, 32–34, 38, 43, 51, 55, 57, 63, 79, 89, 94, 127, 186, 209, 210, 245, 261, 278
   conflict 1, 14, 22, 29, 61, 69, 79, 159, 255, 256, 279, 288
   hatred 35, 83, 257, 289, 292
   identity 1, 3, 5, 6, 9, 56, 63, 157, 208, 209, 262, 272, 280, 282, 284, 288

unity 79
violence 10, 12, 13, 23, 51, 56, 59,
        60, 75–78, 230
ethnicity 1–5, 7, 9, 12, 16, 19, 22,
        29, 31, 32, 35, 47, 48, 53, 65,
        71, 73, 78, 79, 81, 87, 125,
        159, 184, 186, 208, 225, 253,
        257, 261, 279, 284
ethnicization of politics 58, 186
ethnocentrism 1, 8, 13, 14, 31, 59,
        65, 66, 69, 87, 94, 95, 280,
        289
ethnopolitical cohesion 1, 3, 4, 14,
        28, 29, 87, 89, 131, 132, 153,
        159, 201, 210, 230, 232, 255,
        259, 261, 287, 290–292
ethnopolitical conflict 1–3, 8, 12, 14,
        24, 27–29, 31, 47, 63, 65, 77,
        79, 87, 127, 200, 231, 259,
        261, 262, 289, 290, 291
ethnopolitical violence 13, 24, 27,
        128, 289
Evangelical Alliance of Kenya 27,
        66, 86
Evangelical Fellowship of Kenya.
        See Evangelical Alliance of
        Kenya
exclusion 4, 7, 94, 128, 166, 236,
        257
ex nihilo 112, 115

F
Forum for the Restoration of
        Democracy, Kenya 57

G
GEMA 52, 60, 62
Gikuyu, Embu, and Meru Association
        52, 60, 62

I
Internally Displaced Persons 11, 15

K
KADU. *See* Kenya African
        Democratic Union
Kalenjin 26, 32, 34, 42–44, 46,
        50–54, 56–58, 62, 65, 73, 78,
        79, 94, 95, 134, 209
KAMATUSA 55, 58, 62
Kamba 9, 33, 34, 39, 42, 51, 54, 65,
        73, 94, 95, 209, 210
KANU. *See* Kenya African National
        Union
Kenya African Democratic Union
        47, 53
Kenya African National Union 47,
        48, 53
Kenya African Union 46, 47
Kenya Catholic Episcopal
        Conference. *See* Kenya
        Conference of Catholic
        Bishops
Kenyan Conference of Catholic
        Bishops 87
Kenya People's Union 49
Kikuyu 10, 33, 34, 36–38, 42, 45,
        47, 50–54, 57, 58, 59, 62, 65,
        78, 79, 94, 127, 209
Kipsigis 39, 42, 43
Kisii 33, 54, 56, 58

L
Lausanne conference 183
Lausanne Congress 211
Lausanne Covenant 211, 212, 219
Luhya 32–34, 40, 41, 43, 44, 54, 58,
        62, 65, 78, 95
Luo 9, 33, 34, 41, 47, 49–51, 53, 54,
        56–58, 62, 65, 79, 82, 128,
        209

M

Maasai 33, 38, 39, 41, 54, 55, 78

madoadoa 127

majimbo 47, 58, 59, 81

majimboism. See majimbo

Majority World 93, 212

mali ya umma 188

Mau Mau 8, 31, 44–48, 52

Meru 33, 42, 51, 52, 54

moral ethnicity 8

multiparty democracy 2, 55, 58, 68, 80, 186, 210, 213, 229, 237

Mwakenya 68

N

Nandi 33, 38, 40, 43, 44, 52, 56, 78, 79

National Council of Churches of Kenya 13, 27, 28, 66, 202

NCCK. *See* National Council of Churches of Kenya

Ndungu Commission 12

Négritude 234, 274

neo-Calvinism 162

Nyayo 54, 226

O

Operation Okoa Maisha 40

P

paideia 134, 148

palaver 153

Pan-Africanism 234–236, 254, 270, 274, 287

political theology 8, 19, 75, 92, 166, 204, 218, 227, 253, 292

politics as eating 183, 187, 190

post-election 1, 62, 83, 84, 86, 87

  violence 10, 11, 60, 62, 76, 77, 127, 128, 130, 254

Presbyterian Church of East Africa 66, 93

R

Rainbow Coalition 59

Reformed Church of East Africa 93, 95

Reformed theology 8, 24, 91, 93, 259, 291, 292

S

Sabaot 38–40, 43, 265

Sabaot Land Defense Force 40

sanctification 107, 131, 133–135, 142, 144, 146, 147, 149, 152

SLDF. *See* Sabaot Land Defense Force

social cohesion 3, 4, 50, 54, 66, 70

T

theocracy 161, 162

the peaceful village 155

TJRC. *See* Truth, Justice, and Reconciliation Commission

tribalism 1, 3, 7, 8, 14, 31, 63, 66, 67, 70, 94, 203, 204, 207–209, 246

Truth, Justice, and Reconciliation Commission 12, 26, 45, 60

Two Kingdoms theology 159

U

ubuntu 25, 273, 283, 293

Ufungamano Initiative 80

utu 130, 283

V

vivification 141

W

Waki Commission 12, 26

Index of Names

A

Annan, Kofi 61
Arap Moi, Daniel Toroitich 50, 53
Archbishop David Mukuba Gitari.
    See David Gitari
Augustine 104, 113, 168, 169, 191

B

Birech, Ezekiel 73

C

Cortez, Marc 22

D

de Gruchy, John 2

G

Gama Pinto, Pio 49
Gathogo, Julius 210, 252
Gitari, David 14, 66, 68, 201, 210
Grenz, Stanley J. 19
Gushee, David P. 21

H

Hall, Douglas John 19, 27

I

Imathiu, Lawi 69, 86

K

Kaggia, Bildad 48

Karanja, Peter 85
Katongole, Emmanuel 157, 187, 268
Kenyatta, Jomo 46, 47, 53, 59, 211,
    212, 265
Kenyatta, Uhuru 59, 62, 187
Kewasis, Stephen 78, 79
Kibaki, Mwai 57–60, 62, 79, 254
Kitonga, Arthur 73, 75
Kivuitu, Samuel 61
Klopp, Jacqueline M. 10, 188
Korir, Cornelius 71
Kuria, Manasses 66, 68, 71, 72, 78,
    79
Kuyper, Abraham 162, 164, 173,
    195

L

Lonsdale, John 8
Luther, Martin 23, 90, 169, 208

M

Matiba, Kenneth 57, 68, 79
Mbiti, John 14, 25, 29, 232, 236,
    238, 261, 264, 272, 274, 287,
    288, 290
Mboya, Tom 48–51, 219
McGrath, Alister E. 89
Middleton, J. Richard 21, 103
Moi, Daniel Toroitich Arap 28, 31,
    50, 51, 53-63, 65, 67, 69, 72,

74, 75, 79, 80, 82, 189, 207,
212, 213, 223, 226, 227
Moynihan, Daniel P. 3
Mugambi, Jesse 14, 29, 230–232,
264, 290
Muge, Alexander 55, 78, 184, 203
Muite, Paul 68
Musyimi, Mutava 80, 82
Musyoka, Kalonzo 59, 60
Mutai, Chelagat 49
Mwangi, Josiah 49

N
Ndingi a'Nzeki, Rafael 70
Niebuhr, Richard 168
Njogu, Kimani 3
Njoka, Peter 69, 86
Njoka, Timothy 66
Njue, John 70, 72, 81
Noll, Mark 212

O
Odinga, Jaramogi Odinga 48
Odinga, Raila 58–60, 62, 80, 82,
187, 254
Oduyoye, Mercy Amba 15
Ogot, Bethwell 10, 32
Okoth, Zacchaeus 70, 71, 81
Okullu, Henry. *See* Okullu, John
Henry
Okullu, John Henry 66, 202
Otunga, Mourice Michael 70
Ouko, Robert 55, 219

S
Schreiner, Susan 99, 101, 110, 120
Servetus, Michael 99, 112, 193, 290
Shikuku, Martin 49
Smith, James K. A. 124, 148
Stott, John 183, 211, 212, 214, 227,
230

T
Thiong'o, Ngugi wa 49

V
VanDrunen, David 163
Volf, Miroslav 128

W
Walls, Andrew 195, 282
Wamwere, Koigi 13, 49
Wright, N. T. 116
Wrong, Michela 33

Langham
PARTNERSHIP

Langham Literature, with its publishing work, is a ministry of Langham Partnership.

Langham Partnership is a global fellowship working in pursuit of the vision God entrusted to its founder John Stott –

> *to facilitate the growth of the church in maturity and Christ-likeness through raising the standards of biblical preaching and teaching.*

Our vision is to see churches in the majority world equipped for mission and growing to maturity in Christ through the ministry of pastors and leaders who believe, teach and live by the Word of God.

Our mission is to strengthen the ministry of the Word of God through:
- nurturing national movements for biblical preaching
- fostering the creation and distribution of evangelical literature
- enhancing evangelical theological education

especially in countries where churches are under-resourced.

Our ministry

Langham Preaching partners with national leaders to nurture indigenous biblical preaching movements for pastors and lay preachers all around the world. With the support of a team of trainers from many countries, a multi-level programme of seminars provides practical training, and is followed by a programme for training local facilitators. Local preachers' groups and national and regional networks ensure continuity and ongoing development, seeking to build vigorous movements committed to Bible exposition.

Langham Literature provides majority world preachers, scholars and seminary libraries with evangelical books and electronic resources through publishing and distribution, grants and discounts. The programme also fosters the creation of indigenous evangelical books in many languages, through writer's grants, strengthening local evangelical publishing houses, and investment in major regional literature projects, such as one volume Bible commentaries like the *Africa Bible Commentary* and the *South Asia Bible Commentary*.

Langham Scholars provides financial support for evangelical doctoral students from the majority world so that, when they return home, they may train pastors and other Christian leaders with sound, biblical and theological teaching. This programme equips those who equip others. Langham Scholars also works in partnership with majority world seminaries in strengthening evangelical theological education. A growing number of Langham Scholars study in high quality doctoral programmes in the majority world itself. As well as teaching the next generation of pastors, graduated Langham Scholars exercise significant influence through their writing and leadership.

To learn more about Langham Partnership and the work we do visit **langham.org**

* 9 7 8 1 7 8 3 6 8 5 8 0 6 *